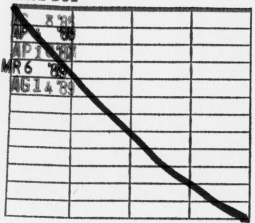

BUREAUCRATIC POWER
IN NATIONAL POLITICS

Second Edition

BUREAUCRATIC POWER
IN NATIONAL POLITICS

Readings Edited by

FRANCIS E. ROURKE
The Johns Hopkins University

LITTLE, BROWN AND COMPANY   *Boston*

Published simultaneously in Canada
by Little, Brown & Company (Canada) Limited

PRINTED IN THE UNITED STATES OF AMERICA

CONTENTS

v

VI

PUBLIC CONTROL OVER BUREAUCRATIC POWER   311

VII

CITIZEN PARTICIPATION IN BUREAUCRACY   377

EDITOR'S INTRODUCTION

The power of executive agencies and officials over the direction and development of public policy in the United States has grown remarkably in recent years. With the blessing of liberals in Democratic administrations and of conservatives when Republicans hold the presidency, ours has increasingly become an "executive-centered" political system. The press may still continue to feature the activities of legislators or the struggle for power within party organizations, but the center of gravity in American politics has clearly moved to the executive branch where politicians, bureaucrats, and outside advisors meet to hammer out the policies by which the lives of Americans are governed.

Of course, many policy decisions made within executive agencies are shaped or limited by forces outside these institutions. An agency's policy positions often mirror its expectations of what legislators, the courts, or the public will accept, and external groups frequently have the power to veto actions that agencies wish to pursue. But the fact remains that bureaucratic organizations exercise strategic influence over policy decisions in the American political system through their ability to identify issues, plan and administer programs to cope with emerging problems, and generate public support for policies they regard as desirable.

The selections in this book focus on the role of executive organizations in the policy process. The literature in this area is growing, but it is still meager compared with, for example, that written in recent years on voter attitudes and behavior. Although the new tools of social science have given us rich insight into the characteristics and behavior of the electorate, they have not been applied with equal success to chart the patterns and forces shaping the decisions of policymakers at the upper reaches of the American political system.

Yet the impact of voters upon executive decision-making is in many ways far less significant than the effects of executive decisions upon voters themselves. This is particularly true in foreign policy and national defense, where in recent years government decisions with far-ranging impact on Americans have increasingly been produced by bureaucratic, rather than electoral, politics. Definitions of American interests abroad and of the commitments necessary to protect these interests have been made within the executive apparatus and have only become objects of public discussion when the decisions made by executive officials have proved costly for the general public.

But in all areas of policy, domestic as well as foreign, the power of bureaucratic organizations has aroused growing concern, not only because of its scope but also because of the manner of its exercise. For one thing, the decisions of bureaucracy are reached in the sanctuaries of government agencies remote from the citizens' view. These decisions are less visible in their conception and often their execution than legislative policies, which are commonly decided under the limelight of public debate.

The exercise of bureaucratic power, moreover, often has intensely personal effects. Though legislatures ordinarily regulate categories of people or classes of things, adverse decisions by an executive agency can inflict severe hardship on individuals, for example, through denying a benefit or imposing a penalty. In extreme cases, citizens may even be required to risk their lives in a distant war for purposes they only dimly understand or share with the agency that decided to send them there.

The following selections illuminate how bureaucratic organizations influence public policy. Though these readings show the leading role that executive organizations play as instruments of government, they also put this power in proper perspective — as a formidable, but not unlimited, influence. No single executive agency operates as a pure monopoly. It shares power in the policy area in which it is located with other organizations, both governmental and nongovernmental — pressure groups, legislative committees, or, at the very least, other executive institutions.

Also, the power of any executive agency varies greatly over time, and its leverage may fluctuate. A decade or so ago, the executive organizations concerned with scientific research and development, such as the National Science Foundation and the National Aeronautics and Space Administration, were regarded as an unassailable power elite. Recent years, however, have seen a substantial contraction of their influence as their appropriations have been trimmed and their recommendations often ignored. Nothing seems so perishable a commodity as power in American politics.

ACKNOWLEDGEMENTS

Several persons were of great help in preparing the second edition of this book. At Johns Hopkins University, Paul Schulman performed a wide variety of tasks with uncommon skill. Marjorie Morrissette at the University of California, Berkeley, typed the editorial sections of the manuscript. The library facilities at both Johns Hopkins and the University of California, Berkeley, provided indispensable resources. I am also indebted to several very competent and patient editors with whom I have worked at Little, Brown: Donald R. Hammonds, Alfred L. Browne, Basil G. Dandison, and Freda Alexander.

I

ADMINISTRATIVE AGENCIES
AND THEIR CONSTITUENCIES

Executive agencies in the United States derive their power from essentially two sources: their ability to create and nurse constituencies and the technical skills that they command and can focus on complicated issues of public policy. This first section centers on how agencies build their influence through cultivating public support, whereas the next section, "The Power of Bureaucratic Expertise," emphasizes the professional or technical skills so important in developing bureaucratic power in all societies.

I

In Norton E. Long's analysis, "Power and Administration," the influence of bureaucratic organizations rests primarily on their capacity for "public relations and the mobilization of political support." A legal mandate conferring specific statutory authority is by itself insufficient. "Agencies and bureaus more or less perforce are in the business of building, maintaining, and increasing their political support. They lead and in large part are led by the diverse groups whose influence sustains them."

From the perspective of Long's essay, the bureaucrat's power is not easily distinguishable from the politician's. His success, like the elected official's, depends upon mobilizing a political following. According to Long, this kind of politicized bureaucracy springs from the decentralized character of the American political system. In the absence of centrally organized and disciplined political parties, or of a presidential cabinet backed by a cohesive legislative majority, each executive agency must fend for itself in the political arena. Executive officials cannot assume that the programs they administer will have political backing, as would ordinarily be the case in a parliamentary democracy. Instead, each agency must constantly create a climate of acceptance for its activities and negotiate alliances with powerful legislative and community groups to sustain its position. It must, in short, master the art of politics as well as the science of administration.

The bureaucratic apparatus in the United States largely emerged in an environment of a vigorously functioning system of democratic politics during the late nineteenth and early twentieth centuries. In Western Europe the bureaucrat's authority was originally derived from his membership in the king's household and his share of the awe and deference usually accorded the monarch. In this country, on the other hand, legitimate political power came from the consent of the governed. Hence, as executive agencies moved toward positions of power in the political system, they could greatly strengthen their authority by showing that it was popularly accepted. The drive for constituency support by administrative agencies in the United States can thus be interpreted as being, in part at least, a quest for political legitimacy in a highly egalitarian democratic society.

II

J. Leiper Freeman in "The Bureaucracy in Pressure Politics" does not attempt so much to explain why executive agencies in the United States assiduously cultivate public favor as he does to mark out the channels through which this support is sought. Foremost among such techniques is cultivating friendly relations with legislators, particularly those on strategic committees, and with attentive outside publics interested in the agency's work.

In "The Struggle for Organizational Survival," Herbert A. Simon, Donald W. Smithburg, and Victor A. Thompson tie the executive agencies' involvement in building outside support to basic organizational survival needs. Powerful legislators must be won over because they control resources vital to an agency's continued existence, and similar considerations dictate the negotiation of alliances with outside publics. The interaction resulting from this activity, however, may modify an agency's power even as it insures its survival; the bargain thus struck may not always be advantageous for the agency.

An illustration of such a bargain is provided by Philip Selznick's "TVA and the Grass Roots." In this case a close and cooperative relationship between an agency and its environment resulted not only from concern for organizational survival but also from the agency's ideological commitment. From its inception, the Tennessee Valley Authority felt it should be intimately familiar with the problems of the communities it served and responsive to the needs of local citizens. This "grass-roots" philosophy won the agency broad support, both in the Valley and outside the area among those who saw the TVA as a demonstration that a national agency could be just as close to the public as units of state and local government. Instead of being remote and "bureaucratic," the national government could in fact decentralize itself through its own institutions.

However, Selznick's study also shows that the agency's grass-roots approach had unanticipated and disadvantageous consequences. Not the least of these was the fact that the TVA was forced to modify its own goals to attract the support of groups dominant in the Valley area. As Selznick points out, "The significance of a constituency relation depends in part upon the fact that the character of the constituency will tend to define and shape the character of the agency." In such cases the price of administrative popularity may come very high if it can only be purchased by adulterating or shifting the agency's goals.

Of course a multi-purpose water development agency like the TVA has by its very nature varied objectives. As Selznick was later to concede,[1] it made some sense for TVA to modify its agricultural aims for the Valley area in order not to alienate the constituency support needed to achieve its

[1] See Philip Selznick, *Leadership in Administration* (Evanston, Ill.: Row, Peterson, 1957), p. 44.

highly ranked goal of bringing electricity to the region through the development of public power facilities. The critical question in such cases is whether an agency is obliged to "sell out" fundamental program commitments to win the support it seeks, or whether it is only required to sacrifice secondary goals to achieve primary objectives. As an essential characteristic of democratic politics, compromise is as appropriate for bureaucratic organizations as it is for political parties.

1 *Power and Administration*

Norton E. Long

I

There is no more forlorn spectacle in the administrative
world than an agency and a program possessed of statutory life,
armed with executive orders, sustained in the courts, yet stricken
with paralysis and deprived of power. An object of contempt to its
enemies and of despair to its friends.

The lifeblood of administration is power. Its attainment, maintenance, increase, dissipation, and loss are subjects the practitioner
and student can ill afford to neglect. Loss of realism and failure are
almost certain consequences. This is not to deny that important
parts of public administration are so deeply entrenched in the habits of the community, so firmly supported by the public, or so clearly
necessary as to be able to take their power base for granted and
concentrate on the purely professional side of their problems. But
even these islands of the blessed are not immune from the plague
of politics. . . . To stay healthy one needs to recognize that health
is a fruit, not a birthright. Power is only one of the considerations
that must be weighed in administration, but of all it is the most overlooked in theory and the most dangerous to overlook in practice.

The power resources of an administrator or an agency are not
disclosed by a legal search of titles and court decisions or by examining appropriations or budgetary allotments. Legal authority

From Norton E. Long, "Power and Administration," reprinted by permission of
the author and The American Society for Public Administration from *Public
Administration Review* 9 (Autumn 1949):257–264.

and a treasury balance are necessary but politically insufficient bases of administration. Administrative rationality requires a critical evaluation of the whole range of complex and shifting forces on whose support, acquiescence, or temporary impotence the power to act depends.

Analysis of the sources from which power is derived and the limitations they impose is as much a dictate of prudent administration as sound budgetary procedure. The bankruptcy that comes from an unbalanced power budget has consequences far more disastrous than the necessity of seeking a deficiency appropriation. The budgeting of power is a basic subject matter of a realistic science of administration.

It may be urged that for all but the top hierarchy of the administrative structure the question of power is irrelevant. Legislative authority and administrative orders suffice. Power adequate to the function to be performed flows down the chain of command. Neither statute nor executive order, however, confers more than legal authority to act. Whether Congress or President can impart the substance of power as well as the form depends upon the line-up of forces in the particular case. A price control law wrung from a reluctant Congress by an amorphous and unstable combination of consumer and labor groups is formally the same as a law enacting a support price program for agriculture backed by the disciplined organizations of farmers and their Congressmen. The differences for the scope and effectiveness of administration are obvious. The presidency, like Congress, responds to and translates the pressures that play upon it. The real mandate contained in an executive order varies with the political strength of the group demand embodied in it, and in the context of other group demands.

Both Congress and President do focus the general political energies of the community and so are considerably more than mere means for transmitting organized pressures. Yet power is not concentrated by the structure of government or politics into the hands of a leadership with a capacity to budget it among a diverse set of administrative activities. A picture of the presidency as a reservoir of authority from which the lower echelons of administration draw life and vigor is an idealized distortion of reality.

A similar criticism applies to any like claim for an agency head in his agency. Only in varying degrees can the powers of subordinate officials be explained as resulting from the chain of command. Rarely is such an explanation a satisfactory account of the sources of power.

To deny that power is derived exclusively from superiors in the hierarchy is to assert that subordinates stand in a feudal relation in which to a degree they fend for themselves and acquire support peculiarly their own. A structure of interests friendly or hostile, vague and general or compact and well-defined, encloses each significant center of administrative discretion. This structure is an important determinant of the scope of possible action. As a source of power and authority it is a competitor of the formal hierarchy.

Not only does political power flow in from the sides of an organization, as it were; it also flows up the organization to the center from the constituent parts. When the staff of the Office of War Mobilization and Reconversion advised a hard-pressed agency to go out and get itself some popular support so that the President could afford to support it, their action reflected the realities of power rather than political cynicism.

It is clear that the American system of politics does not generate enough power at any focal point of leadership to provide the conditions for an even partially successful divorce of politics from administration. Subordinates cannot depend on the formal chain of command to deliver enough political power to permit them to do their jobs. Accordingly they must supplement the resources available through the hierarchy with those they can muster on their own, or accept the consequences in frustration — a course itself not without danger. Administrative rationality demands that objectives be determined and sights set in conformity with a realistic appraisal of power position and potential.

II

The theory of administration has neglected the problem of the sources and adequacy of power, in all probability because of a distaste for the disorderliness of American political life and a belief that this disorderliness is transitory. An idealized picture of the British parliamentary system as a Platonic form to be realized or approximated has exerted a baneful fascination in the field. The majority party with a mandate at the polls and a firmly seated leadership in the cabinets seems to solve adequately the problem of the supply of power necessary to permit administration to concentrate on the fulfillment of accepted objectives. It is a commonplace that the American party system provides neither a mandate for a platform nor a mandate for a leadership.

Accordingly, the election over, its political meaning must be explored by the diverse leaders in the executive and legislative branches. Since the parties have failed to discuss issues, mobilize majorities in their terms, and create a working political consensus on measures to be carried out, the task is left for others — most prominently the agencies concerned. Legislation passed and powers granted are frequently politically premature. Thus the Council of Economic Advisors was given legislative birth before political acceptance of its functions existed. The agencies to which tasks are assigned must devote themselves to the creation of an adequate consensus to permit administration. The mandate that the parties do not supply must be attained through public relations and the mobilization of group support. Pendleton Herring and others have shown just how vital this support is for agency action.

The theory that agencies should confine themselves to communicating policy suggestions to executive and legislature, and refrain from appealing to their clientele and the public, neglects the failure of the parties to provide either a clear-cut decision as to what they should do or an adequately mobilized political support for a course of action. The bureaucracy under the American political system has a large share of responsibility for the public promotion of policy and even more in organizing the political basis for its survival and growth. It is generally recognized that the agencies have a special competence in the technical aspects of their fields which of necessity gives them a rightful policy initiative. In addition, they have or develop a shrewd understanding of the politically feasible in the group structure within which they work. Above all, in the eyes of their supporters and their enemies they represent the institutionalized embodiment of policy, an enduring organization actually or potentially capable of mobilizing power behind policy. The survival interests and creative drives of administrative organizations combine with clientele pressures to compel such mobilization. The party system provides no enduring institutional representation for group interest at all comparable to that of the bureaus of the Department of Agriculture. Even the subject matter committees of Congress function in the shadow of agency permanency.

The bureaucracy is recognized by all interested groups as a major channel of representation to such an extent that Congress rightly feels the competition of a rival. The weakness in party structure both permits and makes necessary the present dimensions of the political activities of the administrative branch — permits because it fails to protect administration from pressures and fails to provide adequate direction and support, makes necessary because it fails to develop a consensus on a leadership and a program that makes possible administration on the basis of accepted decisional premises.

Agencies and bureaus more or less perforce are in the business of building, maintaining, and increasing their political support. They lead and in large part are led by the diverse groups whose influence sustains them. Frequently they lead and are themselves led in conflicting directions. This is not due to a dull-witted incapacity to see the contradictions in their behavior but is an almost inevitable result of the contradictory nature of their support.

Herbert Simon has shown that administrative rationality depends on the establishment of uniform value premises in the decisional centers of organization. Unfortunately, the value premises of those forming vital elements of political support are often far from uniform. These elements are in Barnard's and Simon's sense "customers" of the organization and therefore parts of the organization whose wishes are clothed with a very real authority. A major and most time-consuming aspect of administration consists of the wide range of activities designed to secure enough "customer" acceptance to survive and, if fortunate, develop a consensus adequate to program formulation and execution.

To varying degrees, dependent on the breadth of acceptance of their programs, officials at every level of significant discretion must make their estimates of the situation, take stock of their resources, and plan accordingly. A keen appreciation of the real components of their organization is the beginning of wisdom. These components will be found to stretch far beyond the government payroll. Within the government they will encompass Congress, Congressmen, committees, courts, other agencies, presidential advisors, and the President. The Aristotelian analysis of constitutions is equally applicable and equally necessary to an understanding of administrative organization.

The broad alliance of conflicting groups that makes up presidential majorities scarcely coheres about any definite pattern of objectives, nor has it by the alchemy of the party system had its collective power concentrated in an accepted leadership with a personal mandate. The conciliation and maintenance of this support is a necessary condition of the attainment and retention of office involving, as Madison so well saw, "the spirit of party and faction in the necessary and ordinary operations of government." The President must in large part be, if not all things to all men, at least many things to many men. As a consequence, the contradictions in his power base invade administration. The often criticized apparent cross-purposes of the Roosevelt regime cannot be put down to inept administration until the political facts are weighed. Were these apparently self-defeating measures reasonably related to the general maintenance of the composite majority of the administration? The first objective — ultimate patriotism apart — of the administrator is the attainment and retention of the power on which his tenure of office depends. This is the necessary pre-condition for the accomplishment of all other objectives.

The same ambiguities that arouse the scorn of the naive in the electoral campaigns of the parties are equally inevitable in administration and for the same reasons. Victory at the polls does not yield either a clear-cut grant of power or a unified majority support for a coherent program. The task of the presidency lies in feeling out the alternatives of policy which are consistent with the retention and increase of the group support on which the administration rests. The lack of a budgetary theory (so frequently deplored) is not due to any incapacity to apply rational analysis to the comparative contribution of the various activities of government to a determinate hierarchy of purposes. It more probably stems from a fastidious distaste for the frank recognition of the budget as a politically expedient allocation of resources. Appraisal in terms of their political contribution to the administration provides almost a sole common denominator between the Forest Service and the Bureau of Engraving.

Integration of the administrative structure through an overall purpose in terms of which tasks and priorities can be established is an emergency phenomenon. Its realization, only partial at best, has been limited to war and the extremity of depression. Even in wartime the Farm Bureau Federation, the American Federation of Labor, the Congress of Industrial Organizations, the National Association of Manufacturers, the Chamber of Commerce, and a host of lesser interests resisted coordination of themselves and the agencies concerned with their interests. A presidency temporarily empowered by intense mass popular support acting in behalf of a generally accepted and simplified purpose can, with great difficulty, bribe, cajole, and coerce a real measure of joint action. . . . Only in crises are the powers of the executive nearly adequate to impose a common plan of action on the executive branch, let alone the economy.

In ordinary times the manifold pressures of our pluralistic society work themselves out in accordance with the balance of forces prevailing in Congress and the agencies. Only to a limited degree is the process subject to responsible direction or review by President or party leadership. . . .

III

The difficulty of coordinating government agencies lies not only in the fact that bureaucratic organizations are institutions having survival interests which may conflict with their rational adaptation to overall purpose, but even more in their having roots in society. Coordination of the varied activities of a modern government almost of necessity involves a substantial degree of coordination of the economy. Coordination of government agencies involves far more than changing the behavior and offices of officials in Washington and the field. It involves the publics that are implicated in their normal functioning. To coordinate fiscal policy, agricultural policy, labor policy, foreign policy, and military policy, to name a few major areas, moves beyond the range of government charts and the habitat of the bureaucrats to the marketplace and to where the people live and work. This suggests that the reason why government reorganization is so difficult is that far more than government in the formal sense is involved in reorganization. One could overlook this in the limited government of the nineteenth century but the multi-billion dollar government of the mid-twentieth permits no facile dichotomy between government and economy. Economy and efficiency are the two objectives a laissez faire society can prescribe in peacetime as over-all government objectives. Their inadequacy either as motivation or standards has long been obvious. A planned economy clearly requires a planned government. But, if one can afford an unplanned economy, apart from gross extravagance, there seems no compelling and therefore, perhaps, no sufficiently powerful reason for a planned government.

Basic to the problem of administrative rationality is that of or-

ganizational identification and point of view. To whom is one loyal
— unit, section, branch, division, bureau, department, administration, government, country, people, world history, or what? Administrative analysis frequently assumes that organizational identification should occur in such a way as to merge primary organization
loyalty in a larger synthesis. The good of the part is to give way
to the reasoned good of the whole. This is most frequently illustrated in the rationalizations used to counter self-centered demands
of primary groups for funds and personnel. Actually the competition between governmental power centers, rather than the rationalizations, is the effective instrument of coordination.

Where there is a clear common product on whose successful production the subgroups depend for the attainment of their own satisfaction, it is possible to demonstrate to almost all participants the
desirability of cooperation. The shoe factory produces shoes, or
else, for all concerned. But the government as a whole and many of
its component parts have no such identifiable common product on
which all depend. Like the proverbial Heinz, there are fifty-seven
or more varieties unified, if at all, by a common political profit and
loss account.

Administration is faced by somewhat the same dilemma as economics. There are propositions about the behavior pattern conducive to full employment — welfare economics. On the other hand,
there are propositions about the economics of the individual firm —
the counsel of the business schools. It is possible to show with considerable persuasiveness that sound considerations for the individual
firm may lead to a depression if generally adopted, a result desired
by none of the participants. However, no single firm can afford by
itself to adopt the course of collective wisdom; in the absence of a
common power capable of enforcing decisions premised on the supremacy of the collective interest, *sauve qui peut* is common sense.

The position of administrative organizations is not unlike the position of particular firms. Just as the decisions of the firms could be
coordinated by the imposition of a planned economy so could those
of the component parts of the government. But just as it is possible
to operate a formally unplanned economy by the loose coordination
of the market, in the same fashion it is possible to operate a government by the loose coordination of the play of political forces through
its institutions.

The unseen hand of Adam Smith may be little in evidence in

either case. One need not believe in a doctrine of social or administrative harmony to believe that formal centralized planning — while perhaps desirable and in some cases necessary — is not a must. The complicated logistics of supplying the city of New York runs smoothly down the grooves of millions of well adapted habits projected from a distant past. It seems naive on the one hand to believe in the possibility of a vast, intricate, and delicate economy operating with a minimum of formal overall direction, and on the other to doubt that a relatively simple mechanism such as the government can be controlled largely by the same play of forces. . . .

IV

It is highly appropriate to consider how administrators should behave to meet the test of efficiency in a planned polity; but in the absence of such a polity and while, if we like, struggling to get it, a realistic science of administration will teach administrative behavior appropriate to the existing political system.

A close examination of the presidential system may well bring one to conclude that administrative rationality in it is a different matter from that applicable to the British ideal. The American presidency is an office that has significant monarchical characteristics despite its limited term and elective nature. The literature on court and palace has many an insight applicable to the White House. Access to the President, reigning favorites, even the court jester, are topics that show the continuity of institutions. The maxims of La Rochefoucauld and the memoirs of the Duc de Saint Simon have a refreshing realism for the operator on the Potomac.

The problem of rival factions in the President's family is as old as the famous struggle between Jefferson and Hamilton. . . . Experience seems to show that this personal and factional struggle for the President's favor is a vital part of the process of representation. The vanity, personal ambition, or patriotism of the contestants soon clothes itself in the generalities of principle and the clique aligns itself with groups beyond the capital. Subordinate rivalry is tolerated if not encouraged by so many able executives that it can scarcely be attributed to administrative ineptitude. The wrangling tests opinion, uncovers information that would otherwise never rise to the top, and provides effective opportunity for decision rather than mere ratification of prearranged plans. Like most judges, the executive needs to hear argument for his own instruction. The alternatives presented by subordinates in large part determine the freedom and the creative opportunity of their superiors. The danger of becoming a Merovingian is a powerful incentive to the maintenance of fluidity in the structure of power.

The fixed character of presidential tenure makes it necessary that subordinates be politically expendable. The President's men must be willing to accept the blame for failures not their own. Machiavelli's teaching on how princes must keep the faith bears rereading. Collective responsibility is incompatible with a fixed term of office. As it tests the currents of public opinion, the situation on the Hill, and the varying strength of the organized pressures, the White House alters and adapts the complexion of the administration. Loyalties to programs or to groups and personal pride and interest frequently conflict with whole-souled devotion to the presidency. In fact, since such devotion is not made mandatory by custom, institutions, or the facts of power, the problem is perpetually perplexing to those who must choose.

The balance of power between executive and legislature is constantly subject to the shifts of public and group support. The latent tendency of the American Congress is to follow the age-old parliamentary precedents and to try to reduce the President to the role of constitutional monarch. Against this threat and to secure his own initiative, the President's resources are primarily demagogic, with the weaknesses and strengths that dependence on mass popular appeal implies. The unanswered question of American government — "who is boss?" — constantly plagues administration. . . .

2   *The Bureaucracy in Pressure Politics*

J. LEIPER FREEMAN

It is not a novel statement that we live in a society of "organization men," but we have yet to comprehend adequately the implications of this fact. Today's bureaucratic world is a reality within which the vast majority of Americans are enmeshed. Large, complex, specialized, hierarchical organizations are means of achieving the mass production, communications, services, regulation, and destruction possible in modern society. These bureaucracies are both public and private, large and small, demanding and lenient; but in any case they are the dominating form of social organization in America today.

Although bureaucracies are primarily regarded as organizations which execute policies assigned to them by society, they must also be reckoned with as sources of influence upon social policies. The nature of this influence is basically twofold. First, members of bureaucracies can give shape to stated policies through the exercise of choice and judgment in administering them. Second, in attempting to affect the objectives and working conditions which society will authorize for their organizations, members of bureaucracies necessarily engage in pressure politics.

It is with this second aspect of bureaucratic behavior that this article is chiefly concerned. Furthermore, it is confined to pressure politics engaged in by governmental, as opposed to private, bureaucracies and to pressure politics aimed at influencing official governmental policies.

Public bureaucracies — national, state, and local — today employ about one-eighth of the labor force of the United States. About 3 million of these members of public bureaucracies are in the armed

From J. Leiper Freeman, "The Bureaucracy in Pressure Politics," reprinted by permission of the author and The American Academy of Political and Social Science from *Annals of the American Academy of Political and Social Science* 319 (September 1958):11–19.

The Bureau of the Budget mentioned here and in later selections became the Office of Management and Budget in 1970. In the same year the Post Office Department became the United States Postal Service.

forces; slightly more than 2.2 million are civilian employees of the federal government; more than 1.1 million are classroom teachers in the public schools; about 3.5 million are otherwise employed by the state and local governments. If these bureaucrats, numbering between 9 and 10 million, formed one large group sharing a common identity, they would constitute a force in pressure politics to defy the imagination. But public bureaucrats are divided into many bureaucracies by levels of government, by special functions, by special technologies, by differing clienteles, and by territories. The result is a patchwork of official organizations devoted to limited, specialized interests.

Bureaucracies as Pressure Groups

Since a public bureaucracy is concerned with special and limited aspects of public policy, to a degree it resembles the ordinary private pressure group. It is a congregating place for individuals concerned with the same subjects. Some of these interested individuals become members of the administrative agency while others join groups which look to that organization as a rallying point, and the agency takes a leading part in representing their interests. In this representative process perhaps the bureaucracy's most important function is to promote the idea that its special area of concern is important — be it education, air power, or mental health. The bureaucracy also promotes special solutions to policy problems in its area. Finally, it promotes objectives which are of particular interest to its members *as bureaucrats*. These are matters such as their working conditions, status, and compensation, as well as the maintenance and survival of their organization.

A public bureaucracy, as part of the official government, is subject to some controls over its pressure politics which do not apply to private groups. There are laws at the federal level to restrict the public relations and legislative activities of bureaucrats. Federal agencies are forbidden by an act passed in 1913 to use public funds to compensate "any publicity expert unless explicitly appropriated for that purpose." [1] Another act, passed in 1919, provides that appropriations shall not be used, unless explicitly authorized by Congress, "directly or indirectly to pay for any personal service, advertisement, telegram, telephone, letter, printed or written matter, or other device, intended or designed to influence in any man-

[1] 38 Stat. L. 212.

ner a Member of Congress, to favor or oppose, by vote or otherwise, any legislation or appropriation by Congress, whether before or after the introduction of any bill or resolution proposing such legislation or appropriation. . . ." [2]

These general restrictions, however, have served mainly as policy statements to be used as threats against agency officials rather than as bases for actual cases. "Publicity experts" have not been hired, but "information," "education," and "publication" officers have been employed in good quantity.[3] Although these publicists have often been flayed in the halls of Congress, no cases have arisen in which they have been held as violators of the law. Furthermore, despite the prohibitions against spending public funds to influence a member of Congress, there has remained a great latitude for legislative activity by public administrators. The expectations of Congressmen in this regard were well summarized by Representative Frank Buchanan in his committee's investigation of bureaucratic lobbying in 1950:

. . . It is equally necessary for the executive branch of Government to be able to make its views known to Congress on all matters in which it has responsibilities, duties, and opinions. The executive agencies have a definite requirement to express views to Congress, to make suggestions, to request needed legislation, to draft proposed bills or amendments, and so on. And there is, of course, the power centered in the executive branch to overrule by veto any action of Congress which is not supported by a clear two-thirds majority of both Houses.[4]

CHIEF EXECUTIVE CONTROLS

It is safe to conclude that such statutory restrictions are not important limitations upon administrative propagandizing and lobbying in the federal government, and they are even less so in state and local governments where laws governing political activities of bureaucrats are generally less numerous and less stringent. Instead, more meaningful controls over bureaucratic pressure politics are to be found in the powers of the chief executive.

At all levels of government today there is a tendency toward giving the chief executive more effective authority over finance, or-

[2] 41 Stat. L. 68.

[3] James L. McCamy, *Government Publicity* (Chicago, 1939), p. 7; V. O. Key, Jr., *Politics, Parties and Pressure Groups* (New York, 1952), pp. 731–732.

[4] United States Congress, House, Select Committee on Lobbying Activities, *Legislative Activities of Executive Agencies,* Hearings, 81st Congress, 2d Session, Part 10 (Washington, D.C., 1950).

ganization, and personnel to help him control the actions of administrative agencies. These sanctions do not necessarily remove bureaucrats from the arena of pressure politics, but they tend to channel their activities along lines amenable to the chief executive. The stronger these sanctions are — as in the case of the city manager or strong mayor form of municipal executive, or the strong governorship, or the presidency — the smaller the relative autonomy allowed bureaucrats in legislative and public relations.

In the federal government, the Bureau of the Budget and the provisions of the Budgeting and Accounting Act of 1921 aid the President in establishing central control over tendencies toward agency autonomy in seeking appropriations. Executive departments and bureaus are prohibited from seeking amounts larger than those requested for them in the President's budget when they appear before appropriations committees of Congress. Nevertheless, there have been instances in which questioning by committee members has brought into the record a bureau's original requests which perhaps the Budget Bureau had eliminated or curtailed. This device for circumventing the prescribed budget procedure is probably welcomed by an administrator, with friendly committee members and sympathetic interest groups doing the prodding. Yet, on the whole, the executive budget is a significant means of coordinating administrative requests for funds.

In proposals for legislation, the Bureau of the Budget is also of some help to the President since it has the power to require that agencies' legislative requests should be submitted to it to determine whether they are "in accord with the program of the President." This does not prevent an agency from submitting proposals to Congress which are not "in accord," but it is supposed to enable Congress to know whether measures are consonant with the President's program when it takes action on them. There is no clear agreement among persons who have studied the effectiveness of this procedure, but the most recent evaluation indicates that in recent years it has become somewhat more effective in curbing autonomous action by the various agencies.[5]

---

[5] Richard E. Neustadt, "Presidency and Legislation: The Growth of Central Clearance," *The American Political Science Review* 48 (September 1954): 641 ff. For a different point of view, see Arthur A. Maass, "In Accord with the Program of the President?" in Carl J. Friedrich and J. K. Galbraith (Eds.), *Public Policy* (Cambridge, Mass., 1953), pp. 77–93.

The organizational status of a bureaucracy in the executive hierarchy determines to some degree the autonomy its members will have in their public and legislative relations. The more independently an agency is located in the structure of executive authority, the less formal power the chief executive can exercise over its political activities as well as on its administration of the laws. Thus, independent commissions and government corporations may enjoy some measure of independence from central direction of their political entrepreneurship which is not available to regular departments.

Personnel and Schedule C. Under the kind of government most often found in the United States, with a popularly elected chief executive having constitutional authority separate from the legislative branch, the President needs and usually has a coterie of political appointees. They serve both as political directors of the agencies and as leaders of the bureaucracies in their attempts to promote policies in their special spheres of interest.

The federal government under the Eisenhower administration enlarged the number of offices in this category by creating the so-called Schedule C positions for policy-making personnel in order to give the Republicans a larger crew of high-echelon officials. The major rationale for this enlargement was that the huge bureaucracies inherited from the previous administration, largely protected by Civil Service status, would otherwise be so intractable that the new administration would not be able to curb their autonomous tendencies. The results of this measure are not yet clear, although it has led to the removal of certain posts at the bureau-chief level from merit system status and to the creation of a number of new assistant secretaries and administrative assistants, who are patronage appointees. They compose an enlarged group of party representatives engaged in legislative liaison, public relations, and policy development at higher levels of the administration. They may have also reduced the political leeway of officials at lower levels.[6]

BUREAUCRATIC AUTONOMY

Despite the restrictions which may be placed upon bureaucracies because they are part of the government, they still have consider-

---

[6] Herman Miles Somers, "The President, the Congress, and the Federal Government Service" in *The Federal Government Service* (New York, 1954), p. 71.

able autonomy within the executive structure to engage in pressure politics. They enjoy certain advantages by being in the official family which help to offset the restrictions placed upon them. One advantage is the fact that they are expected by legislators to make recommendations to the legislative body on a continuing, legitimate basis. Furthermore, they may have the blessings of the chief executive in their legislative operations and consequently can speak with considerable force as the administration's specialists.

When Representative Buchanan voiced the thought that bureaucrats should "make their views known" to Congress, he was speaking with restraint. Virtually no piece of legislation of any consequence reaches any advanced stage of the legislative process without at least one administrative agency making some statement concerning it. On many bills, the chances are great that the proposal originated in an executive agency. Furthermore, in the highly decisive stage of the legislative process — committee hearings — officials from the administration are invariably among the most regular and most crucial witnesses. Legislators at all levels of government, despite their defensiveness toward bureaucracy, like to hear from the bureaucrats most intimately concerned when making up their minds about proposed legislation, and the bureaucrats oblige them energetically.

The various bureaucracies are also expected by the chief executive and top leaders of the administration to carry a good deal of the burden of legislative leadership for the executive branch in their own special areas. This aspect of lobbying by administrative agencies is sometimes overlooked or unduly subordinated by students of the subject because of a preoccupation with the desirability of integrated executive leadership. In reality the chief executive cannot personally get involved in every legislative skirmish without tending to reduce his effectiveness and dissipating his resources for political leadership. On lesser matters and indeed on many that are of considerable importance, the bureaucracies are depended upon by the top level of the executive branch to work out the proposals, to secure their introduction, to mobilize support from the public and elsewhere, and to negotiate with the committees and the leaders of the legislative branch to secure favorable action.[7]

[7] In connection with the above and some of the following points, see J. Leiper Freeman, *The Political Process: Executive Bureau — Legislative Committee Relations* (New York, 1955), chaps. 3–5.

GENERAL LEGISLATIVE LIAISON

Administrative agencies do not wait until a specific proposal is to be urged upon the legislature to cultivate harmonious relations with legislators. A continuous process of legislative liaison is maintained. This may be found at all levels of government and at all tiers of administration within these levels, although it is most marked at the higher echelons of federal administration. In the federal government, the growth of this process is reflected in recent institutional developments in which the major agencies have appointed high ranking officials with sizable staffs to spend their full time on it. Every bureau is also equipped to consider requests from Congressmen and to furnish them information speedily. In the field offices, major headquarters follow the same pattern.

Accommodating legislative requests and inquiries where legitimately possible serves to keep agencies in the good graces of legislators and opens the way for suggestions and requests from administrators in return. Field officials usually work with Representatives and Senators from their own area. In Washington, where the liaison machinery is more elaborate and more concerned with agency-wide problems, particular attention is focused upon congressional leaders and members of key committees.

While a good part of this activity is precautionary in that it is intended to keep legislators from becoming annoyed with an agency, it is also part of the agency's attempt to "cast bread upon the waters," to maintain a reservoir of good will, and to keep the solons aware of the important work the agency is doing.

At the state and local levels, legislative liaison has not become as highly organized and institutionalized as it has at the national level, but the essential ingredients are the same.

STRATEGY WITH COMMITTEES

Because so much of the meaningful work of legislative bodies is done in committees rather than in the full assemblies, the relations of spokesmen for the bureaucracies with committee members specializing in given policy areas are crucial aspects of administrative pressure politics. Committee members and agency officials who work together on common problems can build up the kind of understanding which maximizes the effect of agency opinions upon committee decisions. Committee recommendations in turn have a primary effect upon the content of laws passed by the parent body. Committee hearings therefore are not merely means by which legislative groups exert control over bureaucracies, they are also critical opportunities for bureaucrats to influence legislation.

In general, committee members need information on policy questions and administrative officials are in a position to have a vast store of it to present. This information, derived from the elaborate network of a bureaucracy, is a source of power. By presenting it strategically, leaders from the bureaucracy can use hearings to good advantage. Since hearings are usually covered by the press, the information presented may not only make a direct impression upon the committee members but also furnish ammunition to the agency's friends among the public.

Using Higher-Echelon Support. Leaders of a bureaucracy who appear before legislators to advocate any new laws or changes in policy which their agency desires usually try to enlist the support of others. In many instances one of the most helpful sources of support is the chief executive or others in the higher echelons of the administration. Many things that an agency desires are not regarded as being of vital importance to the top leaders of the administration, even though the chief executive and his advisors may have nothing against their passage. If, however, the bureau chief and department officials seeking the legislation can secure from the chief executive a statement to the legislative committee, or a comment to the press, or a paragraph in a speech favorable to their proposal, they may very well enhance its possibilities of adoption.

The effectiveness of this action is, of course, related to the state of the chief executive's popularity and prestige with the legislators. If the bureaucrats decide that the chief executive would in a given instance be more of an albatross than a guardian angel, they will naturally hope that he will not associate himself with their legislative project in any way.

The use of higher-echelon support is also available to bureaucrats as a defense against unwanted legislation. Their advice is given much weight in questions regarding the use of the chief executive's veto power on legislation falling within their special spheres of competence.

Mobilizing Employee Support. One of the great reservoirs of political strength available to agency leaders in certain kinds of leg-

islative activities lies in their organization's employees. This is naturally more true of the larger organizations since elected officials tend
to be impressed by numbers. In the federal government, the
[United States Postal Service] (with over 500,000 employees) is
a good example of an agency which tends to profit appreciably
from employee support.

There is no particular evidence, however, that employees are
necessarily helpful to their agency leaders on *all* legislative matters.
Detailed studies of municipal department heads' legislative strategies show that they are not inclined to view their employees as
important sources of support in dealing with the city council except
on matters such as salaries, job conditions, and the like.[8] The reason
is that public employee organizations tend to concentrate their
efforts on their interests as bureaucrats, often relegating larger policy questions to a secondary position. For this reason, agency leaders
are often faced with the problem of tying employee benefits to
other policy objectives and thereby evoking a maximum effort by
the mass of the bureaucrats in their organizations to influence the
legislative body.

At the federal level, [an] . . . example of the linking of employee interests with broader policy objectives was seen in the fight
waged by the Post Office Department [in the late 1950s] to secure
a modernization of the postal service and the most comprehensive
revision of postage rates in over twenty years. Within the postal
service, postmasters and postal employees were convinced that new
buildings and equipment and increases in salaries were not to be
obtained without the revision, and they contributed to the effort to
obtain it. Legislative representatives from state and national organizations of postmasters conferred with the legislators. Organizations
of postal employees lobbied and propagandized for it heavily.

The employees of the Brooklyn Post Office paid for a full-page
advertisement in *The New York Times* to reprint an article by Senator Olin D. Johnston, Chairman of the Senate Committee on Post
Office and Civil Service, which in general advocated modernization

[8] Based on interviews and observations in the "Bay City" project, conducted
at the Harvard Graduate School of Education under a grant from the W. K.
Kellogg Foundation. "Bay City" is a pseudonym for a Massachusetts city of
nearly 50,000 population where a series of related research inquiries was conducted on local decision-making during the period 1952–55 by a professional
staff consisting chiefly of Peter H. Rossi, Alice S. Rossi, James M. Shipton, and
the present writer.

of the service and increasing the postage rates. Readers were urged to clip the article and mail it to their Senators.[9]

Mobilizing Clientele Support. Employees are, after all, not always the most appropriate pleaders in behalf of a bureaucracy in the legislative arena. Legislators are inclined to regard employees as pleading their own cases and therefore may discount their contentions. Consequently, administrative leaders seek to have their proposals endorsed by private groups who carry weight with legislators.

The easiest groups of this type for most agencies to mobilize are the so-called clientele groups. In many instances they are highly organized and easily identified. The Veterans Administration counts heavily on the American Legion and to a lesser extent on other veterans organizations to support its recommendations to Congress. In fact, it seldom tends to make a recommendation to Congress that is not reasonably acceptable to these organizations, so strong is their partnership in all pressure politics dealing with veterans affairs.

The pattern is similar with many other agencies and their clienteles such as the Commerce Department and business organizations; the Labor Department and the unions; and the Agriculture Department and the Farm Bureau, the Grange, and other farmer organizations. These other groups do not, however, always show the same degree of collaboration as that evinced by the Veterans Administration and its customers. . . .

Other Group Support. Bureaucracies welcome and at times aid the organization of groups to serve as their sponsors. These groups are not necessarily composed of steady customers of an agency, but they are made up of people who for various reasons are interested in its aims and its existence. Some of these groups are completely unofficial in nature; but many are given some official recognition in the agency's operations, rendering them quasi-public in character. By elaborating their administrative structure, public bureaucracies at all levels of American government have enlisted the participation of interested and often influential citizens in their business to give them advice and sometimes even to help them set and administer policies. In turn, the bureaucracies expect and usually receive support for their legislative objectives.

Among the many groups of this type to be found at the federal

---

[9] *The New York Times,* Tuesday, February 18, 1958, p. 13.

level are, for example, the various reserve officer associations of the military branches, or the very exclusive advisory committee of the Commerce Department, or any of the many other advisory committees in other units. Over the years the Agriculture Department has built up one of the most complex systems of citizen participation in administration at the local level that could be imagined. Some of its major programs are handled at the county level by committees elected by farmers and working in conjunction with full-time paid employees of the Department. In this way, for example, the Agricultural Stabilization and Conservation Service enlists sponsors composed of local farm leaders in county after county across the nation.[10]

In local governments, outstanding examples of sponsor groups are to be found in Parent-Teacher Associations or in "Friends of the Library." And at a more official and formal level they may be found in the plethora of boards and commissions which are officially charged with setting policies for various municipal agencies. . . .

Pressure by Administrative Decision. Bureaucrats can often generate pressure upon legislators through the exercise of their legitimate discretion in the course of conducting the public's business. One of the most . . . widely argued examples was furnished by Postmaster General Arthur Summerfield. He gave orders to curtail mail deliveries one day a week . . . when Congress was showing reluctance to appropriate some funds which Mr. Summerfield said were necessary to prevent deficiencies in his agency. Despite outraged cries, Congress gave Mr. Summerfield the money. After all, people wanted their mail on Saturdays.

Looking again at the municipal level, the Water Commissioner of a New England city used his administrative powers to help arouse public support and pressure upon the Council for a bond issue to expand the water supply — a measure which certain industries in the city favored. Although it was a hot and dry summer, the Commissioner helped the drought along for some people by diverting water to the country club from a main which served many residences in a high part of the city. When the residents on this main could not draw bath water, not knowing that their water was being siphoned off to the golfers' showers, they were even more emphatic

[10] Reed L. Frischknecht, "The Democratization of Administration: The Farmer Committee System," *The American Political Science Review* 47 (September 1953):704 ff.

than the Water Commissioner and his industrialist supporters that the water supply needed expansion. Eventually the Council voted the bonds.[11]

GENERAL PUBLICITY ACTIVITIES

The ultimate aim of bureaucratic publicity is in large measure to create a climate of opinion which will be favorable to its objectives. Some of an agency's publicity is necessary to the administrative process of making more acceptable to the public the things it has already been assigned to do. But the cultivation of favorable public images also may serve to build up support for legislation which the agency desires but does not have, and it is difficult to separate one function of bureaucratic publicity from the other.

The many books and articles written about the exploits of the Federal Bureau of Investigation agents, the continuous, favorable publicity accorded to Mr. J. Edgar Hoover, and the speeches and writings of Mr. Hoover himself all help to make the jobs which are assigned to the FBI easier to accomplish. Yet this publicity also makes the agency more successful in its relations with Congress, for Congressmen are sensitive to the image maintained among the public at large.

Of course, the FBI is unusually fortunate in comparison with other federal bureaus in the nature and extent of its publicity, but many administrative units get a good deal of coverage on a fairly steady basis. There are abundant opportunities for members of the higher echelons of the bureaucracy not only to release news through regular channels and to talk to reporters, but also to make addresses, write articles, and in other ways create publicity for their organizations. Furthermore, in the field offices, regional press coverage is generally well maintained, especially for the larger agencies, and this substantially supplements the publicity emanating from Washington. Since nine-tenths of federal employees are not in Washington, there is immense opportunity for publicity to be generated at local levels, where it can often affect the constituents of Congressmen most directly.

There is also usually a network of friendly media especially interested in the subjects dealt with by an agency and willing to help carry the propaganda battle. Some of these are "trade" publications,

[11] See footnote 8.

which, combined with official publications and reports, give bureaucracies ample outlets to reach the most interested audiences. Due to the limited nature of general public interest in most public problems, it is frequently more important to reach the highly concerned portion of the public than to try to publicize in general.

Bureaucrats can become victims of their own overzealous publicity tactics. Legislators are capable of being very sensitive to what they regard as improper administrative propagandizing, especially if it encroaches on their domains. It does not help administrative leaders and the agencies they represent to become branded as propagandists. The kinds of retribution they suffer in such instances vary from oratorical chastisement in the legislative halls to denial of the very objects which they seek to have the legislators bestow — funds and authority.

3   *The Struggle for Organizational Survival*

HERBERT A. SIMON, DONALD W. SMITHBURG, AND VICTOR A. THOMPSON

It is now necessary to see how organizations adjust themselves to the world about them; their relations with other and competing organizations, with Congress, and with the general public. These adjustments and relations are essentially of a political character, and indeed, the topics we are about to discuss are sometimes referred to as "the politics of administration."

Which organizational relations are "internal" and which "external" depends on the standpoint. From the standpoint of the Chief

From *Public Administration,* by Herbert A. Simon, Donald W. Smithburg, and Victor A. Thompson. Copyright 1950 by Herbert A. Simon, Donald W. Smithburg, and Victor A. Thompson. Reprinted by permission of Alfred A. Knopf, Inc.

of the Forest Service, his relations with the Secretary of Agriculture are external; from the standpoint of the Secretary, these same relations are internal. We will be concerned largely with relations that are external to major organizational units — departments and bureaus. . . .

KINDS OF EXTERNAL SUPPORT NEEDED

Among the participants, other than employees, with whom we shall be concerned are the legislature, the chief executive, other governmental organizations, groups regulated or served by the organization ("clientele" groups), and the general public.

Legislative Support. No administrative organization in this country can come into being or long exist without the support of the legislature and usually the chief executive. The legislature provides the legal authority and the funds for the organization. The legal basis of the organization includes not only the definition of its goal or objective, but very often also a rather detailed description of the organizational structure. The legislative body also passes many laws that stipulate how the organization may carry out its objective — laws relating to the management of personnel, accounting for funds, expenditures, procurement, the rights of the citizen as against the organization, and many others. In most cases these laws or statutes, which provide the legal basis for administration, must be approved by the chief executive before they go into effect.

In addition to laws of this kind, the legislature and the executive pass appropriation bills which allow the organization to spend money for personnel and for other purposes and without which it could spend no money. In some cases the chief executive has various kinds of legal authority, either in his own right under the Constitution or by delegation from the legislature, that he may redelegate to an administrative organization. Given this legal framework, it is clear that an administrative organization must have the support of the legislature or the executive — and usually both — if it is to come into existence and continue to exist.

Support of Other Organizations. From this ultimate dependence of administrative organizations on the legislature and the chief executive there develops in a democracy a dependence upon many other persons and groups in the society. In the first place, other governmental organizations, such as a central budget agency or a civil service commission, will have considerable power to hinder or aid any administrative organization in the accomplishment of its goals. Thus the support of these other governmental organizations also becomes necessary.

Clientele Support. In the second place, the backing of groups or individuals that can influence the behavior of the legislature and the executive must also be sought. For some administrative organizations there are groups within society whose support, working through their representatives in the legislature, can guarantee the survival of the organization against almost any odds and whose opposition, in like fashion, is tantamount to the death of the organization or at least considerable modification of its objective and methods. Thus farmer organizations working through the farm bloc in the Federal Congress can often make or unmake agriculture programs and the agencies that administer them.

The group within society that is most immediately interested in an organization's program may be called its *clientele*. Thus, organized labor is more directly concerned with the activities of the Department of Labor than is any other segment of the community. American business is more directly concerned with the activities of the Department of Commerce than is any other segment of the community. The railroads and the shippers are directly concerned with the activities of the Interstate Commerce Commission, and so forth. If the clientele group is large, united in interest, and well organized, it can have an impact on the legislature that makes its support or at least acquiescence important, if not necessary, to the existence of the administrative agency in question.

There is another reason why the support of outside groups must be sought. The administrative organization plans and carries out programs that require the cooperation of segments of the public or even the whole public. If the required amount of cooperation is not forthcoming, the organization will fail to accomplish its objectives and hence to satisfy its supporters. Those who are regulated must generally approve of, or at least accede to, these programs. Administrative regulations can not be enforced against a generally hostile public. The reader can appreciate this point if he will try to imagine an attempt to enforce a draft law toward which most of the people were actively hostile. Even in dictatorships administrative organizations must cultivate some general feeling of support or acquiescence in their programs or they will not be able to carry them out.

The General Public. Finally, the general public through its vote may become a source of support or opposition to an administrative organization. The party in power may come to feel that the activities of a particular agency are so affecting general public opinion that it must interfere with the operations or objectives (or even the existence) of that agency.

Since public opinion concerning any particular governmental agency is generally rather vague, groups with specific interests in an agency's activities will usually have more effect than an incoherent general public. Thus it sometimes happens that opinion polls will show a majority of the people in favor of some activity which nevertheless is abolished or greatly modified by the legislature or the executive or both. A good example is the ill-fated Veteran's Emergency Housing Program of 1946 which got almost nowhere against solid blocks of opposition both within and without the government.

Although public opinion is usually not as influential as are pressure groups in affecting an agency's programs, still an enthusiastic general public support could probably not be negated by any pressure group. Likewise a general public hostility would probably result in abolition or substantial modification of any governmental program. . . .

THE MOTIVES FOR EXTERNAL SUPPORT

In general, the inducements to external supporters come from the goals and objectives of governmental organizations or the values created by them. Even as the customer of a commercial organization is interested in its product, so the "customers" of governmental organizations are interested in the products of governmental action. They give their support, their contribution to the organization, in return for the satisfactions they derive from the values created by the organization, whether these be increased educational opportunity or national defense.

When a group of people in a society becomes aware of an opportunity to achieve certain of the values that it holds either by supporting or opposing a governmental program, we call this set of values an *interest,* and the group that is organized around the promotion of the values an *interest group.* The activities of any particular governmental organization promote certain interests that have developed in society, are irrelevant to many interests, and are antagonistic to still others. Thus, for every administrative organization there are groups whose interests are promoted by the organization's activities, and who give in return their political support (e.g., the support of the American Legion for the Veterans' Administration). Other people and groups will be indifferent to the organization because it does not affect their interests (e.g., the Bureau of Foreign and Domestic Commerce has generally received neither support nor opposition from farm groups). Still others may develop an interest in its abolition or the modification of its activities because these activities challenge or destroy some of the values of the groups in question (e.g., a rent control agency becomes a target for landlord groups; pacifist groups oppose appropriations to the military departments).

The Changing Environment. Since the structure of interests in society is dependent upon the physical and social environment, when these environmental conditions change, the pattern of interests in society changes with them. A change in environment may create a new group of interests; it may intensify or diminish old ones; it may cause an interest to disappear. An environmental change may greatly increase or decrease the number of persons sharing an interest; or it may shift the interest to an entirely new group of people.

As fire hazards increase, the fire department receives more support. As good land runs out, an interest in public irrigation appears. As floods become worse, an interest in flood control intensifies. When depressions occur, interest in relief becomes much stronger. As employment rises, the support of relief agencies and unemployment insurance agencies wanes. As the dependence of business upon technical knowledge increases, an interest in cheap technical education appears. As war becomes total and more terrible and imminent, an interest in the health of young men and the development of skills in the labor force begins to appear. As the economic situation of the railroad industry deteriorates, hostility toward the Interstate Commerce Commission decreases.

Conflicts of Interests. For most goals in society there are antithetical or conflicting interests. Hence programs that satisfy one group of people often reduce satisfactions of other groups. Regulating prices in the interest of consumers decreases profits of producers and sellers. Protecting and strengthening the collective bargaining interest of unions destroys the advantages many employers derive from weak unions or from power over working conditions. Protecting the interests of shippers in fair and uniform rates reduces earnings of railroad companies derived from the ability to impose high and discriminatory rates. Protecting the broadcasting industry (and the listening public) by licensing broadcasters interferes with people who would like to enter the industry but are not allowed to by the Federal Communications Commission.

Which interest will be protected and which sacrificed is determined by the political process. In fact, many political scientists would take this as the very definition of politics — in the words of Harold Lasswell, politics determines "who gets what, when, how."

When one interest is politically strong and well organized and its opponents are weak and unorganized, the answer is simple — as witness the defeat of the public housing program in the Eightieth Congress. Sometimes, however, the conflicting interests are of roughly the same strength, and the conflict resolves itself in some sort of compromise. Subsequent shifts in the relative strengths of conflicting groups then are reflected, from time to time, in program changes. Thus, successive changes in labor legislation over the past generation have reflected changes in the strength and degree of organization of labor and employer groups.

Few, indeed, are the administrative agencies that have all friends and no enemies. There is almost certain to be some hostility towards any administrative organization and its program. To survive with any given program of activities, an agency must find friendly groups whose political support is strong enough to overcome the opposition of hostile groups. To preserve its friends, it must to some degree adapt its program to their interests. To neutralize its enemies, it must sometimes sacrifice elements in its program that attract the most effective political opposition. Hence, organizations are in a continual process of adjustment to the political environment that surrounds them — an adjustment that seeks to keep a favorable balance of political support over political opposition. . . .

Resistance to Adjustment. We find among organizational members, then, three sets of motives that tend to make the organization adapt to the demands of external forces, if these demands are sufficiently strong. The first is a tactical opportunism which arises out of a desire to preserve the organization as an effective means of goal accomplishment, even at the cost of a partial modification of goals and program. The second is an opportunism that seeks to preserve the organization as an object of the pride of membership. The third is a self-protective opportunism which arises out of a desire of the individual to protect his position, power, prestige, and salary.

On the other side of the picture, we find two forces within organizations that resist adjustment to external pressures. The first of these — goal attachment — may countenance adjustment, but only grudgingly and with minimum sacrifice of goals, as we have just seen. The second may be described as "inertia" — resistance due to the painfulness of altering habitual and accustomed ways of doing things. This inertia is derived from a number of psychological forces, including the disinclination to admit that the old ways are not the best ways and the personal cost of thinking out and trying new ways.

A good illustration of the inertia factor is the appeal made to the Congress in 1903 by General Miles, Commanding General of the Army, in opposition to the establishment of the General Staff.

More than 100 years ago our Army was organized by the genius of Washington, Steuben, Hamilton, and others. In all the wars in which we have been engaged it has in the end been victorious. It has withstood intrigue and contaminating influence from without and has absorbed the injurious elements that have been forced upon it, sustaining the honor of the Nation, and the glory of American arms in every campaign and in its present organization is best adapted to our great Republic. In my judgement a system that is the fruit of the best thought of the most eminent patriots and ablest military men that this country has produced should not be destroyed by substituting one that is more adapted to the monarchies of the Old World. . . .[1]

THE EXECUTIVE AND ORGANIZATIONAL ADJUSTMENT

The principal organ of adjustment within an organization is the executive hierarchy. There are several reasons why the executives (increasingly so as we mount the hierarchy) are normally more adjustive, more compromising, than the bulk of the organization's members.

"*Natural Selection.*" In the first place, a sort of natural selection brings about this phenomenon. The executive hierarchy has a much greater influence on the organization than the bulk of its members, and so, if that hierarchy were incapable of adjustment, the organiza-

---

[1] Quoted in [Otto L.] Nelson, [Jr.,] *National Security and the General Staff* [Washington, D.C.: Infantry Journal Press, 1946], pp. 53–54.

tion would cease to exist. In other words, if an organization continues to exist it is a safe conclusion that its hierarchy is adjustable.

Mobility of Executives. Highly mobile individuals — individuals with very strong personal ambitions — gravitate into positions of power. In order to mount the ladder of hierarchical success it is often necessary to take actions or make decisions of a somewhat cold-blooded kind. One must "go to lunch with the right people." Sometimes friends must be by-passed. Occasionally someone must be fired who badly needs his job. Yearnings and aspirations of incapable people must sometimes be disregarded. Most persons, except those who have strong personal ambitions or unusually strong attachments to a goal, find such behavior difficult. Consequently, many highly mobile people climb upward in organizational hierarchies by a kind of self-selection.

Identifications of Executives. There is yet another reason why the executive hierarchy is usually increasingly adjustable or compromising as we go up toward the highest levels. The head of an agency, if he identifies with anything, is likely to identify with the whole agency, with its total program rather than with any of its parts. If it is necessary to sacrifice one branch or the program it administers to obtain the necessary support for the whole agency, that sacrifice may appear to the top executive merely a means to an end — and not the sacrifice of the end itself, as it may appear to the branch personnel. This difference in the breadth of identification between the executive and the people below him will usually be evident from the lowest supervisory level to the highest.

External Contacts of Executives. A final reason for executive adaptability is that the executive is less insulated from the rest of the world than those below him. He must answer questions and justify the operations of his staff to his superiors. Higher-level executives must often justify the operations of their agencies or bureaus to legislative committees. Interested groups and individuals and other administrative agencies will usually make their demands known through the executives; and it is the executives who are often singled out for criticism by the press. This wide range of interests and influences that play upon the executives sharpens their awareness of other points of view, and the political consequences of the agency's decisions will have a special impact on them. It is easy to be firm and uncompromising only when one is remote from the political consequences of his own actions.

The executive hierarchy has a particularly important role to play both in adjustment and in resistance to adjustment. Both because of the expectations of their staffs and because of their own desires, executives will play a leading part in warding off external dangers. Because of position and prestige they will have influence with external groups and individuals, be they the Civil Service Commission, the chief executive, or a legislative committee. A good deal of their attention will usually be given to preventing actions within the organization that might stimulate the antagonism of external individuals and groups. Frequently the very top executive of an administrative organization, whether he is elected or appointed, is a representative of an important political constituency.

The importance of the opportunistic or compromising element in the satisfactions of the executive hierarchy is that it renders the executive more flexible and adjustable; it enables him to see the importance of, and to act on the principle of, "doing a little wrong to do a great right." Through his efforts persons interested in the organization's goals, both within and without the organization, may accomplish part of their desires whereas otherwise they might accomplish nothing. . . .

The Conditions of Survival

We have seen that various groups and individuals, both within and outside of administrative organizations, make contributions to them in return for satisfactions derived from them. Groups and individuals outside contribute political support in return for satisfactions derived from the accomplishment of the organization's goal. Members of the organization contribute time, skills, and knowledge in return for the satisfaction of personal and organizational goals to which they are attached.

Survival for Whom? However, as we have also seen, the satisfaction-contribution equilibria of various organizational members may not all be the same, so that a readjustment to the external world which is desired by some may not be acceptable to others. Even as some individuals and groups outside the organization gain at the expense of others, so within an organization the survival of one set of satisfactions may be at the expense of another. Prestige and power may not survive unless goals are modified; but goal modifications may be impossible unless some accustomed ways of doing and thinking are sacrificed. For organizations to survive there must be a continuous and delicate adjustment of several different sets of satisfactions and contributions to the conditions that determine the shifting interests within society.

Adjustment to What? The problems of survival are not the same for all administrative organizations. Some promote or protect newly recognized interests that have struggled long for recognition, such as the interest of labor unions in worker organization and collective bargaining. Here the external support is enthusiastic and the external opposition bitterly hostile. Here also strong goal attachments within the organization are likely. Such organizations are quite insecure because a shift in the political tide may bring the organization's enemies into political power. In the 1946 elections, the enemies of the National Labor Relations Board secured political power and vastly modified its program (through the Taft-Hartley Act), turning it to some extent into an enemy of organized labor. Many employees of the Board found it difficult to accept the new orientation and resigned or were shunted into positions of relative unimportance.

Other organizations promote interests so thoroughly accepted that no one questions the organization's goals any longer. Such is the case with fire and police departments, the Post Office Department, and many others. Here, strong goal attachments are more difficult, though not impossible, to maintain. External "dangers" are more likely to consist in demands for better, more courteous, or more efficient service.

Some interests are obviously and admittedly short-lived, and it is expected that the organizations established to promote them will disappear when their objectives are completed. Here, although organizational members may wistfully wish that their agency could be continued, the fact that it cannot is so absolute as to be acceptable. Organizations in this class include emergency agencies dealing with floods, wars, and the like. Even in this kind of agency there may sometimes be a struggle for continuance. An example is the difficulty of disarming after a war — a difficulty not ascribable solely to the "dangers of the international situation."

Whereas some organizational goals represent a clear triumph of one interest over conflicting ones, many represent compromises among conflicting interests. In this category we would include much governmental regulatory activity. For example, railroad regulation is always a shifting compromise among the interests of the road managements, the shippers, the passengers, railroad labor, the small stockholders, railroad suppliers, and railroad financial control groups.[2] In this kind of organization, the attempts of the conflicting external interests to get complete control are constant, and the organizational members are, for this reason, constantly embroiled in the politics of survival.

Whether or not there are external conflicts of interest in an organization's goals, the problem of survival is continuous. A new high executive may have ideas about reorganizing or "improving operations"; or a citizens' group may demand a "shakeup"; or some executive, agency, or bureau may begin to acquire more power within the whole government or the whole organization. Any of these may threaten the survival of satisfactions derived from accustomed methods, from prestige and other personal opportunities, and even from the values reflected by the organization's operations.

CONCLUSION

The material set forth in this chapter gives considerable credence to the charge often made by critics of government that government agencies are exceedingly hardy and long-lived. But our analysis does not lend support to the doctrine that this longevity is due to some bureaucratic "will to survive." To be sure, there are many strong motivations at work within organizations that lead these organizations to adapt their activities to the requirements of survival. But government agencies cannot exist without appropriations or enabling statutes. They can survive only so long as they can continue to secure the support of politically effective groups in the community and continue through these groups to secure legislative and executive support. "Bureaucrats" can wish to survive, but they do not determine the conditions of survival.

[2] See Merle Fainsod and Lincoln Gordon, *Government and the American Economy* (New York, 1941), chap. 9.

4   TVA and the Grass Roots

PHILIP SELZNICK

The Tennessee Valley Authority was created by Congress in May, 1933, as a response to a long period of pressure for the disposition of government-owned properties at Muscle Shoals, Alabama. During the First World War, two nitrate plants and what was later known as Wilson Dam were constructed, at a cost of over $100,000,000. For the next fifteen years, final decision as to the future of these installations hung fire. The focal points of contention related to the production and distribution of fertilizer and electric power, and to the principle of government versus private ownership. Two presidential commissions and protracted congressional inquiries recorded the long debate. At last, with the advent of the Roosevelt administration in 1933, the government assumed responsibility for a general resolution of the major issues.

The TVA Act as finally approved was a major victory for those who favored the principle of government operation. The Muscle Shoals investment was to remain in public ownership, and this initial project was to be provided with new goals and to be vastly extended. A great public power project was envisioned, mobilizing the "by-product" of dams built for the purpose of flood control and navigation improvement on the Tennessee River and its tributaries. Control and operation of the nitrate properties, to be used for fertilizer production, was also authorized, although this aspect was subordinated in importance to electricity. These major powers — authority to construct dams, deepen the river channel, produce and distribute electricity and fertilizer — were delegated by Congress to a corporation administered by a three-man board of directors.

If this had been all, the project would still have represented an important extension of government activity and responsibility. But what began as, and what was generally understood to be, primarily

From Philip Selznick, *TVA and the Grass Roots* (Berkeley, 1949), pp. 4–5, 37–41, 69, 72–74, 145–147, 217. Originally published by the University of California Press; reprinted by permission of The Regents of the University of California.

the solution of a problem of fertilizer and power emerged as an institution of far broader meaning. A new regional concept — the river basin as an integral unit — was given effect, so that a government agency was created which had a special responsibility neither national nor statewide in scope. This offered a new dimension for the consideration of the role of government in the evolving federal system. At the same time, the very form of the agency established under the Act was a new departure. There was created a relatively autonomous public corporation free in important aspects from the normal financial and administrative controls exercised over federal organs. Further, and in one sense most important, a broad vision of regional resource development — in a word, planning — informed the conception, if not the actual powers, of the new organization.

The Message of the President requesting the TVA legislation did much to outline that perception: "It is clear," wrote Mr. Roosevelt, "that the Muscle Shoals development is but a small part of the potential public usefulness of the entire Tennessee River. Such use, if envisioned in its entirety, transcends mere power development: it enters the wide fields of flood control, soil erosion, afforestation, elimination from agricultural use of marginal lands, and distribution and diversification of industry. In short, this power development of war days leads logically to national planning for a complete river watershed involving many States and the future lives and welfare of millions. It touches and gives life to all forms of human concerns." To carry out this conception, the President recommended "legislation to create a Tennessee Valley Authority — a corporation clothed with the power of government but possessed of the flexibility and initiative of private enterprise. It should be charged with the broadest duty of planning for the proper use, conservation, and development of the natural resources of the Tennessee River drainage basin and its adjoining territory for the general social and economic welfare of the Nation." . . .

THE PARTNERSHIP OF TVA AND THE PEOPLE'S INSTITUTIONS

After some difficulties and initial disagreements, but still very early in its history, the Authority defined its approach to cooperation with the agencies and institutions already existing in the Valley. The alternatives seemed to be two: either to take a line which assumed that the TVA itself could and should carry out its programs by direct action; or to accept as legitimate and efficient a method which would seek out and even establish local institutions to mediate between the TVA and the people of the area. It was felt that an imposed federal program would be alien and unwanted, and ultimately accomplish little, unless it brought together at the grass roots all the agencies concerned with and essential to the development of a region's resources: the local communities, voluntary private organizations, state agencies, and cooperating federal agencies. The vision of such a working partnership seemed to define "grass-roots democracy at work."

In the Authority's view, the fundamental rationale of the partnership approach is found in its implications for democracy. If the TVA can be "shaped by intimate association with long-established institutions,"[1] that will mean that its vitality is drawn from below. By working through state and local agencies, the Authority will provide the people of the Valley with more effective means by which to direct their own destinies. The TVA may then become more integrally a part of the region, committed to its interests and cognizant of its needs, and thus removed in thought and action from the remote impersonal bureaucracy of centralized government.

The moral dimension of the grass-roots approach has been emphasized many times. The methods of TVA are proffered as more than technical means for the achievement of administrative objectives. They include and underline the responsibility of leadership in a democracy to offer the people alternatives for free choice rather than ready-made prescriptions elaborated in the fastnesses of planning agencies. . . .

The orientation toward local agencies is also a product of the conception that the resources of a region include its institutions, in particular its governmental agencies. The Authority deems it part of its obligation in connection with resource development that these local governmental institutions be strengthened rather than weakened, that they be supplemented rather than supplanted. In doing so, the Authority directs its effort toward developing a sense of responsibility on the part of the local organs and, what is equally important, toward providing them with a knowledge of the tools available to put that responsibility into action. . . .

[1] H. A. Morgan, Chairman, TVA, "Some Objectives and End Results of TVA," address before annual meeting of the American Society of Agricultural Engineers, Knoxville, Tenn., June 23, 1941 (mimeo.).

A list of agencies with which the TVA has maintained some form of cooperative relationship includes nearly all of the governmental institutions in the area: municipal power boards, rural electric cooperatives, school and library boards; state departments of health, conservation, and parks; state and local planning commissions, agricultural and engineering experiment stations, state extension services, and others. In developing these relationships TVA has applied the rule that "wherever possible, the Authority shall work toward achieving its objectives by utilizing or stimulating the developing of state and local organizations, agencies and institutions, rather than conducting direct action programs." [2] In addition, a number of federal agencies, notably technical bureaus of the U.S. Departments of Agriculture and the Interior, the Army Engineers, and the Coast Guard, have cooperative arrangements with the TVA. Notable also are the ad hoc organizations and conferences which have been established as vehicles for cooperation among the administrative agencies within the Valley. These include, among others, a semiannual conference of directors of extension services and of agricultural experiment stations of the seven Valley states, the U.S. Department of Agriculture, and the TVA; the Tennessee Valley Trades and Labor Council, bringing together fifteen international unions of the American Federation of Labor Building and Metal Trades; an annual conference of contractors and distributors of TVA power; and the Tennessee Valley Library Council. Such gatherings help to lay a sound foundation for regional unity, focusing the efforts of many agencies on the region as a central problem.

The form of cooperation with state and local agencies varies, but the pattern of intergovernmental contract has been most fully developed. Such contracts often include reimbursement by the Authority for personnel and other facilities used by the state in carrying on the cooperative program. In many cases, the ideal outcome is viewed as the tapering off of TVA contributions until, as TVA's responsibilities recede in importance, the local agency carries on by itself. Thus the states have in some cases begun planning work through their own commissions with the material help of TVA; later, state funds have been secured with a view to continuing the work when TVA's responsibilities for the readjustment of reservoir-affected urban com-

[2] As formulated at an Administrative Conference of TVA staff members, April 21, 1943.

munities would terminate. In cooperating with the local governments, TVA attempts to establish a pattern which may be continued after TVA aid has ceased.

The objective of stimulating local responsibility among governments and associations within the area is basic to the grass-roots approach. But there are other reasons which support it as sound administrative policy. The existing facilities of the states, even though they may be inadequate, are used to capacity, thus avoiding the establishment of duplicate services and personnel with parallel functions. The TVA is not anxious to have its own men in the field and is willing to forego the prestige that comes from identification as "TVA men" of agents performing services paid for out of TVA funds. The staff is educated to feel most satisfied when it can show evidence that a local organization has carried on TVA work and been permanently strengthened by the experience and in the eyes of its public. In addition, utilization of existing agencies permits TVA to shape its program in conformity with the intimate knowledge of local conditions which such agencies are likely to have; at the same time it is possible to restrict the size of the Authority's direct working force.

The attempt to create a working partnership between the TVA and the people in carrying out a common program for regional development goes beyond the strengthening of existing governmental agencies, though this objective is vital. The meaning of the partnership is contained as well in the use of the voluntary association as a means of inviting the participation of the people most immediately concerned in the administration of the program. In this way, the farmer or the businessman finds a means of participating in the activities of government supplemental to his role on election day. If there is fertilizer to be distributed, farmers are invited, on a county and community basis, to participate in locally controlled organizations which will make decisions as to the most effective means of using that fertilizer in the local area. If government land is to be rented, a local land-use association is organized so that the conditions of rental can be determined with maximum benefit for the community. If power is to be sold in a rural area, a cooperative provides a consumer ownership which retains profits in the community and makes possible a management guided by community problems and local needs. If the business area of a city must be modified because of newly flooded lands, let a locally organized planning

commission work out the best possible adjustment of special interests and long-range planning goals. Thus, at the end-point of operation, the specific consequences of a federal program may be shaped
and directed by local citizens so that its impact at the grass roots
will be determined in local terms. This procedure is not only democratic and just, but undoubtedly adds measurably to the effectiveness of the programs, which will be conjoined to the special desires
of those affected and thus have the benefit of their support and aid.

The policy of consciously working with and through local institutions is, in the Authority's view, integrally related to its relatively
autonomous position within the federal system. It is precisely the
flexibility accorded to the TVA management which has enabled it to
keep in mind its broad concept of regional development and at the
same time to seize upon whatever opportunities might arise to implement the concept concretely. Nationally directed restrictions as
to employment of personnel, a host of regulations framed in national
terms, would doubtless greatly restrict the ability of TVA to establish procedures attuned both to its substantive objectives and to the
grass-roots methods by which they are carried out. It would surely
inhibit the freedom to search out techniques uniquely adapted to
the special situations of some particular state government or community if TVA did not have the power to make its own decisions
and to take the initiative in fostering cooperative relationships.
Moreover, the absence of discretion might well be psychologically
decisive in hobbling the TVA staff by binding it to the customs and
traditional modes of action laid down by the broader hierarchy into
which it might be absorbed. . . .

INHERENT DILEMMAS

Tension and dilemma are normal and anticipated corollaries of the
attempt to control human institutions in the light of an abstract doctrine. . . . Practical leadership cannot long ignore the resistance of
social structure, and is often moved thereby to abandon concern for
abstract goals or ideas — for which it is often criticized out of hand
by the moralists and idealists who lack experience with the vicissitudes of practical action.[3] But a leadership which, for whatever reason, elects to be identified with a doctrine and professes to use it in

[3] Cf. Robert K. Merton, "The Role of the Intellectual in Public Bureaucracy,"
Social Forces 23 (May 1945):413.

action, is continuously faced with tensions between the idea and the act. Ideological symbols may fulfill useful functions of communication and defense and may be long sustained as meaningful even when effective criteria of judgment remain lacking; but an act entails responsibility, establishing alliances and commitments which demand attention and deference. . . .

The TVA, in relation to its policy of grass-roots administration, is not immune to such difficulties. Though seldom made explicit, sources of tension are recognized by members of the staff, and have already entered into the process of administrative decision. Among these may be noted: . . .

Emphasis on existing institutions as democratic instruments may wed the agency to the status quo. A procedure which channels the administration of a program through established local institutions, governmental or private, tends to reinforce the legitimacy of the existing leadership. This is especially true when a settled pattern claims the exclusive attention of the agency, so that other groups striving for leadership may find their position relatively weakened after the new relationships have been defined. In strengthening the land-grant colleges in its area, the TVA has bolstered the position of the existing farm leadership. There is some evidence that in the process of establishing its pattern of cooperation, TVA refrained from strengthening independent colleges in the area not associated with the land-grant college system. Again, the relatively dominant role of the American Federation of Labor unions in TVA labor relations, especially as constituting the Tennessee Valley Trades and Labor Council, is objectively a hindrance to the development of labor groups having other affiliations. In general, to the extent that the agency selects one set of institutions within a given field as the group through which it will work, the possibility of freezing existing social relationships is enhanced. At least in its agricultural program, TVA has chosen to limit its cooperative relationships to a special group, so that the potential or inherent dilemma has been made explicit. . . .

Commitment to existing agencies may shape and inhibit policy in unanticipated ways. When the channels of action are restricted, programs may be elaborated only within the limits established by the nature of the cooperating organizations. The traditions and outlook of an established institution will resist goals which appear to be alien, and the initiating agency will tend to avoid difficulties by restricting its own proposals to those which can be feasibly carried out by the grass-roots organization. Where the grass-roots method is ignored, new institutions may be built, shaped *ab initio* in terms of the desired program. An attempt to carry forward a policy of nondiscrimination (as against Negroes) will not proceed very far when the instrument for carrying out this policy — usually as an adjunct of some broader program — has traditions of its own of a contrary bent. Moreover, the grass-roots policy voluntarily creates nucleuses of power which may be used for the furtherance of interests outside the system of cooperation originally established. Thus the TVA distributes electric power through electric power boards which are creatures of municipalities, with the contractual reservation that surplus income shall be used only for improvements in the system or for the reduction of rates. But the question has been raised: what if pressure arises to use surpluses for general purposes, that is, to finance nonpower functions of the municipal governments? And what if the state governments undertake to tax these surpluses, because of a restricted tax base and unwillingness to institute a state income tax? The logic of the grass-roots policy might force the Authority to agree. However, it is perhaps more likely that the Authority's commitment to function as a successful power project would take precedence over the grass-roots method.

Existing agencies inhibit a direct approach to the local citizenry. The participation of local people always takes place through some organizational mechanism, notably voluntary associations established to involve a public in some measure of decision at the end-point of operation. But such associations are commonly adjuncts of an administrative agency which jealously guards all approaches to its clientele. If, therefore, a federal agency establishes cooperative relations with such an agency, it will be committed as well to the system of voluntary associations which has been established. Hence the channels of participation of local people in the federal program will be shaped by the intermediary agency. In respect to its closeness to the people, the status of the federal government may not, in such circumstances, be materially altered. Viewed from this perspective, the grass-roots method becomes an effective means whereby an intrenched bureaucracy protects its clientele, and also itself, from the encroachments of the federal government. . . .

An Administrative Constituency

. . . The relationship between the TVA and the farm leadership in the Valley area may be summarized in the concept of the administrative constituency. . . . A constituency is a group, formally outside a given organization, to which the latter (or an element within it) has a special commitment. A relation of mutual dependence develops, so that the agent organization must defend its constituency and conversely. This relation gains strength and definition as precedents are established in behavior and in doctrine, and especially as the constituency itself attains organized form. A group which finds its coherence in common interest, but remains unorganized, may enforce its demands in subtle ways, but a leadership and a machinery serve to mobilize its resources. At the same time, however, this machinery may become separated from its popular base and itself become the effective constituency.

The idea of an administrative constituency, however it may be phrased, is familiar to students of public administration,[4] and in general may be thought of as a normal mechanism of social control whereby formal organizations are made responsive to relevant publics. Or, put in other terms, the creation of the constituency relationship is a form of cooptation, the informal involvement of local elements in the process of policy determination. One TVA staff member felt that the TVA's agricultural constituency operated as "one element in the general trend in the Authority toward conservatism and adjustment to Valley institutions." It is this adjustment which is one of the significant implications of the process of cooptation in administration.

The constituency relation varies widely in source, in intensity, and

[4] See Avery Leiserson, *Administrative Regulation* (Chicago, 1942), p. 9; also V. O. Key, Jr., "Politics and Administration," in L. D. White (Ed.), *The Future of Government in the United States* (Chicago, 1942), p. 151: "In one respect individual parts of the administration tend to become like private pressure groups in that they have their own particularistic and parochial interests to defend and promote. . . . The association of the agency with its clientele sometimes makes for a 'representative bureaucracy.' The policy drives of the hierarchy arising from the immediate interests of its members are reinforced and colored by the power and wishes of outside groups concerned with the work of the agency. Through administrative determination of delegated policy questions and through administrative influence on new policy, the desires of private groups may be effectively projected into the governmental machinery. In extreme circumstances something in the nature of a guild may be approached."

in meaning. One form may arise simply out of the need felt by an organization, public or private, to defend its continuing working relations with an outside group or agency. Interest may focus only accidentally upon the particular outside group involved, for it is the smooth avenue of operation which is being defended, and will not be readily jeopardized in the interests of a program in which the organization may have no great stake. It is often inconvenient and difficult to alter established procedures, so that a given form of cooperation may be defended in order to preserve the integrity and equilibrium of operations. This situation is analytically quite different from that in which the outside organization is defended for its own sake, as occurs in the relation between the TVA Agricultural Relations Department and the land-grant colleges. There is also a distinction to be drawn between short-run pressures upon an agency and the long-run strategy by which a measure of continuing control is achieved. In connection with the administrative relations analyzed above, the land-grant colleges have sought and gained a significant measure of influence upon the TVA; moreover, the TVA agriculturists do defend the colleges as valuable, and even indispensable, in themselves. That a constituency relation in this advanced form exists is well known in the higher circles of TVA, and is the subject of much comment.

The significance of a constituency relation depends in part upon the fact that the character of the constituency will tend to define and shape the character of the agency. This may involve the recruitment of personnel from the ranks of the constituency and, in an extreme form, the assumption by elements within the agency of a leadership status with respect to the constituency. The representatives of the constituency within the agency then come to define their role as one of leading a broad struggle for the furtherance of the interests of the constituency, and sometimes may be more conscious of those interests than members of the outside group themselves. Where the outside group is not the formal source of public policy, the constituency relation may remain more or less covert, and its representatives may find it necessary to devise and rely upon some doctrine or ideology to cover and defend the real relationships. An adequate comprehension of the full meaning of the grass-roots policy does not appear to be possible apart from some such principle as this.

In the relation of TVA to the land-grant colleges, the mechanics of representation include attempts by the Agricultural Relations Department of TVA to (1) channel all activities which may possibly be interpreted as within their subject-matter field through the land-grant colleges; (2) make itself the sole point of contact by the Authority with the institutions; (3) actively oppose all encroachments on the prerogatives of the colleges; and (4) further the policies of the colleges within the Authority, as opportunity may arise. . . .

The construction of an administrative constituency, whereby the dominant agricultural leadership in the Tennessee Valley area was afforded a place within the policy-determining structure of the TVA, is an example of the process of *informal* cooptation. . . . The unacknowledged absorption of nucleuses of power into the administrative structure of an organization makes possible the elimination or appeasement of potential sources of opposition. At the same time, as the price of accommodation, the organization commits itself to avenues of activity and lines of policy enforced by the character of the coopted elements. Moreover, though cooptation may occur with respect to only a fraction of the organization, there will be pressure for the organization as a whole to adapt itself to the needs of the informal relationship. Viewed thus broadly, the process of informal cooptation represents a mechanism of comprehensive adjustment, permitting a formal organization to enhance its chances for survival by accommodating itself to existing centers of interest and power within its area of operation. . . .

II

THE POWER
OF BUREAUCRATIC EXPERTISE

Max Weber's "Essay on Bureaucracy" is the classic analysis of expertise as a source of bureaucratic power. Weber contends that the power of executive officials is rooted in the technical or professional skills that distinguish administrators from amateur politicians. Bureaucratic power thus reflects the technological revolution and the growing influence of specialized knowledge in modern civilization. Executive organizations provide a superior way of grouping people together to achieve results and also are a major source of employment for experts in various fields. Thus, as well as being an environment attractive to experts, such organizations create expertise.

"Under normal conditions," Weber writes, "the power position of a fully developed bureaucracy is always overtowering. The 'political master' finds himself in the position of the 'dilettante' who stands opposite the 'expert,' facing the trained official who stands within the management of administration." Weber's analysis does not always fit the contours of American society. His discussion of administrative secrecy, for example, overstates the tendency of public agencies in this country to withhold information. Many agencies spend more time publicizing themselves than they do concealing information; their path to power is publicity rather than secrecy.

In the United States, moreover, the continuity in office of legislative committee chairmen often exceeds that of executive agency heads. So it sometimes becomes a moot point who is the "dilettante" and who the "expert" in confrontations between Congress and the executive. But Weber does correct any tendency to regard administrative power in the United States entirely as the mobilizing of a constituency. In this country as elsewhere, expertise is still a vital factor in the influence that bureaucratic organizations exert. The Surgeon-General's impact on public policy in the United States does not rest exclusively on his skill at mobilizing public support; it stems initially from the fact that his office both embodies and reflects the prestige and skills of medical science.

In past years the National Institutes of Health have frequently received more generous appropriations from Congress than they have requested, an unusual circumstance in executive-legislative relations. While this success can be traced in part to political considerations, especially to the Congressmen's belief that nothing is more important to their constituents than their health, it also rests on the impressive achievements of medical research in the modern world. In the field of health, the power of executive agencies is grounded on deference to professional skill as well as the political following that health organizations command.

I

"The Knowledge-Power Relationship: The Council of Economic Advisers" by Edward S. Flash, Jr., clearly shows that although the administrators' expertise enables them to influence elected officials, these officeholders in turn can expand their own power by surrounding their decisions with the aura of scientific knowledge. Without their access to the President the economists on the Council would have great difficulty in exerting any influence on public policy; hence, they serve their own interests by serving him. At the same time, the President uses the professional skills of his economic advisors to buttress his positions on issues of economic policy.

To some extent Flash's analysis suggests a constant relationship between the President and his staff advisers, a relationship that can be described as an exchange system. The

President has certain needs that his economic staff can satisfy, mainly professional skills to help legitimize his decisions. The staff in turn obtains a resource only the President can provide, entry to the highest councils of government, an access determined not by an ability to win elections but by a capacity to provide answers on major questions of public policy.

Yet Flash's discussion also suggests that the nature of this relationship is very much colored by each President's distinctive style and temperament, as well as by the professional orientation of the Council chairmen. The relationship is also affected by the economic conditions of the moment. If vigorous government action is needed to bolster a sagging economy, then the President turns increasingly to the Council for advice. When the economy is relatively stable, the Council's opportunity to play a leading role in the policy process diminishes. The interaction between the President and the Council, therefore, reflects both constant factors present in the relationship between policymaker and adviser and dramatic alterations from administration to administration or from one economic setting to another.

II

The expertise of an administrative agency like the Council of Economic Advisers stems from the fact that it provides an organizational habitat within which skilled professionals such as economists can practice their craft as government officials. In this case, administrators have acquired their expertise prior to entering the public service.

In Graham T. Allison's "The Power of Bureaucratic Routines: The Cuban Missile Crisis," however, we see the extent to which bureaucratic expertise may be an attribute of the organization itself, not something its members possess as a personal skill. To be sure, the military professionals about whom Allison writes are, in Harold Lasswell's phrase, "specialists in violence." [1] But the routines they have mastered are a product of their service with the organization, and these routines require concerted action by an organization

[1] Harold Lasswell, *Politics: Who Gets What, When, How* (New York: Meridian Books, 1958), pp. 46–61.

for their effective execution, or what is called in the language of organizations "standard operating procedures."

As Allison's account of the Cuban missile crisis reveals, these standard procedures limit the policy options of elected officials to the actions that the organizations themselves are prepared to carry out, and such routines may, because of their inflexibility, produce consequences that the policymakers would prefer to avoid. In addition, organizations have vested interests in choosing policy alternatives that will aggrandize their own power, and because of these interests, may pursue certain courses of action even after they have proved unprofitable from the nation's viewpoint.

Thus, while political leaders are served by bureaucratic expertise, they may also be victimized by it, and their political careers can be shortened as a result. This fact forces them to develop defenses against the influence of their experts. Warner Schilling deals with these defenses in "Scientists, Foreign Policy, and Politics." He focuses on bureaucratic advice, the reasons why policymakers should regard it with a measure of skepticism, and the methods by which they can avoid becoming entirely captive to it. As his analysis reveals, the advisory process may result in serious distortions in policy, not only because of certain professional biases limiting the perspective of advisory groups, but also because Presidents have a predisposition to believe advice that conforms to their prejudices and to screen out information that does not.

5   *Essay on Bureaucracy*

Max Weber

Characteristics of Bureaucracy

Modern officialdom functions in the following specific manner.

I. There is the principle of fixed and official jurisdictional areas, which are generally ordered by rules, that is, by laws or administrative regulations.

1. The regular activities required for the purposes of the bureaucratically governed structure are distributed in a fixed way as official duties.

2. The authority to give the commands required for the discharge of these duties is distributed in a stable way and is strictly delimited by rules concerning the coercive means, physical, sacerdotal, or otherwise, which may be placed at the disposal of officials.

3. Methodical provision is made for the regular and continuous fulfilment of these duties and for the execution of the corresponding rights; only persons who have the generally regulated qualifications to serve are employed.

In public and lawful government these three elements constitute "bureaucratic authority." In private economic domination, they constitute bureaucratic "management." Bureaucracy, thus understood, is

Abridged from *From Max Weber: Essays in Sociology,* edited and translated by H. H. Gerth and C. Wright Mills. Copyright 1946 by Oxford University Press, Inc. Reprinted by permission.

53

fully developed in political and ecclesiastical communities only in the modern state, and, in the private economy, only in the most advanced institutions of capitalism. Permanent and public office authority, with fixed jurisdiction, is not the historical rule but rather the exception. This is so even in large political structures such as those of the ancient Orient, the Germanic and Mongolian empires of conquest, or of many feudal structures of state. In all these cases, the ruler executes the most important measures through personal trustees, table-companions, or court-servants. Their commissions and authority are not precisely delimited and are temporarily called into being for each case.

II. The principles of office hierarchy and of levels of graded authority mean a firmly ordered system of super- and subordination in which there is a supervision of the lower offices by the higher ones. Such a system offers the governed the possibility of appealing the decision of a lower office to its higher authority, in a definitely regulated manner. With the full development of the bureaucratic type, the office hierarchy is monocratically organized. The principle of hierarchical office authority is found in all bureaucratic structures: in state and ecclesiastical structures as well as in large party organizations and private enterprises. It does not matter for the character of bureaucracy whether its authority is called "private" or "public."

When the principle of jurisdictional "competency" is fully carried through, hierarchical subordination — at least in public office — does not mean that the "higher" authority is simply authorized to take over the business of the "lower." Indeed, the opposite is the rule. Once established and having fulfilled its task, an office tends to continue in existence and be held by another incumbent.

III. The management of the modern office is based upon written documents ("the files"), which are preserved in their original or draught form. There is, therefore, a staff of subaltern officials and scribes of all sorts. The body of officials actively engaged in a "public" office, along with the respective apparatus of material implements and the files, make up a "bureau." In private enterprise, "the bureau" is often called "the office."

In principle, the modern organization of the civil service separates the bureau from the private domicile of the official, and, in general, bureaucracy segregates official activity as something distinct from the sphere of private life. Public monies and equipment are divorced from the private property of the official. This condition is everywhere the product of a long development. Nowadays, it is found in public as well as in private enterprises; in the latter, the principle extends even to the leading entrepreneur. In principle, the executive office is separated from the household, business from private correspondence, and business assets from private fortunes. The more consistently the modern type of business management has been carried through the more are these separations the case. The beginnings of this process are to be found as early as the Middle Ages.

It is the peculiarity of the modern entrepreneur that he conducts himself as the "first official" of his enterprise, in the very same way in which the ruler of a specifically modern bureaucratic state spoke of himself as "the first servant" of the state. The idea that the bureau activities of the state are intrinsically different in character from the management of private economic offices is a continental European notion and, by way of contrast, is totally foreign to the American way.

IV. Office management, at least all specialized office management — and such management is distinctly modern — usually presupposes thorough and expert training. This increasingly holds for the modern executive and employee of private enterprises, in the same manner as it holds for the state official.

V. When the office is fully developed, official activity demands the full working capacity of the official, irrespective of the fact that his obligatory time in the bureau may be firmly delimited. In the normal case, this is only the product of a long development, in the public as well as in the private office. Formerly, in all cases, the normal state of affairs was reversed: official business was discharged as a secondary activity.

VI. The management of the office follows general rules, which are more or less stable, more or less exhaustive, and which can be learned. Knowledge of these rules represents a special technical learning which the officials possess. It involves jurisprudence, or administrative or business management.

The reduction of modern office management to rules is deeply embedded in its very nature. The theory of modern public administration, for instance, assumes that the authority to order certain matters by decree — which has been legally granted to public authorities — does not entitle the bureau to regulate the matter by commands given for each case, but only to regulate the matter abstractly. This stands in extreme contrast to the regulation of all relationships through individual privileges and bestowals of favor, which is absolutely dominant in patrimonialism, at least in so far as such relationships are not fixed by sacred tradition. . . .

TECHNICAL ADVANTAGES OF BUREAUCRATIC ORGANIZATION

The decisive reason for the advance of bureaucratic organization has always been its purely technical superiority over any other form of organization. The fully developed bureaucratic mechanism compares with other organizations exactly as does the machine with the nonmechanical modes of production.

Precision, speed, unambiguity, knowledge of the files, continuity, discretion, unity, strict subordination, reduction of friction and of material and personal costs — these are raised to the optimum point in the strictly bureaucratic administration, and especially in its monocratic form. As compared with all collegiate, honorific, and avocational forms of administration, trained bureaucracy is superior on all these points. And as far as complicated tasks are concerned, paid bureaucratic work is not only more precise but, in the last analysis, it is often cheaper than even formally unremunerated honorific service.

Honorific arrangements make administrative work an avocation and, for this reason alone, honorific service normally functions more slowly; being less bound to schemata and being more formless. Hence it is less precise and less unified than bureaucratic work because it is less dependent upon superiors and because the establishment and exploitation of the apparatus of subordinate officials and filing services are almost unavoidably less economical. Honorific service is less continuous than bureaucratic and frequently quite expensive. This is especially the case if one thinks not only of the money costs to the public treasury — costs which bureaucratic administration, in comparison with administration by notables, usually substantially increases — but also of the frequent economic losses of the governed caused by delays and lack of precision. The possibility of administration by notables normally and permanently exists only where official management can be satisfactorily discharged as an avocation. With the qualitative increase of tasks the administration has to face, administration by notables reaches its limits — today, even, in England. Work organized by collegiate bodies causes friction and delay and requires compromises between colliding interests and views. The administration, therefore, runs less precisely and is more independent of superiors; hence, it is less unified and slower. All advances of the Prussian administrative organization have been and will in the future be advances of the bureaucratic, and especially of the monocratic, principle.

Today, it is primarily the capitalist market economy which demands that the official business of the administration be discharged precisely, unambiguously, continuously, and with as much speed as possible. Normally, the very large, modern capitalist enterprises are themselves unequalled models of strict bureaucratic organization. Business management throughout rests on increasing precision, steadiness, and, above all, the speed of operations. This, in turn, is determined by the peculiar nature of the modern means of communication, including, among other things, the news service of the press. The extraordinary increase in the speed by which public announcements, as well as economic and political facts, are transmitted exerts a steady and sharp pressure in the direction of speeding up the tempo of administrative reaction towards various situations. The optimum of such reaction time is normally attained only by a strictly bureaucratic organization.[1]

Bureaucratization offers above all the optimum possibility for carrying through the principle of specializing administrative functions according to purely objective considerations. Individual performances are allocated to functionaries who have specialized training and who by constant practice learn more and more. The "objective" discharge of business primarily means a discharge of business according to *calculable rules* and "without regard for persons."

"Without regard for persons" is also the watchword of the "market" and, in general, of all pursuits of naked economic interests. . . .

The second element mentioned, "calculable rules," also is of paramount importance for modern bureaucracy. The peculiarity of modern culture, and specifically of its technical and economic basis, demands this very "calculability" of results. When fully developed, bureaucracy also stands, in a specific sense, under the principle of *sine ira ac studio.* Its specific nature, which is welcomed by capital-

---

[1] Here we cannot discuss in detail how the bureaucratic apparatus may, and actually does, produce definite obstacles to the discharge of business in a manner suitable for the single case.

ism, develops the more perfectly the more the bureaucracy is "de-humanized," the more completely it succeeds in eliminating from official business love, hatred, and all purely personal, irrational, and emotional elements which escape calculation. This is the specific nature of bureaucracy and it is appraised as its special virtue.

The more complicated and specialized modern culture becomes, the more its external supporting apparatus demands the personally detached and strictly "objective" *expert,* in lieu of the master of old social structures, who was moved by personal sympathy and favor, by grace and gratitude. Bureaucracy offers the attitudes demanded by the external apparatus of modern culture in the most favorable combination. As a rule, only bureaucracy has established the foundation for the administration of a rational law conceptually systematized on the basis of such enactments as the latter Roman imperial period first created with a high degree of technical perfection. During the Middle Ages, this law was received along with the bureaucratization of legal administration, that is to say, with the displacement of the old trial procedure which was bound to tradition or to irrational presuppositions, by the rationally trained and specialized expert. . . .

The Permanent Character of the Bureaucratic Machine

Once it is fully established, bureaucracy is among those social structures which are the hardest to destroy. . . . bureaucracy has been and is a power instrument of the first order — for the one who controls the bureaucratic apparatus.

Under otherwise equal conditions, a "societal action," which is methodically ordered and led, is superior to every resistance of "mass" or even of "communal action." And where the bureaucratization of administration has been completely carried through, a form of power relation is established that is practically unshatterable.

The individual bureaucrat cannot squirm out of the apparatus in which he is harnessed. In contrast to the honorific or avocational "notable," the professional bureaucrat is chained to his activity by his entire material and ideal existence. In the great majority of cases, he is only a single cog in an ever-moving mechanism which prescribes to him an essentially fixed route of march. The official is entrusted with specialized tasks and normally the mechanism cannot be put into motion or arrested by him, but only from the very top. The individual bureaucrat is thus forged to the community of all the functionaries who are integrated into the mechanism. They have a common interest in seeing that the mechanism continues its functions and that the societally exercised authority carries on.

The ruled, for their part, cannot dispense with or replace the bureaucratic apparatus of authority once it exists. For this bureaucracy rests upon expert training, a functional specialization of work, and an attitude set for habitual and virtuoso-like mastery of single yet methodically integrated functions. If the official stops working, or if his work is forcefully interrupted, chaos results, and it is difficult to improvise replacements from among the governed who are fit to master such chaos. This holds for public administration as well as for private economic management. More and more the material fate of the masses depends upon the steady and correct functioning of the increasingly bureaucratic organizations of private capitalism. The idea of eliminating these organizations becomes more and more utopian.

The discipline of officialdom refers to the attitude-set of the official for precise obedience within his *habitual* activity, in public as well as in private organizations. This discipline increasingly becomes the basis of all order, however great the practical importance of administration on the basis of the filed documents may be. The naive idea of Bakuninism of destroying the basis of "acquired rights" and "domination" by destroying public documents overlooks the settled orientation of *man* for keeping to the habitual rules and regulations that continue to exist independently of the documents. Every reorganization of beaten or dissolved troops, as well as the restoration of administrative orders destroyed by revolt, panic, or other catastrophes, is realized by appealing to the trained orientation of obedient compliance to such orders. Such compliance has been conditioned into the officials, on the one hand, and, on the other hand, into the governed. If such an appeal is successful it brings, as it were, the disturbed mechanism into gear again.

The objective indispensability of the once-existing apparatus, with its peculiar, "impersonal" character, means that the mechanism — in contrast to feudal orders based upon personal piety — is easily made to work for anybody who knows how to gain control over it. A rationally ordered system of officials continues to function smoothly after the enemy has occupied the area; he merely needs to change the top officials. This body of officials continues to operate because it is to the vital interest of everyone concerned, including above all the enemy.

During the course of his long years in power, Bismarck brought his ministerial colleagues into unconditional bureaucratic dependence by eliminating all independent statesmen. Upon his retirement, he saw to his surprise that they continued to manage their offices unconcerned and undismayed, as if he had not been the mastermind and creator of these creatures, but rather as if some single figure had been exchanged for some other figure in the bureaucratic machine. With all the changes of masters in France since the time of the First Empire, the power machine has remained essentially the same. Such a machine makes "revolution," in the sense of the forceful creation of entirely new formations of authority, technically more and more impossible, especially when the apparatus controls the modern means of communication (telegraph, et cetera) and also by virtue of its internal rationalized structure. In classic fashion, France has demonstrated how this process has substituted coups d'état for "revolutions": all successful transformations in France have amounted to coups d'état. . . .

THE POWER POSITION OF BUREAUCRACY

Everywhere the modern state is undergoing bureaucratization. But whether the *power* of bureaucracy within the polity is universally increasing must here remain an open question.

The fact that bureaucratic organization is technically the most highly developed means of power in the hands of the man who controls it does not determine the weight that bureaucracy as such is capable of having in a particular social structure. The ever-increasing "indispensability" of the officialdom, swollen to millions, is no more decisive for this question than is the view of some representatives of the proletarian movement that the economic indispensability of the proletarians is decisive for the measure of their social and political power position. If "indispensability" were decisive, then where slave labor prevailed and where freemen usually abhor work as a dishonor, the "indispensable" slaves ought to have held the positions of power, for they were at least as indispensable as officials and proletarians are today. Whether the power of bureaucracy as such increases cannot be decided a priori from such reasons. The drawing in of economic interest groups or other nonofficial experts, or the drawing in of nonexpert lay representatives, the establishment of local, interlocal, or central parliamentary or other representative bodies, or of occupational associations — these *seem* to run directly against the bureaucratic tendency. How far this appearance is the truth must be discussed in another chapter rather than in this purely formal and typological discussion. In general, only the following can be said here:

Under normal conditions, the power position of a fully developed bureaucracy is always overtowering. The "political master" finds himself in the position of the "dilettante" who stands opposite the "expert," facing the trained official who stands within the management of administration. This holds whether the "master" whom the bureaucracy serves is a "people," equipped with the weapons of "legislative initiative," the "referendum," and the right to remove officials, or a parliament, elected on a more aristocratic or more "democratic" basis and equipped with the right to vote a lack of confidence, or with the actual authority to vote it. It holds whether the master is an aristocratic, collegiate body, legally or actually based on self-recruitment, or whether he is a popularly elected president, a hereditary and "absolute" or a "constitutional" monarch.

Every bureaucracy seeks to increase the superiority of the professionally informed by keeping their knowledge and intentions secret. Bureaucratic administration always tends to be an administration of "secret sessions": in so far as it can, it hides its knowledge and action from criticism. Prussian church authorities now threaten to use disciplinary measures against pastors who make reprimands or other admonitory measures in any way accessible to third parties. They do this because the pastor, in making such criticism available, is "guilty" of facilitating a possible criticism of the church authorities. The treasury officials of the Persian shah have made a secret doctrine of their budgetary art and even use secret script. The official statistics of Prussia, in general, make public only what cannot do any harm to the intentions of the power-wielding bureaucracy. The tendency toward secrecy in certain administrative fields follows their material nature: everywhere that the power interests of the domination structure toward *the outside* are at stake, whether it is an economic competitor of a private enterprise, or a foreign, potentially hostile polity, we find secrecy. If it is to be successful, the management of diplomacy can only be publicly controlled to a very limited extent. The military administration must insist on the concealment of its most important measures; with the increasing significance of purely technical aspects, this is all the more the case. Political parties do not proceed differently, in spite of all the ostensible publicity of Catholic congresses and party conventions. With the increasing bureaucratization of party organizations, this secrecy will prevail even more. Commercial policy, in Germany for instance, brings about a concealment of production statistics. Every fighting posture of a social structure toward the outside tends to buttress the position of the group in power.

The pure interest of the bureaucracy in power, however, is efficacious far beyond those areas where purely functional interests make for secrecy. The concept of the "official secret" is the specific invention of bureaucracy, and nothing is so fanatically defended by the bureaucracy as this attitude, which cannot be substantially justified beyond these specifically qualified areas. In facing a parliament, the bureaucracy, out of a sure power instinct, fights every attempt of the parliament to gain knowledge by means of its own experts or from interest groups. The so-called right of parliamentary investigation is one of the means by which parliament seeks such knowledge. Bureaucracy naturally welcomes a poorly informed and hence a powerless parliament — at least in so far as ignorance somehow agrees with the bureaucracy's interests.

The absolute monarch is powerless opposite the superior knowledge of the bureaucratic expert — in a certain sense more powerless than any other political head. All the scornful decrees of Frederick the Great concerning the "abolition of serfdom" were derailed, as it were, in the course of their realization because the official mechanism simply ignored them as the occasional ideas of a dilettante. When a constitutional king agrees with a socially important part of the governed, he very frequently exerts a greater influence upon the course of administration than does the absolute monarch. The constitutional king can control these experts better because of what is, at least relatively, the public character of criticism, whereas the absolute monarch is dependent for information solely upon the bureaucracy. The Russian czar of the old regime was seldom able to accomplish permanently anything that displeased his bureaucracy and hurt the power interests of the bureaucrats. His ministerial departments, placed directly under him as the autocrat, represented a conglomerate of satrapies, as was correctly noted by Leroy-Beaulieu.

These satrapies constantly fought against one another by all the means of personal intrigue, and, especially, they bombarded one another with voluminous "memorials," in the face of which, the monarch, as a dilettante, was helpless.

With the transition to constitutional government, the concentration of the power of the central bureaucracy in one head became unavoidable. Officialdom was placed under a monocratic head, the prime minister, through whose hands everything had to go before it got to the monarch. This put the latter, to a large extent, under the tutelage of the chief of the bureaucracy. Wilhelm II, in his well known conflict with Bismarck, fought against this principle, but he had to withdraw his attack very soon. Under the rule of expert knowledge, the actual influence of the monarch can attain steadiness only by a continuous communication with the bureaucratic chiefs; this intercourse must be methodically planned and directed by the head of the bureaucracy.

At the same time, constitutionalism binds the bureaucracy and the ruler into a community of interests against the desires of party chiefs for power in the parliamentary bodies. And if he cannot find support in parliament the constitutional monarch is powerless against the bureaucracy. The desertion of the "Great of the Reich," the Prussian ministers and top officials of the Reich in November 1918, brought a monarch into approximately the same situation as existed in the feudal state in 1056. However, this is an exception, for, on the whole, the power position of a monarch opposite bureaucratic officials is far stronger than it was in any feudal state or in the "stereotyped" patrimonial state. This is because of the constant presence of aspirants for promotion, with whom the monarch can easily replace inconvenient and independent officials. Other circumstances being equal, only economically independent officials, that is, officials who belong to the propertied strata, can permit themselves to risk the loss of their offices. Today as always, the recruitment of officials from among propertyless strata increases the power of the rulers. Only officials who belong to a socially influential stratum, whom the monarch believes he must take into account as personal supporters, like the so-called *Kanalrebellen* in Prussia, can permanently and completely paralyze the substance of his will.

Only the expert knowledge of private economic interest groups in the field of "business" is superior to the expert knowledge of the bureaucracy. This is so because the exact knowledge of facts in their field is vital to the economic existence of businessmen. Errors in official statistics do not have direct economic consequences for the guilty official, but errors in the calculation of a capitalist enterprise are paid for by losses, perhaps by its existence. The "secret," as a means of power, is, after all, more safely hidden in the books of an enterpriser than it is in the files of public authorities. For this reason alone authorities are held within narrow barriers when they seek to influence economic life in the capitalist epoch. Very frequently the measures of the state in the field of capitalism take unforeseen and unintended courses, or they are made illusory by the superior expert knowledge of interest groups. . . .

6   The Knowledge-Power Relationship:
The Council of Economic Advisers

EDWARD S. FLASH, JR.

For the Council [of Economic Advisers], the relationship between its knowledge and the President's power is one of many relationships, but it is the one of greatest importance to the Council because it is, in fact, the reason for its existence. For the President, the relationship is also one of many. In absolute terms it is important to him; it is accepted, and it is valued. Although it is in relative terms, unique among the President's advisory relationships, it is not, however, one of his major relationships. The terms most descriptive of the essential relationship between the Council and President are "interdependent" and "variable." The first describes the reciprocal nature of the relationship between respective specialties of expert

From Edward S. Flash, Jr., *Economic Advice and Presidential Leadership: The Council of Economic Advisers* (New York: Columbia University Press, 1965), pp. 308–325, reprinted by permission of the author and the publisher.

economic analysis and power-laden political leadership and the relationship between the President's perceived need for the Council and the Council's reaction to that perception. The second term describes the changeable and intermittent nature of the Council-President relationship in its response to the evolving issues, events, and personalities that influence the nature of presidential leadership.

The reciprocity of the Council-President relationship is based upon the paralleling of their concerns and the mutually reinforcing nature of their respective attributes of knowledge and power. As previously recognized, the pervasive nature of the Council's economic analysis matches the nationwide, even worldwide, scope of the President's political responsibilities. Macropolitics and macroeconomics complement one another. The most natural application of the Council's expertise is to presidential problems and opportunities; the whole focus of aggregative analysis is on the national economy. The information, rationale, and advice that the Council gives the President, on both the economy as a whole and on particular issues as they fit into the national picture, strengthen political leadership. In this sense, knowledge is power; knowledge enables the President to enlarge his own specialties of innovation, synthesis, and control. It increases his ability to take the initiative relative to that of the departments and the Congress. The expert information and advice available to the President help him close the gap between the specialized knowledge and sovereignty of departmental programs and responsibilities. At a minimum cost to the President's leadership resources, the Council can speak for him and thereby identify him with what he may want to espouse without being necessarily committed to a particular course of action. In short, the Council strengthens the President's hand; it adds to his coercive power however he may wish to apply it (for example, in the steel-price dispute).

The acceptance of the Council's expertise as the President's economists increases the acceptance of his authority in matters of economic policy, and where applicable it adds economic persuasion to his strategies of influence. In return, the President provides the principal market for the Council's expertise. However circumscribed and tenuous the force of the Council's knowledge, such force is enhanced by affiliation with presidential leadership. Each is strengthened with the special attributes of the other; each can play a stronger role in the decision-making process than would otherwise be the case.

That the Council exists for the President does not deny the support its existence gets from him. It is doubtful that Eisenhower's and Kennedy's endorsements of their respective tax programs would have had the political force that they had had it not been evident that each President had understood and adopted the rationale of his economic advisers. It is equally doubtful that the respective Councils would have had significant impact on their President's thinking had they operated with the detachment typical of one of the Council's predecessors, NRPB [National Resources Planning Board].

The occasional outward appearances of rejection of the Council's advice — of victory for some other adviser or of noneconomic factors overruling economic considerations — do not so much represent differences of opinion between the President and the Council as they do the existence of different values pressed upon a President who must decide. Reciprocity between expertise and power does not require complete agreement or constant association; rather, reciprocity depends upon the use the President decides to make of the Council and the reaction of the Council to his wishes. Thus, the operations of the Council are dependent upon the value the President attaches to them in terms of his own operations. Sorensen argues that "each President must determine for himself how best to elicit and assess the advice of his advisers." [1] The Council's experience bears out Maass's "tentative requirement" for policy staffs suggested some years ago:

First, the President must personally desire such facilities and must always be fully free to alter or abolish them. . . . A second requirement is that to a considerable extent . . . the policy staff must be flexible as regards both its organization and the permanence of status of its personnel. [2]

In his reflections upon his own experiences, Nourse states that "the success of the Council as an institution, the importance of the place it occupies and the value of its work will be just what the President makes of them." [3] Although the reference is to the White

[1] [Theodore C. Sorensen], *Decision-Making in the White House* [New York: Columbia University Press, 1963], p. 58.

[2] "In Accord with the Program of the President?" in [Carl J.] Friedrich and [J. K.] Galbraith (Eds.), *Public Policy* [Cambridge, Mass.: Harvard University Press, 1953], IV, 90–92.

[3] [Edwin Griswold Nourse], *Economics in the Public Service* [New York: Harcourt Brace, 1953], p. 378.

House Office, the following remark by a former Budget Director quoted by Neustadt is similarly applicable to the Council and characterizes its relationship to the President:

"Thank God I'm here and not across the street. If the President doesn't call me, I've got plenty I can do right here and plenty coming up to me, by rights, to justify my calling him. But those poor fellows over there, if the boss doesn't call them, doesn't ask them to do something, what *can* they do but sit?" [4]

In truth, the Council, perhaps more than the White House Office, has succeeded in doing a good deal of independent work, but each chairman has in large measure depended upon his President's view of the Council in directing the type, direction, and extent of the Council's operations. This situation is little influenced by requirements of the Constitution, the Employment Act, other statutes, and custom. Truman's passive acceptance of the Council and his coolness to economics and economists were conditioners of the Keyserling Council's activities as Eisenhower's military concept of staff assistance and his reliance upon a "doctor" to aid his ailing economy were of Burns and his Council. By the same token, Kennedy's thirst for knowledge, his grasp of modern economics, and his style of hard pragmatic analysis shaped the use he made of the Heller Council and of its response to that use.

The interdependent nature of the knowledge-power relationship, the terms of which depend largely on what is acceptable to the President, means that the relationship is also extremely variable. As the President must respond to the developing pressures and opportunities, so must the relationship. It is changeable and intermittent rather than stable and regular. Not only is the relationship active in one crisis and dormant in another but the balances also vary between direct and indirect participation in decision-making, in the different paces and purposes of consultation between the Council, the President, and other members of his administration, and with shifts in the Council's own operation. In the turbulence of current affairs, it is often the changes in rather than the existence of economic policy issues that activate the Council-President relationship.

The persistence of unemployment and the priority given to its solution by the President and his administration may be important

[4] [Richard E. Neustadt], *Presidential Power* [New York: John Wiley, 1960], p. 41.

factors in shaping the President's approach to economic policy, his choice of Council members, and, in turn, the composition and operation of the Council staff. It is, however, the unfolding *changes* in the levels and areas of unemployment that produce either urgency or relaxation on both sides of the relationship. The balance of payments and economic growth in other countries are continuing concerns of the Council on behalf of the President, but it is the *changes* in these areas that set off new questions from the President, that pull his attention from other matters, that propel the Council into some new activity, and that alter its operations and staffing patterns. It is these incremental alterations that set the order of priorities of opportunities and pressures by which both the Council and President work. The degree and importance of changes within areas and the impact of the changes on each other and upon the whole complex of issues facing the President can either effect a major change in Council-President relations or balance out to produce no significant change at all.

The degree of the Council's vulnerability to such variableness is less than that of the White House staff, faced as it is with the alternation of crises and minutiae of the President's daily activities. By the same token, the Council's vulnerability is greater than that of the Budget Bureau with its vast coordinating activities and greater still than that of the operating agencies. The variableness of the Council-President relationship is in most obvious contrast to the stable relations the President maintains or is required to maintain with department heads, upon whom he depends to carry out the laws that must be faithfully executed. Although the relationship between the President and the department heads, who are both advisers and executives, is also affected by changing circumstances, the departments have a depth of continuing programs as well as independent strength sufficient for them to sustain and regulate a relationship through the vagaries of current issues. Thus, change does not work the same leverage on the totality of the relationship. Even changes among Cabinet members and the consequent variations in personal relations between the President and his advisers take on the coloration of departmental operations and traditions; they assume some of the same regularity and predictability.

In the final analysis, the interdependent and variable aspects of the relationship between the Council and the President combine to produce a relationship that is moved more by the President's acceptance of the Council than by his dependence upon it. It has become habitual for the President to depend on the Council, but it is because he wants to depend upon it rather than because he has to. The overlap of political and analytical pressures does not necessarily mean that the President will use the Council but simply that its use could be relevant and helpful.

THE RELATIONSHIP PROCESS

The interdependent and variable nature of the relationship between the Council and the President tells us little of how the relationship is maintained; the dependence of the Council upon the President's perception of his need for its services reveals little of the Council's reaction to this dependence. Without denying the Council's dependence upon the President, it can also be concluded that the Council's operations have been determined less by what the President wants the Council to do than by what he does not object to its doing. The performances of the Keyserling, Burns, and Heller Councils reveal that the character of a Council is very much what the Council itself makes it and that, in fact, the Council does much to create and maintain the President's perception of his need for it. The fact that the Council, as an advisory body with no independent power and no independence of program operations, has discretion is essential to an understanding of the process underlying its relations with the President. The nature of this process can be presented in four related propositions.

1. The relationship is maintained primarily through the Council's initiative.

2. The factors that make the Council dependent upon its own initiative in maintaining the relationship also permit the Council a wide latitude in the choice of its objectives and in the techniques of its initiative. The selection of objectives and of techniques of initiative is determined by the interaction of internal resources, convictions, and conduct with underlying and immediate features of the external political, economic, and administrative situations.

3. The most important technique of initiative is a process of intentional involvement, the degree and nature of which is determined by the Council's objectives and resources as well as the nature of the issue in which it seeks involvement.

4. Involvement is characteristically a process of opportunistic accommodation rather than forceful impingement.

The Council's Initiative. A variety of factors have persuaded the Council that the effectiveness of its operations depends in large measure upon the exercise of its own initiative. These factors have included the relatively asymmetrical dependence of the Council upon the President, the high level of policy generality at which the Council operates, which frequently results in a peripheral role in specific economic policy formulation, and the Council's perennial problem of maintaining a demand for its services. The pervasiveness of its involvement in economic policy and the subjective values supporting its economic expertise, to say nothing of its instincts for organizational self-preservation, have given it a willingness and a need to fend for itself. Consequently, the Council has to a large degree been able to set its own sights; it has made its own assessment of its resources in terms of what it has conceived as its objectives, opportunities, and problems, and it has apportioned its resources accordingly.

It has been the Council's initiative in interpreting its function more than the President's delegation that has maintained the relationship of knowledge and power. The President's original appointment of a chairman and two other members, all of whose views have been more or less in harmony with his, and his instructions to them certainly have set the stage of the relationship and of the Council's potential ultimate contribution. These elements may even have thrown the ignition switch, but they have been too general and intermittent to provide sustaining current for an active relationship.

The significance of the Council over time has emerged from relations operated by its own rather than the President's direction. The original Nourse Council would not have gone far on Truman's original marching orders of "now you fellows just keep national income up to $200 billion." The early precedents of the Council could be established by Nourse and subsequently by Keyserling because the President offered no objections. Keyserling's series of monthly and quarterly reports were volunteered, not requested. ABEGS [Advisory Board on Economic Growth and Stability] was a Burns creation; the weekly meetings with the President were developed by him. Heller seldom missed an opportunity to inform the President of something that Heller thought appropriate; in large measure, he interpreted the size and nature of Kennedy's appetite for economic information and argument. Certainly, the stimulants of the President-Council relationship have been complementary, but the concern here is to identify the relationship's most important and constant source of energy. It appears to have been the Council.

Latitude of Objectives and Initiative. Characterized by a lack of operating momentum — that is, endowed with no formal authority, combined with institutional permanence limited to a maximum of one presidential administration, and committed to only a few command performances other than the preparation of the *Economic Report* — the Council has had little to inhibit its adoption of widely different programs and practices from situation to situation and Council to Council. It has been able to vary the style and degree of its initiative from blatant aggression to defensive avoidance. The same sorts of factors that permitted a Nourse to avoid testifying before committees of Congress for three years permitted a Keyserling to fight for economic expansion wherever possible, a Burns to act with restraint on behalf of conservative and inductive economics, and a Heller to attack existing tax policy prior to the President's public endorsement. The same sorts of factors that have permitted concentration on attempts to participate in formulating policy on grand or limited scales have permitted concentration on factual reporting or on research or on combinations thereof. The same factors that have allowed a Council to risk all have permitted it to risk nothing. These have not been changes of approach or objectives limited to the top level with little significant impact on the professional level but have been basic changes altering the character and operations of the entire Council organization.

These same factors that have allowed the Council initiative and flexibility have extracted their price by making it vulnerable to isolation. The Council has seldom been far from the risk of exclusion from policy formulation, reduced acceptance, frustration, punishment, and insignificance. Certainly, the Council's strategic determinations of its objectives and of its techniques of initiative have been based on necessary assessments of the opportunities and risks presented internally by its own capabilities and interests and externally by its relationship with the President and the presidency, the prevailing economic philosophy, the bureaucratic environment, and the policy issue at hand. Similarly, determination of objectives and of techniques of initiative have had to be varied in accordance with the more immediate internal and external changes, such as personnel turnover within the Council and sudden or short-term economic and noneconomic developments. In short, the factors adhering to the Council have created the extensive and responsive latitude within which the Council's strategic objectives and techniques of initiative have been determined and executed and the Council's relationship with the President maintained. The Council has been given ample rope with which to make, save, or hang itself.

The Process of Conscious Involvement. The Council's major techniques of initiative to maintain the relationship have been those seeking involvement in economic policy affairs; that is, the Council's operations have been more typically motivated by the desire to become involved than to achieve disengagement. The history of the Council can in large measure be seen as an attempt to fulfill this motivation, to offset rather than extend its inherent detachment. Keyserling, Burns, and Heller each endeavored to have their Councils participate in what they considered important [activities]. Involvement requiring considerable amounts of time, energy, and emotion has been necessitated by the competitive nature of advice and by the complexity and depth of the economic policymaking process that extends well back into departments and agencies. Depending upon its objectives, the Council's desire has been to link its expertise and convictions to the power centers of decision in order to maximize its impact upon economic policy.

The Council's influence has often depended upon its degree of success in waging an uphill fight to participate in the decision-making process during the formulative stages. Granted that involvement creates the risk of miring the Council in operating details and of burying that which has been one of its chief strengths, presidential perspective, the Council's effectiveness has nevertheless depended upon "getting to the board" and not trying to play solely from its own hand within the executive office. Withholding advice or being excluded from advising until decisions have reached the White House for approval has often presented the Council with an already closed issue. Positions have been taken, advisory battles fought and settled, support developed, and commitments made. Although the chairman occasionally may have preconditioned the President's thinking, the Council's opportunity to influence specific decisions has often shrunk to the job of rationalizing decisions already formed. In other words, there has been a rough correlation between the nature and extent of the Council's influence and the degree to which its involvement has been to formulate policy or to ratify it.

The Council's involvement in particular issues has also depended upon the relevance of its objectives and beliefs to the issue at hand and to the Council's range of discretion. The more anxious the Council has been to shape economic policies in terms of its own economic rationale, the more aggressive and alert it has become regarding opportunities to get to the President, to add permanent staff and consultants in relevant areas, to participate in committees, to consult and be consulted, to associate with fellow policymakers rather than with technicians. The more crucial a situation has been in national economic terms, such as unemployment or inflation, the more the President has looked to the Council and the more reluctant the Council has been to have decisions take place without its involvement. When the Council has emphasized fact-finding or research, it has adjusted its involvement tactics accordingly; it has focused on different agencies and on different sorts of people; and its pace has changed with the change in pressures and deadlines. But still the Council has sought involvement and not detachment.

Opportunistic Accommodation. The Council's asymmetrical power relationships with its environment and the elasticity of the demand for its services have required that its processes of involvement be characteristically accommodative rather than forceful. The Council's processes have been carried on primarily at the sufferance of the departments and agencies with which the Council has done business. Depending upon its objectives and its assessment of the decision-making situation, the Council has taken advantage of opportunities by being available, by filling vacuums, by purveying expertise, by educating, and by competing with constraint and tact. It has "sold" rather than imposed.

Certainly, accommodation has not meant abject surrender by the Council, for knowledge is not without its intrinsic value, conviction is not without its competitiveness. Advice based on knowledge and urged through conviction carries weight; successful advice helps create its own demand. Expert technical service to an agency has developed into a continuing project, as in the case of the Council's relations with the NSRB [National Security Resources Board] in 1950 and with the Labor Department in 1953. Success as an ally to operating agencies that independently are weak in top policy councils has strengthened the Council's impact on program operations. When, in 1954, recession made the revenue aspect of tax policy less significant than its impact on disposable income, the Council was able to move into the middle of the stage with its involvement fully expected. When, in 1962, the commitment to a new tradition was made, the Council, as its prime exponent, was recognized as a leader. When, as exemplified by the Burns and Heller Councils in particular, the Council and the chairman have been accepted by the President, cabinet members and aides have listened to what the chairman has to say; he has been part of top-level informal and ad hoc policy groups, and agency representation on Council-sponsored committees has been by high-level political appointees and career officials.

Although these achievements have tended to be cumulative and reinforcing and although they have strengthened the Council, they have not allowed it to exchange the open hand of accommodation for the mailed fist or to exchange persuasion for sanction. In a showdown on a specific decision, whether concerning the decision itself or the question of the participation of particular agencies, the Council has seldom been able to force its way into deliberations; as in the case of the Treasury–Federal Reserve accord in 1951, Council participation has often not been invited. In these instances, the necessity or advantage for agencies to deal with the Council has been minimized by their direct higher priority access to the President and their vast institutional resources, as well as their clientele support and pressures. The Council has had to adjust to these factors.

Although the adjustment process is common to interorganizational relations, the nature of the process in the case of the Council has been characterized not so much by reciprocity as by the Council's having to take the initiative to fit its objectives and operations to those of other agencies. There has been no evidence that the other major agencies have altered their operations to suit the Council. Thus, the Council has had to accommodate to the other agencies because, relative to them, it has lacked the resources of forceful impingement.

THE CONSEQUENT QUALITY OF UNIQUENESS

The description of the nature and process of the Council-President relationship implies that the Council under the different chairmen have been virtually different Councils. In fact, they have. They have been almost as different as have been the presidencies of which they have been a part. Similarities in their responsibilities and functions, in their experience with success and failure, and in the nature of their influence on economic policy do not hide unique aspects of each Council that are important to an appreciation of the presidential advisory function. Because of their respective interpretations of the Employment Act, each of the three Councils studied was recognizably different in composition, in method of operation, and in the way it was received by its administration. Their uniqueness appears to have been greater than the uniqueness of the Budget Bureau under different directors or of the Treasury Department under different secretaries.

The relative stability of the composition of the Keyserling Council, made up as it was of veteran economic analysts was in marked contrast to the temporary service of academicians and part-time consultants that characterized the Burns and, even more, the Heller Council. Whereas the relatively permanent staff of the Keyserling Council was geared to the pace of government operations and to the undertaking of long-term projects, those of the more temporary Burns and Heller Councils were geared more to special projects, with those of long duration being handled by a succession of economists. Experience, continuity, and regularity of pace were in contrast to repeated infusion of fresh viewpoints, problems of operating continuity, and peak work loads for short periods of time. In external operations, Burns's centralized control of relations with the White House, the agencies, Congress, and nongovernmental groups is in marked contrast to the Keyserling pattern of extensive external operations by the other Council members and by staff members as much as by the chairman. Although external contacts were for the most part maintained by the Council members and one or two senior staff members, the Heller Council's external operations resembled those of Keyserling far more than those of Burns.

No factors had greater influence in creating the individuality of each Council than the differences in each Council's approach to economic analysis, which was manifested by both Council members and staff professionals in the Council's operations. Just as each President wished and was committed by political philosophy to be different from his predecessor, each new Council sought to apply a different economic philosophy and correspondingly different methods from those of its predecessor. Following Nourse, Keyserling wanted to reset the Council's course toward full-employment objectives. Aware of both the problems and the promise of setting precedents for a new agency, Keyserling strove for involvements and operations opposite from those advocated by Nourse. Both Burns and Heller felt the need to revitalize the approach of the Council because, to Burns's eyes, the Council had fallen into disrepute with the economics profession, while, in Heller's opinion, it had not lived up to its responsibilities under the Employment Act.

The differences in composition and approach to economic analysis contributed to differences in working relationships. The informal but recognized delineation between senior and junior staff members, the formality among the Council members themselves, and the chairman's balance between direction and delegation in the Keyserling Council were all in contrast to the centralized restraint more typical of the Burns Council. Burns's dominance of his Council, his filtering out of policy considerations from the staff's work assignments, and his cross-checking of the staff work through duplication of assignments were in contrast to the informal crash program policy of the Heller Council. Reminiscent of the activity of the Keyserling Council, the Heller group none the less differed from it in the more equal division of work among the Council members themselves and in the shifting of assignments among the staff. Despite marked similarities in the preparation of the President's *Economic Report*, Heller appears to have made it something more of a joint undertaking in both development of content and in drafting than did Keyserling and especially Burns. Clearance of *Economic Report* recommendations was apparently less detailed under Burns and Heller than under Keyserling. Heller returned to the Nourse and Keyserling practice of separating the President's *Report* and the Council's *Report* into two different documents bound within one cover. Under Burns, the two were combined into one report introduced by a brief summarizing letter of transmittal from the President.

In the process of establishing the economic rationale of their respective presidential administrations and of contributing to particular economic policy decisions, each Council created different reputations and images. All three were aggressive but each in his own fashion. Keyserling, the career New Dealer, pressed the Council's viewpoint with tenacity in an administration which, tentative at best in its embrace of the new advisory body and its ideology, accorded him formal rather than intimate access to the inner circles. Burns, the respected expert on business cycles, articulated modern conservatism and influenced policy decisions in an administration that, thankful for having avoided deep depression, welcomed him as a professional "in house" consultant. Heller as the worldly and whirlwind academician promoted a new economic rationale for pragmatists of the New Frontier, who, recognizing an operator of their own kind, accorded him full membership in their policymaking circles.

The reasons for the differences lie in precisely the same sorts of factors that explain the political quality of the Council's advisory function and the interdependent and variable nature of the Council-President relationship. Each Council has served Presidents of widely differing ideological persuasions and styles, different priorities and concepts of office, and different views of the role of the Council. Each Council has helped create and reflect the environment unique to its administration. The Democratic Fair Deal's wheeling and dealing, its activity and confusion, its social concern for a postwar world, its palace guard — all reminiscent of the Roosevelt era — were quite different from the characteristics of the Democratic New Frontier and very different from the business formality of Eisenhower's "New Republicanism." The significance to the Heller Council of its serving an administration whose twentieth-century leaders accepted and understood the principles of Keynesian economics cannot be overemphasized.

Both the political conflicts and the policies in which each Council became involved were vastly different. The emergency growing out of the Korean War and the apparent proximity of World War III caused fear and pressures for the government and population at large that were different from those growing out of the 1953–54 recession, which were, in turn, different from those that developed in 1961–62. The visceral as well as intellectual reaction to inflation was far different after four years of war production and forced saving than it was after four years of peacetime price stability. Heller was not burdened by Keyserling's problem of the postwar return to normalcy nor by Burns's bugbear of a return to 1929, but neither Keyserling nor Burns had Heller's difficulties with both the internal paradox of sustained prosperity and persistent unemployment and the external competition of relatively rapid economic growth in other democratic countries.

Each Council competed with its advice in the manner it believed possible and necessary, given the complex circumstances obtaining at that time. The crucial difference between the approaches to competition was that the set of strategies and tactics used by Keyserling and later by Heller led to opportunities and risks of commission, while the set used by Burns led to opportunities and risks of omission. The Keyserling Council was part of an active presidency, and, consistent with its interpretation of the Employment Act, it believed that "maximum employment, production and purchasing power" were not achieved by inside analysis carried on within a suite of offices on the third floor of "Old State." The Council chose to make the most of its environment by participating as aggressively and as comprehensively as possible in an action-packed emergency situation. Consequently, the Council ran the risk of overplaying its hand, of attempting too much, of poaching on the preserves of others, and of creating antagonisms. In part, the Council fell victim of its own choice. Having originally assumed the risks that accompanied opportunity for aggressive participation, the changed situation in 1951 made its decrease in influence inevitable and pronounced. Not having the force to impose its views, the Council could escape neither virtual exclusion by the administration nor a share in the severe criticism of the Truman Administration.

The Burns Council was not inclined nor did it have the opportunity to function in a manner similar to its predecessor. As part of a less active presidency, which adopted a more conservative interpretation of the Employment Act, the Council chose to operate as a consultant to the administration in a gradually evolving and mildly recessionary situation in which minimal governmental direction of the nation's economic life was a primary policy objective. The very practice of limited outside contact and concentration on inside analysis coincided with the free enterprise approach of minimum government activity characteristic of the Eisenhower Administration. Consequently, the Council's basic orientation was toward doing the least necessary rather than the most possible. Its risks were not of doing too much but of doing too little — of being silent rather than protesting, of simply endorsing the status quo rather than recommending modification or change, and of inhibiting rather than helping recovery. The success of the Burns Council lay in avoiding these pitfalls. By its own interpretation of the Employment Act and by its analysis of the 1953–54 situation, the Council maintained fundamental agreement with the administration; it endorsed a basic policy of noninterference while recommending and gaining acceptance for some limited countermeasures.

As with the Keyserling Council, the Heller Council was part of an active presidency. In choosing to participate aggressively and over a broad area of economic policy, it also ran the risk of overplaying its hand. It did not primarily because it concentrated on developing broad rationale and analysis upon which decisions could be considered and on resisting becoming too enmeshed in specific decision-making processes. It was the combination of an activist philosophy and operations that helped produce a multitude of analyses and recommendations on behalf of the New Frontier.

To be meaningful, these comparisons must be seen in the perspective of their respective times. Keyserling's aggressiveness and advocacy stood out in part because they were blatant but primarily because they conflicted with the then current expectations that the Council display professional objectivity and passivity. To be formally trained as a lawyer rather than as a professional economist, to head a new agency that defended as well as analyzed economic policy, and to expound Keynesian economics made Keyserling and the Council all the more suspect. Burns's restraint was consistent with prevailing values of minimal government interference in economic activity. A decade after Keyserling, Heller's tactful but equally aggressive activity on many fronts was acknowledged as a natural attribute of professional advice.

Both Burns and Heller benefited from all their respective predecessors' experiences. In addition to the advantages of the fresh approach made possible by the complete change in philosophy from the Truman to the Eisenhower Administration, Burns recognized Keyserling's experience by avoiding conflicts between himself and his fellow Council members . . . and by centralizing the Council's internal and external operations. The acceptance of Heller's aggressive approach grows not only out of the manner in which he pursued it but also out of the general change in relevant values. Keyserling had already fought a number of battles that did not need to be fought again — the testifying, speech-making, and policy involvement for which he was severely criticized were taken as a matter of course in the case of Heller. The consensus favoring an active government, the recognized need to plan and coordinate government programs, the general acceptance of Keynesian principles, the advances in economic analysis, the adoption of economic growth as a legitimate political objective, and, finally, Kennedy's perception of the Council's role all accumulated to make the Heller Council uniquely a synthesis combining maximum benefit from both the experiences of his predecessors and the more general economic policy developments of the previous twenty years.

CONCLUSION: THE COUNCIL'S EMERGING TRADITION

The nature of the knowledge-power relationship between the Council and the President, the Council's process of maintaining that relationship, and the uniqueness of each Council combine to indicate the Council's emerging tradition as part of the American presidency. In the case of the Council, the "right relation of knowledge and power" has become substantive and not procedural, complementary and not conflicting, active and not neutral, and personal rather than institutional. The Council's emerging approach to the advisory function is characterized by pragmatism and variety, by education and subjectivity, rather than by norm and consistency or by coordination and scientific objectivity. The Council has supplied information and analysis, but even more it has articulated the concepts needed for determination and defense of policy. The value of such economic rationale has been gradually recognized and accorded legitimacy by politician and bureaucrat, by economist and layman.

However one feels about the substantive economics of particular Councils and however one judges the importance or value of the Councils' actions, each Council's convictions and conduct will none the less continue uniquely to initiate, facilitate, and rationalize economic policy formulation for its own particular administration. As in the past, the Council's activities will vary from creating a philosophical rationale to providing specialized technical abilities, from recommending specific ideas of its own to promoting those of others, from making formal presentations to the President to kibitzing someone else's hand. As both integral parts and catalysts, these expert activities will be essential to the functioning of leadership and to the process of making policy at the White House level, within the executive office, and among various echelons of the operating agencies.

7   *The Power of Bureaucratic Routines:*
The Cuban Missile Crisis

GRAHAM T. ALLISON

For some purposes, governmental behavior can be usefully summarized as action chosen by a unitary, rational decision-maker: centrally controlled, completely informed, and value maximizing. But this simplification must not be allowed to conceal the fact that a "government" consists of a conglomerate of semi-feudal, loosely allied organizations, each with a substantial life of its own. Government leaders do sit formally, and to some extent in fact, on top of this conglomerate. But governments perceive problems through organizational sensors. Governments define alternatives and estimate consequences as organizations process information. Governments act as these organizations enact routines. Government behavior can therefore be understood . . . less as deliberate choices of leaders and more as *outputs* of large organizations functioning according to standard patterns of behavior.

To be responsive to a broad spectrum of problems, governments consist of large organizations among which primary responsibility for particular areas is divided. Each organization attends to a special set of problems and acts in quasi-independence on these problems. But few important problems fall exclusively within the domain of a single organization. Thus government behavior relevant to any important problem reflects the independent output of several organizations, partially coordinated by government leaders. Government leaders can substantially disturb, but not substantially control, the behavior of these organizations.

To perform complex routines, the behavior of large numbers of individuals must be coordinated. Coordination requires standard

From Graham T. Allison, "Conceptual Models and the Cuban Missile Crisis," reprinted by permission of the author and The American Political Science Association from *The American Political Science Review* 63 (September 1969): 689–718. This extract covers pp. 698–707; footnotes are renumbered.

An expanded version of this article appears in Graham T. Allison, *Essence of Decision: Explaining the Cuban Missile Crisis* (Boston: Little, Brown and Company, 1971).

operating procedures: rules according to which things are done. Assured capability for reliable performance of action that depends upon the behavior of hundreds of persons requires established "programs." Indeed, if the eleven members of a football team are to perform adequately on any particular down, each player must not "do what he thinks needs to be done" or "do what the quarterback tells him to do." Rather, each player must perform the maneuvers specified by a previously established play which the quarterback has simply called in this situation.

At any given time, a government consists of *existing* organizations, each with a *fixed* set of standard operating procedures and programs. The behavior of these organizations — and consequently of the government — relevant to an issue in any particular instance is, therefore, determined primarily by routines established in these organizations prior to that instance. But organizations do change. Learning occurs gradually, over time. Dramatic organizational change occurs in response to major crises. Both learning and change are influenced by existing organizational capabilities.

Borrowed from studies of organizations, these loosely formulated propositions amount simply to *tendencies*. Each must be hedged by modifiers like "other things being equal" and "under certain conditions." In particular instances, tendencies hold — more or less. In specific situations, the relevant question is: more or less? But this is as it should be. For, on the one hand, "organizations" are no more homogeneous a class than "solids." When scientists tried to generalize about "solids," they achieved similar results. Solids tend to expand when heated, but some do and some don't. More adequate categorization of the various elements now lumped under the rubric "organizations" is thus required. On the other hand, the behavior of particular organizations seems considerably more complex than the behavior of solids. Additional information about a particular organization is required for further specification of the tendency statements. . . .

ORGANIZATIONAL PROCESS PARADIGM [1]

I. Basic Unit of Analysis: Policy as Organizational Output

The happenings of international politics are, in three critical senses, outputs of organizational processes. First, the actual occur-

[1] The formulation of this paradigm is indebted both to the orientation and

rences are organizational outputs. For example, Chinese entry into the Korean War — that is, the fact that Chinese soldiers were firing at United Nations' soldiers south of the Yalu in 1950 — is an organizational action: the action of men who are soldiers in platoons which are in companies, which in turn are in armies, responding as privates to lieutenants who are responsible to captains and so on to the commander, moving into Korea, advancing against enemy troops, and firing according to fixed routines of the Chinese army. Government leaders' decisions trigger organizational routines. Government leaders can trim the edges of this output and exercise some choice in combining outputs. But the mass of behavior is determined by previously established procedures. Second, existing organizational routines for employing present physical capabilities constitute the effective options open to government leaders confronted with any problem. Only the existence of men, equipped and trained as armies and capable of being transported to North Korea, made entry into the Korean War a live option for the Chinese leaders. The fact that fixed programs (equipment, men, and routines which exist at the particular time) exhaust the range of buttons that leaders can push is not always perceived by these leaders. But in every case it is critical for an understanding of what is actually done. Third, organizational outputs structure the situation within the narrow constraints of which leaders must contribute their "decision" concerning an issue. Outputs raise the problem, provide the information, and make the initial moves that color the face of the issue that is turned to the leaders. As Theodore Sorensen has observed: "Presidents rarely, if ever, make decisions — particularly in foreign affairs — in the sense of writing their conclusions on a clean slate . . . The basic decisions, which confine their choices, have all too often been previously made." [2] If one understands the structure of the situation and the face of the issue — which are determined by the organizational outputs — the formal choice of the leaders is frequently anti-climactic.

---

insights of Herbert Simon and to the behavioral model of the firm stated by Richard Cyert and James March, *A Behavioral Theory of the Firm* (Englewood Cliffs, 1963). Here, however, one is forced to grapple with the less routine, less quantified functions of the less differentiated elements in government organizations.

[2] Theodore Sorensen, "You Get to Walk to Work," *New York Times Magazine,* March 19, 1967.

II. Organizing Concepts

A. *Organizational Actors*. The actor is not a monolithic "nation" or "government" but rather a constellation of loosely allied organizations on top of which government leaders sit. This constellation acts only as component organizations perform routines.[3]

B. *Factored Problems and Fractionated Power*. Surveillance of the multiple facets of foreign affairs requires that problems be cut up and parcelled out to various organizations. To avoid paralysis, primary power must accompany primary responsibility. But if organizations are permitted to do anything, a large part of what they do will be determined within the organization. Thus each organization perceives problems, processes information, and performs a range of actions in quasi-independence (within broad guidelines of national policy). Factored problems and fractionated power are two edges of the same sword. Factoring permits more specialized attention to particular facets of problems than would be possible if government leaders tried to cope with these problems by themselves. But this additional attention must be paid for in the coin of discretion for *what* an organization attends to, and *how* organizational responses are programmed.

C. *Parochial Priorities, Perceptions, and Issues*. Primary responsibility for a narrow set of problems encourages organizational parochialism. These tendencies are enhanced by a number of additional factors: (1) selective information available to the organization, (2) recruitment of personnel into the organization, (3) tenure of individuals in the organization, (4) small group pressures within the organization, and (5) distribution of rewards by the organization. Clients (e.g., interest groups), government allies (e.g., congressional committees), and extra-national counterparts (e.g., the British Ministry of Defense for the Department of Defense, ISA, or the British Foreign Office for the Department of State, EUR) galvanize this parochialism. Thus organizations develop relatively stable propensities concerning operational priorities, perceptions, and issues.

D. *Action as Organizational Output*. The preeminent feature of

[3] Organizations are not monolithic. The proper level of disaggregation depends upon the objectives of a piece of analysis. This paradigm is formulated with reference to the major organizations that constitute the United States government. Generalization to the major components of each department and agency should be relatively straightforward.

organizational activity is its programmed character: the extent to which behavior in any particular case is an enactment of preestablished routines. In producing outputs, the activity of each organization is characterized by:

1. Goals: Constraints Defining Acceptable Performance. The operational goals of an organization are seldom revealed by formal mandates. Rather, each organization's operational goals emerge as a set of constraints defining acceptable performance. Central among these constraints is organizational health, defined usually in terms of bodies assigned and dollars appropriated. The set of constraints emerges from a mix of expectations and demands of other organizations in the government, statutory authority, demands from citizens and special interest groups, and bargaining within the organization. These constraints represent a quasi-resolution of conflict — the constraints are relatively stable, so there is some resolution. But conflict among alternative goals is always latent; hence, it is a quasi-resolution. Typically, the constraints are formulated as imperatives to avoid roughly specified discomforts and disasters.[4]

2. Sequential Attention to Goals. The existence of conflict among operational constraints is resolved by the device of sequential attention. As a problem arises, the subunits of the organization most concerned with that problem deal with it in terms of the constraints they take to be most important. When the next problem arises, another cluster of subunits deals with it, focusing on a different set of constraints.

3. Standard Operating Procedures. Organizations perform their "higher" functions, such as attending to problem areas, monitoring information, and preparing relevant responses for likely contingencies, by doing "lower" tasks, for example, preparing budgets, producing reports, and developing hardware. Reliable performance of these tasks requires standard operating procedures (hereafter SOPs). Since procedures are "standard" they do not change quickly or easily. Without these standard procedures, it would not be possible to perform certain concerted tasks. But because of standard procedures, organizational behavior in particular instances often appears unduly formalized, sluggish, or inappropriate.

---

[4] The stability of these constraints is dependent on such factors as rules for promotion and reward, budgeting and accounting procedures, and mundane operating procedures.

4. Programs and Repertoires. Organizations must be capable of performing actions in which the behavior of large numbers of individuals is carefully coordinated. Assured performance requires clusters of rehearsed SOPs for producing specific actions, e.g., fighting enemy units or answering an embassy's cable. Each cluster comprises a "program" (in the terms both of drama and computers) which the organization has available for dealing with a situation. The list of programs relevant to a type of activity, e.g., fighting, constitutes an organizational repertoire. The number of programs in a repertoire is always quite limited. When properly triggered, organizations execute programs; programs cannot be substantially changed in a particular situation. The more complex the action and the greater the number of individuals involved, the more important are programs and repertoires as determinants of organizational behavior.

5. Uncertainty Avoidance. Organizations do not attempt to estimate the probability distribution of future occurrences. Rather, organizations avoid uncertainty. By arranging a *negotiated environment*, organizations regularize the reactions of other actors with whom they have to deal. The primary environment, relations with other organizations that comprise the government, is stabilized by such arrangements as agreed budgetary splits, accepted areas of responsibility, and established conventional practices. The secondary environment, relations with the international world, is stabilized between allies by the establishment of contracts (alliances) and "club relations" (United States State and United Kingdom Foreign Office or United States Treasury and United Kingdom Treasury). Between enemies, contracts and accepted conventional practices perform a similar function, for example, the rules of the "precarious status quo" which President Kennedy referred to in the missile crisis. Where the international environment cannot be negotiated, organizations deal with remaining uncertainties by establishing a set of *standard scenarios* that constitute the contingencies for which they prepare. For example, the standard scenario for Tactical Air Command of the United States air force involves combat with enemy aircraft. Planes are designed and pilots trained to meet this problem. That these preparations are less relevant to more probable contingencies, e.g., provision of close-in ground support in limited wars like Vietnam, has had little impact on the scenario.

6. Problem-directed Search. Where situations cannot be con-

strued as standard, organizations engage in search. The style of search and the solution are largely determined by existing routines. Organizational search for alternative courses of action is problem-oriented: it focuses on the atypical discomfort that must be avoided. It is simple-minded: the neighborhood of the symptom is searched first; then, the neighborhood of the current alternative. Patterns of search reveal biases which in turn reflect such factors as specialized training or experience and patterns of communication.

7. Organizational Learning and Change. The parameters of organizational behavior mostly persist. In response to nonstandard problems, organizations search and routines evolve, assimilating new situations. Thus learning and change follow in large part from existing procedures. But marked changes in organizations do sometimes occur. Conditions in which dramatic changes are more likely include: (1) Periods of budgetary feast. Typically, organizations devour budgetary feasts by purchasing additional items on the existing shopping list. Nevertheless, if committed to change, leaders who control the budget can use extra funds to effect changes. (2) Periods of prolonged budgetary famine. Though a single year's famine typically results in few changes in organizational structure but a loss of effectiveness in performing some programs, prolonged famine forces major retrenchment. (3) Dramatic performance failures. Dramatic change occurs (mostly) in response to major disasters. Confronted with an undeniable failure of procedures and repertoires, authorities outside the organization demand change, existing personnel are less resistant to change, and critical members of the organization are replaced by individuals committed to change.

E. Central Coordination and Control. Action requires decentralization of responsibility and power. But problems lap over the jurisdictions of several organizations. Thus the necessity for decentralization runs headlong into the requirement for coordination. (Advocates of one horn or the other of this dilemma — responsive action entails decentralized power vs. coordinated action requires central control — account for a considerable part of the persistent demand for government reorganization.) Both the necessity for coordination and the centrality of foreign policy to national welfare guarantee the involvement of government leaders in the procedures of the organizations among which problems are divided and power shared. Each organization's propensities and routines can be disturbed by government leaders' intervention. Central direction and persistent control of organizational activity, however, is not possible. The relation among organizations, and between organizations and the government leaders depends critically on a number of structural variables including: (1) the nature of the job, (2) the measures and information available to government leaders, (3) the system of rewards and punishments for organizational members, and (4) the procedures by which human and material resources get committed. For example, to the extent that rewards and punishments for the members of an organization are distributed by higher authorities, these authorities can exercise some control by specifying criteria in terms of which organizational output is to be evaluated. These criteria become constraints within which organizational activity proceeds. But constraint is a crude instrument of control.

Intervention by government leaders does sometimes change the activity of an organization in an intended direction. But instances are fewer than might be expected. As Franklin Roosevelt, the master manipulator of government organizations, remarked:

> The Treasury is so large and far-flung and ingrained in its practices that I find it is almost impossible to get the action and results I want. . . . But the Treasury is not to be compared with the State Department. You should go through the experience of trying to get any changes in the thinking, policy, and action of the career diplomats and then you'd know what a real problem was. But the Treasury and the State Department put together are nothing compared with the Na-a-vy . . . To change anything in the Na-a-vy is like punching a feather bed. You punch it with your right and you punch it with your left until you are finally exhausted, and then you find the damn bed just as it was before you started punching.[5]

John Kennedy's experience seems to have been similar: "The State Department," he asserted, "is a bowl full of jelly." [6] And lest the McNamara revolution in the Defense Department seem too striking a counter-example, the navy's recent rejection of McNamara's major intervention in naval weapons procurement, the F-111B, should be studied as an antidote.

   F. Decisions of Government Leaders. Organizational persistence does not exclude shifts in governmental behavior. For government

---

[5] Marriner Eccles, *Beckoning Frontiers* (New York, 1951), p. 336.
[6] Arthur M. Schlesinger, Jr., *A Thousand Days* (Boston, 1965), p. 406.

leaders sit atop the conglomerate of organizations. Many important issues of governmental action require that these leaders decide what organizations will play out which programs where. Thus stability in the parochialisms and SOPs of individual organizations is consistent with some important shifts in the behavior of governments. The range of these shifts is defined by existing organizational programs.

III. Dominant Inference Pattern

If a nation performs an action of this type today, its organizational components must yesterday have been performing (or have had established routines for performing) an action only marginally different from this action. At any specific point in time, a government consists of an established conglomerate of organizations, each with existing goals, programs, and repertoires. The characteristics of a government's action in any instance follows from those established routines, and from the choice of government leaders — on the basis of information and estimates provided by existing routines — among existing programs. The best explanation of an organization's behavior at t is $t - 1$; the prediction of $t + 1$ is t. . . .

IV. General Propositions

A number of general propositions have been stated above. . . . This section formulates several more precisely.

A. *Organizational Action*. Activity according to SOPs and programs does not constitute farsighted, flexible adaptation to "the issue" (as it is conceived by the analyst). Detail and nuance of actions by organizations are determined predominantly by organizational routines, not government leaders' directions.

1. SOPs constitute routines for dealing with *standard* situations. Routines allow large numbers of ordinary individuals to deal with numerous instances, day after day, without considerable thought, by responding to basic stimuli. But this regularized capability for adequate performance is purchased at the price of standardization. If the SOPs are appropriate, average performance, i.e., performance averaged over the range of cases, is better than it would be if each instance were approached individually (given fixed talent, timing, and resource constraints). But specific instances, particularly critical instances that typically do not have "standard" characteristics, are often handled sluggishly or inappropriately.

2. A program, i.e., a complex action chosen from a short list of programs in a repertoire, is rarely tailored to the specific situation in which it is executed. Rather, the program is (at best) the most appropriate of the programs in a previously developed repertoire.

3. Since repertoires are developed by parochial organizations for standard scenarios defined by that organization, programs available for dealing with a particular situation are often ill-suited.

B. *Limited Flexibility and Incremental Change.* Major lines of organizational action are straight, i.e., behavior at one time is marginally different from that behavior at $t - 1$. Simple-minded predictions work best: Behavior at $t + 1$ will be marginally different from behavior at the present time.

1. Organizational budgets change incrementally — both with respect to totals and with respect to intraorganizational splits. Though organizations could divide the money available each year by carving up the pie anew (in the light of changes in objectives or environment), in practice, organizations take last year's budget as a base and adjust incrementally. Predictions that require large budgetary shifts in a single year between organizations or between units within an organization should be hedged.

2. Once undertaken, an organizational investment is not dropped at the point where "objective" costs outweigh benefits. Organizational stakes in adopted projects carry them quite beyond the loss point.

C. *Administrative Feasibility.* Adequate explanation, analysis, and prediction must include administrative feasibility as a major dimension. A considerable gap separates what leaders choose (or might rationally have chosen) and what organizations implement.

1. Organizations are blunt instruments. Projects that require several organizations to act with high degrees of precision and coordination are not likely to succeed.

2. Projects that demand that existing organizational units depart from their accustomed functions and perform previously unprogrammed tasks are rarely accomplished in their designed form.

3. Government leaders can expect that each organization will do its "part" in terms of what the organization knows how to do.

4. Government leaders can expect incomplete and distorted information from each organization concerning its part of the problem.

5. Where an assigned piece of a problem is contrary to the exist-

ing goals of an organization, resistance to implementation of that piece will be encountered.

V. Specific Propositions

1. Deterrence. The probability of nuclear attack is less sensitive to balance and imbalance, or stability and instability . . . than it is to a number of organizational factors. Except for the special case in which the Soviet Union acquires a credible capability to destroy the United States with a disarming blow, United States superiority or inferiority affects the probability of a nuclear attack less than do a number of organizational factors.

First, if a nuclear attack occurs, it will result from organizational activity: the firing of rockets by members of a missile group. The enemy's *control system*, i.e., physical mechanisms and standard procedures which determine who can launch rockets when, is critical. Second, the enemy's programs for bringing his strategic forces to *alert status* determine probabilities of accidental firing and momentum. At the outbreak of World War I, if the Russian Czar had understood the organizational processes which his order of full mobilization triggered, he would have realized that he had chosen war. Third, organizational repertoires fix the range of effective choice open to enemy leaders. The menu available to Czar Nicholas in 1914 had two entrees: full mobilization and no mobilization. Partial mobilization was not an organizational option. Fourth, since organizational routines set the chessboard, the training and deployment of troops and nuclear weapons is crucial. Given that the outbreak of hostilities in Berlin is more probable than most scenarios for nuclear war, facts about deployment, training, and tactical nuclear equipment of Soviet troops stationed in East Germany — which will influence the face of the issue seen by Soviet leaders at the outbreak of hostilities and the manner in which choice is implemented — are as critical as the question of "balance."

2. Soviet Force Posture. Soviet force posture, i.e., the fact that certain weapons rather than others are procured and deployed, is determined by organizational factors such as the goals and procedures of existing military services and the goals and processes of research and design laboratories, within budgetary constraints that emerge from the government leader's choices. The frailty of the Soviet air force within the Soviet military establishment seems to have been a crucial element in the Soviet failure to acquire a large bomber force in the 1950s (thereby faulting American intelligence predictions of a "bomber gap"). The fact that missiles were controlled until 1960 in the Soviet Union by the Soviet ground forces, whose goals and procedures reflected no interest in an intercontinental mission, was not irrelevant to the slow Soviet build-up of ICBMs (thereby faulting United States intelligence predictions of a "missile gap"). These organizational factors (Soviet ground forces' control of missiles and that service's fixation with European scenarios) make the Soviet deployment of so many MRBMs that European targets could be destroyed three times over, more understandable. Recent weapon developments, e.g., the testing of a Fractional Orbital Bombardment System (FOBS) and multiple warheads for the SS-9, very likely reflect the activity and interests of a cluster of Soviet research and development organizations, rather than a decision by Soviet leaders to acquire a first strike weapon system. Careful attention to the organizational components of the Soviet military establishment (strategic rocket forces, navy, air force, ground forces, and national air defense), the missions and weapons systems to which each component is wedded (an independent weapon system assists survival as an independent service), and existing budgetary splits (which probably are relatively stable in the Soviet Union as they tend to be everywhere) offer potential improvements in medium and longer term predictions.

THE UNITED STATES BLOCKADE OF CUBA . . .

Organizational Intelligence. At 7:00 P.M. on October 22, 1962, President Kennedy disclosed the American discovery of the presence of Soviet strategic missiles in Cuba, declared a "strict quarantine on all offensive military equipment under shipment to Cuba," and demanded that "Chairman Khrushchev halt and eliminate this clandestine, reckless, and provocative threat to world peace." [7] This decision was reached at the pinnacle of the United States government after a critical week of deliberation. What initiated that precious week were photographs of Soviet missile sites in Cuba taken on October 14. These pictures might not have been taken until a week later. In that case, the President speculated, "I don't think probably we would have chosen as prudently as we finally did." [8]

[7] U.S. Department of State, *Bulletin* 47:715–720.
[8] Schlesinger, *op. cit.*, p. 803.

United States leaders might have received this information three weeks earlier — if a U-2 had flown over San Cristobal in the last week of September.[9] What determined the context in which American leaders came to choose the blockade was the discovery of missiles on October 14.

There has been considerable debate over alleged American "intelligence failures" in the Cuban missile crisis.[10] But what both critics and defenders have neglected is the fact that the discovery took place on October 14, rather than three weeks earlier or a week later, as a consequence of the established routines and procedures of the organizations which constitute the United States intelligence community. These organizations were neither more nor less successful than they had been the previous month or were to be in the months to follow.[11]

The notorious "September estimate," approved by the United States Intelligence Board (USIB) on September 19, concluded that the Soviet Union would not introduce offensive missiles into Cuba.[12] No U-2 flight was directed over the western end of Cuba (after September 5) before October 4.[13] No U-2 flew over the western end of Cuba until the flight that discovered the Soviet missiles on October 14.[14] Can these "failures" be accounted for in organizational terms?

On September 19 when USIB met to consider the question of Cuba, the "system" contained the following information: (1) shipping intelligence had noted the arrival in Cuba of two large-hatch Soviet lumber ships, which were riding high in the water; (2) refugee reports of countless sightings of missiles, but also a report that Castro's private pilot, after a night of drinking in Havana, had boasted: "We will fight to the death and perhaps we can win because we have everything, including atomic weapons"; (3) a sight-

---

[9] Theodore Sorensen, *Kennedy* [New York, 1965], p. 675.

[10] See U.S. Congress, Senate, Committee on Armed Services, Preparedness Investigation Subcommittee, *Interim Report on Cuban Military Build-up*, 88th Congress, 1st Session, 1963, p. 2; Hanson Baldwin, "Growing Risks of Bureaucratic Intelligence," *The Reporter* (August 15, 1963), pp. 48–50; Roberta Wohlstetter, "Cuba and Pearl Harbor," *Foreign Affairs* [43] (July 1965):706.

[11] U.S. Congress, House of Representatives, Committee on Appropriations, Subcommittee on Department of Defense Appropriations, *Hearings*, 88th Congress, 1st Session, 1963, p. 25 ff.

[12] R. Hilsman, *To Move a Nation* (New York, 1967), pp. 172–173.

[13] Department of Defense Appropriations, *Hearings*, p. 67.

[14] *Ibid.*, pp. 66–67.

ing by a CIA agent of the rear profile of a strategic missile; (4) U-2 photos produced by flights of August 29, September 5 and 17 showing the construction of a number of SAM sites and other defensive missiles.[15] Not all of this information was on the desk of the estimators, however. Shipping intelligence experts noted the fact that large-hatch ships were riding high in the water and spelled out the inference: the ships must be carrying "space consuming" cargo.[16] These facts were carefully included in the catalogue of intelligence concerning shipping. For experts sensitive to the Soviets' shortage of ships, however, these facts carried no special signal. The refugee report of Castro's private pilot's remark had been received at Opa Locka, Florida, along with vast reams of inaccurate reports generated by the refugee community. This report and a thousand others had to be checked and compared before being sent to Washington. The two weeks required for initial processing could have been shortened by a large increase in resources, but the yield of this source was already quite marginal. The CIA agent's sighting of the rear profile of a strategic missile had occurred on September 12; transmission time from agent sighting to arrival in Washington typically took 9 to 12 days. Shortening this transmission time would impose severe cost in terms of danger to subagents, agents, and communication networks.

On the information available, the intelligence chiefs who predicted that the Soviet Union would not introduce offensive missiles into Cuba made a reasonable and defensible judgment.[17] Moreover, in the light of the fact that these organizations were gathering intelligence not only about Cuba but about potential occurrences in all parts of the world, the informational base available to the estimators involved nothing out of the ordinary. Nor, from an organizational perspective, is there anything startling about the gradual

[15] For (1) Hilsman, *op. cit.*, p. 186; (2) [Elie] Abel [*The Missile Crisis* (Philadelphia, 1966)], p. 24; (3) Department of Defense Appropriations, *Hearings*, p. 64; Abel, *op. cit.*, p. 24; (4) Department of Defense Appropriations, *Hearings*, pp. 1–30.

[16] The facts here are not entirely clear. This assertion is based on information from (1) "Department of Defense Briefing by the Honorable R. S. McNamara, Secretary of Defense, State Department Auditorium, 5:00 P.M., February 6, 1963." A verbatim transcript of a presentation actually made by General Carroll's assistant, John Hughes; and (2) Hilsman's statement, *op. cit.*, p. 186. But see R. Wohlstetter's interpretation, "Cuba and Pearl Harbor," *op. cit.*, p. 700.

[17] See Hilsman, *op. cit.*, pp. 172–174.

accumulation of evidence that led to the formulation of the hypothesis that the Soviets were installing missiles in Cuba and the decision on October 4 to direct a special flight over western Cuba.

The ten-day delay between that decision and the flight is another organizational story.[18] At the October 4 meeting, the Defense Department took the opportunity to raise an issue important to its concerns. Given the increased danger that a U-2 would be downed, it would be better if the pilot were an officer in uniform rather than a CIA agent. Thus the air force should assume responsibility for U-2 flights over Cuba. To the contrary, the CIA argued that this was an intelligence operation and thus within the CIA's jurisdiction. Moreover, CIA U-2s had been modified in certain ways which gave them advantages over air force U-2s in averting Soviet SAMs. Five days passed while the State Department pressed for less risky alternatives such as drones and the air force (in Department of Defense guise) and CIA engaged in territorial disputes. On October 9 a flight plan over San Cristobal was approved by COMOR [Committee on Overhead Reconnaissance], but to the CIA's dismay, air force pilots rather than CIA agents would take charge of the mission. At this point details become sketchy, but several members of the intelligence community have speculated that an air force pilot in an air force U-2 attempted a high altitude overflight on October 9 that "flamed out," i.e., lost power, and thus had to descend in order to restart its engine. A second round between air force and CIA followed, as a result of which air force pilots were trained to fly CIA U-2s. A successful overflight took place on October 14.

This ten-day delay constitutes some form of "failure." In the face of well-founded suspicions concerning offensive Soviet missiles in Cuba that posed a critical threat to the United States' most vital interest, squabbling between organizations whose job it is to produce this information seems entirely inappropriate. But for each of these organizations, the question involved the issue: "*Whose* job was it to be?" Moreover, the issue was not simply, which organization would control U-2 flights over Cuba, but rather the broader issue of ownership of U-2 intelligence activities — a very long standing territorial dispute. Thus though this delay was in one sense a "failure," it was also a nearly inevitable consequence of two facts:

---

[18] Abel, *op. cit.*, pp. 26 ff.; Weintal and Bartlett, *Facing the Brink* (New York, 1967), pp. 62 ff.; *Cuban Military Build-up;* J. Daniel and J. Hubbell, *Strike in the West* (New York, 1963), pp. 15 ff.

many jobs do not fall neatly into precisely defined organizational jurisdictions; and vigorous organizations are imperialistic.

Organizational Options. Deliberations of leaders in ExCom meetings produced broad outlines of alternatives. Details of these alternatives and blueprints for their implementation had to be specified by the organizations that would perform these tasks. These organizational outputs answered the question: What, specifically, *could* be done?

Discussion in the ExCom quickly narrowed the live options to two: an air strike and a blockade. The choice of the blockade instead of the air strike turned on two points: (1) the argument from morality and tradition that the United States could not perpetrate a "Pearl Harbor in reverse"; (2) the belief that a "surgical" air strike was impossible.[19] Whether the United States *might* strike first was a question not of capability but of morality. Whether the United States *could* perform the surgical strike was a factual question concerning capabilities. The majority of the members of the ExCom, including the President, initially preferred the air strike.[20] What effectively foreclosed this option, however, was the fact that the air strike they wanted could not be chosen with high confidence of success.[21] After having tentatively chosen the course of prudence — given that the surgical air strike was not an option — Kennedy reconsidered. On Sunday morning, October 21, he called the air force experts to a special meeting in his living quarters where he probed once more for the option of a *"surgical"* air strike.[22] General Walter C. Sweeny, Commander of Tactical Air Forces, asserted again that the air force could guarantee no higher than 90 percent effectiveness in a surgical air strike.[23] That "fact" was false.

The air strike alternative provides a classic case of military estimates. One of the alternatives outlined by the ExCom was named "air strike." Specification of the details of this alternative was delegated to the air force. Starting from an existing plan for massive United States military action against Cuba (prepared for contingencies like a response to a Soviet Berlin grab), air force estimators

[19] Schlesinger, *op. cit.*, p. 804.
[20] Sorensen, *Kennedy,* p. 684.
[21] *Ibid.,* pp. 684 ff.
[22] *Ibid.,* pp. 694–697.
[23] *Ibid.,* p. 697; Abel, *op. cit.,* pp. 100–101.

produced an attack to guarantee success.[24] This plan called for extensive bombardment of all missile sites, storage depots, airports, and, in deference to the navy, the artillery batteries opposite the naval base at Guantanamo.[25] Members of the ExCom repeatedly expressed bewilderment at military estimates of the number of sorties required, likely casualties, and collateral damage. But the "surgical" air strike that the political leaders had in mind was never carefully examined during the first week of the crisis. Rather, this option was simply excluded on the grounds that since the Soviet MRBMs in Cuba were classified "mobile" in United States manuals, extensive bombing was required. During the second week of the crisis, careful examination revealed that the missiles were mobile, in the sense that small houses are mobile: that is, they could be moved and reassembled in six days. After the missiles were reclassified "movable" and detailed plans for surgical air strikes specified, this action was added to the list of live options for the end of the second week.

Organizational Implementation. ExCom members separated several types of blockade: offensive weapons only, all armaments, and all strategic goods including POL (petroleum, oil, and lubricants). But the *"details"* of the operation were left to the navy. Before the President announced the blockade on Monday evening, the first stage of the navy's blueprint was in motion, and a problem loomed on the horizon.[26] The navy had a detailed plan for the blockade. The President had several less precise but equally determined notions concerning what should be done, when, and how. For the navy the issue was one of effective implementation of the navy's blockade — without the meddling and interference of political leaders. For the President, the problem was to pace and manage events in such a way that the Soviet leaders would have time to see, think, and blink.

A careful reading of available sources uncovers an instructive incident. On Tuesday the British Ambassador, Ormsby-Gore, after having attended a briefing on the details of the blockade, suggested to the President that the plan for intercepting Soviet ships far out of reach of Cuban jets did not facilitate Khrushchev's hard deci-

[24] Sorensen, *Kennedy,* p. 669.
[25] Hilsman, *op. cit.,* p. 204.
[26] See Abel, *op. cit.,* pp. 97 ff.

sion.[27] Why not make the interception much closer to Cuba and thus give the Russian leader more time? According to the public account and the recollection of a number of individuals involved, Kennedy "agreed immediately, called McNamara, and over emotional navy protest, issued the appropriate instructions."[28] As Sorensen records, "in a sharp clash with the navy, he made certain his will prevailed."[29] The navy's plan for the blockade was thus changed by drawing the blockade much closer to Cuba.

A serious organizational orientation makes one suspicious of this account. More careful examination of the available evidence confirms these suspicions, though alternative accounts must be somewhat speculative. According to the public chronology, a quarantine drawn close to Cuba became effective on Wednesday morning, the first Soviet ship was contacted on Thursday morning, and the first boarding of a ship occurred on Friday. According to the statement by the Department of Defense, boarding of the *Marcula* by a party from the *John R. Pierce* "took place at 7:50 A.M., E.D.T., 180 miles northeast of Nassau."[30] The *Marcula* had been trailed since about 10:30 the previous evening.[31] Simple calculations suggest that the *Pierce* must have been stationed along the navy's original arc which extended 500 miles out to sea from Cape Magsi, Cuba's eastern most tip.[32] The blockade line was *not* moved as the President ordered, and the accounts report.

What happened is not entirely clear. One can be certain, however, that Soviet ships passed through the line along which American destroyers had posted themselves before the official "first contact" with the Soviet ship. On October 26 a Soviet tanker arrived in Havana and was honored by a dockside rally for "running the blockade." Photographs of this vessel show the name *Vinnitsa* on the side of the vessel in Cyrillic letters.[33] But according to the official United States position, the first tanker to pass through the blockade was the *Bucharest*, which was hailed by the navy on the morning of October 25. Again simple mathematical calculation excludes the

[27] Schlesinger, *op. cit.*, p. 818.
[28] *Ibid.*
[29] Sorensen, *Kennedy*, p. 710.
[30] *The New York Times*, October 27, 1962.
[31] Abel, *op. cit.*, p. 171.
[32] For the location of the original arc see Abel, *op. cit.*, p. 141.
[33] *Facts on File* 22 (1962):376, published by Facts on File, Inc., New York, yearly.

possibility that the *Bucharest* and the *Vinnitsa* were the same ship. It seems probable that the navy's resistance to the President's order that the blockade be drawn in closer to Cuba forced him to allow one or several Soviet ships to pass through the blockade after it was officially operative.[34]

This attempt to leash the navy's blockade had a price. On Wednesday morning, October 24, what the President had been awaiting occurred. The 18 dry cargo ships heading towards the quarantine stopped dead in the water. This was the occasion of Dean Rusk's remark, "We are eyeball to eyeball and I think the other fellow just blinked."[35] But the navy had another interpretation. The ships had simply stopped to pick up Soviet submarine escorts. The President became quite concerned lest the navy — already riled because of presidential meddling in its affairs — blunder into an incident. Sensing the President's fears, McNamara became suspicious of the navy's procedures and routines for making the first interception. Calling on the Chief of Naval Operations in the navy's inner sanctum, the Navy Flag Plot, McNamara put his questions harshly.[36] Who would make the first interception? Were Russian-speaking officers on board? How would submarines be dealt with? At one point McNamara asked Anderson what he would do if a Soviet ship's captain refused to answer questions about his cargo. Picking up the Manual of Navy Regulations the navy man waved it in McNamara's face and shouted, "It's all in there." To which McNamara replied, "I don't give a damn what John Paul Jones would have done; I want to know what you are going to do, now."[37] The encounter ended on Anderson's remark: "Now, Mr. Secretary, if you and your Deputy will go back to your office the navy will run the blockade."[38]

[34] This hypothesis would account for the mystery surrounding Kennedy's explosion at the leak of the stopping of the *Bucharest*. See Hilsman, *op. cit.*, p. 45.

[35] Abel, *op. cit.*, p. 153.

[36] See *ibid.*, pp. 154 ff

[37] *Ibid.*, p. 156.

[38] *Ibid.*

8   *Scientists, Foreign Policy,*
      and Politics

WARNER R. SCHILLING

I

In their general character, the problems occasioned by the participation of scientists in the determination of high policy are not nearly so novel as is generally supposed. The scientist has been brought into the councils of government because he possesses specialized skills and information believed relevant to the identification and resolution of particular policy problems. His relationship to the policy process is therefore a familiar one, that of an expert. Just as Sputnik I precipitated the establishment of a Special Assistant to the President for Science and Technology, so the earlier problems of fighting World War II and insuring postwar employment had brought the Joint Chiefs of Staff and the Council of Economic Advisors into the offices of the President.

The central problems in policymaking posed by the entry of scientists into the policy process are thus formally no different from those associated with any other expert involved in the determination of national security policy. In particular, four such problems can be noted. (1) Like all experts, scientists will at times disagree, and the nonscientist (be he politician, administrator, or an expert in some other field) will confront the problem of choosing a course of action in the face of conflicting scientific advice. (2) Like all experts, scientists will at times evince certain predispositions toward the resolution of the policy problems on which their advice is sought, and the nonscientist will confront the problem of identifying the policy predilections peculiar to scientists and being on his guard against them. (3) The nonscientist and scientist will confront one problem in common, and that is how to organize them-

From Warner R. Schilling, "Scientists, Foreign Policy, and Politics," reprinted by permission of the author and The American Political Science Association from *The American Political Science Review* 56 (June 1962):287–300. Footnotes are renumbered.

selves to maximize the contribution that science can make to the government's programs, opportunities, and choices. Finally, (4) the scientist will confront a problem common to all experts who participate in the American policy process, and that is how to engage in politics without debasing the coinage of his own expertise.

II

The difficulties the nonscientist confronts in choosing a course of action in the face of conflicting scientific advice seem inherently no more formidable than those a nonexpert would face in deciding what to do in the event of conflicting advice from economists, soldiers, or specialists on Soviet foreign policy. There are at least seven procedures that the nonexpert can follow in such circumstances, singly or in combination, and they appear to have about the same promise, for better or for worse, regardless of the kind of experts involved.[1]

The first step the nonscientist can take is to make certain that it is really conflicting *scientific* advice he is receiving. In the fall of 1949 President Truman asked Secretary Acheson to look into the disputes then current within the Atomic Energy Commission and elsewhere about the consequences of undertaking an intensive effort to make an H-bomb. Upon investigation the Secretary of State concluded that the scientists involved were not really very far apart except on the foreign policy issues that were his and Truman's responsibility to decide.[2]

Procedures two and three are simple: the nonscientist may be guided by quantitative or qualitative features of the division (he can side with the majority, or with that side whose past record is the more confidence-inspiring). Failing these, there is, four, the "principle of least harm" and, five, the "principle of minimal choice." In the former, one chooses that course of action which appears to involve the least cost if the technical premise on which it is based proves to be wrong. Thus in World War II, given the American be-

[1] Cf. the implication in the following remarks of Glenn T. Seaborg, the Chairman of the Atomic Energy Commission: "Scientists don't necessarily have to make the final political decisions, but it might be easier to let a capable scientist learn political reality than to teach a politician science." Quoted in the *Bulletin of the Atomic Scientists*, February 1961, p. 79.

[2] In this and subsequent undocumented references the present writer has drawn upon personal interviews during 1956–1958 with participants in the H-bomb decision.

lief that the Germans were hard at work on an A-bomb, it seemed more sensible to spend $2 billion on the assumption that the bomb could be made than to do little or nothing on the assumption that it could not. In the case of the "principle of minimal choice," one chooses that course of action which seems to close off the least number of future alternatives. This was the character of President Truman's first decision on the H-bomb. He decided to go ahead in the effort to explore the feasibility of an H-bomb, but nothing was decided about technical steps of a greater political or military consequence (for example, testing a device if one were fabricated, or preparing to produce the materials that would be required for weapons production in the event of a successful test).[3]

In the case of procedure six the nonscientist can make his choice among conflicting scientists on the basis of whichever technical estimate is most in accord with policy on which he was already intent. (In contrast to the first procedure, where the nonscientist endeavors to factor out of the conflict the policy preferences of the scientists, here he is factoring into the conflict his own policy preferences.) In the spring of 1942, the British scientists Henry Tizard and F. A. Lindemann (Lord Cherwell) diverged greatly in their estimates of the destruction that could be accomplished by an intensive bombing of the homes of the German working class. There was general agreement among the soldiers and politicians involved that if the lower estimate were correct there were better military uses for the resources the bombing campaign would require, but in the end the campaign was made in the expectation that the higher estimate would prove to be the more accurate (which it did not). This choice was clearly influenced by Churchill's interest in presenting the Russians with a dramatically visible contribution to the war against Germany and by the fact that British air doctrine had long presumed the efficacy of strategic bombing.[4]

[3] For the "principle of least harm," see Bernard Brodie, "Strategy as a Science," *World Politics,* July 1949, p. 479n. On the H-bomb choice, see the present writer's "The H-Bomb Decision: How to Decide without Actually Choosing," *Political Science Quarterly,* March 1961, pp. 37–38.

[4] See C. P. Snow, *Science and Government* (Cambridge: Harvard University Press, 1961), pp. 47–51, the review of this book by P. M. S. Blackett in *Scientific American,* April 1961, pp. 192–194, and Winston S. Churchill, *The Second World War: The Hinge of Fate* (Boston: Houghton Mifflin Company, 1950), p. 281. For British air doctrine see also Herbert S. Dinnerstein, "The Impact of Air Power on the International Scene, 1933–1940," *Military Affairs,* Summer 1955, pp. 67–68.

In procedure seven the nonscientist is guided by his own sense for the scientific and technical problems involved. In the 1949 H-bomb debate, some of the politicians involved were little deterred by the fact that the scientists were by no means confident that they could make such a weapon and by the possibility that an all-out but failing effort might entail very high costs for the A-bomb program. These politicians were willing to press ahead in part because of their belief that the scientists were not really aware of their own potential. Similarly, when the German soldiers, scientists, and engineers engaged in the development of the V-2 divided on the question of whether it should be launched from mobile or fixed batteries, Hitler's own technical enthusiasm for large, hardened bunkers led him, unwisely as it turned out, to decide on behalf of the latter.[5]

In concluding this survey of the problem of conflicting advice, it should be noted that one of the more likely outcomes is that the actions of the contending scientists may prove much more influential than the procedures followed by the nonscientist. Divided experts will not always be equal in their physical or personal access to the decision-maker, in the persistence with which they state their case, or in the force and clarity of their arguments. Thus, in the H-bomb debate, there were instances where equally qualified scientists differed greatly in the time and energy they spent circulating their views of the technical (and political) prospects, and such differences were by no means without consequence for the judgments of others.[6]

---

[5] Maj. Gen. Walter Dornberger, *V-2* (New York: Ballantine Books, 1954), pp. 97, 158–160, and Lt. Gen. James M. Gavin, *War and Peace in the Space Age* (New York, 1958), pp. 76–77.

[6] Note should also be taken of the problem the policymaker faces when all his experts are *agreed*. The present writer is unable to suggest a useful procedure here (other than variations on numbers five, six, and seven above); but that the problem is a real one can be seen in the conclusion of the German physicists that it would be infeasible for any Power to develop an atomic bomb during World War II. Some of the German scientists later stated that political considerations were partly responsible for their advice and for the fact that they made so little progress themselves on an A-bomb (cf. procedure one).

The German work on the A-bomb during World War II is described in Samuel A. Goudsmit, *Alsos* (New York: Henry Schuman, Inc., 1947). For various appraisals of the influence exercised by political considerations, see Robert Jungk, *Brighter than a Thousand Suns* (New York: Harcourt, Brace and Company, 1958), pp. 88–104, Hans Bethe in the *Bulletin of the Atomic Scientists*, December 1958, p. 427, and William L. Laurence, *Men and Atoms* (New York: Simon and Schuster, 1959), pp. 90–93.

III

The discussion of the policy predispositions displayed by scientists must be entered with considerable caution. The major theoretical premise involved is that all experts will evidence certain predilections with regard to policy and policymaking which are the result of the character of their expertise: their skills, knowledge, and experience. Since experts differ in the skills, knowledge, and experience they command (or in the responsibilities with which they are charged), they will differ in the biases they characteristically exhibit. Thus scientists, soldiers, and diplomats jointly concerned with a policy problem are likely to approach the question of how and in what manner it should be resolved with rather dissimilar predispositions.

These points, however, are easier stated than demonstrated. To begin with, it should be clear that, insofar as policy is concerned, "the scientific mind" is as much a chimera as "the military mind." Scientists, like soldiers and the rest of us, differ greatly in the ideas they have about the political world and the things that will (or ought to) happen in it, and their views on foreign policy matters are far more likely to be reflective of these differences than conditioned by their common professional skills and interests. Moreover, even if differences in expertise or responsibility were the only factors determining the views of policymakers (and they certainly are not), one would still have to take account of the fact that scientists are as varied in their professional skills and pursuits as soldiers. The perspectives of a theoretical physicist engaged in basic research are no more to be equated with those of an organic chemist engaged in applying extant knowledge to the improvement of an industrial product than is the outlook of a staff officer in Washington drafting a war plan to be considered identical with that of a general in charge of a theatre of operations.

In addition to these difficulties, analysis must also contend with the fact that it is directed toward a moving target. The policy perspectives that a physicist may have developed as a result of two decades in a university laboratory are unlikely to endure without change after a few years on a Washington advisory committee. Many American scientists are well along the same route that transformed the policy perspectives of large numbers of the American military profession during the war and immediate postwar years. As a result of new problems and new responsibilities, these soldiers acquired new skills, knowledge, and experience. In consequence, with regard to their approach to foreign policy, some are, for all practical purposes, interchangeable between the Pentagon and the State Department, and one could wish that there were more diplomats equally well equipped to work on both sides of the Potomac.

With these reservations in mind, six policy perspectives will be presented here which seem moderately characteristic of many scientists, most of them physicists, who have participated in national security policy in recent times. Most of these predispositions were first evidenced during their work with the military during World War II, and the extent and manner in which they have been later operative in reference to larger foreign policy issues is not always easy to document, since most of the sources are still classified. Needless to say, in outlining these predispositions, one is presenting a cross between a caricature and a Weberian ideal type, not describing real people. In discussing these predispositions, the present writer does not mean to convey the impression that they are either "good" or "bad" from the point of view of policy or policymaking, or that one or another of these predispositions may not also be evidenced by groups other than scientists. The point to this discussion is that if certain orders of scientists are indeed prone to these or other policy predispositions, the nonscientist will be wise to be alert to them, even if . . . he should conclude that they are all for the good.

Naive Utopianism or Naive Belligerency. C.P. Snow has described the scientist as an impatient optimist in his approach to social wrongs; he is quick to search for something to do and inclined to expect favorable results.[7] Certainly, the scientist's profession inclines him to look at problems in terms of searching for a solution to them. When this perspective is turned to problems of international politics, however, the scientist's approach often appears open to the characterization of "naive utopianism or naive belligerency."[8] His approach to international relations appears simplistic and mechanistic. It is almost as if he conceives of policy being

[7] C. P. Snow, *The Two Cultures and the Scientific Revolution* (New York: Cambridge University Press, 1959), pp. 9–11.

[8] I am indebted to Hans Speier for the phrasing of this point.

made primarily by forward-looking, solution-oriented, rational-thinking types like himself.

In these perspectives the scientist is likely to find little in common with the diplomat (who is inclined to believe that most of his problems have no solution, and who is in any event too busy with the crises of the day to plan for tomorrow), or with the politician (whose approach to problems is so spasmodic as to seem neither analytical nor rational, and whose policy positions are anyway soon blurred by his efforts to accommodate to the positions of others), or with the professional student of international politics (who, when the opportunity permits, lectures the scientist on the elegant complexity of the political process, but who never seems, to the scientist at least, to have any really good ideas about what to do). It is perhaps these differences in perspective that lead the scientist on occasion to seem "intellectually arrogant"; it is as if he concludes that those who have no promising solutions or are not seeking them cannot be very bright. In his predisposition toward action and solutions, the scientist comes closest to sharing the predilection of the soldier for decision, which may be one reason why their partnership has been so spectacularly successful.

The Whole Problem Approach. The first grant made by the United States government for experimental research was in 1832 to the Franklin Institute. The scientists were asked to investigate the reasons for explosions in steamboat boilers. They reported back not only with a technical explanation but with a draft bill to provide for federal regulation of steamboats.[9] In this they evidenced the scientist's predilection for the "whole problem approach." The reluctance of scientists to apply their expertise to mere fragments of the total problem, especially under conditions where those who prescribe the fragments do not reveal the whole of which they are a part, was evident in the work of both British and American scientists during World War II. Military officials initially approached the scientists with requests for the development of particular weapons and devices without revealing the military problems or reasoning responsible for their requests. The scientists objected to this procedure, and they were eventually able to persuade the soldiers to inform them of the general military problems involved in order

[9] Don K. Price, *Government and Science* (New York: New York University Press, 1954), pp. 10–11.

that the scientists might reach their own conclusions about the kinds of weapons and devices the military would need to meet those problems.[10]

In 1952, in connection with an air force project on air defense, a group of American scientists was asked to review the prospects for improving the nation's continental air defense. The scientists concluded that some new and promising systems were possible, and they submitted an estimate of what the developments might cost. They also recommended that the money be spent. The air force did not approve the recommendation, and as is customary in Washington the disputants on both sides began to search for allies and to leak their cases to the press. Certain air force officials, who feared that additional funds for air defense would come at the expense of dollars otherwise available for the Strategic Air Command and who were convinced that this would be militarily undesirable, charged that the scientists by entering into matters of military strategy and budget policy had exceeded both their assignment and their expertise. Commenting on this charge, one of the scientists involved later explained that he would have little interest in working on a study project that did not have the potential for leading into the question of whether the conclusions should be acted upon.[11]

The predisposition to want to be told and to deal with the whole problem no doubt has its base in the professional experience

[10] This persuasion was largely accomplished through demonstrations of the military utility of the scientists' taking such an approach, although in the early history of the M.I.T. Radiation Laboratory a certain amount of polite bargaining was apparently practiced. One scientist involved, whenever told that the reason for a request was a problem for Washington, not him, to worry about, adopted the practice of working on something else until he was given a description of the problem involved. For a brief summary of the British experience, see Alexander Haddow, "The Scientist as Citizen," *Bulletin of the Atomic Scientists,* September 1956, p. 247.

[11] Cf. the following exchange between Gordon Gray and Jerrold Zacharias during the Oppenheimer hearing. Gray: "If you were directing a study which had to do with electronics, a pretty clearly defined field, and it started to come up with recommendations with respect to foreign policy, would you feel that an official of the Defense Department who urged that you stick to electronics was acting with impropriety?" Zacharias: "I think I would not direct a project that was as restrictive as that, sir, as to be restricted only to electronics." U. S. Atomic Energy Commission, *In the Matter of J. Robert Oppenheimer, Transcript of Hearing before Personnel Security Board,* Washington, 1954, p. 930.

For some of the issues involved in the 1952 air defense study, see *ibid.,* pp. 598–599, 749–750, 763–765, 923–924, 930–931, 935, 938, and also the account in Price, *Government and Science,* pp. 136–138.

of scientists (and one of the central credos of science) that good ideas on a problem may come from the most unexpected quarters and that the widest possible dissemination of information about a problem will significantly enhance its chances for an early solution.[12] Still, there are problems and problems; some are open to determinate solutions, and others can be resolved only through the exercise of political power. The point about the "whole problem approach," as the air defense example illustrates, is that it not only helps propel the scientists from an advisory to a political role but it serves to make the scientist somewhat blind to the fact that he is so moving. In its most extreme form, the "whole problem approach" coupled with the "intellectual arrogance" perspective can lead to such instances as when, on one high-level advisory committee concerned with several areas of national security policy, a scientist whose formal claim to participation was a knowledge of infra-red ray phenomena was reportedly quite free with his proposals for what political policies should be adopted with regard to the United Nations.

Quantum Jumps versus Improvements. A number of scientists have advanced the proposition that the military tend to be more interested in improving existing weapons than in developing radically new ones, and they have urged that a separate civilian agency be established to undertake such development. Both scientists and soldiers have explained this difference in their approach to military research and development, "quantum jumps versus improvements," with the hypothesis that the soldier's interest in developing entirely new weapons must always be inhibited by his concern for the possibility that war may come in the near future, since in this event his interests are best served by improving existing weapons. It has also been suggested that military leaders, who must be prepared at any time to ask others to take up the weapons at hand and fight with them, cannot afford to let themselves or others become too im-

[12] General Leslie Groves, who directed the Manhattan project, was especially sensitive to the scientists' tendency to take on the whole problem. (Some even advised him on how the garbage should be collected at Los Alamos, an act which may possibly have reflected self- rather than scientific interest.) One reason for his effort to compartmentalize the work scientists were doing was his fear that "if I brought them into the whole project, they would never do their own job. There was just too much of scientific interest, and they would just be frittering from one thing to another." *Oppenheimer Transcript,* p. 164.

pressed with the deficiencies of those weapons as compared with others that might have been had.[13]

An explanation less flattering to the military for this difference is the occasional assertion by scientists that theirs is a profession which stimulates original and creative thought, while that of the military tends to develop minds which accept the existing situation without too much question. As indicated in the discussion of the first predilection, this is a judgment which the scientist may extend to the diplomat and the politician as well. The structure of both the domestic and the international political process is normally such as to make "quantum jumps" in policy infeasible. Diplomats and politicians are accustomed to seeing the same old policy problems come around year after year, and they are generally intent on policies which promise only slow and modest change. Scientists, on the other hand, have been demanding and searching for quantum jumps in foreign policy ever since the end of World War II. It is symptomatic that the first proposal developed by the Advisory Committee on Science and Technology to the Democratic National Advisory Council, established in 1959, was for the creation of a new scientific agency, independent of the State and Defense Departments, whose function would be "to face all the problems of disarmament." [14]

Technology for Its Own Sweet Sake. In the summer of 1945, after the A-bomb had been tested but before the first drop on Japan, the Director of the Los Alamos Laboratory, J. Robert Oppenheimer, suggested to his superior, General Leslie Groves, that if some improvements were made in the design of the bomb it would be more effective. Groves decided against the improvements because he did not want to incur any delay in the use of the bomb, which he expected would end the war with Japan. In the summer of 1943, after the Director of the German V-2 project, General Dornberger, had finally secured a first-class priority for the use of the weapon, those responsible for producing it in quantity were increasingly handicapped by the scientists and engineers who kept improving but changing its design. Dornberger was finally obliged to issue a flat order against any further improvements.[15]

---

[13] See, for example, Lloyd V. Berkner, "Science and National Strength," *Bulletin of the Atomic Scientists*, June 1953, pp. 155, 180.

[14] See the *Bulletin of the Atomic Scientists*, December 1959, p. 412.

[15] *Oppenheimer Transcript*, p. 33, and Dornberger, *V-2*, pp. 134–137.

There was nothing irresponsible in these scientists' actions. Charged with the technical development of weapons, they would have been remiss in their responsibilities if they had failed to call attention to the prospects for improvement. The point to the examples is that scientists and engineers, in the pursuit of their own responsibilities and interests, may easily lose sight of those of the policymaker.

The scientists on the General Advisory Committee to the Atomic Energy Commission who recommended against the development of an H-bomb in 1949 did so in part because of their concern for the foreign-policy consequences of introducing a weapon of such destructive power into the world. Oppenheimer, the Chairman of the Committee, later stated that the thermonuclear design developed by Edward Teller in 1951 was "technically so sweet" that, if it had been available in 1949, the Committee would probably not have made the recommendation that it did. Since, with a technically more promising design at hand, one might suppose that the Committee's foreign-policy concerns would have been all the greater, some observers have concluded that in the pursuit of his technical interests the scientist can also easily lose sight of his own policy concerns.[16]

Such a judgment ignores the complexity of the Committee's position. For example, one of the reasons why the Committee thought the United States should take the initiative in renouncing the H-bomb was precisely because the device then in view seemed likely to be both difficult to make and of dubious military value. It was thought that for this reason the Russians might be willing to follow the American example and that, if they did not, the United States would not have risked much by the delay. These were considerations which obviously would have been changed if a technically more promising design had been available in 1949.[17] Still, the comments of several scientists close to these events are not without relevance. It is their feeling that there are times when the technician does take over, that when the scientist is faced with an interesting and challenging problem his inclination is to get to work on it, and

[16] *Oppenheimer Transcript*, p. 251. For an extreme judgment, see Jungk, *Brighter than a Thousand Suns*, p. 296.

[17] See Oppenheimer's statements in *Oppenheimer Transcript*, pp. 81, 251, 897, and "The H-Bomb Decision: How to Decide Without Actually Choosing," *loc. cit.*, pp. 30–36.

that under these circumstances he should not be the first person to be expected to keep larger policy considerations in balance.

This predisposition, "technology for its own sweet sake," appears to have its roots in two more of science's central credos: the belief in the value of pursuing knowledge for its own sake, and the belief that the best motivation for the direction of research is the strength and character of individual curiosities. But the direction and strength of scientific interests and curiosities is not necessarily coincident with the requirements of military or foreign policy. One of the most recent examples of the scientist's capacity to get caught up in a challenging problem (assigned, to be sure, by policymakers) is afforded by the ingenious techniques scientists conceived for evading nuclear-test detection systems and for the design of new systems to meet those evasions. In the light of the later course of negotiations, an American statesman who believed there was considerable foreign-policy gain in a test-ban treaty and who believed that the Russians were at one time seriously interested in such a treaty might well conclude that the formula developed by Watson-Watt, the scientist who fathered radar, with reference to the problem of meeting wartime military requirements was not without its implications for meeting peacetime foreign policy requirements: "Give them the third best to go with; the second comes too late, the best never comes."[18] This observation is not intended as an argument that the interests of the United States would have been better served by a test-ban treaty with a "third best" detection system than by no treaty at all. The point is that the policymaker must be sensitive to the prospect that, because of the constant advance of technology, his only real choices may be of this order.

The Sense for Paradise Lost. This predisposition is likely to be more characteristic of the scientists who had their graduate training and early professional experience in the years before World War II than of those who have known only war or Cold War conditions.[19] The prewar scientists took it as an article of faith that certain conditions were essential for the progress of science, in particular

[18] Sir Robert Watson-Watt, *Three Steps to Victory* (London: Odhams, 1957), p. 74.

[19] In 1955 slightly more than half of the active research physicists in the United States were under forty years of age and had received their doctorates after December 7, 1941. Lee A. DuBridge, "The American Scientist: 1955," *Yale Review*, September 1955, p. 1.

that scientists be free to select their research problems and that both scientists and scientific information be free to move among as well as within nations.[20] All of these conditions were violated during World War II, and as a result of the Cold War they were never fully reestablished. The nuclear physicists had had perhaps the most highly developed sense of international community. They were relatively few in number, had intimate personal relationships at home and abroad, and had been experiencing an exciting exchange of discoveries since Rutherford identified the nucleus in 1911. They also lost the most, for theirs was militarily the most sensitive knowledge, and the pages of the *Bulletin of the Atomic Scientists* offer eloquent testimony to their ideological disturbance.

The result is that the senior scientists tend to be especially sensitive to possibilities which hold some promise for restoring the former order. They may usually be found on the side (or in front) of those urging freer exchange of scientific and military information with allied governments, less secrecy in the circulation of scientific (and sometimes military) information, and more extensive cultural, and especially scientific, exchanges with the Soviet Union. Similarly, the major activities of the Foreign Policy Panel of the President's Science Advisory Committee and of the Office of the Science Advisor to the Secretary of State have been in connection with the Science Attaché program, the facilitation of international scientific programs and conferences, and the exchange of scientists with the Soviet Union.[21]

Science Serves Mankind. For at least 300 years the western scientific tradition has assumed that the unrestricted generation of new knowledge about the world was a social good. Over these years science in its purest form (the discovery of the facts of nature for knowledge's sake alone) became increasingly an autonomous social institution; research scientists were largely disassociated from the practical applications of their discoveries, but they took it for

---

[20] These assumptions are excellently set forth in Margret Smith Stahl, "Splits and Schisms: Nuclear and Social," unpublished doctoral dissertation, University of Wisconsin, 1946, chap. 4.

[21] For the activities of the Panel and the Office see James R. Killian, "Science and Public Policy," Address to the American Association for the Advancement of Science, December 29, 1958, as printed in *Science Program — 86th Congress*, Report of the Senate Committee on Government Operations, 86th Congress, 1st Session (1959), pp. 12–13, and *The Science Adviser of the Department of State*, Department of State Publication 7056 (Washington, D.C., 1960).

granted that these discoveries would ultimately benefit mankind.[22] The advent of nuclear and bacteriological weapons systems which have the potential of destroying so much of mankind and his works has called this faith sharply into question. It does not take much imagination to wonder if man, in view of his apparent inability to escape from the order of conflicts which have historically resulted in war, would not be better off in a world where the knowledge that has made the new weapons possible did not exist. For some of the senior nuclear physicists this is more than a philosophical question. They are unable to avoid a sense of real personal responsibility; they reason from the premise that they were few, and if they had acted differently weapons development might not have taken the turn it did.

In the immediate postwar years, the apparent contradiction between the good of science and the evil of war was resolved by the expectation that the very destructiveness of the new weapons would lead man to renounce at last the folly of war. The course of foreign policy in later years has weakened these expectations but not destroyed them, as the recent flurry of arms-control proposals premised on the rational self-interest of both sides in avoiding mutual destruction testifies.

The need to preserve their sense of service to mankind led some American scientists to refuse to work on weapons. Similarly, there are reports that several Russian scientists were imprisoned, exiled, or placed under surveillance for refusing to participate in weapons work between 1945 and 1953, and in 1957 a number of Germany's elite physicists announced that they would have no part in nuclear weapons work.[23] Such cases are dramatic, but nowhere have they prevented the development of weapons on which governments were determined. The more consequential resolutions have been those in which scientists have simply identified the good of mankind with the strength of their nation or have endeavored to develop new weapons systems which would be as effective as the old in promoting national policy but which would result in less

---

[22] See Stahl, *op. cit.*, chap. 4.

[23] See Arnold Kramish, *Atomic Energy in the Soviet Union* (Stanford: Stanford University Press, 1959), p. 105. Kramish states that it is not certain whether the objections of the Russian scientists were technical or political. For the declaration of the German physicists, see the *Bulletin of the Atomic Scientists,* June 1957, p. 228.

slaughter if used. This was part of the rationale behind the recommendation made by a group of American scientists in 1951 that the government undertake the development and production of a large number of A-bombs for tactical use in the ground defense of Western Europe. Their hope was that such an innovation would relieve the United States of the burden of having to rely solely on the threat of strategic bombing to contain the Red Army.[24]

The failure of the United States to orbit a satellite before the Soviet Union did was the result of the State Department's insensitivity to the political implications of the event and the decision of the President and the Secretary of Defense not to let a satellite program interfere with military missile programs. A small part of the story, however, is to be found in the reluctance of some of the American scientists involved in the programming of the International Geophysical Year to see an American IGY satellite propelled by an operational military weapon. Their preference for the less developed but nonmilitary Vanguard over the army's Redstone appears to have reflected a combination of the "sense for paradise lost" and the "science serves mankind" predispositions, in this case an interest in showing the world the peaceful side of science and in demonstrating that the scientists of the world could cooperate in the interests of knowledge as well as compete in the interests of nations.[25]

IV

With regard to the two remaining problems to be discussed — how to organize relations between science and government, and how the scientist can participate in policymaking and still keep his expert standing — four points seem deserving of special emphasis: (A) the problem of organization, especially in the area of foreign policy, is still very much in the research and development stage, and so it may long remain, considering the precedent set by the problem of how to relate military experts and foreign policy; (B) in many areas of policy it will never be possible to specify what constitutes "the best" organization; the way in which policymakers are organized is not without influence on the kind of policies they will produce, and so long as there are differences over policy there

24 *Oppenheimer Transcript*, pp. 584, 594–595, 891–894.
25 See Walter Sullivan, *Assault on the Unknown* (New York: McGraw-Hill, 1961), pp. 79–81.

will be no agreement about organization; (C) in the American political system, at least, the science expert at the high-policy level has no real hope of keeping out of politics; his only choice is in the character of his political style; and finally, (D) it should not be forgotten that organization and policymaking are not the same as policy; successful instances of foreign policy capitalizing on or guiding developments in science and technology will not automatically follow just because scientists have been liberally injected into the policymaking process.

Organization. Current American organization in the area of science and foreign policy still reflects the emergency responses to the Russian ICBM and Sputnik I. One effect of the events was that scientists were rushed to the most important single center of power, the Office of the President, by means of the creation of the Special Assistant to the President for Science and Technology and the President's Science Advisory Committee.

The President certainly needs men around him sensitive to the areas of interaction between science and foreign policy. But a case can be made for the proposition that the center of gravity for the input of scientific advice into the policymaking process should be at a lower level than the White House. The President's political interests lie in keeping the staff about him small and generalized. Well-developed plans and programs will have a better chance of maturing in the larger and more diversified facilities that departments and agencies can provide. Secondly, as C. P. Snow concludes in his account of the differences between Tizard and Lindemann, there are risks in having a single science advisor sitting next to the center of political power. Although it should be noted that Churchill fared better with a single science advisor than Hitler did with none ("The Führer has dreamed," Dornberger was told, "that no [V-2] will ever reach England"), Snow's point has merit and it holds for institutions as well as for individuals.[26] The President will generally find his choices facilitated by the existence of multiple and independent sources of scientific advice. . . .

Organization and Purpose. Since administrative organizations exist for the purpose of serving policy goals and implementing policy programs, it is to be expected that those who differ on the goals and programs of policy will differ about the proper design of admin-

[26] Snow, *Science and Government*, pp. 66–68, and Dornberger, *V-2*, p. 87.

istrative organizations. The desire of many scientists in 1945 to see atomic energy used for peaceful rather than military purposes was one of the reasons for their political campaign to place the postwar atomic energy program in the hands of a civilian commission instead of the War Department. Similarly, more recent differences about how to organize the government's space effort reflect, in part, policy differences about whether space will or should be an area for major military operations.

The same point can be seen in the proposal to create a Department of Science and Technology which would include the variety of "little" science programs now scattered throughout the executive structure (for example, those of the Weather Bureau, National Bureau of Standards, the Antarctic Office) but would exclude those of the Department of Defense, the Atomic Energy Commission, and the Space Administration. The hope behind this proposal is that, combined together, the "little" programs would be able to compete more effectively in the struggle for government dollars with the "big" science programs of the military, atomic energy, and space organizations.[27]

The question of the "best" science organization is thus inescapably tied to the question of what is the "best" science policy. But who can demonstrate whether science and foreign policy would be better served by allocating dollars to a program to control weather or to a program to explore Mars? There are no determinate solutions to problems of this order. Neither, for that matter, is there any "one right amount" of the nation's scientific resources that should be allocated to basic as compared to applied research. Differences on policy questions such as these are unavoidable among scientists and nonscientists alike, and they can be resolved in but one manner: through the interplay of power and interest in a political arena.

This condition, plus the increasing dependence of scientific programs and research on government funds, plus the increasing consequences of the choices the government makes in allocating those funds, all promise to put the politicians and the scientists under increasing pressure. As the opportunities for further development in

[27] See Lloyd V. Berkner, "National Science Policy and the Future," Address at Johns Hopkins University, December 16, 1958, as printed in *Science Program — 86th Congress*, pp. 116–118.

each of a thousand different scientific fields mushroom with the acceleration of scientific knowledge, whatever the government decides to support, it will be deciding *not* to support more. Indeed, it is not too difficult to see the scientists becoming practiced advocates and lobbyists for the government's support of their cherished fields and projects, or to imagine the day when the politicians start to complain about "interscience rivalry" and begin to fancy that, if only there were a single Chief of Science, competition and duplication could be ended and the nation could have an integrated science policy.

Scientists in Politics. The American political system is not one that insulates its experts from the politics of choice.[28] The scientist involved in high-policy matters is likely to find himself propelled into the political arena, either by a push from behind or by his own interest in seeing that the "right" choices are made. Some of the incentives the scientist may have, to follow up his advice with an effort to see that it is accepted (and to take a hand in a few other matters while he is at it), were outlined and illustrated in the preceding section. It is equally important to recognize that the scientist may find himself on the political firing line, placed there by a politician interested in using the scientist's prestige as an "expert" to disarm the critics of his (the politician's) choices.

Thus, prior to the moratorium on nuclear tests, the Eisenhower administration appeared to be using scientists and their scientific facts on fall-out as a means of justifying and defending a policy that was obviously compounded of a variety of considerations besides that of the radiological hazard. The comparison with Truman's use of the prestige of the Joint Chiefs of Staff to defend his choices in the Korean War comes easily to mind. So, too, do the statements of various Republican leaders that they had lost confidence in the Joint Chiefs and their determination, when they came to power, to get rid of the "Democratic" Chiefs and to appoint Chiefs in sympathy with Republican policies.

The scientist, in short, is not likely to orbit the centers of political power emitting upon request "beeps" of purely technical informtion. He will inevitably be pulled into the political arena. If his par-

[28] This point, especially as it relates to science experts, is discussed in Price, *Government and Science*, pp. 61–62, and in Herman Finer, "Government and the Expert," *Bulletin of the Atomic Scientists*, November 1956, pp. 331–332.

ticipation there is to be either productive or personally satisfying, both the scientist and the nonscientist need to be highly conscious of the character of their activity and the problems involved. The scientist (and many a nonscientist) must learn that the making of foreign policy is not a quest for the "right" answers to the problems of our time. There are only hard choices, the consequences of which will be uncertain and the making of which will often seem interminable in time and irrational in procedure.

The debate and disagreement over these choices will be heated and confused under the best of circumstances, but emotion and misunderstanding can be eased if scientists and nonscientists are both alert to the limits as well as the potential of the scientist's contribution. On the scientist's part, there is the obvious need to exercise the utmost care in making clear to himself and to others the areas where he speaks as a concerned citizen and those where he speaks as a professional expert. More difficult will be the task of learning how and to whom to address himself in each of these capacities when he is dissatisfied with the outcome of a policy decision in which he has participated. There is, as Don Price has pointed out, no clear code in Washington to govern the conduct of dissenting experts, only a "flexible" set of possible relationships with one's immediate superiors and those whose authority competes with or exceeds that of one's superiors. In contrast to the soldier, who can find some although not complete guidance in the doctrine of "civilian control," the very nature of the scientist's intellectual habits and many of his policy predispositions may make especially difficult his task in determining the limits to which he can stretch his dissent.[29]

On their part, the nonscientists need to recognize that scientists can hardly be expected to remain politically indifferent or inactive about the policy issues with which they are involved (especially when no one else in Washington practices such restraint). It was the naivete of this expectation that was so appalling in the conclusion of the Gray Board that Oppenheimer was a security risk because (among other reasons) "he may have departed his role as scientific advisor to exercise highly persuasive influence in matters in which his convictions were not necessarily a reflection of technical judgment, and also not necessarily related to the protection of the

[29] See the discussion in Price, *Government and Science*, pp. 131, 133, 138–142. The point about the scientists' lacking a tradition of "civilian control" was suggested by William T. R. Fox.

strongest offensive military interests of the country." [30] It is unlikely that "civil-scientist" relations will ever get any worse than this. With time and experience one can expect many of these problems to be eased, but it would be unrealistic to expect them to disappear. Military experts have participated in the making of foreign policy far longer than scientists, and the question of how they can best do so is still the subject of more than a little disagreement. . . .

[30] U. S. Atomic Energy Commission, *In the Matter of J. Robert Oppenheimer, Texts of Principal Documents and Letters* (Washington, 1954), pp. 19–20. Note the policy predisposition in the phrase "strongest offensive military interests."

It should not be comfortable for an American to reflect on the career of Peter Kapitsa, a Soviet physicist who was a student of Rutherford and who worked in England from 1922 to 1934 and then returned to the Soviet Union. Kapitsa was placed under house arrest in 1947 and remained there until Stalin's death. Kapitsa has told Western scientists and newsmen that his arrest was the result of his refusal to work on nuclear energy for military purposes. Kramish believes that his arrest was due to the government's dissatisfaction with his advice on certain technical approaches to weapons development. In either event, it is noteworthy that Kapitsa is believed to have recently been, on an informal basis, one of Khrushchev's main science advisors.

On the matter of his arrest, see the report by Harrison Salisbury in *The New York Times,* July 11, 1956; the *Bulletin of the Atomic Scientists,* January 1957, p. 38; and Kramish, *Atomic Energy in the Soviet Union,* pp. 109–110. The information on his recent activity was supplied by the staff of the Subcommittee on National Policy Machinery, Senate Committee on Government Operations.

III

POLITICAL AND
BUREAUCRATIC ELITES

As the preceding selections have indicated, executive agencies derive their power to influence public policy from resources that politicians cannot easily duplicate. Policy only becomes legitimate in a democratic society, however, when it is supported by laws enacted by elected officials, or at least when these officials do not choose to oppose the programs bureaucratic organizations wish to put into effect. Consequently, agencies have a high stake in winning the approval of political officials in both the executive branch and the legislature, for policy preferences and jurisdictional ambitions cannot easily be gratified in the face of opposition from these officeholders. The search for such approval generates interaction between bureaucratic and political elites that plays a central role in developing public policy in the United States.

I

On paper at least, the President holds a position of unrivaled eminence in the American political system, having under his domain a bureaucratic apparatus that commands constantly expanding technical capacities and skills. The abilities of the bureaucrats over whom he presides, however, may represent for the President such impenetrable mysteries that he may become the prisoner rather than the master of his own executive establishment. Indeed, he may feel himself in the position of the Russian czar who, as noted by

121

Weber, "was seldom able to accomplish permanently anything that displeased his bureaucracy and hurt the power interests of the bureaucrats." [1]

Asserting mastery of his own executive house thus becomes a prime responsibility of presidential leadership. Arthur M. Schlesinger, Jr., in "Roosevelt as Chief Administrator" describes how Franklin D. Roosevelt performed this task. Roosevelt's method essentially maintained a system of checks and balances within the executive branch — preventing a single agency or official from monopolizing his attention in any area of public policy. In this way he could draw advice from various sources, playing one expert off against another, and in the end maintaining that most precious of a leader's prerogatives — freedom of action.

This account of presidential relations with the bureaucracy also illuminates how intensely administrators vie with one another in their efforts to gain direct access to the chief executive. When an agency succeeds in securing such access, the President may be led to give preferential treatment to it in assigning responsibility for the administration of new programs, or the agency may be able to shape his outlook on matters of public policy that are important to it.

II

The interaction between bureaucratic organizations and Congress in the formation of public policy reveals a sharp dichotomy between traditional theory and actual practice. In theory, the assumption has been that Congress spells out broad objectives through legislation, confining itself to the major goals of policy and leaving it to administrators to fill in the details. In practice, however, the relationship often is the reverse of this theoretical model. Congressmen have an incurable tendency to concern themselves with the details of administration, particularly when these details directly affect a legislature's home district — for example, the establishment of a new federal installation in a Congressman's

[1] *From Max Weber: Essays in Sociology,* ed. and trans. by H. H. Gerth and C. Wright Mills (New York: Oxford University Press); see *infra,* p. 62.

constituency or — less happily — the closing of such a facility.

Recently, there has been an increasing tendency to justify congressional preoccupation with the details of administration on the grounds that legislators are not properly equipped to work out the grand design of policy, and that this burden will inevitably be assumed by executive agencies that have the staff and technical resources for such planning and policy development. Legislators make their most effective contribution to the policy process, it is argued, when they subject executive projects to searching scrutiny, bringing to bear on these activities their own critical judgment and keen sense of political feasibility and effect.

This latter model presupposes an adversary relationship between Congress and administration, and in the case of agencies that have tangible benefits to dispense, the relationship is often much more congenial than that. In "Congress and Water Resources," Arthur A. Maass explores the efforts of legislators to secure Corps of Engineers' approval for river and harbor ("pork-barrel") projects in their own districts. Because it can grant such approval, the Corps has developed powerful sources of support both in Congress and the community at large. In recent years military procurement activities by defense agencies have rivalled such rivers and harbors appropriations as a source of hard currency in administrative relations with Congress. Many other agencies, however, have only modest favors to award in return for legislative support, and they are much more dependent on decisions made in Congress than the legislature is upon their favorable determinations.

III

At the frontiers separating political and administrative institutions in American national government stand the heads of the great executive departments. They preside over vast bureaucratic establishments that generate formidable pressures for particular policy viewpoints, while at the same time they are responsible to the White House and Congress for policies favored in each of these other centers of power. Many a cabinet member has been a casualty of this system, for, as Richard F. Fenno, Jr., reveals in "The Role of the

Cabinet," it requires administrative statecraft of the highest order to avoid being capsized in these turbulent crosscurrents of national politics. The retirement of two cabinet officers during the first two years of the Nixon administration was traced to their inability to maintain favor simultaneously with the President and the members of their own department.

Often the heads of executive agencies give their first loyalty to their own bureaucratic establishments or to the groups in society that their agencies serve. As a result, Presidents are obliged to bring into the government a cadre of appointees whose primary commitment is to the chief executive rather than to agency or group interests. These "in-and-outers," as Richard E. Neustadt calls them in "White House and Whitehall," represent a third force in the executive establishment, being neither as political as agency heads nor as bureaucratic as career civil servants. Because they have well-established positions outside the government in, for example, universities and law firms, these in-and-outers can bring to executive discussions an independence of judgment that might otherwise be missing. The comparison Neustadt makes between in-and-outers in the American system and high-level civil servants in Great Britain is a provocative one, but a British observer might question whether the temporary status of the in-and-outer in the United States gives him anything like the continuing power of his well-entrenched counterpart at Whitehall.

The most conspicuous and powerful of the in-and-outers in American politics are the presidential staff members. In "The Presidents' Men," Patrick Anderson traces the factors that led to the emergence of this super-staff in Washington. These presidential assistants enjoy assets denied to ordinary cabinet members. They have easier access to the President, are not subject to senatorial confirmation, and, under the doctrine of executive privilege, are immune from the necessity of responding to congressional interrogation.

These White House Assistants also lack the independent power base that cabinet members possess; thus they are wholly dependent on the President's goodwill for continued influence. One recent White House staff member charged that executive aides are primarily interested in currying favor with the chief executive.[2] When this is the case, White House staff members cannot perform the indispensable function of telling the President unpleasant truths about mistakes or failures in his policies. Indeed, they may seek to bolster his ego and protect their own position by concealing the truth. Worth noting is the fact that cabinet members have recently seemed to be the most independent and critical of the President's executive advisors — Secretary of Defense Clark Clifford in the case of President Lyndon B. Johnson, and Secretary of the Interior Walter Hickel under President Richard M. Nixon.

[2] George E. Reedy, *The Twilight of the Presidency* (New York: World Publishing Co., 1970).

9   *Roosevelt as Chief Administrator*

Arthur M. Schlesinger, Jr.

Little fascinated Franklin Roosevelt more than the tasks of presidential administration. And in few things was he more generally reckoned a failure.

This verdict against Roosevelt derived ultimately from a philosophy of public administration — a philosophy held for many years after by Civil Service professionals, expounded in departments of political science, and commending itself plausibly to common sense. This school's faith was in logical organization of government, founded on rigid definitions of job and function and maintained by the sanctity of channels. It weapons were the job description and the organization chart. Its unspoken assumption was that the problems of administration never change; and its consuming fear was improvisation, freewheeling, or unpredictability — which is nearly to say creativity — in the administrative process. From this point of view, it need hardly be said, the Roosevelt government was a textbook case of poor administration. At one time or another, Roosevelt must surely have violated every rule in the sacred texts of the Bureau of the Budget.

And this conventional verdict found apparent support in much of the literature written by men who worked for Roosevelt. Though these reports differed on many other things, one thing on which they very often agreed was in their complaint about Roosevelt as an ad-

From *The Coming of the New Deal.* Copyright © 1958 by Arthur M. Schlesinger, Jr. Reprinted by permission of the publisher, Houghton Mifflin Company.

ministrator. They agreed on one other thing too — the perspective from which they were written. Nearly all exhibited the problems of the presidency from below — from the viewpoint of the subordinate rather than from that of the President. The picture created by this mass of individual stories, while vivid and overwhelming, was inevitably distorted and too often querulous. For no subordinate ever got what he wanted or thought he needed. In later years, George C. Marshall would talk of "localitis" — the conviction ardently held by every theater commander that the war was being won or lost in his own zone of responsibility, and that the withholding of whatever was necessary for local success was evidence of blindness, if not of imbecility, in the high command. "Localitis" in one form or another was the occupational disease of all subordinate officials; and, in a sense, it had to be, for each of them ought to demand everything he needed to do the best job he can. But "localitis" offered no solid ground for judgment of superiors, whose role it must inevitably be to frustrate the dreams of subordinates. The President occupied the apex of the pyramid of frustration. The essence of his job was to enforce priorities — and thereby to exasperate everybody. And, in Roosevelt's case, there is little left in the literature to emphasize the view from the summit, where any President had to make his decisions. As Grace Tully (whose book does something to redress the balance) commented on other memoirists, "None of them could know that for each minute they spent with the President he spent a hundred minutes by himself and a thousand more with scores of other people — to reject, improvise, weigh and match this against that until a decision was reached on a public policy."

The question remains whether the true test of an administrator may be, not his ability to design and respect organization charts, not his ability to keep within channels, but his ability to concert and release the energies of men for the attainment of public objectives. It might be argued that the essence of successful administration is: first, to acquire the ideas and information necessary for wise decisions; second, to maintain control over the actual making of the decisions; and, third, to mobilize men and women who can make the first two things possible — that is, who can provide effective ideas and information, and who can reliably put decisions into effect. It is conceivable that these things may be more important than preserving the chastity of administrative organization — that, indeed, an excessive insistence on the sacredness of channels and charts is likely to end in the stifling of imagination, the choking of vitality, and the deadening of creativity.

I

Franklin Roosevelt, at any rate, had some such philosophy of administration. The first task of an executive, as he evidently saw it, was to guarantee himself an effective flow of information and ideas. And Roosevelt's first insight — or, at least, his profound conviction — was that, for this purpose, the ordained channels, no matter how simply or how intricately designed, could never be enough. An executive relying on a single information system became inevitably the prisoner of that system. Roosevelt's persistent effort therefore was to check and balance information acquired through official channels by information acquired through a myriad of private, informal, and unorthodox channels and espionage networks. At times, he seemed almost to put his personal sources against his public sources. From the viewpoint of subordinates, this method was distracting when not positively demoralizing. But Roosevelt, with his voracity for facts and for ideas, required this approach to cross-check the official system and keep it alert as well as to assure himself the balanced and various product without which he could not comfortably reach decisions.

The official structure, of course, maintained a steady flow of intelligence. Roosevelt was, for a President, extraordinarily accessible. Almost a hundred persons could get through to him by telephone without stating their business to a secretary; and government officials with anything serious on their minds had little difficulty in getting appointments. In addition, he read an enormous number of official memoranda, State Department cables, and government reports, and always tried to glance at the *Congressional Record*. The flow was overwhelming, and he sought continually to make it manageable. "I learned a trick from Wilson," he remarked to Louis Brownlow. "He once told me: 'If you want your memoranda read, put it on one page.' So I, when I came here, issued a similar decree, if you want to call it that. But even at that I am now forced to handle, so the oldsters around tell me, approximately a hundred times as many papers as any of my predecessors." Certainly his subordinates paid little attention to the one-page rule.

What gave Roosevelt's administrative practice its distinctive quality was his systematic effort to augment the official intelligence.

The clutter of newspapers on his bed each morning marked only the first stage in his battle for supplementary information. In this effort, reading was a useful but auxiliary weapon. Beyond government documents and newspapers, he read little. So far as current magazines were concerned, the President, according to Early, "sketches the field," whatever that meant. As for books, Roosevelt evidently read them only on holiday, and then not too seriously. When Frances Perkins sent him the Brookings study *America's Capacity to Produce*, he replied, "Many thanks. . . . I am taking it on the trip and will guarantee to browse through it but not of necessity to read every word!" On the whole, he preferred to acquire both information and ideas through conversation.

Many visitors, it is true, left Roosevelt with the impression that he had done all the talking. This was markedly less true, in his first term, however, than it would be later. Indeed, Henry Pringle, reporting the Washington view in 1934, wrote, "He is a little too willing to listen." And the complaint against Roosevelt's overtalking meant in some cases only that a visitor had run into a deliberate filibuster (thus William Randolph Hearst's baffled lament after a session with Roosevelt in 1933, "The President didn't give me a chance to make suggestions. He did all the talking"). "Words are a good enough barrage if you know how to use them," Roosevelt told one visitor. Like many talkers, moreover, Roosevelt absorbed attitudes and ideas by a mysterious osmosis on occasions when the visitor complained he hadn't got a word in edgewise.

Conversation gave him an indispensable means both of feeling out opinion and of clarifying his own ideas. He talked to everybody and about everything. His habits of conversation out of channels were sometimes disconcerting. He had little hesitation, if he heard of a bright man somewhere down the line in a department, about summoning him to the White House. Ickes complained bitterly in his diary about "what he does so frequently, namely, calling in members of my staff for consultation on Department matters, without consulting me or advising with me." And often he bewildered visitors by asking their views on matters outside their jurisdiction. "He had a great habit," said Jesse Jones, "of talking to one caller about the subject matter of his immediately preceding interview." "I would go to see the President about something," wrote James P. Warburg, "and the fellow who was there before me talking about cotton would be told by the President, 'Well, why don't you stay.'

Before we were through the guy who was there talking about cotton was telling him what to do about gold." All this, irritating as it was to tidy minds, enlarged the variety of reactions available to him in areas where no one was infallible and any intelligent person might make a contribution.

Moreover, at this time, at least, conversation around him was unusually free and candid. Always sensitive to public criticism, Roosevelt could take a large measure of private disagreement. Moley describes him as "patient, amenable to advice, moderate and smilingly indifferent to criticism." "In those days," wrote Richberg, "he enjoyed the frankness and lack of deference with which the original 'brain trusters' and I discussed problems." When people disagreed they said so plainly and at length. "I had numerous quarrels with him," wrote Ed Flynn, who once (in 1940) hung up on him in the midst of a phone conversation. "However, as with sincere friends, the quarrels never impaired our friendship."

II

In seeking information, Roosevelt took care not to confuse the capital with the nation. "Pay no attention to what people are saying in Washington," he once told Molly Dewson. "They are the last persons in the country to listen to." He loved going out to the country himself and got infinite stimulus from faces in crowds, from towns quietly glimpsed out of the windows of slow-moving trains, from chance conversations with ordinary people along the way. But polio and the presidency limited his mobility. Instead, he had to urge others to get out of Washington. "Go and see what's happening," he told Tugwell. "See the end product of what we are doing. Talk to people; get the wind in your nose."

His first reliance was on his wife. From the first days after his disability, he trained her to do his looking for him. "That I became, as the years went by, a better and better reporter and a better and better observer," she later wrote, "was largely owing to the fact that Franklin's questions covered such a wide range. I found myself obliged to notice everything." While he sometimes doubted her judgment on policy and especially on timing, he had implicit faith in her observations. He would say at cabinet, "My Missus says that they have typhoid fever in that district," or "My Missus says that people are working for wages way below the minimum set by NRA in the town she visited last week." "It was not unusual," said

Grace Tully, "to hear him predicate an entire line of reasoning upon a statement that 'my Missus told me so and so.'" In addition, he liked detailed reports of the kind Lorena Hickok and Martha Gellhorn rendered on the situation of people on relief. And he listened with interest to any reasonably succinct account of human conditions anywhere.

Another great source of information was the mail. Five to eight thousand letters a day came normally to the White House; in times of anxiety, of course, many more. The mail was regularly analyzed in order to gauge fluctuations in public sentiment. From time to time, the President himself called for a random selection of letters in order to renew his sense of contact with raw opinion. As the White House mail clerk later wrote, "Mr. Roosevelt always showed a keen interest in the mail and kept close watch on its trend."

In all these ways, Roosevelt amassed an astonishing quantity of miscellaneous information and ideas about the government and the country. "No President," wrote Alben Barkley, "has ever surpassed him in personal knowledge of the details of every department"; and he could have added that probably no President surpassed him in specific knowledge of the geography, topography, and people of the nation. Roosevelt took inordinate pride in this mastery of detail and often displayed it at length when those around him wished to get down to business. But, at the same time, the information — and the pride in it — signified the extraordinary receptivity which was one of his primary characteristics.

This receptivity produced the complex of information systems by which he protected himself from White House insulation. It oriented the administrative machinery away from routine and toward innovation. It made possible the intellectual excitement of the New Deal; it helped provoke a tempest of competing ideas within government because everyone felt that ideas stood and fell at the White House on their merit, not on whether they arrived through the proper channels. Good ideas might pop up from anywhere. "You sometimes find something pretty good in the lunatic fringe," Roosevelt once told his press conference: after all, America today was remade by "a whole lot of things which in my boyhood were considered lunatic fringe." Anyone with new theories had a sense that they were worth developing because, if good, they would find their way to the center. Sometimes this caused problems: Roosevelt was occasionally sold on harebrained ideas which more orderly procedures would have screened out and which taxed responsible officials before he could be unsold. But, on balance, benefits far outweighed disadvantages. H. G. Wells, who saw in Roosevelt's union of openness of mind and resolution of will the realization of his old dream of the Open Conspiracy, wrote with admiration in 1934, "He is, as it were, a ganglion for reception, expression, transmission, combination and realization, which I take it, is exactly what a modern government ought to be."

III

If information was the first responsibility of the executive, the second was decision. American Presidents fall into two types: those who like to make decisions, and those who don't. One type designs an administrative system which brings decisions to him; the other, a system which keeps decisions away from him. The second technique under its more mellifluous designation of "delegation of authority," is regarded with favor in the conventional theory of public administration. Yet, pressed very far, "delegation of authority" obviously strikes at the roots of the presidency. One can delegate routine, but one cannot delegate any part of the serious presidential responsibility. The whole theory of the Constitution makes the chief executive, in the words of Andew Jackson, "accountable at the bar of public opinion for every act of his Administration," and thus presumably accountable in his own conscience for its every large decision.

Roosevelt, in any case, was preeminently of the first type. He evidently felt that both the dignity of his office and the coherence of his administration required that the key decisions be made by him, and not by others before him. He took great pride, for example, in a calculation of Rudolph Forster's that he made at least thirty-five decisions to each one made by Calvin Coolidge. Given this conception of the presidency, he deliberately organized — or disorganized — his system of command to insure that important decisions were passed on to the top. His favorite technique was to keep grants of authority incomplete, jurisdictions uncertain, charters overlapping. The result of this competitive theory of administration was often confusion and exasperation on the operating level; but no other method could so reliably insure that in a large bureaucracy, filled with ambitious men eager for power, the decisions, and the power to make them, would remain with the President. This was in part on

Roosevelt's side an instinct for self-preservation; in part, too, the temperamental expression of a restless, curious, and untidy personality. Coexistence with disorder was almost the pattern of his life. From the day of his marriage, he had lived in a household of unresolved jurisdictions, and it had never occurred to him to try to settle lines finally as between mother and wife. As Assistant Secretary of the Navy, he had indulged happily in the kind of administrative freewheeling which he was not much concerned to penalize in others now. As his doctor once said, Roosevelt "loved to know everything that was going on and delighted to have a finger in every pie."

Once the opportunity for decision came safely into his orbit, the actual process of deciding was involved and inscrutable. As Tugwell once put it, "Franklin allowed no one to discover the governing principle." He evidently felt that clear-cut administrative decisions would work only if they expressed equally clear-cut realities of administrative competence and vigor. If they did not, if the balance of administrative power would not sustain the decision, then decision would only compound confusion and discredit government. And the actualities of administrative power were to be discovered, not by writing — or by reading — executive orders, but by apprehending through intuition a vast constellation of political forces. His complex administrative sensibility, infinitely subtle and sensitive, was forever weighing questions of personal force, of political timing, of congressional concern, of partisan benefit, of public interest. Situations had to be permitted to develop, to crystallize, to clarify; the competing forces had to vindicate themselves in the actual pull and tug of conflict; public opinion had to face the question, consider it, pronounce upon it — only then, at the long, frazzled end, would the President's intuitions consolidate and precipitate a result.

Though he enjoyed giving the impression of snap decisions, Roosevelt actually made few. The more serious complaint against him was his weakness for postponement. This protraction of decision often appeared a technique of evasion. And sometimes it was. But sometimes dilemmas did not seem so urgent from above as they seemed below — a proposition evidently proved when they evaporated after the passage of time. And Roosevelt, in any case, justified, or rationalized, delay in terms of his own sense of timing. He knew from hard experience that a person could not regain health in a day or year; and he had no reason to suppose that a nation would mend any more quickly. "He could watch with enormous patience as a situation developed," wrote his wife, "and would wait for exactly the right moment to act." When people pressed proposals on him, he often answered (as he did to Frank Walker in 1936), "You are absolutely right. . . . It is simply a question of time." The tragedy of the presidency in his view was the impotence of the President. Abraham Lincoln, Roosevelt said, "was a sad man because he couldn't get it all at once. And nobody can." He was responding informally to an important young questioner. "Maybe you would make a much better President than I have. Maybe you will, some day. If you ever sit here, you will learn that you cannot, just by shouting from the housetops, get what you want all the time." . . .

As a President's conquest of the problem of information makes decision possible, so his conquest of the problem of decision leads on to the third responsibility of administration: execution. Success in administration obviously stands or falls on skill in execution. Execution means, above all, the right people — it means having men and women capable of providing the information and carrying out the decision. Nothing is more important for a President than to command the necessary abundance of understanding, loyalty, and ardor on the part of able and imaginative subordinates.

Different Presidents want different things from their subordinates. Some want fidelity, some diligence, some flattery, some no more than the undemanding competence which will take things off their own back. Roosevelt no doubt wanted all of these at various times. What he evidently wanted most was liveliness, vitality, vision. He sought out men who had ideas and drive; and he designed the kind of administrative system which would bring him the men he wanted. Again, as in the case of information, the competitive approach to administration best served his purposes. The men around Roosevelt were not easily contented or contained. They were always fanning out, in ideas and in power. A government well organized in the conventional sense would have given them claustrophobia. The looseness of the New Deal gave them the feeling of scope and outlet which made public service for them tolerable and amusing.

IV

To guarantee the scope, Roosevelt had to revamp the structure of government. By orthodox administrative theory, the antidepression activities should have been brought in under the appropriate old-line departments — Agriculture, Commerce, Labor, the Treasury. But Roosevelt felt that the old departments, even with new chiefs, simply could not generate the energy and daring the crisis required. "We have new and complex problems. We don't really know what they are. Why not establish a new agency to take over the new duty rather than saddle it on an old institution?" Hence the resort from the start to the emergency agency, an essential instrument in the Rooseveltian technique of administrative improvisation. If the obvious channel of action was blocked and it was not worth the political trouble of dynamiting it open, then the emergency agency supplied the means of getting the job done nevertheless. And the new agencies simplified the problem of reversing direction and correcting error. "We have to be prepared to abandon bad practices that grow out of ignorance. It seems to me it is easier to use a new agency which is not a permanent part of the structure of government. If it is not permanent, we don't get bad precedents."

The New Dealers, particularly those of the Brandeis-Frankfurter school, talked a good deal about the importance of a first-class civil service on the British model. Roosevelt accepted this as an aspiration. "Public service," he said proudly in 1934, "offers better rewards in the opportunity for service than ever before in our history." But in practice the professional civil service often seemed an arsenal of obfuscation. It had become, said Tugwell, "a way of choosing and keeping 'the best of the worst,' of making certain that, barring revolution, war or economic disater, the chosen dullards could have a long uneventful, thoroughly secure working life." More than that, the civil service register for upper-grade positions reflected the generally Republican character of the professional and business classes. Mathematics thus indicated that staffing the New Deal through the civil service would fill key positions with anti-New Dealers. In consequence, the new agencies did their best to bypass the civil service. By 1936 the proportion of employees under the "merit system" had materially declined.

The new agencies were plainly indispensable. They tended to have an administrative dash and *élan* which the old departments, sunk in the lethargy of routine, could not match. Yet the theory could be pushed too far. At times Roosevelt acted as if a new agency were almost a new solution. His addiction to new organizations became a kind of nervous tic which disturbed even avid New Dealers.

By 1936 we find Tugwell pleading with him not to set up new organizations. "My experience — and Harry's — is that it takes almost a year to perfect a country-wide administrative organization and that while it is being done there is political turmoil over the jobs, criticisms of procedure from the field, jealousy on the part of old organizations which fancy their prerogatives are threatened and other sources of irritation."

Each new agency had its own distinct mission. But in many cases jurisdictions overlapped each other and even spilled into cabinet departments. This was sloppy and caused much trouble. Yet this very looseness around the joints, this sense of give and possibility which Henry Stimson once called the "inherently disorderly nature" of Roosevelt's administration, made public service attractive to men of a certain boldness and imagination. It also spurred them on to better achievement. Roosevelt liked the competitive approach to administration, not just because it reserved the big decisions for the President, but perhaps even more because it enabled him to test and develop the abilities of his subordinates. How to tell which man, which approach was better? One answer was to let them fight it out. This solution might cause waste but would guarantee against stagnation. "There is something to be said," Roosevelt once observed ". . . for having a little conflict between agencies. A little rivalry is stimulating, you know. It keeps everybody going to prove that he is a better fellow than the next man. It keeps them honest too. An awful lot of money is being handled. The fact that there is somebody else in the field who knows what you are doing is a strong incentive to strict honesty." One can see, for example, in the diaries of Harold Ickes how the overhanging presence of Hopkins and Morgenthau caused Ickes to spend hours and days in intrigue and invective. One can also see how the feuding stimulated him and them to more effective accomplishment and kept every part of the relief and public works effort forever on its toes.

Sometimes the competitive theory could meet political needs too. Roosevelt, as the leader of a coalition, had to keep a variety of interests satisfied, or at least hopeful. What better way than to give each representation where decisions were made? Some agencies seemed to be staffed on the ancient Persian theory of placing men who did not trust each other side by side, their swords on the table. Everywhere there was the need to balance the right and the left — let Cohen and Corcoran write the act establishing the Securities and Exchange Commission, but let Joe Kennedy administer it, but flank him with Jim Landis and Ferdinand Pecora. Rather than sitting on creative vitality anywhere, give each faction something of a head and try to cope with the results. "He had an instinct," wrote Frances Perkins with insight, "for loose, self-directed activity on the part of many groups."

Competition in government, inadequately controlled, would mean anarchy. Adequately controlled, it could mean exceptional creativity. One consequence under the New Deal was a darkling plain of administrative confusion, where bureaucrats clashed by night. Another was a constant infusion of vitality and ideas. In a quieter time, when problems were routine, there would have been every reason to demand tight and tidy administration. But a time of crisis placed a premium on initiative and innovation — and on an organization of government which gave these qualities leeway and reward.

V

Getting bold and imaginative subordinates, however, by itself hardly solves the problem of execution. The worst error a President can make is to assume the automatic implementation of his own decisions. In certain respects, having able subordinates aggravates that problem, since strong personalities tend to have strong ideas of their own. Civil government operates by consent, not by command; the President's task, even within his own branch of government, is not to order but to lead. Students of public administration have never taken sufficient account of the capacity of lower levels of government to sabotage or defy even a masterful President. Somehow, through charm, cajolery, and the communication of ideals, as well as through pressure, discipline, and coercion, the President must make the executive branch *want* to carry out his policies.

The competitive approach to administration gave Roosevelt great advantages. It brought him an effective flow of information; it kept the reins of decision in his own hands; it made for administrative flexibility and stimulated subordinates to effective performance.

At the same time it exacted a price in morale. It placed those close to him under incessant strain. Even for men who could have operated in no other way, it was at best nerve-wracking and often positively demoralizing. Yet this too Roosevelt turned to his own purposes of control. Their insecurity gave him new opportunities for manipulation, which he exploited with cruel skill, while looking blandly in the opposite direction. He pretended not to know what was going on around him; but, said Tugwell, "those who knew his weakness for not grasping really nasty nettles knew from small signs that he was peeking through his fingers." In a way he liked the agony below: "he gave" said Cordell Hull a bit dolefully, "the impression almost of being a spectator looking on and enjoying the drama." "If he seemed to ignore the heaving bosoms presented to him," said Tugwell, "it did not mean that he did not know all about the agitation, or . . . did not enjoy it."

"You know," Harry Hopkins once said, "he is a little puckish." Puckish at times must have seemed an inadequate description. What Roosevelt could regard with equanimity from his place at the summit was often unbearable for those beneath. And it was not just that he seemed oblivious or entertained; at times he appeared to take a light and capricious pleasure in intensifying anxieties. His sometimes unfeeling ribbing of his associates expressed a thin streak of sadism of which he was intermittently aware and for which he was intermittently remorseful. "However genial his teasing," said Francis Biddle, "it was often . . . pointed with a prick of cruelty, because it went to the essence of a man, hit him between the ribs into the heart of his weakness, which might often be his unreasonable affection for his chief." Others shared Biddle's apprehension "that if we came too close I might suffer from his capacity to wound those who loved him." . . .

10   Congress and Water Resources

ARTHUR A. MAASS

Should Twitch Cove, Maryland, be improved at Federal expense for the protection of the few crabbers who live near this Eastern Shore community? This past May, Congress decided yes; they confirmed a recommendation of the Chief of Engineers, United States Army. The United States Engineer Department, as the Corps of Engineers is called in the exercise of civil functions, recommended in favor of Twitch Cove after evaluating alternative plans of improvement and selecting that one which appeared to balance best the factors of "economic feasibility" — i.e., the ratio of benefits to costs, "engineering feasibility," and the "desires of local interests."

This last item is of interest for the moment. For any major improvement, even for Twitch Cove, there will be many groups of "local interests," and their "desires" will differ, may even conflict. Thus, the Engineers seek to adjust these interests and to come up with a recommendation that will maximize the total desires of the community.

Congress for a great number of years has followed a procedure of legislative self-restraint with respect to water resources developments. It will not authorize any improvement which has not received a favorable report from the Chief of Engineers. And since the Engineers attempt to maximize local desires, it may be said that Congress has transferred important responsibility for the adjustment of group interests from its own body to the United States Engineer Department, an executive agency.

The Engineers have recognized the nature of the responsibility which Congress has delegated to them. They have conducted their organization and operations in a manner designed to allow a rather full articulation of local group interests. The project-planning procedure, from the time Congress authorizes the Corps to undertake

From Arthur A. Maass, "Congress and Water Resources," reprinted by permission of the author and The American Political Science Association from *The American Political Science Review* 44 (September 1950):576–593.

an examination of a given area, involves twenty distinct stages at which group interests are able to present their views to the Corps. At three of these twenty, public hearings are regularly provided for; at two additional stages, Engineer Department instructions require consultation with local interests; and at the remaining fifteen, the extent of consultation varies with particular circumstances, but the necessity of a constant awareness of the current attitudes of local interests is emphasized in all Engineer Department publications.

Recently, the Chief of Engineers said:

> The authorization of a river and harbor or flood control project follows a definitely prescribed, democratic course of action. It is based upon the activation of the desires of local interests, who are most vitally interested. Local interests, as individuals or groups through the actions of their representatives in Congress, make request for an item to be included in a rivers and harbors or flood control bill (i.e., authorization to conduct an examination). . . . The District Engineer, mindful of the need for developing all public opinion, holds an open public hearing at which not only those interests that are active in obtaining authorization of the proposed work but also all other views are obtained and encouraged. Having thus developed the desires of the local citizens, the District Engineer makes a study. . . .

PRESENT ARRANGEMENTS AND THE LEGISLATIVE PROCESS [1]

Several important consequences for the legislative process flow from this project planning procedure. These include the participation by members of Congress in the "executive" planning process; legislation by committee resolution; service by the Corps of Engi-

---

[1] Arrangements relating to Congress, the Corps of Engineers, and the President are discussed. No effort is made to deal in any detail with the relations of Congress and the Bureau of Reclamation because of space limitations and the fact that Corps arrangements constitute the more controlling factors in legislation for water resources. This has become more the case in the last few years. Where the Bureau and the Corps have been in competition since 1936, the Secretary of Interior has sought support of the President's office to offset support which the Corps has gotten from Congress. But even with the President's support, the Secretary has not had great success in getting his programs adopted. As a result, the Bureau of Reclamation and its supporters in Congress, the Western irrigation bloc, have begun to use the same legislative techniques which have meant such "success" for the Engineers. Adoption of these techniques has been limited, however, by the fact that support of the reclamation program of the Bureau is restricted in Congress to the Western bloc; whereas support of the navigation and flood control programs of the Corps is found in representatives from all areas.

neers as consultants to, and contractors for, the Congress, certain congressional committees, and individual members of Congress; by-passing of the President and friction among executive agencies; and the interlocking of pressure groups, the Corps, and members of Congress.

Though Congress as a group has largely disassociated itself from the process of project planning by transferring responsibility for adjustment of group interests to the Engineer Department, individual members of Congress have not been so abstentious. Representatives and Senators, knowing they cannot obtain congressional authorization for projects they are sponsoring without a favorable report from the Engineers, have attempted to pressure them into approving these projects by appealing to District Engineers and to the Board of Engineers for Rivers and Harbors in Washington in public hearings.

The following quotations from members of Congress indicate the importance which the legislators attach to their appearances at Engineer Department hearings:

Rep. Dockweiler (Calif.). I have appeared before the Board of Army Engineers in behalf of a harbor in my district and I made what I thought was a pretty good case for improvement of Santa Monica Harbor. . . . And I think the conclusion of the Board of Army Engineers was that no work should be done there because there was not enough business there. . . .

Of course we must abide by the decision of somebody, and the Army Engineers decided against me in that case.

Rep. Harris (Ark.). Mr. Speaker, the Army Engineers, of the Vicksburg district, who are doing a fine work in that area (*sic*), held a public meeting at Hot Springs, Ark., Friday, December 12, investigating the construction by the Federal Government of Blakely Mountain Dam and Reservoir, on the Ouachita River. I had accepted their invitation to appear before the engineers at that meeting, but, due to the emergency and declaration of war, I did not have the privilege. My remarks, however, were read for me and I insert them here in the *Record*.

Colonel Sturgis and gentlemen, on behalf of the people of the Seventh District of Arkansas, I am glad to appear before you in the interest of the construction of the Blakely Mountain Dam and Reservoir for flood control and power development. Needless to say the greater part of the Ouachita River in Arkansas runs through my district, affecting directly 8 of the 11 counties. . . .

I wish to express my appreciation and the appreciation of the people throughout this whole area for the fine work the Army engineers are doing in the development of these projects for flood control and power facilities as well. The people are intensely interested and not only asking but pleading for this protection and development. . . .

If the Engineers submit an unfavorable or partially favorable report, the proponents of a project seek a reexamination, for the Congress will, as noted, not authorize an improvement without a favorable Corps recommendation. At the same time, the Corps by law may not initiate a survey unless Congress has specifically authorized it, usually in an omnibus rivers and harbors or flood control bill. However, to make it easier for members of Congress to require the Engineers to reexamine unfavorable reports in the hope that "changed conditions" may justify a favorable recommendation, the Congress has devised a truly unique procedure amounting to legislation by committee resolution.

After a report of the Chief of Engineers is one year old, any Representative or Senator may present a resolution to the appropriate congressional committee [2] which, if adopted by the committee, requires the "Board of Engineers for rivers and harbors . . . to review the report with a view to determining whether any modification should be made at this time in the recommendation heretofore made." The committee resolution has the effect of law, and, it should be noted, is not subject to presidential veto.

Review solutions have been quite common. As the Congressmen proposing the reviews enjoy no opposition to their requests in most cases, and as the Engineer Department has not been called upon often to report on the desirability of conducting reviews, the committees have been disposed to grant the requests, on occasion disregarding even the one-year waiting period. It is physically impossible for any one member of a committee to be informed on the history of all navigation and flood control projects. The Representative from Arkansas, for example, in all probability never heard of Mill Creek, Virginia, to say nothing of having any judgment as to whether or not the Engineers should be asked to review the report on this Creek; he will vote, Yes. Of 83 investigations completed by the Corps in fiscal year 1946, 20 were authorized by regular legislation and 63 were reexaminations submitted in response to committee resolutions.

[2] In the House, Committees on Rivers and Harbors or on Flood Control prior to 80th Congress; now Committee on Public Works. In the Senate, Committee on Commerce prior to 80th Congress; now Committee on Public Works.

The new House Committee on Public Works in 1947 resolved to cut down on this indiscriminate use of legislation by committee resolution. It adopted a rule extending the waiting period to three years and requiring the Chief of Engineers to report on the estimated costs of conducting the proposed reviews. The Senate Committee failed to follow suit.

It is difficult to evaluate the review resolution as a technique for pressuring the Corps to give its approval to the projects which the members of Congress desire. Available data, however, are rather impressive in showing the importance of the resolution in getting water projects approved, expanded in scope, or modified in terms of reducing the local contributions required.

The Congress, in its long history of legislating internal improvements, has developed close relations with the Corps. (The Corps was the engineering department of the Government which planned and executed the national internal improvement programs of the 1820s.) Congress considers the Corps to be *directly* responsible to it. By resolution Congress directs the Board of Engineers for Rivers and Harbors, an advisory board to the Chief of Engineers, to conduct reviews of surveys. It does not direct the chief executive officer, the President; nor does it even provide the President with an opportunity for veto.

The Corps concurs heartily in this relationship. The Engineers call themselves "the engineer consultants to, and contractors for, the Congress of the United States." The theoretical consequences of such a direct legislative-agency relationship are familiar to students of government and administration; they need not be repeated here.[3]

As might be expected, Congress as a whole is not equipped to exercise direct responsibility over the conduct of Engineer Corps civil functions. It is rather certain congressional committees — those with competence over navigation and flood control matters — that attempt to hold the Corps accountable. It is to them that the Engineers are directly responsible. Witness the review resolution procedure in which Congress in effect allows a committee to legislate for it.

Traditionally members of Congress from the Mississippi delta

[3] A recent restatement of the major issues by Laurence I. Radway and this author can be found in "Gauging Administrative Responsibility," *Public Administration Review* 9 (1949):182–193.

area, where flood protection, drainage, and river navigation problems assume great importance, seek positions on the committees which handle Corps legislation. Through regular reelection they attain positions of seniority. Will M. Whittington of Mississippi, Chairman of the House Committee on Public Works, was for years prior to the establishment of this committee Chairman of the Committee on Flood Control. Judge Whittington, a hard-hitting committee chairman, has always had Corps legislation closely under his control. More than anyone in the executive or legislative establishments, he is in close contact with, and almost in a position of supervision over, the Chief of Engineers and the USED. Until his recent death, John Overton of Louisiana was number one man in the Senate on navigation and flood control legislation.

Direct relations between these committees of Congress and the Corps have developed into a close identity of interests between the two. The Committees on Public Works feel a proprietary interest in the Corps of Engineers and in the direct relations which prevail. In terms of policies for the development of resources, the important consequences of this will be stated later.

In some respects the Engineer Department is more nearly responsible to individual members of Congress directly than to Congress as a whole or to certain congressional committees. It is the member of Congress who initiates the legislative proposal for survey; he is first contacted by the District Engineer to determine the scope of the desired improvement and interested parties; he is first to be informed of any change in the status of the investigation. The nature of the authorization process — the enactment of omnibus rivers and harbors and flood control bills — is such as further to encourage direct responsibility to individual Congressmen. When hearings are held by congressional committees on favorably reported projects to be included in omnibus bills, the testimony of the member of Congress from the district in which the project is located is usually corroborated and supplemented by the army engineer present at the hearing. All of these techniques have led to a sense of direct responsibility on the part of the Engineer Department to the individual member of Congress.

Direct relations between Congress and the Corps mean, of course, that the Engineers bypass the President. This is obviously bad, for the only place where related executive functions can be coordinated effectively is in the President's office. Prior to the 1930s there was no major problem as most river improvements were for single purposes and did not impinge directly on the activities of other agencies. In the early thirties, however, the Corps began planning multiple-purpose projects throughout the country involving flood control, power, irrigation, drainage, and other uses, and coordination in order to produce the best multiple purpose plan for the development of major drainage basins seemed essential. The history of resources legislation and of the development of planning procedures between 1934 and this date constitutes very largely the history of efforts by Presidents Roosevelt and Truman to break down direct agency responsibility to the Congress and to substitute for it a pattern of responsibility to the chief executive. Only in these terms can recent developments in the resources field be interpreted.

The agency with which the Corps has had greatest friction due to lack of coordination is the Bureau of Reclamation in the Department of the Interior. In this inter-agency feud, which has been really intense since 1939, the Corps, for reasons already indicated, has enjoyed the strong support of the Congress. The Secretary of the Interior and the Bureau of Reclamation, on the other hand, have received less consistent congressional support and have sought to balance the advantage of the Corps of Engineers in this respect by obtaining the support of the President and his executive office. The general pattern may be expressed as follows: Corps of Engineers + Congress v. Secretary of the Interior + Executive Office of the President.

The fact that Congress as a body has transferred to the Engineers responsibility for adjusting group interests in proposing water developments, but that individual members of Congress continue to take an active part in the planning and adjusting process is revealed in an interesting manner by the national water pressure groups — particularly the National Rivers and Harbors Congress. This comprehensive lobby counts in its membership the "local interests" (state and local officials, local industrial and trade organizations, contractors), the United States Congress (Representatives and Senators are honorary members), and the Corps of Engineers (officers of the Corps engaged in rivers and harbors work are all ex-officio members). The members of Congress, though they are in a real sense the lobbied, take a very active part in the Rivers Congress. Today, for example, the President is Senator John McClellan of Arkansas, a member of the Public Works Committee and of the subcommittee of the Committee on Appropriations which handles Engineer Corps funds, and Chairman of the Committee on Expenditures in the Executive Departments — to which the Hoover Commission recommendations proposing reorganization of the Corps of Engineers have been referred. McClellan, as a member of the Hoover Commission, dissented from those recommendations which would divest the army of rivers and harbors functions. The national vice presidents of the pressure group are Senator Wherry of Nebraska, Republican floor leader and a member of the Appropiations sub-committee on Engineer Corps funds; Representative Whittington of Mississippi, identified earlier; and Representative Case of South Dakota, a member of the Committee on Appropriations and, at the time of his selection as vice-president, of the subcommittee which considered appropriations for the Corps.

In the past the ex-officio members, officers of the Corps, also have taken part in the proceedings of the lobby, though today they are somewhat more circumspect. The Rivers Congress remains, however, the most active pressure group in support of the USED.

Perhaps the most interesting and important aspect of the Rivers and Harbors Congress is the work of the Projects Committee. When the National Congress was formed in 1901, its slogan was "a policy, not a project." The purpose was not to urge any specific waterway improvements but to interest the public and the federal Congress in the development of waterways in general. In 1935, however, the Rivers and Harbors Congress reversed its policy, agreed to promote certain waterway improvements actively, and for that purpose organized a Projects Committee. The Committee meets once a year for several days preceding the annual convention to act upon all applications for endorsement. It holds hearings on each project, classifies it in one of several orders of priority, and presents its recommendations to the full Rivers and Harbors Congress for adoption.

Senators and Congressmen who are sponsoring waterway improvements in their districts appear before the Committee in order to obtain from that organization of which they are honorary members favorable recommendations for their projects. The following excerpts, in the April, 1940, issue of the *National Rivers and Har-*

bors News, are from a report of the annual meeting of the Projects Committee:

Congressman Joe Hendricks of Florida presented testimony on the Cape Canaveral Harbor, which he stated will serve the $5,000,000 citrus fruit belt, which is now without proper harbor facilities.

Congressman John Jennings, Jr. of Tennessee, urged approval of the project for the construction of dams in the vicinity of Oakdale and Harriman, Tennessee.

Representative Edith Nourse Rogers, of Massachusetts, asked approval of the Merrimac River project. The project will help protect the city of Lowell, Massachusetts, from disastrous floods, as well as the rest of that area, she said.

It is difficult to place a value on the general effectiveness of the Rivers and Harbors Congress because of the fact that it serves as a clearinghouse for uniting and coordinating the activities of local and sectional interests. The Congress itself puts forth bold claims as to its influence:

The influence of the National Rivers and Harbors Congress has been perhaps a more controlling force on legislation approved than that of any other organization. . . . Thus far there has been no adverse criticism of any of the recommendations made by the Congress in its resolutions and reports, and virtually every bill passed by the federal Congress for the improvement of harbors and waterways has been composed almost in toto of projects previously investigated and recommended by the National Rivers and Harbors Congress.

The [Rivers and Harbors] Congress is the country's oldest and largest water organization and occupies *semi-official status* by reason of its close liaison with the governmental agencies, legislative and executive, responsible for public works. . . .

Though the group may be correct in making these claims, we shall be content to accredit it with being certainly one of the most effective lobbies in Washington today. . . .

CONGRESS AND EXECUTIVE BRANCH ORGANIZATION

The fact that organization for water resources development is so inadequate today is in large part a result of the congressional attitudes we have outlined.

Theodore Roosevelt, Herbert Hoover, Franklin Roosevelt — all have tried to bring rationale into administration of water functions. And all have failed, failed because Congress will brook no interference whatsoever in its direct relations with the Corps. As one writer has said, "The civil functions of the Army Corps of Engineers constitute a veritable Rock of Gibraltar against all executive attempts to introduce any organizational integration of flood control and river development with the land use, irrigation, and electric-power activities of other federal agencies."

In recent years the Bureau of the Budget, as a coordinating agency for the President, has tried to break into the direct channel between the Corps and Congress. It has required that survey reports (in the same manner as proposed legislation) be submitted to the executive office of the President, prior to submission to Congress, so that the Corps can be informed of the relationship of the reports to the program of the President. But when the executive office informs the Corps that a project does not conform with the President's program, the Engineers pay no heed. They recommend to Congress, nonetheless, that the project be adopted.

The Budget Bureau is the source of statistics to back up this conclusion.[4] Between January, 1941, and September, 1948, the Corps of Engineers submitted to the Budget Bureau 436 reports favorable to construction of federal improvements. Three hundred and sixty were cleared with no objections to the authorization of the projects, and 76 were (a) held by the Bureau to be wholly or partially not in accord with the President's program (44 reports) or (b) were the subject of specific reservations stated in special comments by the Bureau (32 reports).

With regard to the 44 reports held not in accord with the President's program, the Corps of Engineers transmitted reports on all of these projects to Congress with favorable recommendations. Congress authorized 38. Of the total of 76 projects on which the Bureau made some reservations and comments, Congress authorized 62; seven were either abandoned, or considered by Congress and rejected, while seven projects had not yet been formally considered by Congress. The projects authorized by Congress upon which the Bureau had expressed reservations or full opposition had a total estimated cost in 1947 of $2 billion; those not authorized by Congress, a cost of about $500 million.

Senator Douglas's recent publicized effort to reduce by $840 mil-

---

[4] Commission on Organization of the Executive Branch of the Government, *Task Force Report on Natural Resources* (Washington, D.C., 1949), Appendix 5.

lion the authorizations contained in the 1950 rivers and harbors and flood control bill provides another illustration. Most all of the projects which Douglas attacked had been given low priority or held not in accord by the Bureau of the Budget. Yet the Senate, like the Senate and House Committees on Public Works and the House of Representatives before it, adopted the recommendations of the Chief of Engineers and disregarded those of the President.

Under the present planning pattern, the water experts of all agencies of the Federal government do not cooperate to prepare reports on the best uses of water in any drainage basin. Rather the Corps of Engineers (or the Bureau of Reclamation, as the case may be) undertakes a survey for which it assumes sole responsibility. It may or may not call in experts of other agencies during the conduct of the survey. When the report has been completed and tentative recommendations announced to the local interests, then the report is referred to other agencies for comment; but experience has proved that clearance occurs too late in the planning process for effective coordination.

This pattern of uncoordinated planning was set by Congress in enacting the first two national flood-control bills in 1936 and 1938. Although it was known, certainly by 1938, that the President, the National Resources Planning Board, the Budget Bureau, and the Agriculture and Interior Departments all preferred provisions for genuinely cooperative planning, Congress preferred to assign the planning responsibility directly to the Corps, not to the executive branch as a whole through the person of the President.

The NRPB recommended that the President veto each of these bills for this failure, among other reasons. The President approved them, but in each instance stated his opposition to the uncoordinated planning provided and his determination to alter this within the executive branch. He said in 1938:

> I have approved this bill with some reluctance. . . .
> It is not a step in the right direction in the setup provided for general government planning.
> I am in doubt as to the value of some of the projects provided for and it is unwise to place recommendations to the Congress solely in the hands of the Engineer Corps of the Army in some cases and of the Department of Agriculture in other cases.
> Coordination of all such public works involves a wider survey and the examination of more national problems than any one bureau or department is qualified for.

In these respects future legislation will be vitally important, in order to give to the Congress and to the country a complete picture which takes all factors into consideration.

For the coming year, however, I shall try to obtain this coordination by asking for complete consultation between all groups and government agencies affected. In this way the whole of the problem can be made more clear. I have, however, approved the bill because it accomplishes a number of good things, with, however, the reservation that its deficiencies should be corrected as early as possible.

The President was unsuccessful in this resolve, due largely to those congressional-Corps relations we have been discussing. The same obstacle prevents the President from consolidating important resources functions. Theodore Roosevelt recommended to Congress in 1908 that responsibility for water development be centralized. Congress, expressing full confidence in the Corps of Engineers, failed to implement his recommendation. Herbert Hoover proposed to Congress in 1932 that the civil functions of the Corps of Engineers be transferred to the Department of Interior. His reorganization plan, submitted under the Economy Act of 1932, was roundly defeated in the House. The members of the House Committees on Flood Control and on Rivers and Harbors, Democrats and Republicans alike, opposed the reorganization. Franklin Roosevelt in 1937 proposed that Congress enact legislation permitting him to effect reorganizations within the executive branch. No agencies of government were to be excluded. When in 1939 Congress finally passed the Reorganization Bill authorizing the President to submit plans to Congress which would become law unless vetoed by both Houses of Congress within 60 days, the Corps of Engineers was one of a very few purely executive agencies placed beyond application of the legislation. Harry Truman in 1945 asked that Congress reenact reorganization legislation (it had lapsed some years previously) and that no agencies be exempted from its provisions. Congress did exempt some eight agencies, seven of them independent commissions or boards, and the eighth, the Corps of Engineers.

The Hoover Commission in 1949 proposed that the water resources functions of the Corps of Engineers and the Bureau of Reclamation be consolidated in a Water Development and Use Service and that this Service be organized within the Department of Interior or, as three commissioners urged, within a new Department of Natural Resources. In proposing this consolidation, the Commission's task force on Natural Resources said:

Perhaps the most imposing argument against transferring the civil functions of the Corps of Engineers to another agency is found in the intense
opposition with which any such proposal is likely to be met. There is no
need to emphasize the powerful local and congressional support of the
Corps. . . . The history of past reorganization efforts reveals the difficulties encountered when measures have been proposed involving any
change whatsoever in the civil functions of the Army Engineers.

To implement this proposal and many others, President Harry
Truman and former President Herbert Hoover urged Congress in
1949 to enact a general reorganization bill. The legislation was to
be similar to earlier reorganization bills in that plans submitted by
the President would become law unless vetoed by both Houses of
Congress within 60 days. It was to differ from earlier legislation in
that both Truman and Hoover insisted on a "clean bill," one con-
taining no exemptions, and on a permanent bill, not one that ex-
pired within a few years.

The supporters of the Corps of Engineers, both in and out of
Congress objected strenuously to the proposed legislation. Herbert
Hoover lashed out at these supporters and their demand for exemption for the Corps. Despite considerable opposition, the House
passed the bill with no outright exemptions. The Senate, too, passed
a "clean bill," no exemptions. But the Senate bill has a joker, one to
which the House had to agree to get any bill at all. This joker provides that any reorganization plan submitted by the President shall
become law unless vetoed by a constitutional majority of *one* House.
This constitutes a major reverse for administrative reorganization;
the bills of 1939 and 1945 had required veto by both Houses.

Why did the Senate insist on this change? Because the congressional supporters of the Corps of Engineers announced that they
would forego outright exemption for the Corps *only if* Congress
would agree to a one-House veto.[5] They were sure that any proposed

[5] The report of the Senate Committee on Expenditures contained the following:

"By far the largest number of witnesses appeared in behalf of the exemption
of the civil functions of the Corps of Engineers, including representatives of
valley improvement, flood control and development associations, chambers of
commerce, and other State and civic organizations: 17 of the 25 witnesses
appearing at the hearings, and 14 of the 23 resolutions and communications
submitted for the record, were in support of such exemption. In addition,
hundreds of telegrams and letters from 44 States and the District of Columbia
were received by the committee, expressing opposition to granting any reorganization authority to the President which would permit the transfer of the
civil functions of the Corps of Engineers to any other department or agency. . . .

transfer of the Corps could not get through Congress under these conditions. And to make sure that future changes in the complexion of Congress might not alter this situation, they provided that the bill expire at the end of Truman's present term of office. The ease with which Congress, under this scheme, can defeat reorganization plans of the President has been demonstrated recently with grim reality. . . .

11   *The Role of the Cabinet*

RICHARD F. FENNO, JR.

    The executive and legislative branches of the government interact within a constitutional framework, which provides for independent bases of power but a sharing of decision-making authority. The President is given the constitutional authority to send messages to Congress, to "recommend to their consideration such measures as he shall judge necessary and expedient," to call special sessions, to exercise a veto power over legislation, and to control certain aspects of our foreign relations. The Congress, on the other hand, has the legal authority to set up executive departments and agencies, to appropriate money for the executive branch, to confirm presidential appointments, to conduct investigations in the execu-

---

    "An amendment to exempt the civil functions of the Corps of Engineers, offered by the chairman [Senator McClellan], was defeated by a vote of 5 to 4. Several members of the committee indicated, however, that in voting against this exemption they reserved the right to favor such exemption should the Senate not approve the amendment providing for disapproval of reorganization plans by either the House of Representatives or the Senate." *Senate Report* 232, 81st Congress, 1st Session (April 7, 1949), pp. 12–15, 17.

Reprinted by permission of the author and the publishers from pp. 196–199, 224–234 of Richard F. Fenno, Jr., *The President's Cabinet,* Cambridge, Mass.: Harvard University Press, Copyright, 1959, by the President and Fellows of Harvard College. Footnotes have been omitted.

tive branch, and to share with the President the control and conduct of foreign relations. This is by no means a complete catalogue of the points of formal contact, but it is sufficient to show the basis of the President's role as chief legislator and the basis of congressional control over the executive branch.

Threaded through and around the formal legal structure are a whole set of informal, less visible relationships which help to shape the character of the President's legislative relations. The subtle threat of a veto, a well-timed distribution of patronage, personal confidence or hostility — all these may be decisive in the making of a legislative decision favorable to the chief legislator. Interpersonal contact between the President and legislative leaders or between members of the executive branch and Congressmen may be most effective in winning cooperation. Nor is the continual interplay of the legislature and the executive branch through interest groups recorded in formal documents. The President needs help in both formal and informal legislative activities, and since the cabinet member is constantly involved in both, he has the opportunity to furnish it.

The cabinet member's position in the context of executive-legislative relations is by no means a consistent one. He will find himself playing two roles at once when he faces Congress — he is a presidential advisor, but he is also a department head. In the first role, he is bound tightly by the power-responsibility relationship to the chief executive. According to the hierarchical or vertical conception of authority, he acts as the agent of the President helping him to carry out his ultimate responsibility. But as a department head, the lines of responsibility are not quite so distinct. His department is subject to *both* presidential direction and legislative control — to both vertical and horizontal lines of responsibility. This conception of the cabinet member's activity is not an internally harmonious one, and opportunities to help the President may also be opportunities to harm.

When Attorney General-designate Herbert Brownell was asked by the congressional committee investigating his nomination to discuss the executive-legislative relationships of cabinet members, he answered blithely that "they would be making a tremendous mistake if they didn't work with the head of the executive division of the government, which I propose to do, and they would also be making a great mistake if they didn't work in close cooperation with the legislative branch of the government, which I propose to do."

Brownell's reply, whether born of diplomacy or naiveté, reveals the dilemma, for the cabinet member cannot always cooperate as closely with one as with the other. Where his ultimate responsibility is concerned, he cannot serve two masters. He confronts this dilemma because the separation of powers, as we have seen, contains within it the seeds of executive-legislative antagonism and at the same time prescribes no patent solution for it. The problem is as old as the republic, as the early behavior of Alexander Hamilton will attest. There is "an unresolved difference concerning the presidential versus the congressional theory of responsibility for administrative action." The cabinet member is caught and torn by this conflict. According to the orthodox, vertical conception of presidential responsibility, department heads are subject to the final control of the chief executive. The "congressional theory," however, takes off from the areas of legislative control over the department heads and proclaims his horizontal responsibility to that body.

Consider this statement by Representative Hay with respect to the Secretary of War: "His office is not a constitutional one. He derives no power from the Executive. He is the creature of the Congress of the United States and as such is amenable to it. He has no power which the Congress does not confer." Or consider this one by Senator Thomas Walsh: "I regard the Secretary of the Navy and the Secretary of the Interior . . . as the agents and representatives of the Congress of the United States. They do what we tell them to do." While Congress accepts the cabinet member as a presidential advisor, they do not view him as the President's man in his extra-cabinet relationships. Thus the cabinet member functions in a twilight region of executive-legislative responsibility with all of the dilemmas of role conflict which that produces. When theoretical conflict is translated into the actual day-to-day functioning of the government, writes Herring, "there is a maze of criss-crossing relationships between the President, Congress and the departments."

Theoretical ambiguities become reinforced by ambiguities in the realm of informal power relationships, and the upshot is that the President-cabinet member, power-responsibility relationship will not suffice as an explanation of the extra-cabinet activity of the cabinet member. The legislative branch is found to be competing with the President for control over the department head's activities. The clientele publics from which the cabinet member draws so much of his support may have easy access to the legislature and may work through it to establish a proprietary relationship with the department. The department head, for his part, knows that from the President alone he cannot get all of the power that he needs to operate his department as he wishes. He frequently responds favorably to legislative control in return for the power which he draws from it. It may be of mutual benefit to the cabinet member and "the legislature," i.e., a committee or a Congressman, to develop horizontal relationships. In formally institutionalized ways, in informal contact, or in combinations of both, department head-legislative-interest group relations develop and become counterweights to presidential control.

Depending on the circumstances, the cabinet member will probably have alternatives of action when he confronts Congress. He may play his role as presidential advisor and department head in such a way that they mutually reinforce one another — in which case he may not only help the President but himself as well. Or, at the other extreme, he may be able to divorce one role from the other. If he appears as the President's man, he may aid his superior and may or may not (probably not) improve his own departmental position. If he operates independently of the President, he may aid his own future and may or may not (probably not) help the President. Between these extremes lie the intermediary positions most often taken — positions which accommodate, with shifting emphasis, one role to the other. The context in which this accommodation goes on is filled with sources of difficulty, as well as help, for the chief legislator. . . .

As requisites to successful departmental administration, the two most important personal qualifications would seem to be administrative experience in a political environment and some acquaintance with the substantive policy problems of the department involved. These are the two elements most prominent in the individual application of the cabinet norm. The vagaries of the appointment process are no more a guarantee of both these elements than they are of anything else. Indeed, the indeterminable interaction of the forces discussed earlier frequently results in the selection of an individual without either. "For the Navy Department [writes Mr. Dooley] you want a Southern Congressman from the cotton belt. A man that ever saw salt water outside of a pork barrel would be disqualified for the place. He must live so far from the sea that he don't know a capstan bar from a sheet anchor."

This facetious description is sometimes more closely related to reality than we would like to think. Consider, for instance, pacifist Josephus Daniels, North Carolina newspaper editor and politician and devoted friend of Wilson's, who became Secretary of the Navy without any knowledge whatsoever of its substantive problems. Or, consider Edwin Denby, ex-Congressman from Michigan, who was plucked out of the blue just before inauguration time to be Harding's Secretary of the Navy. His unwitting acquiescence in the transfer of the oil leases out of his department paved the way for the Teapot Dome scandals. Mark Sullivan's comment is typical, that "His record demonstrated him to be ludicrously unfit for his post. The man merited neither tears nor prosecution. He deserved to be laughed out of the Cabinet." Or, consider Denby's successor, Chief Justice of the California Supreme Court, Curtis Wilbur, a man who knew nothing about the navy, whose policy statements were at times radically opposed to those of the President, and under whose administration the navy was allowed to languish in both organization and construction. It is not to cast aspersions on any positive contributions which these men may have made to say that their qualifications, and in some cases their performances, were not well matched with the criteria of administrative experience and substantive knowledge.

A new cabinet secretary who is unacquainted with his department's organization and/or its policy problems is at an immediate disadvantage. "I was [wrote one] like a sea captain who finds himself standing on the deck of a ship that he has never seen before. I did not know the mechanism of my ship; I did not know my officers — even by sight — and I had no acquaintance with the crew." A Secretary of the Interior said that "When I came to Washington, I didn't know we had charge of territories. I didn't know we had charge of anything exterior." Another Secretary acknowledged, "I recognized that it was a hot seat, but actually I had no conception of its difficulties." Cabinet members who find themselves in this situation may not be able to have as much of an impact on their departments as some with prior acquaintance.

Though previous experience within a department may be an optimum recommendation for the cabinet from an administrative angle, it is often not possible to find individuals who are available. When the White House changes party hands, the likelihood of such a person's being appointed declines. And where it is done, as in the recent case of Secretary of State John Foster Dulles, it may still not produce the administrative ideal. The Dulles example illustrates as well as any other the possibility of conflict even within the administrative aspect of the cabinet norm. An expert in terms of substantive knowledge may turn out to be a very poor departmental administrator. Like Secretary Dulles, he may be so preoccupied with what he considers more important things that he is simply not department-oriented. He may live in the realm of his own ideas, "cut off from his own authority, his colleagues, and his duties." If a secretary does not establish internal lines of communication and does not keep his department apprised of overall policy, the morale of the department will be low and it will be difficult to integrate that department's efforts into the larger goals of the President. In view of these many personal variables, there are a large number of possibilities for less than satisfactory departmental administration, and there is room for considerable uncertainty in chief administrator–department head relations.

We must, however, resist the temptation to overpersonalize organizational activity and to exaggerate the influence which an individual secretary can have on his department. The most ambitious and talented department head confronts a formidable complex of situational limitations on his activity. The new appointee finds himself amid a framework of established relationships, of goals already fixed and of forces long since set in motion. He faces an impersonal bureaucratic structure with great resistance to change. Most of his organization is staffed with career personnel, relatively unaffected by changes in high-level policy. Power relationships among constituent elements of the department, or between departmental units and clusters of interest outside the department, tend to be in an equilibrium which reflects an optimum adjustment for all concerned. Their desire to survive may confront the secretary with serious limitations. He has, of course, some formal controls with which to countervail department resistances, but these are frequently minimized by the very forces he is trying to combat.

One control, for instance, which is a prerequisite to successful departmental management is the power of appointment. Yet the secretary frequently operates under considerable restriction — statutory or otherwise. Harold Ickes complained that, "Without the power to appoint subordinates there is no power of control at all. I think this power should lie with the Secretary because, at least in the public mind, he is charged with the responsibility. As it is now, he has the responsibility without any authority, and that makes for bad administration, bad morale, and misunderstanding."

The appointments of the under secretary and assistant secretaries are subject to many nonsecretarial influences. During party turnovers these positions are eminently suited for the payment of political rewards. Both President and Congressmen may press personal favorites upon the department head. In any case, the result may be unfortunate from the standpoint of internal administration, as, for example, Stimson's experience with Under Secretary Castle will attest. Or, interested groups may lay claim to some of these positions. The desire of the AFL and the CIO for one assistant secretaryship of labor apiece is a case in point. With regard to bureau chiefs, the secretary operates under severe statutory handicaps. Inability to remove these officials follows where the power of appointment is lacking.

The department head's formal managerial weapons may be further blunted by organizational inflexibilities. We have already noted the historical evolution of the so-called "holding company" type of department, which includes Interior, Defense, Commerce, and Health, Education and Welfare. Many constituent units of these departments have their own separate statutory bases, thereby helping to establish an authority with nondepartmental roots. Since built-in unity is lacking, it can come to the "holding company" organization only by super-imposition from above, yet it is part of the organizational pattern that such authority is hard to come by. In an "integrated" type of organization the secretary has substantive grants of authority over the constituent units, whereas in the more loosely structured department he has a vaguely defined responsibility to "direct and supervise" them. In practice, however, such a mandate is "an almost meaningless generality."

This limitation is most obvious in terms of authority to reorganize the relationships of the subordinate units. Frequently, he cannot transfer activities from one unit to another, make adjustments in his field organization, or alter the budget so as to make organizational changes possible. Congress may want to exercise minute supervision over all such organizational changes. When Chairman

Carl Vinson of the House Armed Services Committee proposed that the Secretary of Defense should consult his Committee before making any organizational changes, Secretary Louis Johnson exclaimed, "Why, you would become the Secretary of Defense. That completely ties the hands of the Secretary." Said Vinson in reply, "We don't want Congress bypassed."

What appear, from a bird's-eye view, to be limitations on the secretary's managerial discretion appear from another perspective as the phenomenon of "bureau autonomy." Hoover described the Commerce Department as "a congeries of independent bureaus . . . all old establishments created prior to the Department itself. . . . Each was an inbred bureaucracy of its own. There was little department spirit or *esprit de corps*. Some of the bureaus even placed their own names on their letterheads, without mentioning the Department." Franklin Lane described the Interior Department as "a rather disjointed department [in which] the bureaus have stood up as independent entities." The independence of the Army Corps of Engineers is a classic instance of the pattern of relationships which may develop, and it has been admirably related in another place. The important thing to be noted about bureau autonomy, for our purposes, is that its dynamics are by no means explainable in wholly organizational terms. An administrative organization like a bureau does not hang motionless in a political vacuum waiting to be directed according to statute and hierarchy. In order to gain and hold any degree of autonomy, its position must be shored up by sufficient political support. This usually derives from those groups in the political system to whose advantage it is to maintain such autonomy. In addition to bureau personnel, these groups will ordinarily include the clientele for whom the bureau provides services, and members of the legislature who have an interest, corporate or otherwise, in controlling the activities of an administrative agency. The intimate *rapprochement* which the Corps of Engineers have established with local organizations and with influential Congressmen is a key to their continued administrative independence.

Considered in these broad situational terms, the problems raised by bureau autonomy may arise to some degree in every executive department. Even though a departmental executive may possess considerable authority, a bureau will possess its own independent base of support to which it may appeal. In fact, and this is the point, it must do so in order to get the power to operate. Regardless of statutory relationships with Congress (though these help), direct bureau-legislature relationships will be legion, including appropriations, investigations, appointments, etc. Every governmental bureau has one vested interest, one constant preoccupation — survival. And in the interests of survival, it must cultivate sympathetic attitudes and support on the part of those who can do it harm, which most often means the legislature. In the interests of control, the legislative unit whose relations with the agency are most frequent will encourage and attempt to enforce responsibility to it. This mutuality of interests may create a concentration of power which can undermine the authority of the secretary over his department.

Interwoven with the bureau-legislature "subsystem," and operating on both parties to it, are the interested private groups. Regional labor groups interested in employment may work with both bureau admirals and pork-barreling Congressmen to keep the control of naval shipyard and supply contracts out of the hands of an economy-minded Secretary of the Navy. In the process of administration, policy is made by the operating bureaus. Each bureau develops its own clientele — people interested in the policy questions within the bureau's area of discretion. Thus, "a structure of interests friendly or hostile, vague and general, or compact and well defined encloses each significant center of administrative discretion." If the bureau is to survive and develop a program, it must have support from these sources. To the private groups, on the other hand, the bureaus "represent the institutionalized embodiment of policy, an enduring organization actually or potentially capable of mobilizing power behind policy." Here again, mutual dependence dictates a close relationship, one which may not be logically consistent with the policies or desires of the secretary. Little can be known about these informal power clusters by studying the formal intradepartmental hierarchy, yet they may be in direct competition with it. Where this is so, they impair the secretary's ability to manage his department and to provide the President with good administration just as surely as any lack of adequate formal authority.

Time is still another complicating factor for every cabinet official. If he wishes to help the President by rendering him good departmental administration, he must focus his energies downward into the department. But as he provides this kind of negative assistance, he has little time left for positive and constructive assistance. Men of large vision and extra-departmental enthusiasms like Secretary of the Interior Franklin Lane will often leave, like him, a testament of frustration in office: "Ability is not lacking, but it is pressed to the point of paralysis because of an infinitude of detail. . . . Every man is held to details, to the narrower view which comes too often to be the departmental view or some sort of parochial view . . . there was little opportunity to think of anything more than the immediate." William Redfield, the man who received Wilson's letter of praise for efficient departmental administration, admitted that "I looked at my duties too much as a business matter — too little as the creative counsellor." But, he explained in defense, "My nose is kept closely to the grindstone in my own Department." The tendency to become sucked in and submerged by routine or detail or immediacy has been called "the most insidious hazard both to the executive and his organization." He cannot lift up his head often enough to look at things from a government-wide, i.e. presidential, standpoint. If he is to be of help to the President, his time is a precious resource, easily exploited and difficult to conserve.

Department secretaries live in a world which has many extra-presidential dimensions. We have seen the multiplicity of forces within the political system which impinge upon him — forces built into his department by its history, by forces of the appointment process, by forces emanating from Congress, and by forces generated by the publics which the department serves — forces of interest, of authority, and of partisanship. Up to this point in our discussion we have discussed what might be called a series of objective factors which affect departmental administration, with potentialities for lightening or increasing the President's burden. They are objective factors in the sense that the assumption is made that the overriding concern of the secretary is to manage the internal affairs of his department in the interests of the President. The implicit image of the cabinet member thus far has been something akin to that of a person whose administrative life history is one ceaseless struggle to surmount a veritable network of obstacles, personal and situational, in an effort to act as the agent and servant of his superior. Such may, indeed, be the case. The secretary may be exclusively President-oriented, and instances where he fails to help the President may be written off as the result of forces which he cannot bring under control. But it is an equally likely possibility, in view of the department head's problems of success and survival, that he may deliberately assume postures and adopt positions that are department-oriented, and which may not accord with presidential desires.

Secretaries of Agriculture have frequently faced the problem of reconciling the views of the Farm Bureau with their loyalty to the chief executive. Secretary of Labor James Mitchell has lived amid similar cross-pressures from his union constituency and from President Eisenhower on such matters as right-to-work laws and FEPC [Fair Employment Practices Commission] legislation, and he has taken positions on them which the President himself refused to take. There is present, almost always, this dilemma of competing responsibilities, loyalties, and demands, bringing with it the potentiality of conflict. Conflict may, of course, be avoided, but its presence colors the secretary's whole pattern of behavior. Every department head finds himself caught and torn between alternatives of action — President-oriented or department-oriented — in an environment where the rationale, the means, and the incentives for pursuing either are readily available.

His very position as head of one executive establishment among several carries with it certain attitudes and organizational necessities nonpresidential in character. He inherits an immense bureaucratic structure with its own traditions, its own raison d'être, and its own operating methods. None of these depend on him, nor will he be able to alter them very significantly. He cannot help but become a part of this particular organization, supporting its vested interests, concerned for its esprit de corps, and speaking for it in all of its conflicts.

A Secretary of the Interior will predictably contest the location of the Forest Service (now in Agriculture) with the Secretary of Agriculture. He will do it not because it is a personal or partisan matter, but because it is a long-established, organizational tenet within Interior that the Forest Service belongs there. Secretaries may "defend or [be] governed by bureaus they themselves do not control," which in turn may lead them to "take positions hostile to presidential needs and policy."

The department head is not to be viewed as the unwilling captive of his organization or as someone who "fronts" for bureaus against his own subjective inclinations. No admiral of the navy ever defended bureau autonomy more stubbornly, more vigorously, and more willingly than did Secretary of the Navy Josephus Daniels. If a secretary is to accomplish any of his goals, he must cultivate the support of his own organization. He cannot, as the Hoover Commission seems to think, trade exclusively on the influence of the President in his operations. Beyond his own organization, he must locate his support within the legislature and with interested private groups. Without nonpresidential support of this kind, his department may be decimated — as the Secretary of Labor lost some of his bureaus by congressional action in a period when these units and the department in general had insufficient support from organized labor.

Harold Ickes's attempt to change the name of his Department from "Interior" to "Conservation and Public Works" illustrates how impotent a cabinet official can be when he operates on the assumption that presidential support is all that he needs to run his department. Relying on Roosevelt's assurances that he was interested, that he would request other executive departments (Agriculture, War, and Navy) not to oppose it, and that he would urge congressional leaders to take favorable action, Ickes introduced his measure. When the bill failed to pass even a congressional subcommittee, Ickes was shocked, and interpreted the result as an act of personal perfidy by the President. What happened, actually, was that other executive departments which felt their interests threatened by the change were able to muster congressional support in the person of the Chairman of the subcommittee, and external support from the farm organizations. The President could not have made the difference in any event. More than this, it is not realistic to expect the President to give strong support to those pet projects of a cabinet member which affect so many of his fellows. The cabinet member is left on his own most of the time simply because the President, for most of his time, must remain relatively detached as between competing departments. And where Congress is concerned, if the President exerts his power too frequently he may, by virtue of a familiar political paradox, lose it.

In the interests of effective departmental administration, most cabinet members will be led at one time or another to exploit the presence of the competing lines of authority, running vertically to the President and horizontally to the Congress. The spectacle of Secretary of War George Dern supporting the Corps of Engineers in their autonomous operations is explainable only by looking behind the vertical, hierarchical rationale. Dern did everything he could to resist integrated planning on water resources because he felt it would dilute the functions of one of his bureaus. He even went so far as to claim that the Corps was "an agency of the legislative branch," thereby protecting his department by renouncing his own control over it! Many secretaries, like him, have nourished the notion of horizontal responsibility in order to preserve their organizations. The point is that conflict between President-oriented actions and department-oriented actions inheres in the American political system. It is as evident in the administrative realm as in the legislative. The cabinet member is subject to strong nonpresidential or extra-presidential influences, creating a gap between fact and theory in the formal power-responsibility relationship. . . .

12   *White House and Whitehall*

RICHARD E. NEUSTADT

Cabinet government, so-called, as practiced currently in the United Kingdom, differs in innumerable ways — some obvious, some subtle — from "presidential government" in the United States. To ask what one can learn about our own system by viewing theirs, may seem farfetched, considering those differences. But actually the question is a good one. For comparison should help us to discriminate between shadow and substance in both regimes. A look down Whitehall's corridors of power might suggest a lot of things worth noticing in Washington.

For a President-watcher . . . it is no easy matter to attempt comparison with the internal life of Whitehall. How is one to get a comparable look? Those who govern Britain mostly keep their secrets to themselves. They rarely have incentive to do otherwise, which is

From Richard E. Neustadt, "White House and Whitehall," *The Public Interest*, No. 2 (Winter 1966), pp. 55–69, by permission of the author and the publisher. Copyright ©, 1966, National Affairs, Inc.

among the differences between us. Least of all are they inclined to satisfy the curiosities of academics. Even we colonials, persistent though we are and mattering as little as we do, find ourselves all too frequently treated like Englishmen and kept at bay by those three magic words: "Official Secrets Act." Why not? Nothing in the British Constitution says that anyone outside of Whitehall needs an inside view. Quite the reverse. If academics know, then journalists might learn, and even the back-benchers might find out. God forbid!

In Britain governing is *meant* to be a mystery. And so it is. Only in the memoirs of participants does one get glimpses, now and then, of operational reality. And even the most "indiscreet" of recent memoirs veil the essence of the modern system: the relations between ministers and civil servants in the making of a government decision. . . .

. . . Let me raise two simple points of difference between their system and ours.

First, we have counterparts for their top civil servants — but not in our own civil service.

Second, we have counterparts for their cabinet ministers — but not exclusively, or even mainly, in our cabinet.

If I state these two correctly, and I think I do, it follows that in our conventional comparisons we all too often have been victims of semantics. Accordingly, in our proposals for reform-by-analogy we all too often have confused function with form. I find no functions in the British system for which ours lacks at least nascent counterparts. But it is rare when institutions with the same names in both systems do the same work for precisely the same purpose. . . .

I

"Why are your officials so passionate?" I once was asked in England by a bright, young Treasury official just back from Washington. I inquired with whom he had been working there. His answer: "Your chaps at the Budget Bureau."

To an American, those "chaps" appear to be among the most *dis*-passionate of Washingtonians. Indeed, the Budget staff traditionally prides itself on being cool, collected, and above the struggle, distant from emotions churning in the breasts of importunate agency officials. Yet to my English friend, "They took themselves so seriously . . . seemed to be crusaders for the policy positions they thought made sense . . . seemed to feel that it was up to them to save the day. . . ." If this is how the Budget Bureau struck him, imagine how he would have felt about some circles in our air force, or the European Bureau of the State Department, or the Office of Economic Opportunity, or the Forest Service for that matter, or the Bureau of Reclamation, or the National Institutes of Health!

His inquiry suggests two further queries. First, out of what frame of reference was he asking? And second, is it sensible of him (and most of us) to talk of our own budgeteers as though they were his counterparts? These questions are pertinent because I think we are very far from candid with ourselves about the way we get *his* work done in *our* system.

This young man was a principal-with-prospects at the Treasury. By definition, then, he was a man of the administrative class, the elite corps of the British civil service. More important, he was also an apprentice-member of the favored few, the elite-of-the-elite, who climb the ladder *in* the Treasury. With skill and luck and approbation from his seniors he might someday rise to be a mandarin. And meanwhile he would probably serve soon as personal assistant to a cabinet minister. In short, he had the frame of reference which befits a man whose career ladder rises up the central pillar of the whole Whitehall establishment toward the heights where dwell the seniors of all seniors, moulders of ministers, heads of the civil service, knights in office, lords thereafter: the Permanent Secretaries of the Cabinet and the Treasury.

English civil servants of this sort, together with their foreign office counterparts, make up the inner core of "officials," civilian career men, whose senior members govern the United Kingdom in collaboration with their ministerial superiors, the front-bench politicians, leaders of the parliamentary party which commands a House majority for the time being. Theirs is an intimate collaboration, grounded in the interests and traditions of both sides. Indeed it binds them into a Society for Mutual Benefit: what they succeed in sharing with each other they need share with almost no one else, and governing in England is a virtual duopoly.

This is the product of a tacit treaty, an implicit bargain, expressed in self-restraints which are observed on either side. The senior civil servants neither stall nor buck decisions of the government, once these have been taken in due form. "Due form" means consultation with these senior civil servants, among other things; but having been

consulted, these officials act without public complaint or private evasion, even though they may have fought what they are doing up to
the last moment of decision. They also try to assure comparable
discipline in lower official ranks, and to squeeze out the juniors
who do not take kindly to it.

The senior politicians, for their part — with rare and transient
exceptions — return this loyalty in full measure. The politicians
rarely meddle with official recruitment or promotion: by and large,
officialdom administers itself. The politicians preserve the anonymity of civil servants both in Parliament and in the press. Officials
never testify on anything except "accounts," (an audit of expenditures) and nobody reveals their roles in shaping public policy.
Ministers take all kudos for themselves — likewise the heat. They
also take upon themselves protection for the status of officialdom in
the society: honors fall like gentle rain at stated intervals. They even
let career civil servants run their private offices, and treat their
personal assistants of the moment (detailed from civil-service ranks)
as confidentially as our department heads treat trusted aides im-
ported from outside. More important, the politicians *lean* on their
officials. They *expect* to be advised. Most important, they very often
follow the advice that they receive.

This is an advantageous bargain for both sides. It relieves the
politicians of a difficult and chancy search for "loyal" advisers and
administrators. These are in place, ready to hand. And it relieves
civil servants of concern for their security in terms both of profession and of person. No wonder our career men appear "passionate"
to one of theirs; theirs have nothing at stake except policy!

So a Treasury-type has everything to gain by a dispassionate
stance, and nothing to lose except arguments. To be sure, since he
feels himself with reason to be one of an elite, ranking intellectually
and morally with the best in Britain, this is no trifling loss. If parliamentary parties were less disciplined than they now are, or if he
had back-benchers who identified with him, he could afford to carry
arguments outside official channels, as his predecessors sometimes
did a century ago — and as *military* officers still do, on occasion. But
party discipline calls forth its counterpart in his own ranks. And
party politicians on back-benches have no natural affinities with
civil servants — quite the contrary. The civil servant really has no
recourse but to lose his arguments with grace and wait in patience
for another day, another set of ministers. After all, he stays, they go.

And while he stays, he shares the fascinating game of power, stretching his own mind and talents in the service of a reasonably grateful country.

The Treasury-type is a disciplined man; but a man fulfilled, not frustrated. His discipline is the price he pays for power. Not every temperament can take it; if he rises in the Treasury, he probably can. But there is more to this than a cold compromise for power's sake. Those who rise and find fulfillment in their work do so in part because they are deliberately exposed at mid-career to the constraints, the miseries, the hazards which afflict the human beings who wield power on the political side. They know the lot of ministers from observation at first hand. Exposure makes for empathy and for perspective. It also makes for comfort with the civil servant's lot. Whitehall's elites gain all three while relatively young. It leaves them a bit weary with the weight of human folly, but it rids them of self-righteousness, the bane of *our* career men — particularly endemic, of course, among budgeteers.

A Treasury-type gains this exposure through that interesting device, the tour of duty in a minister's private office as his personal "dogsbody." The private secretary, so called, serves his master-of-the-moment as a confidential aide, minding his business, doing his chores, sharing his woes, offering a crying towel, bracing him for bad days in the House, briefing him for bad days in the office. Etcetera. Remarkably, by our standards, the civil service has preempted such assignments for its own. (Do not confuse a minister's private secretary with mere *parliamentary* private secretaries who are drawn from the back benches of the House.) Still more remarkably, the politicians feel themselves well served and rarely dream of looking elsewhere for the service. I know an instance where a minister confided in his private secretary a secret he told no one else save the Prime Minister, not even his permanent secretary, the career head-of-department, "lest it embarrass him to know." The permanent secretary was the private secretary's boss; yet the secret was kept as a matter of course. This, I am assured, is not untypical: "ministerial secrets" are all in the day's work for dogsbodies.

Accordingly, the one-time private secretary who has risen in due course to be permanent secretary of a department knows far more of what it feels like to perform as a politician than his opposite number, the department's minister, can ever hope to fathom in reverse.

A William Armstrong, for example, now joint-head of Treasury, whose opposite number is the Chancellor of the Exchequer, spent years as private secretary to a previous Chancellor who was among the ablest men in the cabinets of his time. Draw the contrast with our own career civil servants.

Our budgeteers imagine that they are the nearest thing to Treasury civil servants. For this, no one can blame them. Much of our literature suggests that if they are not quite the same as yet, a little gimmickery could make them so. Many American political scientists have bemused themselves for years with plans to borrow nomenclature and procedures from the British side, on the unstated premise that function follows form. But it does not.

Functionally, our counterparts for British Treasury-types are *non*-career men holding jobs infused with presidential interest or concern. They are "in-and-outers" from the law firms, banking, business, academia, foundations, or occasionally journalism, or the entourages of successful Governors and Senators — along with up-and-outers (sometimes up-and-downers) who relinquish, or at least risk, civil-service status in the process. Here is the elite-of-the-elite, the upper crust of our "administrative class." These are the men who serve alongside our equivalents for ministers, and who share in governing. One finds them in the White House and in the *appointive* jobs across the street at the Executive Office Building. One finds them also on the seventh floor of State, and on the third and fourth floors of the Pentagon; these places among others.

Let me take some names at random to suggest the types. First, the prototype of all: Averill Harriman. Second, a handful of the currently employed: David Bell, William Bundy, Wilbur Cohen, Harry McPherson, Paul Nitze. Third, a few recent "outers" almost certain to be back, somehow, sometime: McGeorge Bundy, Kermit Gordon, Theodore Sorensen. Fourth, a long-time "outer" who is never back but always in: Clark Clifford. Three of these men got their start as government career men, two as academics, two in banking, two in law, and one on Capitol Hill. The numbers are but accidents of random choice; the spread is meaningful.

The jobs done by such men as these have no precise equivalents in England; our machinery is too different. For example, McGeorge Bundy as the President's Assistant for National Security Affairs was something more than Principal Private Secretary to the Prime Minister (reserved for rising Treasury-types), a dogsbody-writ-large, and also something different from the Secretary of the Cabinet (top of the tree for them), a post "tradition" turns into an almost Constitutional position, certainly what we would call an "institutional" one. Yet the men in those positions see a Bundy as their sort of public servant. They are higher on the ladder than my young friend with the question; they do not take budgeteers to be their counterparts; they know a senior civil servant when they see one.

Every detail of our practice is un-English, but the general outline fits. One of our men appears on television; another testifies against a bill; a third and fourth engage in semi-public argument; a fifth man feeds a press campaign to change the President's mind; a sixth disputes a cabinet member's views in open meeting; a seventh overturns an inter-agency agreement. So it goes, to the perpetual surprise (and sometimes envy?) of the disciplined duopolists in Britain. Yet by *our* lights, according to *our* standards, under our conditions, such activities may be as "disciplined" as theirs, and as responsive to political leadership. The ablest of our in-and-outers frequently display equivalent restraint and equal comprehension in the face of the dilemmas which confront our presidential counterparts of their cabinet politicians.

The elite of our officialdom is not careerist men in the British sense (although, of course, our in-and-outers have careers); why should it be? Neither is it the President with his department heads. They, too, are in-and-outers. We forget that the duopoly which governs Britain is composed of *two* career systems, official and political. Most ministers who will take office through the next decade are on the scene and well identified in Westminister. The permanent secretaries who will serve with them are on the Whitehall ladders now; a mere outsider can spot some of them. Contrast our situation — even the directorships of old-line bureaus remain problematical. Who is to succeed J. Edgar Hoover?

We have only two sets of true career men in our system. One consists of Senators and Congressmen in relatively safe seats, waiting their turn for chairmanships. The other consists of military officers and civil employees who are essentially technicians manning every sort of specialty (including "management") in the executive establishment. Between these two we leave a lot of room for in-and-outers. We are fortunate to do so. Nothing else could serve as well to keep the two apart. And *their* duopoly would be productive, not of governance, but of its feudal substitute, piecemeal administration. We can only hope to govern in our system by, and through, the presidency. In-and-outers are a saving grace for Presidents.

II

Since 1959, English commentators frequently have wondered to each other if their government was being "presidentialized." In part, this stemmed from electoral considerations following the "personality contest" between Harold Macmillan and Hugh Gaitskell in that year's general election. In part, too, it stemmed from the impression left by Macmillan's active premiership — reenforced this past year by the sight of still another activist in office, Harold Wilson.

Despite their differences of style, personality, and party, both Macmillan and Wilson patently conceived the Cabinet Room in Downing Street to be the PM's office, not a mere board-room. Both evidently acted on the premise that the PM's personal judgment ought, if possible, to be decisive. Both reached out for the power of personal decision on the issues of the day. Macmillan did so through offstage maneuver, while avowing his fidelity to cabinet consensus. With perhaps a bit more candor, Wilson does the same. Hence discussion about trends toward "presidential" government.

Yet between these two Prime Ministers there was another for a year, Sir Alec Douglas-Home. And by no stretch of the imagination could his conduct in office have been characterized as presidential. On the contrary, by all accounts he was a classic "chairman of the board", who resolutely pushed impending issues *out* of Number 10, for initiative elsewhere, by others. He managed, it is said, to get a lot of gardening done while he resided there. I once asked a close observer what became of the initiatives, the steering, the maneuvering, which Home refused to take upon himself. He replied:

When ministers discovered that he really wouldn't do it, they began to huddle with each other, little groups of major figures. You would get from them enough agreement or accommodation to produce the main lines of a government position, something they could try to steer through cabinet. Or if you didn't get it, there was nothing to be done. That's how it began to work, outside of Number 10, around it.

That is how it would be working now, had there been but a slight shift in the popular vote of 1964.

The British system, then, has *not* been presidentialized, or not at least in operational terms. For, as we learned with Eisenhower, the initiatives a President must take to form "the main lines of a government position" cannot survive outside the White House precincts. Toss them out and either they bounce back or they wither away. A President may delegate to White House aides ("ok, S.A."), or to a Foster Dulles, but only as he demonstrates consistently, day-in-and-out, that they command his ear and hold his confidence. Let him take to his bed behind an oxygen tent and they can only go through motions. Eisenhower's White House was a far cry from 10 Downing Street in the regime of Douglas-Home. That remains the distance Britain's system has to travel toward a presidential status for prime ministers.

But even though the system did not make an activist of Douglas-Home, his predecessor and successor obviously relished the part. The system may not have required them to play it, but they did so, and the system bore the weight of their activity. In externals, Number 10 looks no more like the White House under Wilson than it did a year ago. But, in essense, Wilson comes as close to being "President" as the conventions of *his* system allow. He evidently knows it and likes it. So, I take it, did Macmillan.

How close can such men come? How nearly can they assert "presidential" leadership inside a cabinet system? Without endeavoring to answer in the abstract, let me record some impressions of concrete performances.

First, consider Britain's bid for Common Market membership four years ago, which presaged an enormous (if abortive) shift in public policy, to say nothing of Tory party policy. By all accounts, this "turn to Europe" was Macmillan's own. The timing and the impetus were his, and I am told that his intention was to go wholehog, both economically and politically. As such, this was among the great strategic choices in the peacetime politics of Britain. But it never was a "government decision." For those, by British definition, come in cabinet. Macmillan never put the issue there in candid terms. Instead he tried to sneak past opposition there — and on back-benches and in constituencies — by disguising his strategic choice as a commercial deal. The cabinet dealt with issues of negotiation, *en principe* and later in detail, for making Britain part of Europe's economic union without giving up its Commonwealth connections (or farm subsidies). One minister explained to me:

Timing is everything. First we have to get into the Common Market as a matter of business, good for our economy. Then we can begin to look at the political side. . . . Appetites grow with eating. We couldn't hold the Cabinet, much less our back-benchers, if we put this forward now in broader terms. . . .

Accordingly, the move toward Europe had to be played out in its ostensible terms, as a detailed negotiation of a commercial character. This took two years; and while the tactic served its purpose within Tory ranks, these were the years when France escaped from the Algerian war. By the time negotiations neared their end, Charles de Gaulle was riding high at home. Macmillan tiptoed past his own internal obstacles, but took so long about it that his path was blocked by an external one, the veto of de Gaulle.

Second, take the Nassau Pact of 1962, which calmed the Skybolt crisis between Washington and London even as it gave de Gaulle excuses for that veto. Macmillan was his own negotiator at the Nassau Conference. He decided on the spot to drop his claim for Skybolt missiles and to press the substitution of Polaris weaponry. He wrung what seemed to him an advantageous compromise along those lines from President Kennedy. Then and only then did he "submit" its terms to the full cabinet for decision (by return cable), noting the concurrence of three potent ministers who had accompanied him: the Foreign, Commonwealth, and Defense Secretaries. With the President waiting, the cabinet "decided" (unenthusiastically, by all accounts) to bless this fait accompli. What else was there to do? The answer, nothing — and no doubt Macmillan knew it.

Third, consider how the present Labour government reversed its preelection stand on Nassau's terms. Within six weeks of taking office, Wilson and his colleagues became champions of the Polaris program they had scorned in opposition. Their back-benchers wheeled around behind them almost to a man. It is no secret that the Prime Minister was the source of this reversal, also its tactician. So far as I can find, it was his own choice, his initiative, his management, from first to last. He got it done in quick-time, yet he did it by maneuvering on tiptoe like Macmillan in the case of the Common Market (with just a touch of the shotgun, like Macmillan in the Nassau case). When Wilson let Polaris reach the cabinet for "decision," leading ministers, both "right" and "left," already were committed individually. By that time also, Wilson had pretested back-bench sentiment; he had "prematurely" voiced to an acquiescent House what would become the rationale for cabinet action: keeping on with weapons whose production had already passed a "point of no return."

Superficially, such instances as these seem strikingly unpresidential. In our accustomed vision, Presidents do not tiptoe around their cabinets, they instruct, inform or ignore them. They do not engineer faits accomplis to force decisions from them, for the cabinet does not make decisions; Presidents decide. A Kennedy after Birmingham, a Johnson after Selma, deciding on their civil rights bills, or a Johnson after Pleiku, ordering the bombers north, or Johnson last December, taking off our pressure for the multilateral force, or Kennedy confronting Moscow over Cuba with advisers all around him but decisions in his hands — what contrasts these suggest with the maneuvers of a Wilson or Macmillan!

The contrasts are but heightened by a glance at their work forces: Presidents with twenty-odd high-powered personal assistants, and a thousand civil servants in their executive office — Prime Ministers with but four such assistants in their private office (three of them on detail from departments) and a handful more in cabinet office, which by definition is not "theirs" alone. Differences of work place heighten the effect still more: 10 Downing Street is literally a house, comparing rather poorly with the White House before T. R.'s time. The modern White House is a palace, as Denis Brogan keeps reminding us, a physically-cramped version of the Hofburg, or the Tuileries.

Yet beneath these contrasts, despite them, belying them, Americans are bound to glimpse a long-familiar pattern in the conduct of an activist Prime Minister. It is the pattern of a President maneuvering around or through the power-men in his administration *and* in Congress. Once this is seen, all contrasts become superficial. Underneath our images of Presidents-in-boots, astride decisions, are the half-observed realities of Presidents-in-sneakers, stirrups in hand, trying to induce particular department heads, or Congressmen or Senators, to climb abroad.

Anyone who has an independent power-base is likelier than not to get "ministerial" treatment from a President. Even his own appointees are to be wooed, not spurred, in the degree that they have their own attributes of power: expertise, or prestige, or a statute under foot. As Theodore Sorensen reported while he still was at the White House:

In choosing between conflicting advice, the President is also choosing between conflicting advisers. . . . He will be slow to overrule a cabinet officer whose pride or prestige has been committed, not only to save the officer's personal prestige but to maintain his utility. . . . Whenever any President overrules any Secretary he runs the risk of that Secretary grumbling, privately if not publicly, to the Congress, or to the press (or to his diary), or dragging his feet on implementation, or, at the very worst, resigning with a blast at the President.

But it is men of Congress more than departmental men who regularly get from Pennsylvania Avenue the treatment given cabinet ministers from Downing Street. Power in the Senate is particularly courted. A Lyndon Johnson (when he served there), or a Vandenberg in Truman's time, or [in 1966] an Anderson, a Russell, even a Mansfield — to say nothing of a Dirksen — are accorded many of the same attentions which a Wilson has to offer a George Brown.

The conventions of "bipartisanship" in foreign relations, established under Truman and sustained by Eisenhower, have been extended under Kennedy and Johnson to broad sectors of the home-front, civil rights especially. These never were so much a matter of engaging oppositionists in White House undertakings as of linking to the White House men from either party who had influence to spare. Mutality of deference between Presidents and leaders of congressional opinion, rather than between the formal party leaderships, always has been the essence of "bipartisanship" in practice. And men who really lead opinion on the Hill gain privileged access to executive decisions as their customary share of "mutual deference." "Congress" may not participate in such decisions, but these men often do: witness Dirksen in the framing of our recent Civil Rights Acts, or a spectrum of Senators from Russell to Mansfield in the framing of particular approaches on Viet Nam. Eleven years ago, Eisenhower seems to have kept our armed forces out of Indo-China when a projected intervention at the time of Dien Bien Phu won no support from Senate influentials. Johnson now maneuvers to maintain support from "right" to "left" within their ranks.

If one seeks our counterparts for Wilson or Macmillan as cabinet tacticians, one need look no further than Kennedy or Johnson maneuvering among the influentials both downtown *and* on the Hill (and in state capitals, or among steel companies and trade unions, for that matter). Macmillan's caution on the Common Market will suggest the torturous, slow course of JFK toward fundamental changes in our fiscal policy, which brought him to the point of trying for a tax cut only by the end of his third year. Macmillan's fait accompli on Polaris brings to mind the Southeast Asia Resolution Johnson got from Congress after there had been some shooting in the Tonkin Gulf — and all its predecessors back to 1955, when Eisenhower pioneered this technique for extracting a "blank check." Wilson's quiet, quick arrangement for the Labour party to adopt Polaris has a lot in common with the Johnson coup a year ago on Federal aid to education, where a shift in rationale took all sorts of opponents off the hook.

British government may not be presidential, but our government is more prime-ministerial than we are inclined to think. Unhappily for clarity of thought, we too have something called a cabinet. But that pallid institution is in no sense the equivalent of theirs. Our equivalent is rather an informal, shifting aggregation of key individuals — the influentials at both ends of Pennsylvania Avenue. Some of them may sit in what we call the cabinet as department heads; others sit in back rows there, as senior White House aides; still others have no place there. Collectively these men share no responsibility nor any meeting ground. Individually, however, each is linked to all the others through the person of the President (supported by his telephone). And all to some degree are serviced — also monitored — by one group or another on the White House staff. The former "Bundy Office," or the "Sorensen Shop" which one might best describe now as the Moyers "sphere of influence," together with the staff of legislative liaisoners captained until lately by Lawrence O'Brien — these groups, although not tightly interlocked, provide a common reference point for influentials everywhere: "This is the White House calling. . . ." While we lack an institutionalized cabinet along British lines, we are evolving an equivalent of cabinet office. The O'Brien operation was its newest element, with no precursors worthy of the name in any regime earlier than Eisenhower's. Whether it survives, and how and why, without O'Brien become questions of the day for presidency-watchers.

The functional equivalence between a British cabinet and our set of influentials — whether Secretaries, Senators, White House staffers, Congressmen, or others — is rendered plain by noting that, for most intents and purposes, their cabinet members do the work of our congressional committees, our floor leaderships, and our front-offices downtown, all combined. The combination makes for superficial smoothness; Whitehall seems a quiet place. But once again, appearances deceive. Beneath the surface, this combine called "cabinet" wrestles with divergencies of interest, of perspective, of procedure, of personality, much like those we are used to witnessing above ground in the dealings of our separated institutions. Not only is the hidden struggle reminiscent of our open one, but also the results are often similar: "bold, new ventures" actually undertaken are often few and far between. Whitehall dispenses with the grunts and groans of Washington, but both can labor mightily to bring forth mice.

It is unfashionable just now to speak of "stalemate" or of "deadlock" in our government, although these terms were all the rage two years ago and will be so again, no doubt, whenever Johnson's coattails shrink. But British government is no less prone to deadlock than our own. Indeed I am inclined to think their tendencies in that direction more pronounced than ours. A keen observer of their system, veteran of some seven years at cabinet meetings, put it to me in these terms:

The obverse of our show of monolithic unity behind a government position, when we have one, is slowness, ponderousness, deviousness, in approaching a position, getting it taken, getting a "sense of the meeting." Nothing in our system is harder to do, especially if press leaks are at risk. You Americans don't seem to understand that. . . .

In the Common Market case, to cite but one example, the three months from October to December, 1962, were taken up at Brussels, where negotiations centered, by a virtual filibuster from the British delegation. This drove some of the Europeans wild and had them muttering about "perfidious Albion." But London's delegates were not engaged in tactical maneuvering at Brussels. All they were doing there was to buy time for tactical maneuvering back home, around the cabinet table. The three months were required to induce two senior ministers to swallow agricultural concessions every student of the subject knew their government would have to make. But Britain could not move until those influential "members of the government" had choked them down. The time-lag seemed enormous from the vantage point of Brussels. Significantly, it seemed short indeed to Londoners. By Whitehall standards this was rapid motion.

One of the checks-and-balances in Britain's system lies between the PM and his colleagues as a group. This is the check that operated here. A sensible Prime Minister is scrupulous about the forms of collective action: overreaching risks rejection; a show of arbitrariness risks collegial reaction; if they should band together his associates could pull him down. Accordingly, the man who lives at Number 10 does well to avoid policy departures like the plague, unless, until, and if, he sees a reasonable prospect for obtaining that "sense of the meeting." He is not without resources to induce the prospect, and he is at liberty to ride events which suit his causes. But these things take time — and timing. A power-wise Prime Minister adjusts his pace accordingly. So Macmillan did in 1962.

Ministerial prerogatives are not the only source of stalemate or slow motion in this system. If members of a cabinet were not also heads of great departments, then the leader of their party in the Commons and the country might be less inclined to honor their pretensions in the government. A second, reenforcing check-and-balance of the system lies between him and the senior civil servants. To quote again, from the same source:

> The PM has it easier with ministers than with the civil servants. The ranks of civil servants do not work for *him*. They have to be brought along. They are loyal to a "Government Decision" but that takes the form of action in Cabinet, where the great machines are represented by their ministers.

The civil servants can be his allies, of course, if their perceptions of the public interest square with his; then all he needs to do is to bring ministers along. Something of this sort seems to have been a factor in the Labour government's acceptance of Polaris: Foreign Office and Defense officials urged their masters on: Treasury officials remained neutral. The PM who first manages to tie the civil servants tighter to his office than to their own ministries will presidentialize the British system beyond anything our system knows. But that day is not yet. It may never come.

So a British Premier facing cabinet is in somewhat the position of our President confronting the executive departments and Congress combined. Our man, compared to theirs, is freer to take initiatives and to announce them *in advance* of acquiescence from all sides. With us, indeed, initiatives in public are a step toward obtaining acquiescence, or at least toward wearing down the opposition. It is different in Downing Street. With us, also, the diplomatic and defense spheres yield our man authority for binding judgments on behalf of the whole government. Although he rarely gets unquestioning obedience and often pays a price, his personal choices are authoritative, for he himself is heir to royal prerogatives. In Britain these adhere to cabinet members as a group, not to the Prime Minister alone. True, he can take over diplomacy, as Neville Chamberlain did so disastrously, and others since, or he can even run a war like Winston Churchill. But Chamberlain had to change Foreign Secretaries in the process, and Churchill took precautions, making himself Minister of Defense.

Still, despite all differences, a President, like a Prime Minister, lives daily under the constraint that he must bring along *his* "colleagues" and get action from *their* liege-men at both ends of the Avenue. A sensible Prime Minister is always counting noses in cabinet. A sensible President is always checking off his list of "influentials." The PM is not yet a President. The President, however, is a sort of super-Prime Minister. This is what comes of comparative inquiry.

III

For over half a century, a great number of studious Americans have sought to fasten on our system, frankly imitating Britain, both a senior civil service drawn from career ranks and a Cabinet drawn from Congress. Meanwhile, without paying much attention to such formulations, our governmental practice has been building ad hoc counterparts. I have given two examples and could offer many more, but I hope these suffice to make the point.

The in-and-outers on whom we depend to do at presidential level what the Treasury-types of Whitehall do at Cabinet level deserve much more notice than they have so far received. They are a political phenomenon to study. They also are a political resource to nurture. Their care-and-feeding should concern our schools of public service not less but rather more than that of civil servants who remain in career ranks. . . .

13   *The Presidents' Men*

PATRICK ANDERSON

. . . I asked a man who served prominently on a recent President's White House staff if he would be interested in running for the Senate. His reply was candid:

"I had more power over national affairs in a few years in the White House than I could if I spent the rest of my life in the Senate."

Would he like to return to government in one of the cabinet posts?

"Most of them aren't worth having," he said with a shrug.

These are overstatements — the gentleman quoted wouldn't turn down either a Senate or cabinet seat, I suspect — yet they accurately reflect the tremendous influence over governmental affairs that has gravitated in recent years to the President's personal assistants.

The growth of the White House staff into a powerful instrument of government has been an inevitable result of the great expansion of the presidency itself that began in 1933 with Roosevelt's New Deal. The coming of the Welfare State at home and the Cold War abroad has all but overwhelmed the President with powers and responsibilities unimaginable forty years ago. . . .

Fortunately, the presidency is an office of considerable flexibility. In the strict sense of the words, the President alone has power, and cannot delegate it, and his aides have only influence. But as a practical matter, leading presidential assistants do acquire considerable power, as the word is commonly used, even though they do not have the final accountability for their actions.

Traditionally, the members of the President's cabinet have been the prime recipients of his delegated authority. Recent Presidents, however, have increasingly delegated authority to their most favored White House assistants, until several of those assistants have overshadowed the cabinet executives. Essentially, the reason for this is that, as the federal government has grown, a centrifugal force has been pulling the cabinet officers away from the presidential orbit, making them prisoners of their bureaucracies, giving them priorities and loyalties that may not be identical with the President's.

Cabinet members are still often chosen for political reasons — to repay a campaign debt, to please a religious or ethnic group — and they may or may not be men the President knows, likes, or trusts. It has often followed that Presidents, faced with complex issues on which they must make crucial decisions, have relied more heavily upon the judgment of their hand-picked personal staffs than on their cabinet executives. The clear trend of the past thirty-five years is toward increased use of the staff to oversee the agencies and departments of government. This may not be a healthy trend, but it is an unmistakable one.

As the White House staff has increasingly challenged the influence of the cabinet, it has also challenged the status of another time-honored source of advice for Presidents. These are the venerable figures who might be called Distinguished Outsiders — the Senator or party leader or prominent businessman to whom many Presidents have looked for sage counsel in time of adversity. The best known Distinguished Outsiders of this century have been Colonel E. M. House, who advised Woodrow Wilson, Bernard Baruch, who advised numerous Presidents, and, in recent years, Clark Clifford.

The complex, technical, fast-moving nature of today's government is inevitably reducing the importance of outside advisors. By sheer force of personality, the outsider may impress the President with general strategies, but to have a continuing impact, the adviser needs to be on the scene twelve hours a day, reading the cables, studying intelligence documents, sounding out the bureaucracy, digging deeply into the facts and figures a hard-pressed modern President needs. That is why the influence of outsiders is giving way to that of staff insiders — men like McGeorge Bundy, Bill D. Moyers, Theodore Sorensen, Joseph A. Califano, Jr. — whose value to the President rests less on their mastery of affairs of state than on their mastery of the endless details of state. . . .

A wonderful variety of men has made its way to the White House staff in recent years. There have been men of extraordinary ability, clowns, scoundrels, ruthless sons-of-bitches, men of rare sensitivity, even a hero or two. The one factor almost all of them have shared is uncommon ambition, a thirst for power and glory, even reflected power and glory, and a willingness to sacrifice friends, family, and personal health, often to suffer personal and political humiliation, in order to satisfy their ambitions. Sometimes their ambition is cloaked — the courtly manners of Clark Clifford or the determined modesty of Bill Moyers — in other cases, like those of Tom Corcoran, McGeorge Bundy, or Richard Goodwin, the ambition glistens like a dagger in the moonlight. In either event, the yearning is there, the desire to be near the center of decision, to have, in the current phrase, a piece of the action. . . .

Amazing celebrity now accompanies service in the White House. When Pierre Salinger returned to California in 1964 to seek the Democratic nomination for the United States Senate, a public-opinion poll revaled that 85 percent of the voters could identify him, whereas only 35 percent could identify his opponent, the State Controller, Alan Cranston. Similarly, when a leading pollster in 1966 attached Bill Moyers's name to a poll designed to rate public recognition of United States Senators, only three of the 100 Senators — Fulbright of Arkansas and the two Kennedys — proved to be better known nationally than the young Moyers.

Of course, Salinger and Moyers each served as presidential Press Secretary and were necessarily in the public eye, but other aides such as Sherman Adams, Sorensen, Bundy, and O'Brien have become equally well known as a result of countless newspaper and magazine articles and television appearances.

Essentially, the media's spotlights are focused on the President and necessarily illuminate the people around him. Some aides are singled out because they become exceedingly powerful; others, who have little to say about policy, are publicized because they are colorful or controversial, or simply because they are the President's intimates. The press and the nation realize instinctively that a President reveals himself by the sort of men he picks to be his close associates. A President assembling his staff, like a sultan choosing his harem, can indulge his whim — if we are to understand Lyndon Johnson, for example, we must understand how one man, within a few years' time, could bring into his official family four such diverse figures as Moyers, Valenti, Bobby Baker, and Marvin Watson.

A President's trusted aide can attain power and glory, but the power is precarious and the glory may become tinged with notoriety, for there are many dangers inherent in his position.

The scrutiny of the press will magnify both the aide's virtues and his faults. If he has a knack for putting his foot in his mouth, he can quickly make a fool of himself on a worldwide scale. On the other hand, if his President is a jealous master, praise from the press can be equally harmful to him, as aides to Roosevelt and Johnson discovered.

The aide must be willing to be used as a political lightning rod to draw criticism away from the President, for the President's political opponents, not ready to attack him directly, may find it convenient to blame his alleged misdeeds on his advisers. Over the years, the targets of such attacks have included Roosevelt's Rexford G. Tugwell and Harry Hopkins, Eisenhower's Sherman Adams, Kennedy's Arthur M. Schlesinger, Jr., and Johnson's Bill Moyers and Marvin Watson. For such aides, the pain of suffering in silence is magnified by the fear that the President, to quiet the critics and protect his administration, may make a political sacrifice of the controversial assistant.

The powerful presidential assistant will surely have enemies within the President's cabinet, and he must regard them with extreme care, for whatever the cabinet executive's real status within the administration, he has an official, public status that reinforces his position. The presidential favorite must also live with suspicion and animosity from some congressional leaders; this has been the case at least since just after the 1932 election, when Sam Rayburn pointedly informed Raymond Moley, who was then Roosevelt's closest advisor, "I hope we don't have any ——— Rasputins in this Administration!"

Finally, the aide will almost certainly develop an enemy or two among his fellow staff members — his rivals in the harem — for little has changed since the Earl of Rochester, poet and courtier of the English Renaissance, deplored "the mean policy of Court-Prudence, which makes us lie to one another all day, for fear of being betrayed by each other at night."

Most Presidents deliberately balance liberals against conservatives, intellectuals against nonintellectuals, on their staffs, and the certain result is friction, rivalry, and hostility. This is not done, as some have suggested, out of pure sadism on the President's part, but because a President will regard his staff as an important channel of ideas and information and he will want to ensure himself a clash of ideas.

All these forces play upon the White House favorite — a demanding President, the cabinet, staff rivals, the press, congressional critics, a wife and family he too rarely sees — and the history of the White House is replete with men who, in one way or another, succumbed to the pressures. Indeed, although a President's staff can be a source of comfort and encouragement to him, he may be forgiven if he sometimes regards his assistants as a necessary evil, for the chances are excellent that one or more of them will embarrass him by some improbable indiscretion.

If there are dangers in being a presidential aide, there are also dangers in writing about them. One is that in viewing governmental affairs from the vantage point of the presidential assistant, rather than from the President's, one runs the risk of seeming to let the tail wag the dog. So it should be stressed . . . that the final credit or blame for what happens in the White House is, and must be, the President's. If he approves a policy or delivers a speech that is the work of one of his assistants, he makes it his own. Even if the aide makes some mistake of which the President has no knowledge, the President must be willing to bear the blame, if only because he gave the man too large a mandate or failed to exercise enough control over him.

Yet granting that, for example, Roosevelt must get final credit for his New Deal, or Johnson for his Great Society program, the fact remains that the New Deal would have been different without Tugwell and Corcoran, and the Great Society without Moyers and Califano. To ignore their contributions is to miss part of the story. It is, to be sure, a hard story to get at, for the White House is so constructed that credit flows upward and blame downward. The assistant cannot hope for much recognition, either from contemporary accounts or from history. The President's good works are carved in marble; his aides' are writ on water. Perhaps the most influential, and admirable, of the men discussed . . . [here] was FDR's Harry Hopkins, a hero among heroes during the killing years of the Second World War. Yet his fame was fleeting; many members of my generation, asked to identify Harry Hopkins, would venture a guess that he once played shortstop for the Cardinals.

Today's White House aide generally fares better than Hopkins and his contemporaries. His role has achieved respectability. When he leaves the government, high-paying jobs await him. He may advance from the White House staff to the cabinet, as Lawrence F. O'Brien and Clark Clifford have done, and as McGeorge Bundy, Bill Moyers, Ted Sorensen, and several others might do in the future. Or, he may try to convert the fame and experience he gained in the White House into a political career of his own, as Pierre Salinger and Ken O'Donnell did, and as O'Brien, Moyers, Sorensen, and others may in the future. . . .

. . . Yet to some of the more sensitive White House assistants, the pot of gold that awaits them at the rainbow's end is not an unmixed blessing. The aide may find, as he emerges from the White House, that he is not the same man he was a few years earlier and that, as Thomas Wolfe warned, he can't go home again. Clifford could not return to St. Louis, or Moyers to Texas, or Salinger to the city room of the San Francisco *Chronicle,* or Sorensen to those idealistic causes that had inspired his early manhood — if, in fact, any of those men ever wanted to return to those points.

The departing aide will have become acutely aware of status and image. He has spent several years dealing as an equal with the richest, most powerful men in America, and he may have come to savor the best clubs, the best cars, the best cigars, and other amenities of power. He has worked hard for a salary which, compared with his responsibility, is absurdly low. He may be in debt; he probably thinks he deserves some rewards after his years of sacrifice. His wife may have come to enjoy the pleasures of the most fashionable social circles. . . .

Even at best, the transition from the White House to private life is a painful one. The White House is the nerve center of the Western world and after its trials and triumphs a man is likely to find work in a Wall Street firm or a Long Island newspaper office to be weak wine indeed. The President, when he leaves office, has at least been President; the assistant, when he leaves, has been — what? A man who stood in the shadows of power, who played a mysterious role in a complicated process, a man who got little credit for his successes and ample blame for his mistakes, a man who will seem a braggart if he seeks credit, but whose good works will soon be forgotten if he does not. Like T. E. Lawrence or Charles Lindbergh or Jim Thorpe or Scott Fitzgerald he may find that those first years of glory were the best and that those afterward become a long, slow decline. It is hard to think of a presidential advisor whose afteryears, insofar as one can judge from the outside, have equaled the satisfaction of his time in the White House. Clark Clifford, perhaps.

Finally, adding insult to injury, as the aide departs from the White House, bloody but not quite bowed, he must watch with envy as the new President's team marches in — crisp, confident, eager to clean up the mess in Washington, to get the country moving again, to build the Great Society. The departing warrior's only consolation, in this dark hour, lies in the assurance that, as Emmet John Hughes put it, those who come to clean up the mess in Washington will soon *become* the mess in Washington. . . .

There remains, after the personal aspects of the presidential assistants' roles have been considered, the larger equation in which those assistants are simply cogs in the increasingly complex machinery of government.

How do you run the American government? How do you make it work? The Founding Fathers pondered those questions at Philadelphia in 1787, and they are still pondered today by Presidents and the men around them.

A large, powerful White House staff has been one of the tools recent Presidents have built to try to control their ever-expanding bureaucratic empires. From where the President sits, the hard fact is that there isn't time for him to perform all the roles demanded of him — to be chief of state, chief executive, chief legislator, party chief, and commander in chief. He must fix priorities, decide where his time is best invested, and delegate duties accordingly. Inevitably, the men personally and physically closest to the Presidents, best known by them and most fully responsible to them, have been prime recipients of delegated authority.

The nature of the delegation varies with different Presidents, different aides, and different issues. There will be many matters the assistant will decide in the President's name, without consulting the President, but confident that he is acting within his mandate. This is possible because, on countless details brought to the White House for action, what is required is not *presidential* decision but just *decision*.

On other issues that come to the White House, the aide will conduct an investigation, arrive at a recommended course of action, and take it to the President for final approval. If the President skims a covering memorandum, or asks a question or two, before ratifying the aide's decision, it can be argued that the "decision" was his, although to say so is largely a matter of semantics.

Finally, there will be the larger issues, the ones that do demand careful presidential consideration, in which the aide's role will be to investigate and clarify the alternatives open to the President — not to make the President's decision but to make it easier for him. These are, of course, the hardest issues, the ones on which, as Harry Truman often said, the buck stops at the President's desk.

Most recent Presidents, Eisenhower excepted, have tried to maintain the pretense that they read every paper, examine every issue, and make every decision. In fact, at least the last three Presidents have, either by choice or necessity, concentrated their attention on foreign affairs and delegated substantial amounts of authority in domestic affairs to men like Adams, Sorensen, Moyers, and Califano. Moreover, Kennedy, disillusioned by the State Department, partially bypassed it by creating Bundy's "little State Department" in the White House basement.

The insistent question raised by the growth of the White House staff in the past thirty-five years, and particularly by the emergence in the 1960s of a powerful NSC staff and by Califano's staff of domestic specialists, is whether the White House staff has become a new, perhaps permanent instrument of presidential administration, one that is destined to supplant older instruments, notably the powers of cabinet executives.

To an extent, it has. Since the New Deal, it has become normal practice for Presidents to have one or more staff assistants who are among the most influential members of their administration. Moreover, in the 1960s, there has been a clear trend for the leading assistants not only to be powerful individuals, but to direct staffs that in effect institutionalize their authority. Bundy's and Califano's staffs represent a new layer of authority between the President and the agencies of government. Bundy's staff most often seemed to perform usefully in keeping open tangled lines of interdepartmental communication. . . . The unanswered question is whether a massive White House staff, as grew up under Johnson, with a dozen Special Assistants and three or four dozen Assistants' assistants, is in fact an effective instrument of government. The danger of the fast-multiplying assistants to Assistants is that they really aren't the President's men, and they certainly aren't the departments' men, and they may fall into a kind of governmental limbo. There may be a point of diminishing returns . . . at which an over-large White House staff creates more confusion than it eliminates.

The modern White House staff, although it may be big and powerful, has no guarantee of permanence. However efficient, it operates only a heartbeat from obsolescence. It is for this reason that detailed projections as to the future of the presidential staff in American government are unwise. Douglass Cater called the press the fourth branch of government, Arthur Schlesinger called the federal bureaucracy the fourth branch of government, and at times, when it functions as a powerful, semi-autonomous institution, one might call the White House establishment a fourth (or fifth, or sixth) branch of government. But the catch is that, while the press and the bureaucracy are here to stay, the White House apparatus is, and must be, transitory, molded to each President's plans or whims. In theory, at least, a President must be free to fire everyone except one typist if he thinks that's the way he can most effectively administer his government. Eisenhower builds a powerful National Security Council; Kennedy discards the Council and invests power in its staff; Johnson downgrades that staff and bolsters the State Department; each President is right because he is governing in the manner he finds most comfortable.

Still, the large, powerful White House apparatus is probably here to stay. No President is likely to revert to the pre-FDR system of a half dozen clerks and typists. A change in administrations may result in the staff's being reduced from fifty men to thirty, or increased to seventy, but the difference is altogether relative. Thirty or seventy, the question is whether a strong, semi-permanent palace guard is a good thing — beyond the needs of individual Presidents, for the long-range interests of the government. When carried to extremes, it probably isn't.

Clearly, at the simplest level, it is desirable for our President to have men close at hand who are attuned to his personal tastes, and can arrange his schedule, relay his messages, help write his speeches, and otherwise satisfy his personal, immediate needs. Such men, by their knowledge of the President's mind, can do much to conserve his time. They will know what issues he wants to take up personally and what issues he doesn't. They can see visitors for him. They can read government documents for him and summarize their contents.

This passive role as a presidential evaluator, if well performed, will lead to an active one, with the aide moving aggressively as the President's eyes and ears throughout the government, and in the worlds of business, labor, education, and journalism as well.

These are proper functions of a President's assistant. The complication is that intimacy with the President will breed power and knowledge, which will breed more intimacy, and more power, and so on. A President's aide may start as a messenger boy but if he is at all clever he won't stay one. And as his influence escalates, the propriety of his role will come into question. The first point at which controversy arises comes when White House aides emerge as powerful coordinators of governmental affairs. Obviously, someone must assume a coordinative role in foreign affairs. It is everywhere agreed that the State Department, by virtue of its historic status as the first agency of government, *should* do so. Unfortunately, it has failed to do so, and the initiative has passed elsewhere. One result was Bundy's role as a watchdog over political, military, and diplomatic policymaking in the early 1960s.

In foreign affairs, it can at least be said that the State Department *should* assume leadership; in domestic areas there is only the urgent reality of urban problems that grow more serious each day and that require, but rarely get, the most careful coordination among the various federal departments and agencies. But the fact is that these departments will rarely cooperate, and risk surrendering any of their prerogatives, unless required to by some superior force. Since the 1930s, no President has had the time and inclination to immerse himself, on a continuing basis, in domestic affairs, and men like Clifford, Steelman, Adams, Sorensen, Moyers, and Califano have emerged as the presidential coordinators of domestic matters.

In some instances these White House coordinators have simply brought together antagonists to set the stage for decision; in other cases, the President's man is forced to dictate a decision to irreconcilable officials; in either event, his main job is to spare the President the necessity of presiding over endless interagency disputes. As Sherman Adams once told two feuding cabinet members: "Either make up your minds or else tell me and I will do it. We must not bother the President with this. He is trying to keep the world from war."

The role of the presidential assistant comes into serious question when he moves beyond coordination to become the de facto administrator and policymaker for one or more of the departments or programs of the government. To one degree or another, this has happened during every administration since Franklin Roosevelt's. Typically, the powerful White House aide, who has the President's trust, replaces the inept cabinet member who does not. The aide makes the decisions from behind the scenes while the cabinet member lingers on as a figurehead. The trouble with such an arrangement is that it is inherently inefficient and it inevitably demoralizes the officials of the department involved. It may meet the President's immediate needs, but it saps the vitality of an institution that must carry on long after the President has left office. It is far better for the President to remove the inept cabinet executive and install someone who can do the job, as when President Johnson replaced Anthony Celebrezze with John Gardner. One major challenge faced by President Nixon was to find a Secretary of State who would build a strong, viable Department of State.

President Eisenhower, when he left office, urged that the White House staff be endowed with more status. This could be done in various ways: by raising the staff's salaries, by defining their duties more clearly (perhaps by Executive Order), by submitting their appointments to the Senate for confirmation. Yet such moves would probably be unwise. The members of the White House staff should be exclusively the President's men, for him to use, abuse, or discard as he chooses. Insofar as they have independent status or permanent authority, their usefulness to him is lessened. They must remember their true condition: The President has been elected to lead the nation; they have been selected only to serve his convenience. If, in this era of the presidential mystique, there is any extra prestige available for the President to pass out, it would best go to those all but forgotten men, the cabinet secretaries and assistant secretaries, who now often wear the cloak of anonymity that the White House staff in recent years has cast off.

For the most part, the Presidents have brought men of outstanding ability onto their staffs. Sometimes, men of less obvious gifts have grown to meet the challenges of the job, just as Presidents have grown in office. It would be pointless to try outside regulation of the White House staff, as by Senate confirmation; the only way to get good men around a President is to elect good Presidents. And even then, even at best, the President's men will let him down from time to time. They will let old friends pay their hotel bills, or romance their secretaries, or enter into improper business deals, or make outrageous political statements.

Yet the same men will often perform admirably, even heroically, rendering genuine, little-known services to the country, with (in John Kennedy's phrase) a good conscience their only sure reward — and even that not always sure. These seekers of power are also men of paradox. Well-intentioned men generally, with a fair share of vanities and frailties, they operate within a political framework that offers many pitfalls and few protections, a system that does not always reward idealism and candor or punish deception and compromise. It is a system that allows for few whites, few blacks, and an infinity of grays. . . .

IV

THE INTERNAL STRUGGLE WITHIN
THE EXECUTIVE BRANCH

Although, as the readings in the previous section reveal, the development of public policy in the United States is greatly affected by interaction between political officials and career civil servants, it is also determined in significant ways by a dialogue that originates and is carried on within the ranks of bureaucracy itself. Sometimes this dialogue is fueled by rivalries among organizations or the conflicting ambitions of agency executives who take positions designed to protect or advance their own standing and power. But no less often it simply reflects different viewpoints among officials about which course of action will best advance public policy goals.

I

The terms commonly used to describe the struggle for power among executive agencies suggest a close analogy with the rivalries among nations. Bureaucratic organizations are spoken of as "engaging in territorial disputes" or as having "spheres of influence" to protect. Faced with attacks from a common enemy, formerly rival agencies may negotiate alliances designed to counter outside threats.

The title of Matthew Holden, Jr.'s essay, " 'Imperialism' in Bureaucracy," is in this vein. Holden's fundamental interest lies in the factors that cause some agencies to seek to broaden their organizational hegemony, either at the expense of other agencies from which territory must be seized, or by moves into new areas not presently under governmental sovereignty.

New organizations are particularly prone to "imperialist" behavior because they seek missions to perform and thus to attract constituencies through which they can extend their political support. An administrator, Holden writes, "must have the jurisdiction out of which he can tease the suitable combinations of constituency support." Agencies that have long been in existence may be primarily oriented toward maintaining rather than expanding their jurisdiction, especially when extending their authority threatens to disturb well-established patterns of constituency support.

As Holden reveals, an executive agency's search for public support can make bureaucracy more representative of the community than would otherwise be the case because it is in the interest of administrative agencies to welcome and serve clientele groups not presently part of any constituency. In Holden's words, "Agency initiative in a competitive political atmosphere permits the dissatisfied to 'shop around' until they find somewhere in the administrative system agencies responsive to their claims." In the past, however, it has sometimes been necessary to establish new agencies to achieve effective representation for groups not served by the existing bureaucratic apparatus.

The creation of a bureaucratic empire depends on both the existence of favorable opportunities for expansion and an agency's capacity to take advantage of such opportunities when they arise. This capacity for growth can by no means be taken for granted, as Andrew M. Scott demonstrates in "Environmental Change and Organizational Adaptation: The Problem of the State Department." Since World War II, the activities of the executive branch in foreign affairs have multiplied, but State Department jurisdiction has remained relatively stable. The Department has allowed other agencies to encroach on its territory and, in the view of many observers, has yielded primacy in the foreign policy area to the Department of Defense.[1]

---

[1] An agency's growth may also be hampered by its attachment to a constituency that demands its exclusive attention. See, in this connection, Samuel P. Huntington, "The Marasmus of the I.C.C.: The

The principal reason for this loss of power is the ideology of the dominant bureaucratic elite in the State Department, the Foreign Service Officers Corps. The Corps has tended to take a very narrow view of the functions appropriate for the professional diplomat. Young foreign service officers are subject to a process of socialization after becoming department members through which they acquire an attitude of disdain toward research, planning, management, and all other activities considered improper for the diplomatic role. The Department's culture has thus acted as a major constraint on its growth because in the eyes of the foreign service expansion could only be purchased through adulterating the purity of its professional commitments.

II

In scholarly literature at least, the power struggle within the executive branch is most commonly discussed in terms of competition among organizations. In "Bureaucratic Politics," however, Graham T. Allison focuses on the conflicting roles and individual characteristics of top administrators as one means of explaining the dialogue that took place within the executive branch during the Cuban missile crisis in 1962. "Where you [an official] stand," Allison writes, "depends on where you sit." Role is centrally important in determining an administrative executive's policy orientation, which is also affected by his personal attributes.

In his essay, Allison explains foreign-policy decisions as being a product not only of the exigencies of the international environment but also of the role and personality of each official who participates in making major decisions. Only a very few top officials are involved in matters as momentous as the Cuban missile crisis, and decisions of this kind may be greatly affected by the people who happen to participate in the discussion, their perception of their role, and the balance of power among the offices they hold. The

Commissions, the Railroads, and the Public Interest," *Yale Law Journal* 61 (April 1952):467–509. In this case the original constituency of the Interstate Commerce Commission — the railroad industry — prevented it from reaching out to cover new segments of the transportation industry as they developed through technological change.

influence of each participant is thus much greater in critical, nonprogrammed areas of administrative decision-making than in routine programmed areas usually handled by standard organizational procedures.[2]

Agencies differ a great deal in the influence they enjoy within the executive establishment, and the final essay in this section focuses on some of the forces that account for these "Variations in Agency Power." The chief factors discussed are constituency support, the esteem with which an agency's expertise is held by outsiders, an organization's esprit de corps, and the skill of its leadership. But it is well to remember that however useful analytical categories may be, they do not fully capture the uncertainty and flux that attend the pursuit of power by executive organizations and officials. Chance events play no less important a role in bureaucratic struggles than in other spheres of political life.

[2] For a discussion of this distinction between "programmed" and "nonprogrammed" decisions, see Herbert Simon, *The New Science of Management Decision* (New York: Harper & Row, 1960), pp. 14–34.

14   *"Imperialism" in Bureaucracy*

MATTHEW HOLDEN, JR.

I. CONSTITUENCY, JURISDICTION, AND POWER

If an important part of the political scientist's mission is to anticipate and explain "the critical problems that generate turbulence" [1] in that part of the world which attracts his attention, then, in the study of administration, bureaucratic "imperialism" [2] must be of compelling interest. If systematic data directly assembled for the purpose are lacking, and if there are some signal problems of theory which have been little investigated,[3] there is still enough evidence from studies of other political problems [4] that it seems worthwhile

From Matthew Holden Jr., " 'Imperialism' in Bureaucracy," reprinted by permission of the author and the American Political Science Association from *The American Political Science Review* 60 (December 1966):943–951.

[1] Albert B. Martin, *Personal Communication.*

[2] Cf., Gordon Tullock, *The Politics of Bureaucracy* (Washington, D.C,: Public Affairs Press, 1965), pp. 134–136; and Bela Gold, *Wartime Economic Planning in Agriculture* (New York: Columbia University Press, 1949), pp. 530–535.

[3] Cf., Philip Selznick, *Leadership in Administration* (Evanston: Row, Peterson and Company, 1957), p. 11.

[4] Herbert Emmerick, *Essays on Federal Reorganization* (University, Ala.: University of Alabama Press, 1950), chap. 2; Irving K. Fox and Isabel Picken, *The Upstream-Downstream Controversy in the Arkansas-White-Red Basins Survey (ICP, #55)* (University, Ala.: University of Alabama Press, 1960); Samuel P. Huntington, *The Common Defense: Strategic Programs in National Politics* (New York: Columbia University Press, 1961); James Miller Leake, "Conflict over Coordination," [*The American Political Science Review*] 12 (August 1918):365–380; Sidney I. Ploss, *Conflict and Decision-Making in Soviet Russia* (Princeton: Princeton University Press, 1965); F. F. Ridley, "French Technocracy and Comparative Government," *Political Studies* 14 (February 1966):41; Ashley L. Schiff, *Fire and Water: Scientific Heresy in the Forest*

to set out some trial-run ideas in the hope that they will elicit further discussion.

Bureaucratic imperialism seems preeminently a matter of interagency conflict in which two or more agencies try to assert permanent control over the same jurisdiction, or in which one agency actually seeks to take over another agency [5] as well as the jurisdiction of that agency. We are thus primarily concerned with the politics of allocation [6] and shall, except incidentally, bypass some other interesting aspects of interagency politics [7] such as cooperation between agencies sharing missions, competition for favorable "one-time-only" decisions which do not involve jurisdictional reallocation, or the critical problems of the "holding company" administrative organization and its internal politics.[8] For the moment, our concern with the politics of allocation leads to a focus on what would appear to be the likely behaviors of those decisionmakers who have both inclination and opportunity to look after the institutional well-being of agencies. Administrators at this level are really "administrative politicians," and the genesis of their problem is the necessity to increase power if the agency is to survive and flourish in an administrative habitat crowded with other agencies: [9] agencies embryonic or decaying, nascent, adolescent or mature.

Service (Cambridge: Harvard University Press, 1962), chap. 5; Warner R. Schilling, Strategy, Politics, and Defense Budgets (New York: Columbia University Press, 1962), pp. 22–24; and Herman M. Somers, Presidential Agency: The Office of War Mobilization and Reconversion (Cambridge: Harvard University Press, 1950), particularly chaps. 1 and 2.

[5] The well-known case of Interior Secretary Ickes's effort to acquire control over the Forest Service is in point: Harold L. Ickes, The Secret Diary of Harold L. Ickes: The First Thousand Days, 1933–36 (New York: Simon and Schuster, 1953).

[6] Emmette S. Redford, "Perspectives for the Study of Government Regulation," Midwest Journal of Political Science 6 (February 1962):8–9; and Marshall Dimock, "Expanding Jurisdictions: A Case Study in Bureaucratic Conflict," in Robert K. Merton, et al., Reader in Bureaucracy (Glencoe, Ill.: Free Press, 1952), pp. 282–291.

[7] For a pertinent contribution, see William M. Evan, "Toward a Theory of Inter-Organizational Behavior," Management Science 11 (August 1965):B217–230.

[8] Health, Education, and Welfare, and Housing and Urban Development are, at the federal level, particularly good examples of "holding company" orgnizations lacking an integrating goal or mythology.

[9] Norton E. Long, The Polity (edited by Charles Press) (Chicago: Rand, McNally and Company, 1960), chap. 4, remains the best statement on this point; also Herbert Kaufman, "Organization Theory and Political Theory," [The American Political Science Review] 58 (March 1964):12 and note 9 at the same page.

This by no means implies that administrative politicians are pirates out for plunder. But it does imply that the most saintly idealist (if a saintly idealist ever could arise to such a high post) could not function if he abandoned the maxim of "my agency, right or wrong!" The condition of power is a favorable balance of constituencies. Constituency means any group, body or interest to which the administrative politician looks for aid and guidance, or which seeks to establish itself as so important (in his judgment) that he "had better" take account of its preferences even if he finds himself averse to those preferences. The constituency of the agency, like the legislative constituency, includes not only those with whom the politician has a stable *and friendly* relationship, but those who support his ends, those who oppose his ends, and those who wish to intervene for what he regards as "irrelevant" purposes. Moreover, the term "constituency," although only customarily applied to the external groups which make claims upon the administration, is equally applicable to subordinates, employees, and colleagues who constitute internal constituencies.

To achieve a favorable balance of constituencies, in other words, administrative politicians must discover, identify, or manufacture suitable combinations of means and ends to yield effective incentives for the constituents he desires. This is the signal importance of jurisdiction. The goods the administrative politician can deliver, and the penalties he can impose, are a function of jurisdiction. Hence, he must have the jurisdiction (or competence) [10] over those policy issues out of which he can tease the suitable combinations of constituency support.

II. Strategies in Bureaucratic Imperialism

It would be unreasonable to assume that the incentives of agency power always lead to imperialistic behavior.[11] Yet the evidence of such behavior occurs often enough that we can believe it is not rare or trivial. Hence, we have to reach for some greater clarity about agency strategies. By strategy we mean calculation by some "broad" or "general" set of partially explicit, partially implicit "de-

[10] We recall that the "sphere of competence" is an essential criterion of the "administrative organ" as defined in Max Weber, *Theory of Social and Economic Organization* (Glencoe, Ill.: Free Press and Falcon's Wing Press, 1947), p. 330.

[11] Victor A. Thompson, *The Regulatory Process in OPA Rationing* (New York: King's Crown Press, 1950), makes this point by noting the *indisposition* of the OPA's Gasoline Eligibility Committee to grab jurisdiction.

cision rules" which provide clues to action in unforeseen — and often unforeseeable — contingencies.

Strategic patterns will naturally reflect such idiosyncratic features as the disposition of the individual decisionmaker, his sense of purpose, or his sense of agency capability to perform in the area where opportunity exists. But if the basic criterion of agency strategy is power achieved through constituency organized around jurisdiction, then we suggest that the administrative politician tends to adopt the impact on *existing* constituencies as the criterion by which to respond to each potential reallocation of jurisdiction. In this regard, there are at least three major considerations which will govern strategic choice: agency disposition, available occasions for allocation issues, and modes of resolution.

Agency Disposition. Some agencies rather clearly have a greater disposition to take on new jobs than do others which might, in principle, take on the same jobs. One of the critical factors here is the nature of the internal constituency. Administrative empire-building may, of course, be little more than a self-promotion strategy for an agency head to build a reputation and move on. This is somewhat unlikely, it would seem, for administrative empire-building also requires signs of successful performance or evidence that successful performance is likely. If this is to be achieved, the internal constituents have to make a serious decision to produce: the agency and its enterprises must engage their loyalties and enthusiasm. The boss's orders won't be enough!

While the energizing mythology which sustains a disposition to take on new jobs may be found in many different kinds of agencies, it may be suggested that it is most likely in the new organization. A new organization will exist only because someone thought there was something to be "reformed," "improved," or "developed" and this is likely to carry over into the selection of personnel. But there is a vital collective incentive. In the nature of government, there is an almost inevitable mixture of missions between agencies (e.g., a labor department, a commerce department, and a development department). If the old agencies have somewhat come to terms with the mixture of missions, the new agency can vindicate itself only if it finds a substantial share which it can control by itself. This requires energetic pursuit of opportunities and, necessarily, imposes conflicts with previously existent agencies. (Witness OEO in relation to HEW, Labor, etc.) But the very novelty of the situation means that the organization will have on board people who see brilliant opportunities if only they can so extend their reach as to bring all the relevant program fragments under their own agency's control. They lack commitment to existing programs, slots, routines, and schedules and therefore have great mobility.

In the first stages, at any rate, the novel organization is also likely to benefit from the interest of those external constituencies which provided support for its very creation. These constituencies will be inclined to think of all resistance from existing agencies as "old fogeyism" and, equally, will having just gone through the process of creating the agency be much on the alert for possible external threats. Defense politics since World War II would be acutely relevant, since it is *the* best (and *the* test) case of effective reorganization. The military needs of the Cold War were perceived as great enough and specific enough that the most important constituent — the President — had a vested interest in supporting reorganization. These same needs, plus the awareness of presidential support, activated the doctrines of obedience and inhibited potential resisters.

Each time the expanding agency acquires a new constituency, that constituency co-opts [12] part of the agency's money, people, time, skill and working doctrine. If the agency then seeks to shift those resources, it may find itself constrained by the demands of the co-opting constituency which has, so to speak, now acquired a first mortgage on those resources. From this arises a disposition toward maintenance rather than basic expansion. When this process first manifests itself, the agency officials may find it regrettable, and may even console themselves that the lapse from expansion into maintenance is purely temporary. But the fact is that it is difficult to shift funds once committed, to get personnel to interest themselves in new jobs, or even to find the time. Even more, it is virtually impossible to change these commitments without offending or injuring powerful constituencies, so that "temporary" maintenance becomes "permanent" maintenance.

When maintenance-minded agencies are challenged, one common response is to attempt to prove that what it is doing is all that could be done in the area (witness the Triborough Bridge Authority contra Mayor Lindsay) or that it is doing all the new things now desired.

[12] Philip Selznick, *TVA and the Grass Roots* (Berkeley: University of California Press, 1949).

Perhaps the most neglected cases are those in which there is a clear agency disposition toward retrenchment or self-limitation. It is not merely that the agency adopts kid-glove tactics in order to maintain a cooperative relationship with a constituency, but that it actually denies its powers. The history of the Natural Gas Act of 1938, as interpreted by the Federal Power Commission, provides one fairly clear example.[13] The FPC has several times seemed to be faced with a cleavage between the preference of the industry (little or no regulation) and the preferences of others (greater regulation). Recurrently, the Commission chose the strategy of denying (by quasi-judicial interpretation) that the Act conferred those powers which the proregulatory forces desired it to exercise. (The Federal Courts tended to assert exactly the contrary.)

Retrenching agencies may be forced to reorient themselves in order merely to maintain the status quo. This special case of reluctant running just to keep in place seems to be an interpretation one may impose upon the recent responses of the Texas Railroad Commission — an agency regulating oil and gas production [14] — to legislation establishing the Texas Water Pollution Control Board. The new statute (1961) apparently consolidates powers formerly vested in several agencies (not including the Commission).[15] Prior to this legislation, the Commission had disclaimed the power to regulate the discharge of oilfield brines (saline wastes) into water courses, although it did describe such discharges as a necessary incident to production. By this disclaimer, the Commission was freed of any responsibility to impose penalties upon the producing constituency, with which it had a long-standing and protective relationship.

The Commission pursued its policy of self-limitation in a slightly different form when the new legislation first became effective. In

[13] The interpretation is my own, but the evidence is presented in Edith T. Carper, "Lobbying and the Natural Gas Bill," in Edwin A. Bock and Alan K. Campbell (Eds.), *Case Studies in American Government* (Englewood Cliffs, N.J.: Prentice-Hall, Inc., 1962), pp. 178–184.

[14] York Y. Willbern, "Administrative Control of Petroleum Production," in Emmette S. Redford (Ed.), *Public Administration and Policy Development* (Austin: University of Texas Press, 1956), pp. 3–50.

[15] The statute is H.B. No. 24 of the 57th Legislature. First-Called Session, codified as Article 7621d, *Vernon's Annotated Civil Statutes*. It is reprinted in: U.S. House of Representatives, Committee on Government Operations, Subcommittee on Natural Resources and Power, *Hearings on Water Pollution Control and Abatement* (Washington, D.C.: Government Printing Office, 1965), Part 6, p. 3579 *et seq.*

administrative conferences to set up the Control Board machinery, Commission spokesmen agreed that the Board (1) had authority to issue or withhold permits for discharges into watercourses, (2) the Commission itself lacked such authority, and (3) "the Commission would depend upon the Board in regard to the decisions regarding quality to be maintained in the waters of the State in line with the Board's responsibility as the coordinating agency in pollution matters." [16] This administrative treaty, subsequently sanctioned by an Opinion of the Attorney General,[17] became the basis for the Board's new permit system. However, when a producing firm challenged the Board's new permit system, arguing that authority in oilfield matters lay exclusively with the Commission, the Commission intervened on the producer side, thus negating its acceptance of the earlier agreement.

How can this change-about be explained? If we accept the constituency hypothesis of this paper, the following interpretation would appear to be consistent with the facts. In the absence of a competing agency, no problem existed for the Commission, but it could hardly oppose some kind of permit system once the new statute was effective. Nor could it easily accept the controlling role for itself, in view of its previous position. If this were so, then the administrative treaty would seem a reasonable settlement. Once the Board actually began to operate, however, its course seriously disturbed the equilibrium of the Commission-producer relationship by a highly restrictive interpretation of one aspect of the problem. "Grandfather" permits were, under the statute, to be available to producers already in business, but when the Board began to operate, it actually issued "grandfather" permits to only 45 percent of the existing producers. Almost inevitably, one producer brought the lawsuit mentioned and the Commission's choices became much more constricted. It could sustain the original agreement, and violate the basic reciprocity owed its primary constituency, or it could join that constituency. It chose the latter course claiming, in effect, powers broader than any which it had exercised previously. It won the suit in the trial courts, but the legal issue was soon moot, for the legisla-

[16] This recitation of the facts is based upon Board briefs filed in litigation. Since it is of considerable importance and apparently nowhere rebutted, we assume its accuracy.

[17] Opinion No. WW-1465, October 31, 1962, as reprinted in House Committee on Government Operations, *op. cit.*, pp. 3586 *et seq.*

ture amended the law (before the appeal could be heard), making the primacy of the Commission with respect to oilfield matters unmistakable.

This shift from retrenchment indicates what we suspect is a more persistent factor. The disposition toward retrenchment would seem to depend upon the extent to which there is one critical constituency which cannot be changed or which has substantially inflexible ends. When there is at least one such, and the administrative politician does not perceive possibilities for a favorable constituency balance with diverse constituencies, he will tend to seek ways for self-limitation. This is particularly important in agencies where the internal constituency is a relatively homogeneous professional or skill group. For the agency head is more immediately jeopardized by the demoralization or silent sabotage of this internal group than by external criticism.

If the phenomenon of retrenchment is little noted in formal discussion, it is nonetheless apparent in many familiar situations. Political scientists need only consider some of their departmental problems. If, for example, there is a legal requirement that students be taught a course in "the Government of North State," a chairman is very likely to experience difficulty reconciling this with faculty desires to work in an atmosphere of academic high fashion. If the professional constituency is to be satisfied, therefore, it makes sense for a chairman to try to get rid of the requirement. In contemporary urban politics, the relationship between the police departments and the civil rights groups raises this problem. Police departments tend to be highly cohesive bodies in which the normative rules acceptable to the internal constituency are defined primarily from the inside,[18] so that the more responsive the police commissioner is to those who allege "police brutality," the more he will find himself forced to fight his internal constituency. The more responsive he is to his men, the more he must try to get an allocation of responsibility which permits him to ignore the outside. In federal administration,

[18] Wallace S. Sayre and Herbert Kaufman, *Governing New York City* (New York: W. W. Norton & Company, 1965), pp. 285–292; William Westley, "Secrecy and the Police," *Social Forces* 34 (March 1956):254–257; Westley, "Violence and the Police," *American Journal of Sociology* 59 (July 1953): 34–41; William Kephart, *Radical Factors in Urban Law Enforcement* (Philadelphia: University of Pennsylvania Press, 1959); and Murray Kempton, "The Cop as Idealist: The Case of Stephen P. Kennedy," *Harper's Magazine* (March 1962):66–71.

the recent signal example has been the Public Health Service which never wanted serious *police* power over environmental pollution — a power largely inconsistent with the developed tradition of PHS.

Occasions for Allocation Decisions. The administrative politician's strategies must go, of course, far beyond the estimate which he can make of the agency disposition to act. One of the primary considerations must be the "ecology" [19] within which action is to take place, and an important component of this ecology is the state of the competition. What are the alternatives open to those on whom he is dependent if he does not move? What are the alternatives if he does move? If he refuses to take on a new task, will he cut his own throat because some other agency will be given the task to the eventual detriment of his own agency? If his subordinates do not like the course he follows and resign, are there really places they can go, or do they have to stay with him?

Even more, however, he must consider the extent to which there is a consensus about policy or the extent to which there is uncertainty. (1) If we may agree that the ultimate limitation is some arbitrary criterion which makes some possible claims patently "ridiculous", then one critical occasion for making agency claims exists when policies are in their infancy. Doubt and confusion about policy ends lead to similar doubt and confusion about appropriate instruments. There is likely to be an almost primitive uncertainty [20] such that the decisionmaker does not "know what he wants," nor how "to make things turn out right," nor possibly even what "right" is. (2) Fluidity and confusion in a policy area, where there are some major fixed points of substance, but where connecting "threads" of policy have not been worked out so that the area is stable, also permit disputes about allocation. For who gets the job will do much to determine the eventual policy fabric. (3) The commonest situation appears to be that in which policy norms appear to be agreed upon,

[19] John M. Gaus, *Reflections on Public Administration* (University, Ala.: University of Alabama Press, 1947), chap. 1; Kaufman, *op. cit.;* Long, *op. cit.* chap. 10; Fred W. Riggs, *The Ecology of Administration* (London: Asia Publishing House, 1961); and Redford, "Perspectives for the Study of Government Regulation," *op. cit.,* pp. 4–5, all embody literary formulations of the idea of ecology in administration. Evan, *op. cit.,* has contributed a more precise statement in the notion of the "organization-set."

[20] On levels of uncertainty, see Matthew Holden, Jr., "Committee Politics under Primitive Uncertainty," *Midwest Journal of Political Science* 9 (August 1965):236–237.

but in which there is dissatisfaction *superficially* directed to the forms and techniques of administration. When this occurs, the ambitious administrative politician may put forth his agency as the "natural" or "logical" candidate to do the job efficiently.

Under primitive uncertainty, maintenance may be feasible for very strong organizations, but few such are actually likely to exist. Retrenchment, on the other hand, is almost a sure receipe for disaster, for the disposition to retrench actually protects the agency only so long as the constituency which loses thereby does not secure opportunities by other channels to achieve the same ends. Primitive uncertainty gives the freest play to dispositions to expand and this is most likely to be manifest when the governmental system is yet evolving [21] or, even more, when the very basic frame of social order is unsure.[22] But this may be fundamentally akin to the problem of administrative coordination whenever policy problems are severe enough that the existing system, if continued in its dominant mode, cannot accommodate to them. Even in highly stable countries, particular administrative units, whether mature or embryonic, find these seasons of crisis and confusion favorable to attempts to satisfy their most elemental power requirements.[23]

When uncertainties depend mainly upon the fluidity of policy, but where a few major points are more or less fixed, or where there is a presumption of policy consensus so that only administrative technique is overly disputable, the problem of acting on one or another agency disposition is even more complex. In these instances, retrenchment can be successfully pursued only by very strong organizations which jettison what they regard as irritating trivialities,[24] or by weak organizations which can afford only the least measure of turbulence. Organizations which do not tower over all their competitors, but which are still strong enough to be in the competition, have the problem that jettisoning any area of responsibility for

[21] Leonard D. White, *The Federalists* (New York: The Macmillan Company, 1956), particularly chap. 18.

[22] Lucian W. Pye, *Politics, Personality, and Nation-Building* (New Haven: Yale University Press, 1962), chaps. 15, 16.

[23] This seems to me the conclusion supportable by Somers, *op. cit.*, on economic administration during World War II.

[24] See, for example, Leslie Goldner, "Air Pollution Control in the Metropolitan Boston Area: A Case Study in Public-Policy Formulation," in Harold Wolozin (Ed.), *The Economics of Air Pollution* (New York: W. W. Norton and Company, Inc)., 1966, p. 137, n. 11.

which there is support opens the door for other agencies to appeal to the pertinent constituencies. This is particularly important in public as against private administration where the constituency is likely to entertain a presumption that the agency has a responsibility to look after its welfare.[25] (Imagine the fate of a Secretary of Labor who concluded that the major international unions really did not deserve his attention any more and tried to redefine "labor" to mean people largely outside the union movement.) The administrative politician thus has the complicated problem, if he really prefers to act on the retrenchment disposition, of trying to do as little as possible while not vacating the jurisdiction to possible competitors.

On the other hand, situations other than primitive uncertainty impose constraints on *explicit* self-aggrandizement because of the normative doctrine that all governmental agencies are "really" directed to a common purpose. Political ritual thus precludes, as a usual procedure, an open display of ambition or an explicit attack on the opposition. Consequently, the administrative politician is more likely to cooperate with, and sometimes to generate, surrogate or third-party claims in his own behalf, as the Texas law suit or the well-known practice of leaking criticism through a friendly newspaper or legislator. But, in any event, he is likely to appeal to the pertinent constituencies by setting up a straw man. Thus, a limited area of authority may be expanded if it can successfully be argued that "the problem is *really* not X [which is what the competitor presumably can handle] but Y [which is what the claimant can handle]."

Again, water pollution control provides an illustration beyond those equally applicable cases (e.g., defense reorganization) with which there is such common familiarity that the basic process may be missed. Pennsylvania is, for example, a state in which this issue has recently come to be of considerable political value. The main agency contestants are the Health Department and the Mines Department. The rule-making Sanitary Water Board characteristically exercises its authority through, or at the recommendation of, its "enforcement agent": the Department of Health.

Over the years, the more obvious dangers of bacterial pollution

---

[25] In this respect, the idea that there is "ordinarily little or no limit to the amount of inaction an organization can 'undertake' [because] inaction does not absorb resources" seems in error. See James G. March and Herbert A. Simon, *Organizations* (New York: John Wiley and Sons, Inc., 1958), p. 175.

which Health has emphasized have receded, and the relevant external constituency ("the conservationists") has looked more toward ending chemical pollution, mainly associated with the drainage of toxic acids from coal mines, a matter of less importance to the sanitary engineers. Meantime, the Mines Department has had some recent successes with controlling pollution from highly visible bituminous surface (strip) mines. Legislators and newspapers have tended to praise the good faith and efficiency of the Mines Department, while viewing the Health Department with skepticism, if not hostility, for "not enforcing the law."

The Secretary of Mines did not miss the opportunity to advise the legislature that acid drainage was necessarily incident to the mining business, as repugnant to the mine firms as to anyone else, and was actually "a mine problem" and "not a water problem." Having thus established this rationale, the Secretary then proposed to remove the matter from the Sanitary Water Board into an entirely new Mine Drainage Board. The particular proposal failed, but the door was opened. The Sanitary Water Board retained its regulatory power but a Mine Drainage Research Commission was created and, in the normal course of administrative politics, one would expect future efforts to expand its jurisdiction at the expense of the Sanitary Water Board.

For all the effort to place the issue in the perspective of proper administrative techniques to do an agreed job, the opportunity to seek a reallocation existed in 1965 and not some other time precisely because there was a general mystique supporting "clean streams" and considerable dissatisfaction with existing administration.

Modes of Resolution. The third consideration in the strategies of administrative politicians is that they know that issues of jurisdiction can seldom long be resolved, except in very broad terms. This is a point which appears rather obvious, yet is largely missed in existing administrative theory because the latter is largely a theory of kingship, i.e., how the executive-ruler may compel subordinates to do his will ("achieve organizational goals") and no more. If one adopts the regio-centric perspective, autonomous or contradictory agency action is pathological or, as Selznick says, "adventitious and subversive." [26] This is an important consideration in the tendency to

[26] Selznick, *Leadership in Administration,* p. 11.

pursue what Clawson appropriately describes as "the mirage of reorganization," [27] or the effort to give internally consistent settlements of jurisdictional issues.

Unless one could imagine simple free enterprise in the bureaucratic system, there could be only two ways to settle questions of boundaries. One would be some form of interagency bargaining such as the process by which the Corps of Engineers and the Bureau of Reclamation merged their conflicting downstream-flood control and upstream-irrigation interests, thus forestalling deadlock among their respective congressional supporters and obstructing effective presidential advocacy of a "basin authority" for the Missouri basin.[28]

As a general rule, it would seem doubtful that agencies have any great ability to make such deals explicitly. Since each party aims at its own continuance, it is apparent that bargains will not be accepted unless parties consider themselves advantaged by the deals. If party A enters a deal, A must be able to protect itself against such of its followers as are disaffected, or the deal cannot stand. Similarly, A and B must be able jointly to maintain the integrity of their deal by jointly protecting themselves against third-party attack. If the effective deal depends upon the ability of each to assure the other that the deal will more likely be kept than not, the issues at stake must be issues which can have reasonably clear termination points. The division of interests in the Missouri Basin permitted this to some degree by the sheer physical nature of the two areas of activity. Most jurisdictional issues do not lend themselves to specific termination points, simply because of the continued intermixture of missions.

Moreover, differences in agency power become extremely relevant. Given the intermixture of missions, there is a variety of constituency interests often "shopping" from one agency to the next, providing ambitious agencies with incentives to break their deals and defensive agencies with much ground for uncertainty about the consequences of such broken deals. The more firmly an agency is bound to a previous deal, the less opportunity it will have to ward off new challenges or to respond to new opportunities provided by

[27] Marion Clawson, *The Public Lands* (Washington, D.C.: Resources for the Future, Inc., and American Forestry Association, 1965), Part 5.

[28] Henry C. Hart, *The Dark Missouri* (Madison: University of Wisconsin Press, 1957), chap. 7.

the incidence of constituency "shopping." Accordingly, the resolution of agency jurisdictional conflicts must much more often be tacit than explicit, and accordingly much more uncertain of future stability.

The limitations of bargaining must often mean some kind of central decision or arbitration by a third official party — presumably "above" the contending agencies — as to which agency shall occupy a particular jurisdiction. Litigation is the clearest form of arbitration, leading to a decision by a court which says (as in the Texas case) that "this matter lies within the jurisdiction of this agency rather than that." But most of the arbitration lies with other officials, e.g., the President, the Governor, the Congress or the legislature. Insofar as each administrative agency has, or will seek to have, its autonomous base of power, it is evident that such arbitration is not likely to have lasting effect. The resolution of jurisdictional disputes tends to become more like mediation or conciliation in which the disputes are tentatively settled, on incremental terms. In making claims before third parties, agencies may exploit all the ordinary techniques of politics. The extent to which they do so determines whether the third-party officials making the allocation decisions can or cannot be coercive in forcing settlements upon the agencies.

The point now takes on considerable practical relevance because there is a mood in American politics — appropriately symbolized by the idea of systems analysis or the more startling notion of "goals research" [29] — suitable to the idea of "modernization" or "rationalization." [30] One of its manifestations is a revival of the regio-centric notion that bureaucratic imperialism is a form of pathology to be dealt with appropriately by institutional design which eliminates the conflicts and cross-purposes.

Since so much of the rationalization case is based on DOD experience, we have to note how consistent that experience appears to be with the idea that success in reorganization also requires time to wear down the centers of resistance. . . . The Defense experience is highly consistent with the view that reorganization which

[29] See the "Introduction" by Gerhard Colm in Leonard A. Lecht (Ed.), *Goals, Priorities, and Dollars* (New York: Free Press, 1966), pp. 1–16.

[30] Cf. Paul Y. Hammond, "Foreign Policy-Making and Administrative Politics," *World Politics* 17 (July 1965):656–671; and Charles J. Hitch, *Decision-Making for Defense* (Berkeley: University of California Press, 1965).

denies powerful parties' access to the internal decision process of the new organization will itself precipitate a new round of jurisdictional controversies, including new efforts to change the boundaries of the organization. Its product is reality rather than mirage if, and only if, the side being "attacked" can be deprived of alternative channels of influence or if powerful marginal constituents can be brought to the side of the "attacker." Even then, there is no guarantee that the process will stop, nor is it evident that even if, by some criteria, there are critical substantive problems to which appropriate responses are not forthcoming, . . . institutional reorganization is necessarily likely to produce those responses.[31]

Finally, the pressure toward reorganization involves a normative issue to which a postscript reply may be made. It would be improper for us to conclude that bureaucratic imperialism never involves irrationalities. But what we know of administration in an imperfect world suggests two considerations in terms of which bureaucratic imperialism may also have highly rational[32] effects in the policy process.

1. The administrative world in reality is a place of confusion and uncertainty, with false signals strewn about like dandelion seeds in an open meadow. Bureaucratic imperialism is a part of the process of clarification. Decisionmakers need some guides to the needs, preferences, ambitions and hopes of the various and constantly changing constituencies. Competition between agencies, engendered by competition between constituencies, is a vital part of the process of clarification.

2. Since administrative agencies tend to be co-opted by particular constituencies, other constituencies whose interests are affected have difficulty entering the process as agency boundaries are stabilized and, indeed, ossified. This is the source of pathological disinclinations to adapt to new circumstances. The idea that "higher authority" alone could either know enough of all the relevant situations or afford to make continuous readjustments of agency missions simply

[31] For a case demonstration, see Francis E. Rourke, "The Politics of Administrative Organization," *Journal of Politics* 19 (August 1957): 461–478.

[32] For a sympathetic reconsideration by an economist-systems analyst, see Roland N. McKean, "The Unseen Hand in Government," *American Economic Review* 60 (June 1965):496–506; and McKean, "Limitations, Risks, and Problems," in David G. Novick (Ed.), *Program Budgeting* (Cambridge: Harvard University Press, 1965), pp. 295–296.

ignores the complex reality.[33] There must be numerous means of readjustment of missions including agency initiative. Agency initiative in a competitive political atmosphere permits the dissatisfied to "shop around" until they find somewhere in the administrative system agencies responsive to their claims.

Competition through self-aggrandizement may thus enhance the sense of reality and maintain the fluidity of choice which prevents serious error. This phenomenon may be deemed "irrational" or "pathological" if, but only if, one has assumed that there is at some point a central policy mechanism capable of articulating a single "public interest" and that those interests not so articulated ought not to be permitted avenues of realization. Those who advocate this may describe it as "rational planning," but gamblers have a more honest name: they call it stacking the deck.

III. SUMMARY AND COMMENTS

Bureaucratic imperialism arises, it is argued here, from the simple fact that, whatever the purposes of the administrative politician, his first necessity is to maintain sufficient power for his agency. Power is organized around constituency and constituency around jurisdiction. Hence, the conflicts over the allocation of jurisdiction. Since it is obvious that not all administrative politicians move their agencies with the same frequency into efforts to claim jurisdiction, we have to look for clues to their strategies. Among the manifold considerations which may be pertinent, three seem of permanent relevance: agency disposition, occasions for allocation, and modes of resolution.

1. Agencies may have dispositions toward expansion, maintenance, or retrenchment. The disposition to expand is likely to be greatest when the agency is relatively new because the novel organization has (a) the necessity to establish a secure place for itself in relation to other agencies, (b) internal constituencies with little commitment to existing programs, slots, routines, and schedule, and (c) external constituencies still energized, from the effort to get the agency created, to support its claims against the threatening resist-

---

[33] The practical irrelevance of regio-centric approaches is evident when one reviews discussions of the problems of the President — indubitably the public figure most like a king. Richard E. Neustadt, *Presidential Power: The Politics of Leadership* (New York: John Wiley and Sons, Inc., 1960); and Theodore Sorensen, *Decision-Making in the White House* (New York: Columbia University Press, 1963).

ance of older agencies which may otherwise obstruct realization of the desirable results which people had in mind when they sponsored the new agency.

2. Dispositions toward maintenance are a function of the "first mortage" expectations which constituencies develop toward agency resources — money, people, skill, time, working doctrine — as the agency goes through the process of exploiting jurisdiction to build up support.

3. Retrenchment dispositions — dispositions actually to deny agency powers — develop when administrative politicians perceive no opportunity to create favorable constituency balances out of existing jurisdiction and when they possess some critical constituency which cannot be changed and for which the critical incentives are flexible.

4. Administrative politicians' choices of strategies are further determined by the critical occasions for decision. Dispositions toward expansion may most freely be pursued under primitive uncertainty. Under the same condition, very strong organizations may, in principle, pursue a disposition toward retrenchment because the very meaning of primitive uncertainty makes such a disposition trivial. Retrenchment, always dangerous because of the room it leaves for competing organizations, is under these conditions an invitation to organizational disaster.

5. Resolution of interagency jurisdictional conflict would tend to be highly problematical whether the method of resolution were bargaining or central decision (arbitration). Explicit bargaining is feasible mainly when the relevant agencies can fix physical limits to the areas of contention (e.g., the Pick-Sloan Plan). Tacit bargaining will normally be more relevant because the intermixture of agency missions is continual and because agencies will wish to leave open options for reassessing their power relations by future competition for constituencies as circumstances change. The existing of constituencies "shopping around" for places to get satisfaction also constitutes the critical limit on the durability and coerciveness of central decisions.

6. The normative case for reorganization — manifest both in administrative theory as usually known and in the more common version of systems analysis — is not necessarily to be rejected, but it is at least open to doubt. For, assuming that the criteria of judgment are clear, it may also be argued that bureaucratic "imperialism" may

also clarify constituency preferences and disrupt stale or archaic bureaucracies through the emergence of competitors. Moreover, it is open to doubt whether there is any specific relationship between systematic reorganization and improved substantive outputs, beyond the fact that stale and archaic routines are disrupted — a result equally accomplished by the self-aggrandizement of ambitious agencies. . . .

15   Environmental Change and Organizational Adaptation: The Problem of the State Department

ANDREW M. SCOTT

Every organization exists in an environment and interacts with it to some extent. When the environment changes in a significant way, the organization usually goes through a process of adaptation which, allowing for time lag, corresponds in some way to the environmental change. If sufficient adaptation does not take place, strains will develop and the organization will begin to move toward irrelevance, extinction, or some form of abrupt, forced, change. Some organizations adapt to change more readily than others. This article deals with an organization —the Department of State — which has found adaptation extremely difficult.

To note that the Department has been insufficiently adaptive is not to suggest that it has been changeless. The Foreign Service Act

From Andrew M. Scott, "Environmental Change and Organizational Adaptation," reprinted by permission of the author and the Wayne State University Press from *International Studies Quarterly* 14 (March 1970):85–94. Copyright © 1970, Wayne State University Press.

of 1946 and the integration of State Department officers into the Foreign Service in 1953, for example, represented efforts to make the Department and the Foreign Service more effective instruments of American foreign policy. Such changes have usually resulted from external rather than internal pressures.[1]

Interestingly enough, during the period since World War II in which the adaptation of the Department of State was altogether inadequate, the foreign affairs system as a whole showed an impressive capacity for adaptation. Foreign aid began in the post–World War II period with the modest goals of relief and rehabilitation. Governmental agencies were brought into existence to administer aid programs and the concept of what might be done with economic aid gradually expanded to encompass the economic rebirth of one continent and the economic development of others. The concept of technical assistance emerged as a response to felt needs, and when it was given funding and organizational support a new instrument of statecraft was born. The United States government wanted to carry its story to other nations during the Cold War and so yet another instrument of statecraft, the United States Information Agency, came into being. Various forms of military aid were developed — the use of military advisors, the training of foreign officers in the United States, the development of civic action programs, and so on. Just as new weapons altered the nature of war and the way that men thought about it, they also altered the way that men thought about peace, and this period witnessed the creation of the Arms Control and Disarmament Agency. At the same time the White House was organized to play a more important role in the foreign affairs process. But in the midst of all these developments, the Department of State showed only minimal adaptation.

The starting point for understanding the Department lies in an appreciation of the nature and dominance of the Foreign Service corps. Only 15 per cent of the total number of persons employed by the Department of State are Foreign Service officers, but they set the tone for the whole. The Foreign Service has the characteristics of a typical career service including entry at the bottom, resistance to lateral entry, career tenure and regular advancement through

[1] John E. Haar, *The Professional Diplomat* (Princeton, N. J.: Princeton University Press, 1969). See Chapters 2 and 3 for an account of these reform efforts.

grades if qualified, competition with others for advancement, esprit de corps, and a tendency toward corps self-government.[2]

The Foreign Service has developed an internal culture of its own consisting of an interrelated set of ideas, behavioral norms, and operating practices, including several of those enumerated above.[3] The norms and ideology associated with this culture permeate the Department and govern departmental responses in a variety of important areas.

This subculture contains elements which satisfy short-term needs of the career service and individuals in it but which do not necessarily satisfy the long-term needs of the Department of State nor the requirements of American foreign policy. These elements include, for example, hostile or condescending attitudes toward research, planning, management, and "outsiders."[4] Their dysfunctionality often takes the form of promoting attitudes and behavior that tend to insulate the organization from full and free contact with its environment. An organization that is not fully exposed to its environment is under reduced pressure to adapt to it. The short-term functionality of these elements is usually to be found in the way in which they soothe and reassure members of the subculture, protect them from critics and criticism, help smooth interpersonal relations within the Service, and promote discipline and order.

One of the dysfunctional aspects of the Foreign Service subculture is the extent to which it encourages officers to become inward-looking and absorbed in the affairs of the Service. Perhaps all career services tend to do this, but the Foreign Service carries it to an extreme. When an individual finds himself in an environment that places great emphasis upon rank and status, he usually learns to concern himself with matters of assignment, promotion, the impression he makes on fellow officers, the position he takes on shifting alignments in the Service, and the like. Learning to adapt one's be-

[2] See Frederick C. Mosher, "Careers and Career Services in the Public Service," *Public Personnel Review*, January 1963, pp. 46–51.

[3] See Andrew M. Scott, "The Department of State: Formal Organization and Informal Culture," *International Studies Quarterly* 13, No. 1 (March 1969):1–18.

[4] In the Foreign Service, policy is emphasized at the expense of management. John Haar remarks that "management is an alien concept in foreign affairs." ("The Managerial Crisis," *The Annals,* November 1968, p. 33.) Frederick C. Mosher has noted that few career systems give much attention to management even though management is important to them. *Democracy and the Public Service* (New York: Oxford University Press, 1968), p. 160.

havior and reactions to organizational expectations is an important part of being socialized into an organization. The fully socialized individual would be one who has internalized the organization's norms and learned expected behavior patterns so well that he conforms to them without thought. This degree of socialization would be functional in the sense that if all members were fully socialized the internal affairs of the Service would move smoothly and without a hitch. It would, of course, be highly dysfunctional for American foreign policy.

Given the importance to the individual of the internal workings of the Service, it is understandable that he may become as concerned with these workings, and their relation to his career, as with the organization's success in dealing with the external world. If an officer fails to do well in internal competition he will be directly penalized, but if the organization fails to cope effectively with its environment he may not suffer personally at all because the responsiblity for the failure will be diffused throughout the entire organization. It is not surprising, therefore, that an individual may become more concerned with office holding than with organizational accomplishment, more concerned with trying to *be* something rather than with trying to *do* something.[5] There is no invisible hand that makes it inevitable that the internal processes of an organization must produce results that are in harmony with the formal objectives of the organization. The two may easily drift into conflict, and when this happens it is as likely that the formal goals of the organization will suffer as that organizational imperatives will be disregarded. The very absorption with Service matters that socialization encourages, and almost requires, can be counter-productive from the point of view of the conduct of foreign policy.

If an organization is dealing with a relatively stable and unchanging environment, an insulated mode of operation may work fairly well, but if the environment is highly dynamic, as the international environment now is, insulation is likely to entail high costs. For one thing, it hinders the development in the organization of a determination to do what it can to shape events. The attitudes toward planning that are embodied in this particular subculture provide a case

---

[5] "The trouble with most FSOs is that they are too concerned about *being* something or *becoming* something — being a DCM or becoming an Ambassador — and not enough concerned with *doing* anything." A young Foreign Service officer quoted in John E. Haar, *op. cit.*, p. 208.

in point. The ideology teaches that planning is usually futile because each situation is unique and cannot be anticipated. That being the case, the best that one can do is to play things by ear and improvise creatively when events require it. Ideology, therefore, helps explain why the Department appears incapable of a serious planning effort. From time to time senior departmental officers have decreed that the Department will henceforth engage in planning. These efforts have been greeted with profound skepticism and have usually been short-lived.

A nation with widespread interests should be constantly planning for the future. Those responsible for policy must ask what actions should be taken today and tomorrow and next month in order to bring about a desired result some time in the more distant future. If the Department of State is not prepared to undertake this activity, some other organization is likely to try to fill the vacuum. During the McNamara era it was the Department of Defense, to a degree. More important has been the changing role of the President's staff. The White House is not insulated from its environment but is, on the contrary, a focal point for a great many pressures. The members of the White House staff do not belong to the State Department subculture, do not share its attitudes toward planning, and hence are free to engage in that activity. Furthermore, they are at the President's elbow, and a President is likely to feel the need for effective policy planning.

The White House staff has been important in the foreign affairs field since John F. Kennedy assumed office. The explanation for this is to be found only in part in the fact that the Presidents of the 1960s have been strong or interested in foreign affairs. At the outset President Kennedy expected to operate through the State Department and only established the Bundy operation when that expectation was disappointed. Lyndon Johnson had great confidence in Secretary Rusk but that did not prevent W. W. Rostow from becoming a powerful figure in foreign affairs. Henry Kissinger, foreign affairs advisor to President Nixon, is shaping American policy as visibly as the Department of State and has made a point of drawing certain planning functions to himself and his staff.

Foreign affairs staff members in the White House have become important because the times have demanded action and the Department of State has not been able to gear itself for action. There is significance in President Kennedy's happy daydream of "establishing a secret office of 30 people or so to run foreign policy while maintaining the State Department as a facade in which people might contentedly carry papers from bureau to bureau." [6]

It may seem strange to speak of the Department as insulated from its environment when its officers all over the world file millions of words annually, but the term is nevertheless appropriate. If a scale could be developed showing the extent to which public organizations interact with their environments, the Department would be found toward the lower end of that scale. It is insulated in that the Foreign Service is a career service with little lateral entry. It is insulated in that its members have a high level of interaction with one another and a relatively low level of interaction with significant figures in the outside environment — Congressmen, individuals in other departments and agencies, young people, corporate executives, academicians, and certain categories of foreigners. It is insulated in that it is unresponsive to changing circumstances and to the emergence of new skills, new information, new ideas, and new problems. It is insulated in that it defines what is relevant to its mission in a parochial way. It is insulated in that it has developed ways of explaining away outside criticism and has learned to ignore or sidetrack most demands for change.

It is easy to understand why individuals in an organization may act so as to shield the organization from its environment. When the organization is insulated, the need for disruptive adjustments to the environment is reduced and uncertainty and felt pressures are minimized. Isolation makes life easier. Men can do things the way they are accustomed to doing them and they can think accustomed thoughts. The drive toward isolation can be seen in many organizations but has been particularly apparent in the Department of State. Since changes in the international environment in which it operates are many, complex, and follow one another in rapid succession, the attractiveness of holding that environment at arm's length is particularly great. Since the Washington environment is also complex and changing and, in addition, is somewhat threatening and critical, it is not surprising that the Department should have developed fairly elaborate defense mechanisms.

[6] Arthur M. Schlesinger, Jr., *A Thousand Days: John F. Kennedy in the White House* (Boston: Houghton Mifflin, 1966), p. 433.

Structural characteristics of the career system also impede easy adaptation. When entry into the Service is primarily at the bottom, the carriers of new ideas are apt to be young and to be low in rank, status, and influence. Power in the organization will rest in the hands of older men who are likely to be imbued with traditional ideas. During a workshop in 1966 junior Foreign Service officers identified a number of Departmental problems, including the following: [7]

— assignment to jobs is based more on seniority than on competence;
— the Service is not making use of modern organizational, training, and assignment practices;
— older officers prevent progressive, adaptive action by younger officers;
— the Service reserves decisions to the highest levels and suppresses ideas from lower levels;
— fear of criticism and retaliation inhibit dissent and the expression of non-conformist ideas.[8]

Each of these "problems" represents a feature of the Foreign Service system that is functional from the point of view of a senior officer's conception of the smooth operation of the Service, i.e., a seniority system, personalized management, caution and conservatism on the part of senior officers, deference on the part of junior officers, the absence of vigorous debate that might mar interpersonal relations. Yet each of these features is also *dysfunctional* from the point of view of the Service's long-term future and its formal purposes. Order and discipline within the Service are purchased at the cost of imagination, flexibility and organizational drive.

The argument set forth here is that the departmental subculture has served to cripple the Department of State by promoting insulation and by furthering a variety of dysfunctional doctrines. If this line of analysis is correct, it means that the subculture will have to be substantially modified before the Department can play its proper role in foreign affairs. The historical record of the Department would not encourage optimism in this connection. Examples of bu-

[7] John E. Haar, *op. cit.,* pp. 272–274.
[8] Pressure for conformity is a frequent theme in the comments of junior officers. See Chris Argyris, "Some Causes of Organizational Ineffectiveness within the Department of State," Department of State publication 8180, January 1967.

reaucratic self-renewal are few and far between, and certainly the Department of State does not have a history of success.

Nevertheless, in recent years there have been stirrings that may prove to be important. In 1967 a group of "young Turks" in the Foreign Service gained control of the American Foreign Service Association with the idea of using it as an instrument to press for service reform. Some of the reforms that the Association's leadership is concerned with — improved training, more effective use of research, rapid promotion of able younger officers, altered assignment practices — would have the effect of weakening the hold of a number of the dysfunctional doctrines that now tie up the Department.

The leaders of the Association have also indicated that they intend to open the Foreign Service to its environment. One of the ways in which they propose to do this is by giving Foreign Service officers experience in the nongovernmental sectors of the foreign affairs community.

The concept of a foreign affairs community is interesting and potentially significant. There are many individuals who work professionally in foreign affairs outside the government. Together with those in the government, they comprise what might be termed a "foreign affairs community." Members of this community who are not in the government represent a resource that governmental agencies could utilize more fully. Conversely, members of the community in the government represent a resource from the point of view of businesses engaging in overseas activity, foundations concerned with international affairs, banks, nongovernmental organizations with international interests, and academic institutions. If the degree of lateral movement of personnel among the various sectors of the community could be substantially increased, this would be a net gain for all concerned. The attractiveness of the Foreign Service would certainly be increased and its competitive position would be improved if movement in and out of the Service were made much easier. At present the young man considering the Foreign Service is asked to choose a way of life once and for all because the decision to go into the Service usually forecloses other options. An able young man would be more likely to opt for the Service if he knew that he could move out of it for a few years with comparative ease and then back in if he chose. Perhaps, in time, young men may be able to plan for a career in foreign affairs that will involve relatively easy movement among the various sectors of the foreign affairs community. An individual's career would not have to be tied to a particular organization, such as the Foreign Service, but could be planned with an eye to the broad arena of foreign affairs. Perhaps also, in time, the Foreign Service and the other governmental services will be merged into a single foreign affairs service. This would do a good deal to overcome the tendency toward parochialism and would certainly open up the Foreign Service.

The leaders of the Foreign Service Association are interested in opening up the Service by making greater use of the principle of lateral entry. This would have a number of advantages, particularly if it could be coupled with short terms of service. At present the Foreign Service does not have enough technical specialists. Given the Service's predisposition toward the "generalist," such specialists are not likely to be developed within the Foreign Service and must therefore be recruited from outside. Many of the specialist candidates for appointment might not be interested in giving up their professional careers in order to spend a large part of their lives abroad but might be interested in entering the Service for four or five years. The adoption of a different philosophy with regard to lateral entry would make it easier for the Service to draw on the vast reservoir of trained men in the middle years of their lives. More important, these men might be a valuable leaven in the Foreign Service since they would be likely to have perspectives at variance with those normally found in the Service.

Some FSOs have misgivings about the extension of lateral entry on the ground that it will tend to undermine the concept of a career service. Their instincts are probably right. The guild-like characteristics of the Service would be strained by extensive use of lateral entry. If a choice must be made between a closed Service, on the one hand, and an open, adaptive Service on the other, however, there can be no doubt where the long-term interests of the nation and of the Department of State lie. . . .

The external environment in which the Department of State must operate is going to become more rather than less demanding with the passage of time. The Department is charged with conducting the foreign policy of one of the world's most powerful nations, and the insulation and dysfunctionality that were irritating but tolerable in the era before World War II are too costly and dangerous to be tolerated any longer. The costs associated with nonadaptation, errors made, imagination not exercised, problems not understood, and opportunities overlooked are not borne by the Department alone but by many people, in the United States and elsewhere, whose destinies are shaped to some extent by the successes and failures of the Department.

16   *Bureaucratic Politics*

GRAHAM T. ALLISON

The leaders who sit on top of organizations are not a monolithic group. Rather, each is, in his own right, a player in a central, competitive game. The name of the game is bureaucratic politics: bargaining along regularized channels among players positioned hierarchically within the government. Government behavior can thus be understood . . . as outcomes of bargaining games. . . . The bureaucratic politics model sees no unitary actor but rather many actors as players, who focus not on a single strategic issue but on many diverse intranational problems as well, in terms of no consistent set of strategic objectives but rather according to various conceptions of national, organizational, and personal goals, making government decisions not by rational choice but by the pulling and hauling that is politics.

The apparatus of each national government constitutes a complex arena for the intranational game. Political leaders at the top of this apparatus plus the men who occupy positions on top of the critical

From Graham T. Allison, "Conceptual Models and the Cuban Missile Crisis," reprinted by permission of the author and The American Political Science Association from *The American Political Science Review* 63 (September 1969):689–718. This extract covers pp. 707–715; footnotes are renumbered.

An expanded version of this article appears in Graham T. Allison, *Essence of Decision: Explaining the Cuban Missile Crisis* (Boston: Little, Brown and Company, 1971).

organizations form the circle of central players. Ascendancy to this circle assures some independent standing. The necessary decentralization of decisions required for action on the broad range of foreign-policy problems guarantees that each player has considerable discretion. Thus power is shared.

The nature of problems of foreign policy permits fundamental disagreement among reasonable men concerning what ought to be done. Analyses yield conflicting recommendations. Separate responsibilities laid on the shoulders of individual personalities encourage differences in perceptions and priorities. But the issues are of first order importance. What the nation does really matters. A wrong choice could mean irreparable damage. Thus responsible men are obliged to fight for what they are convinced is right.

Men share power. Men differ concerning what must be done. The differences matter. This milieu necessitates that policy be resolved by politics. What the nation does is sometimes the result of the triumph of one group over others. More often, however, different groups pulling in different directions yield a resultant distinct from what anyone intended. What moves the chess pieces is not simply the reasons which support a course of action, nor the routines of organizations which enact an alternative, but the power and skill of proponents and opponents of the action in question.

This characterization captures the thrust of the bureaucratic politics orientation. If problems of foreign policy arose as discreet issues, and decisions were determined one game at a time, this account would suffice. But most "issues," e.g., Vietnam or the proliferation of nuclear weapons, emerge piecemeal, over time, one lump in one context, a second in another. Hundreds of issues compete for players' attention every day. Each player is forced to fix upon his issues for that day, fight them on their own terms, and rush on to the next. Thus the character of emerging issues and the pace at which the game is played converge to yield government "decisions" and "actions" as collages. Choices by one player, outcomes of minor games, outcomes of central games, and "foul-ups" — these pieces, when stuck to the same canvas, constitute government behavior relevant to an issue.

The concept of national security policy as political outcome contradicts both public imagery and academic orthodoxy. Issues vital to national security, it is said, are too important to be settled by political games. They must be "above" politics. To accuse someone of "playing politics with national security" is a most serious charge. What public conviction demands, the academic penchant for intellectual elegance reinforces. Internal politics is messy; moreover, according to prevailing doctrine, politicking lacks intellectual content. As such, it constitutes gossip for journalists rather than a subject for serious investigation. Occasional memoirs, anecdotes in historical accounts, and several detailed case studies to the contrary, most of the literature of foreign policy avoids bureaucratic politics. The gap between academic literature and the experience of participants in government is nowhere wider than at this point.

BUREAUCRATIC POLITICS PARADIGM [1]

I. Basic Unit of Analysis: Policy
as Political Outcome

The decisions and actions of governments are essentially intra-national political outcomes: outcomes in the sense that what happens is not chosen as a solution to a problem but rather results from compromise, coalition, competition and confusion among government officials who see different faces of an issue; political in the sense that the activity from which the outcomes emerge is best characterized as bargaining. Following Wittgenstein's use of the concept of a "game," national behavior in international affairs can be conceived as outcomes of intricate and subtle, simultaneous, over-lapping games among players located in positions, the hierarchical arrangement of which constitutes the government.[2] These games

---

[1] This paradigm relies upon the small group of analysts who have begun to fill the gap. My primary source is the model implicit in the work of Richard E. Neustadt, though his concentration on presidential action has been generalized to a concern with policy as the outcome of political bargaining among a number of independent players, the President amounting to no more than a "super-power" among many lesser but considerable powers. As Warner Schilling argues, the substantive problems are of such inordinate difficulty that uncertainties and differences with regard to goals, alternatives, and consequences are inevitable. This necessitates what Roger Hilsman describes as the process of conflict and consensus building. The techniques employed in this process often resemble those used in legislative assemblies, though Samuel Huntington's characterization of the process as "legislative" overemphasizes the equality of participants as opposed to the hierarchy which structures the game. Moreover, whereas for Huntington, foreign policy (in contrast to military policy) is set by the executive, this paradigm maintains that the activities which he describes as legislative are characteristic of the process by which foreign policy is made.

[2] The theatrical metaphor of stage, roles, and actors is more common than this metaphor of games, positions, and players. Nevertheless, the rigidity con-

proceed neither at random nor at leisure. Regular channels structure the game. Deadlines force issues to the attention of busy players. The moves in the chess game are thus to be explained in terms of the bargaining among players with separate and unequal power over particular pieces and with separable objectives in distinguishable subgames.

II. Organizing Concepts

A. *Players in Positions.* The actor is neither a unitary nation, nor a conglomerate of organizations, but rather a number of individual players. Groups of these players constitute the agent for particular government decisions and actions. Players are men in jobs.

Individuals become players in the national security policy game by occupying a critical position in an administration. For example, in the United States government the players include "Chiefs": the President, Secretaries of State, Defense, and Treasury, Director of the CIA, Joint Chiefs of Staff, and since 1961, the Special Assistant for National Security Affairs; [3] "Staffers": the immediate staff of each Chief; "Indians": the political appointees and permanent government officials within each of the departments and agencies; and "Ad Hoc Players": actors in the wider government game (especially "Congressional Influentials"), members of the press, spokesmen for important interest groups (especially the "bipartisan foreign policy

---

notated by the concept of "role" both in the theatrical sense of actors reciting fixed lines and in the sociological sense of fixed responses to specified social situations makes the concept of games, positions, and players more useful for this analysis of active participants in the determination of national policy. Objections to the terminology on the grounds that "game" connotes nonserious play overlook the concept's application to most serious problems both in Wittgenstein's philosophy and in contemporary game theory. Game theory typically treats more precisely structured games, but Wittgenstein's examination of the "language game" wherein men use words to communicate is quite analogous to this analysis of the less specified game of bureaucratic politics. See Ludwig Wittgenstein, *Philosophical Investigations*, and Thomas Schelling, "What is Game Theory?" in James Charlesworth, *Contemporary Political Analysis* [New York, 1967].

[3] Inclusion of the President's Special Assistant for National Security Affairs in the tier of "Chiefs" rather than among the "Staffers" involves a debatable choice. In fact he is both super-staffer and near-chief. His position has no statutory authority. He is especially dependent upon good relations with the President and the Secretaries of Defense and State. Nevertheless, he stands astride a genuine action-channel. The decision to include this position among the Chiefs reflects my judgment that the Bundy function is becoming institutionalized.

establishment" in and out of Congress), and surrogates for each of these groups. Other members of the Congress, press, interest groups, and public form concentric circles around the central arena — circles which demarcate the permissive limits within which the game is played.

Positions define what players both may and must do. The advantages and handicaps with which each player can enter and play in various games stems from his position. So does a cluster of obligations for the performance of certain tasks. The two sides of this coin are illustrated by the position of the modern Secretary of State. First, in form and usually in fact, he is the primary repository of political judgment on the political-military issues that are the stuff of contemporary foreign policy; consequently, he is a senior personal advisor to the President. Second, he is the colleague of the President's other senior advisors on the problems of foreign policy, the Secretaries of Defense and Treasury, and the Special Assistant for National Security Affairs. Third, he is the ranking United States diplomat for serious negotiation. Fourth, he serves as an administration voice to Congress, the country, and the world, Finally, he is "Mr. State Department" or "Mr. Foreign Office," "leader of officials, spokesman for their causes, guardian of their interests, judge of their disputes, superintendent of their work, master of their careers." [4] But he is not first one, and then the other. All of these obligations are his simultaneously. His performance in one affects his credit and power in the others. The perspective stemming from the daily work which he must oversee — the cable traffic by which his department maintains relations with other foreign offices — conflicts with the President's requirement that he serve as a generalist and coordinator of contrasting perspectives. The necessity that he be close to the President restricts the extent to which, and the force with which, he can front for his department. When he defers to the Secretary of Defense rather than fighting for his department's position — as he often must — he strains the loyalty of his officialdom. The Secretary's resolution of these conflicts depends not only upon the position, but also upon the player who occupies the position.

For players are also people. Men's metabolisms differ. The core of the bureaucratic politics mix is personality. How each man man-

---

[4] Richard E. Neustadt, Testimony, United States Senate, Committee on Government Operations, Subcommittee on National Security Staffing, *Administration of National Security*, March 26, 1963, pp. 82–83.

ages to stand the heat in his kitchen, each player's basic operating style, and the complementarity or contradiction among personalities and styles in the inner circles are irreducible pieces of the policy blend. Moreoever, each person comes to his position with baggage in tow, including sensitivities to certain issues, commitments to various programs, and personal standing and debts with groups in the society.

B. *Parochial Priorities, Perceptions, and Issues.* Answers to the questions: "What is the issue?" and "What must be done?" are colored by the position from which the questions are considered. For the factors which encourage organizational parochialism also influence the players who occupy positions on top of (or within) these organizations. To motivate members of his organization, a player must be sensitive to the organization's orientation. The games into which the player can enter and the advantages with which he plays enhance these pressures. Thus propensities of perception stemming from position permit reliable prediction about a player's stances in many cases. But these propensities are filtered through the baggage which players bring to positions. Sensitivity to both the pressures and the baggage is thus required for many predictions.

C. *Interests, Stakes, and Power.* Games are played to determine outcomes. But outcomes advance and impede each player's conception of the national interest, specific programs to which he is committed, the welfare of his friends, and his personal interests. These overlapping interests constitute the stakes for which games are played. Each player's ability to play successfully depends upon his power. Power, i.e., effective influence on policy outcomes, is an elusive blend of at least three elements: bargaining advantages (drawn from formal authority and obligations, institutional backing, constituents, expertise, and status), skill and will in using bargaining advantages, and other players' perceptions of the first two ingredients. Power wisely invested yields an enhanced reputation for effectiveness. Unsuccessful investment depletes both the stock of capital and the reputation. Thus each player must pick the issues on which he can play with a reasonable probability of success. But no player's power is sufficient to guarantee satisfactory outcomes. Each player's needs and fears run to many other players. What ensues is the most intricate and subtle of games known to man.

D. *The Problem and the Problems.* "Solutions" to strategic problems are not derived by detached analysts focusing coolly on *the* problem. Instead, deadlines and events raise issues in games, and demand decisions of busy players in contexts that influence the face the issue wears. The problems for the players are both narrower and broader than *the* strategic problem. For each player focuses not on the total strategic problem but rather on the decision that must be made now. But each decision has critical consequences not only for the strategic problem but for each player's organizational, reputational, and personal stakes. Thus the gap between the problems the player was solving and the problem upon which the analyst focuses is often very wide.

E. *Action-Channels.* Bargaining games do not proceed randomly. Action-channels, i.e., regularized ways of producing action concerning types of issues, structure the game by preselecting the major players, determining their points of entrance into the game, and distributing particular advantages and disadvantages for each game. Most critically, channels determine "who's got the action," that is, which department's Indians actually do whatever is chosen. Weapon procurement decisions are made within the annual budgeting process; embassies' demands for action cables are answered according to routines of consultation and clearance from State to Defense and White House; requests for instructions from military groups (concerning assistance all the time, concerning operations during war) are composed by the military in consultation with the Office of the Secretary of Defense, State, and White House; crisis responses are debated among White House, State, Defense, CIA, and Ad Hoc Players; major political speeches, especially by the President but also by other Chiefs, are cleared through established channels.

F. *Action as Politics.* Government decisions are made and government actions emerge neither as the calculated choice of a unified group, nor as a formal summary of leaders' preferences. Rather the context of shared power but separate judgments concerning important choices, determines that politics is the mechanism of choice. Note the *environment* in which the game is played: inordinate uncertainty about what must be done, the necessity that something be done, and crucial consequences of whatever is done. These features force responsible men to become active players. The *pace of the game* — hundreds of issues, numerous games, and multiple channels — compels players to fight to "get other's attention," to make them "see the facts," to assure that they "take the time to think seriously about the broader issue." The *structure of the game* — power shared by individuals with separate responsibilities — validates each player's feeling that "others don't see my problem," and "others must be persuaded to look at the issue from a less parochial perspective." The *rules of the game* — he who hesitates loses his chance to play at that point, and he who is uncertain about his recommendation is overpowered by others who are sure — pressures players to come down on one side of a 51–49 issue and play. The *rewards of the game* — effectiveness, i.e., impact on outcomes, as the immediate measure of performance — encourages hard play. Thus, most players come to fight to "make the government do what is right." The strategies and tactics employed are quite similar to those formalized by theorists of international relations.

G. *Streams of Outcomes.* Important government decisions or actions emerge as collages composed of individual acts, outcomes of minor and major games, and foul-ups. Outcomes which could never have been chosen by an actor and would never have emerged from bargaining in a single game over the issue are fabricated piece by piece. Understanding of the outcome requires that it be disaggregated.

III. Dominant Inference Pattern

If a nation performed an action, that action was the *outcome* of bargaining among individuals and groups within the government. That outcome included *results* achieved by groups committed to a decision or action, *resultants* which emerged from bargaining among groups with quite different positions and *foul-ups*. [The] explanatory power [of this model] is achieved by revealing the pulling and hauling of various players, with different perceptions and priorities, focusing on separate problems, which yielded the outcomes that constitute the action in question.

IV. General Propositions

1. *Action and Intention.* Action does not presuppose intention. The sum of behavior of representatives of a government relevant to an issue was rarely intended by any individual or group. Rather separate individuals with different intentions contributed pieces which compose an outcome distinct from what anyone would have chosen.

2. Where You Stand Depends on Where You Sit.[5] Horizontally, the diverse demands upon each player shape his priorities, perceptions, and issues. For large classes of issues, e.g., budgets and procurement decisions, the stance of a particular player can be predicted with high reliability from information concerning his seat. In the notorious B-36 controversy, no one was surprised by Admiral Radford's testimony that "the B-36 under any theory of war, is a bad gamble with national security," as opposed to Air Force Secretary Symington's claim that "a B-36 with an A-bomb can destroy distant objectives which might require ground armies years to take."[6]

3. Chiefs and Indians. The aphorism "where you stand depends on where you sit" has vertical as well as horizontal application. Vertically, the demands upon the President, Chiefs, Staffers, and Indians are quite distinct.

The foreign-policy issues with which the President can deal are limited primarily by his crowded schedule: the necessity of dealing first with what comes next. His problem is to probe the special face worn by issues that come to his attention, to preserve his leeway until time has clarified the uncertainities, and to assess the relevant risks.

Foreign-policy Chiefs deal most often with the hottest issue *de jour*, though they can get the attention of the President and other members of the government for other issues which they judge important. What they cannot guarantee is that "the President will pay the price" or that "the others will get on board." They must build a coalition of the relevant powers that be. They must "give the President confidence" in the right course of action.

Most problems are framed, alternatives specified, and proposals pushed, however, by Indians. Indians fight with Indians of other departments; for example, struggles between International Security Affairs of the Department of Defense and Political-Military of the State Department are a microcosm of the action at higher levels. But the Indian's major problem is how to get the *attention* of Chiefs, how to get an issue decided, how to get the government "to do what is right."

[5] This aphorism was stated first, I think, by Don K. Price.
[6] Paul Y. Hammond, "Super Carriers and B-36 Bombers," in Harold Stein (Ed.), *American Civil-Military Decisions* (Birmingham, 1963).

In policymaking then, the issue looking *down* is options: how to preserve my leeway until time clarifies uncertainties. The issue looking *sideways* is commitment: how to get others committed to my coalition. The issue looking *upwards* is confidence: how to give the boss confidence in doing what must be done. To paraphrase one of Neustadt's assertions which can be applied down the length of the ladder, the essence of a responsible official's task is to induce others to see that what needs to be done is what their own appraisal of their own responsibilities requires them to do in their own interests.

V. Specific Propositions

1. Deterrence. The probability of nuclear attack depends primarily on the probability of attack emerging as an outcome of the bureaucratic politics of the attacking government. First, which players can decide to launch an attack? Whether the effective power over action is controlled by an individual, a minor game, or the central game is critical. Second, though . . . confidence in nuclear deterrence stems from an assertion that, in the end, governments will not commit suicide, [this model] recalls historical precedents. Admiral Yamamoto, who designed the Japanese attack on Pearl Harbor, estimated accurately: "In the first six months to a year of war against the U.S. and England I will run wild, and I will show you an uninterrupted succession of victories; I must also tell you that, should the war be prolonged for two or three years, I have no confidence in our ultimate victory." [7] But Japan attacked. Thus, three questions might be considered. One: could any member of the government solve his problem by attack? What patterns of bargaining could yield attack as an outcome? The major difference between a stable balance of terror and a questionable balance may simply be that in the first case most members of the government appreciate fully the consequences of attack and are thus on guard against the emergence of this outcome. Two: what stream of outcomes might lead to an attack? At what point in that stream is the potential attacker's politics? If members of the United States government had been sensitive to the stream of decisions from which the Japanese attack on Pearl Habor emerged, they would have been aware of a considerable probability of that attack. Three: how might miscalculation and confusion generate foul-ups that yield attack as an out-

[7] Roberta Wohlstetter, *Pearl Harbor* (Stanford, 1962), p. 350.

come? For example, in a crisis or after the beginning of conventional war, what happens to the information available to, and the effective power of, members of the central game.

The United States Blockade of Cuba . . .

The Politics of Discovery. A series of overlapping bargaining games determined both the *date* of the discovery of the Soviet missiles and the *impact* of this discovery on the administration. An explanation of the politics of the discovery is consequently a considerable piece of the explanation of the United States blockade.

Cuba was the Kennedy Administration's "political Achilles' heel."[8] The months preceding the crisis were also months before the congressional elections, and the Republican Senatorial and Congressional Campaign Committee had announced that Cuba would be "the dominant issue of the 1962 campaign."[9] What the administration billed as a "more positive and indirect approach of isolating Castro from developing, democratic Latin America," Senators Keating, Goldwater, Capehart, Thurmond, and others attacked as a "do-nothing" policy.[10] In statements on the floor of the House and Senate, campaign speeches across the country, and interviews and articles carried by national news media, Cuba — particularly the Soviet program of increased arms aid — served as a stick for stirring the domestic political scene.[11]

These attacks drew blood. Prudence demanded a vigorous reaction. The President decided to meet the issue head-on. The administration mounted a forceful campaign of denial designed to discredit critics' claims. The President himself manned the front line of this offensive, though almost all administration officials participated. In his news conference on August 19, President Kennedy attacked as "irresponsible" calls for an invasion of Cuba, stressing rather "the totality of our obligations" and promising to "watch what happens in Cuba with the closest attention."[12] On September 4, he issued a strong statement denying any provocative Soviet action in Cuba.[13] On September 13 he lashed out at "loose talk" calling for an invasion

8 [Theodore] Sorensen, *Kennedy* [New York, 1965], p. 670.
9 *Ibid.*
10 *Ibid.*, pp. 670 ff.
11 *The New York Times*, August, September, 1962.
12 *The New York Times*, August 20, 1962.
13 *The New York Times*, September 5, 1962.

of Cuba.[14] The day before the flight of the U-2 which discovered the missiles, he campaigned in Capehart's Indiana against those "self-appointed generals and admirals who want to send someone else's sons to war."[15]

On Sunday, October 14, just as a U-2 was taking the first pictures of Soviet missiles, McGeorge Bundy was asserting:

I *know* that there is no present evidence, and I think that there is no present likelihood that the Cuban government and the Soviet government would, in combination, attempt to install a major offensive capability.[16]

In this campaign to puncture the critics' charges, the administration discovered that the public needed positive slogans. Thus, Kennedy fell into a tenuous semantic distinction between "offensive" and "defensive" weapons. This distinction originated in his September 4 statement that there was no evidence of "offensive ground to ground missiles" and warned "were it to be otherwise, the gravest issues would arise."[17] His September 13 statement turned on this distinction between "defensive" and "offensive" weapons and announced a firm commitment to action if the Soviet Union attempted to introduce the latter into Cuba.[18] Congressional committees elicited from administration officials testimony which read this distinction and the President's commitment into the *Congressional Record*.[19]

What the President least wanted to hear, the CIA was most hesitant to say plainly. On August 22 John McCone met privately with the President and voiced suspicions that the Soviets were preparing to introduce offensive missiles into Cuba.[20] Kennedy heard this as what it was: the suspicion of a hawk. McCone left Washington for a month's honeymoon on the Riviera. Fretting at Cap Ferrate, he

[14] *The New York Times,* September 14, 1962.

[15] *The New York Times,* October 14, 1962.

[16] Cited by [Elie] Abel [*The Missile Crisis* (Philadelphia, 1966)], p. 13.

[17] *The New York Times,* September 5, 1962.

[18] *The New York Times,* September 14, 1962.

[19] Senate Foreign Relations Committee; Senate Armed Services Committee; House Committee on Appropriation; House Select Committee on Export Control.

[20] Abel, *op. cit.,* pp. 17–18. According to McCone, he told Kennedy, "The only construction I can put on the material going into Cuba is that the Russians are preparing to introduce offensive missiles." See also [Edward] Weintal and [Charles] Bartlett, *Facing the Brink: An Intimate Study of Crisis Diplomacy* (New York, 1967), pp. 60–61.

bombarded his deputy, General Marshall Carter, with telegrams, but Carter, knowing that McCone had informed the President of his suspicions and received a cold reception, was reluctant to distribute these telegrams outside the CIA.[21] On September 9 a U-2 "on loan" to the Chinese Nationalists was downed over mainland China.[22] The Committee on Overhead Reconnaissance (COMOR) convened on September 10 with a sense of urgency.[23] Loss of another U-2 might incite world opinion to demand cancellation of U-2 flights. The President's campaign against those who asserted that the Soviets were acting provocatively in Cuba had begun. To risk downing a U-2 over Cuba was to risk chopping off the limb on which the President was sitting. That meeting decided to shy away from the western end of Cuba (where SAMs were becoming operational) and modify the flight pattern of the U-2s in order to reduce the probability that a U-2 would be lost.[24] USIB's unanimous approval of the September estimate reflects similar sensitivities. On September 13 the President had asserted that there were no Soviet offensive missiles in Cuba and committed his administration to act if offensive missiles were discovered. Before congressional committees, administration officials were denying that there was any evidence whatever of offensive missiles in Cuba. The implications of a National Intelligence estimate which concluded that the Soviets were introducing offensive missiles into Cuba were not lost on the men who constituted America's highest intelligence assembly.

The October 4 COMOR decision to direct a flight over the western end of Cuba in effect "overturned" the September estimate, but without officially raising that issue. The decision represented McCone's victory for which he had lobbied with the President before the September 10 decision, in telegrams before the September 19 estimate, and in person after his return to Washington. Though the politics of the intelligence community is closely guarded, several pieces of the story can be told.[25] By September 27, Colonel Wright

21 Abel, *op. cit.*, p. 23.

22 *The New York Times*, September 10, 1962.

23 See Abel, *op. cit.*, pp. 25–26; and [Roger] Hilsman, [*To Move a Nation* (New York, 1967)], p. 174.

24 [U.S. Congress, House of Representatives], Department of Defense Appropriations, *Hearings*, [88th Congress, 1st Session, 1963], p. 69.

25 A basic, but somewhat contradictory, account of parts of this story emerges in the Department of Defense Appropriations, *Hearings*, pp. 1–70.

and others in DIA [Defense Intelligence Agency] believed that the Soviet Union was placing missiles in the San Cristobal area.[26] This area was marked suspicious by the CIA on September 29 and certified top priority on October 3. By October 4 McCone had the evidence required to raise the issue officially. The members of COMOR head McCone's argument, but were reluctant to make the hard decision he demanded. The significant probability that a U-2 would be downed made overflight of western Cuba a matter of real concern.[27]

The Politics of Issues. The U-2 photographs presented incontrovertible evidence of Soviet offensive missiles in Cuba. This revelation fell upon politicized players in a complex context. As one high official recalled, Khruschev had caught us "with our pants down." What each of the central participants saw, and what each did to cover both his own and the Administration's nakedness, created the spectrum of issues and answers.

At approximately 9:00 A.M., Tuesday morning, October 16, McGeorge Bundy went to the President's living quarters with the message: "Mr. President, there is now hard photographic evidence that the Russians have offensive missiles in Cuba." [28] Much has been made of Kennedy's "expression of surprise," [29] but "surprise" fails to capture the character of his intial reaction. Rather, it was one of startled anger, most adequately conveyed by the exclamation: "He can't do that to *me!*" [30] In terms of the President's attention and priorities at that moment, Khrushchev had chosen the most unhelpful act of all. Kennedy had staked his full presidential authority on the assertion that the Soviets would not place offensive weapons in Cuba. Moreover, Khrushchev had assured the President through the most direct and personal channels that he was aware of the President's domestic political problem and that nothing would be done to exacerbate this problem. The Chairman had *lied* to the President. Kennedy's initial reaction entailed action. The missiles must be removed.[31] The alternatives of "doing nothing" or "taking

[26] Department of Defense Appropriations, *Hearings,* p. 71.
[27] The details of the ten days between the October 4 decision and the October 14 flight must be held in abeyance.
[28] Abel, *op. cit.,* p. 44.
[29] *Ibid.,* pp. 44 ff.
[30] See Richard Neustadt, "Afterword," *Presidential Power* (New York, 1964).
[31] Sorensen, *Kennedy,* p. 676; Schlesinger, *op. cit.,* p. 801.

a diplomatic approach" could not have been less relevant to *his* problem.

These two tracks — doing nothing and taking a diplomatic approach — were the solutions advocated by two of his principal advisors. For Secretary of Defense McNamara, the missiles raised the spectre of nuclear war. He first framed the issue as a straightforward strategic problem. To understand the issue, one had to grasp two obvious but difficult points. First, the missiles represented an inevitable occurrence: narrowing of the missile gap. It simply happened sooner rather than later. Second, the United States could accept this occurrence since its consequences were minor: "seven-to-one missile 'superiority,' one-to-one missile 'equality,' one-to-seven missile 'inferiority' — the three postures are identical." McNamara's statement of this argument at the first meeting of the ExCom was summed up in the phrase, "a missile is a missile." [32] "It makes no great difference," he maintained, "whether you are killed by a missile from the Soviet Union or Cuba." [33] The implication was clear. The United States should not initiate a crisis with the Soviet Union, risking a significant probability of nuclear war over an occurrence which had such small strategic implications.

The perceptions of McGeorge Bundy, the President's Assistant for National Security Affairs, are the most difficult of all to reconstruct. There is no question that he initially argued for a diplomatic track. [34] But was Bundy laboring under his acknowledged burden of responsibility in Cuba I? Or was he playing the role of devil's advocate in order to make the President probe his own initial reaction and consider other options?

The President's brother, Robert Kennedy, saw most clearly the political wall against which Khrushchev had backed the President. But he, like McNamara, saw the prospect of nuclear doom. Was Khrushchev going to force the President to an insane act? At the first meeting of the Ex-Com, he scribbled a note, "Now I know how Tojo felt when he was planning Pearl Harbor." [35] From the outset he searched for an alternative that would prevent the air strike.

The initial reaction of Theodore Sorensen, the President's Special

[32] Hilsman, *op. cit.*, p. 195.
[33] *Ibid.*
[34] Weintal and Bartlett, *op. cit.*, p. 67; Abel, *op. cit.*, p. 53.
[35] [Arthur M.] Schlesinger, Jr., [*A Thousand Days: John F. Kennedy in the White House* (Boston, 1965)], p. 803.

Counsel and "alter ego," fell somewhere between that of the President and his brother. Like the President, Sorensen felt the poignancy of betrayal. If the President had been the architect of the policy which the missiles punctured, Sorensen was the draftsman. Khrushchev's deceitful move demanded a strong countermove. But like Robert Kennedy, Sorensen feared lest the shock and disgrace lead to disaster.

To the Joint Chiefs of Staff the issue was clear. *Now* was the time to do the job for which they had prepared contingency plans. Cuba I had been badly done; Cuba II would not be. The missiles provided the *occasio*n to deal with the issue: cleansing the Western Hemisphere of Castro's Communism. As the President recalled on the day the crisis ended, "An invasion would have been a mistake — a wrong use of our power. But the military are mad. They wanted to do this. It's lucky for us that we have McNamara over there." [36]

McCone's perceptions flowed from his confirmed prediction. As the Cassandra of the incident, he argued forcefully that the Soviets had installed the missiles in a daring political probe which the United States must meet with force. The time for an air strike was now.[37]

The Politics of Choice. The process by which the blockade emerged is a story of the most subtle and intricate probing, pulling, and hauling; leading, guiding, and spurring. Reconstruction of this process can only be tentative. Initially the President and most of his advisors wanted the clean, surgical air strike. On the first day of the crisis, when informing Stevenson of the missiles, the President mentioned only two alternatives: "I suppose the alternatives are to go in by air and wipe them out, or to take other steps to render them inoperable." [38] At the end of the week a sizeable minority still favored an air strike. As Robert Kennedy recalled: "The fourteen people involved were very significant. . . . If six of them had been President of the U.S., I think that the world might have been blown up." [39] What prevented the air strike was a fortuitous coincidence of a number of factors — the absence of any one of which might have permitted that option to prevail.

[36] *Ibid.*, p. 831.
[37] Abel, *op. cit.*, p. 186.
[38] *Ibid.*, p. 49.
[39] Interview, quoted by Ronald Steel, *New York Review of Books,* March 13, 1969, p. 22.

First, McNamara's vision of holocaust set him firmly against the air strike. His initial attempt to frame the issue in strategic terms struck Kennedy as particularly inappropriate. Once McNamara realized that the name of the game was a strong response, however, he and his deputy Gilpatric chose the blockade as a fallback. When the Secretary of Defense — whose department had the action, whose reputation in the cabinet was unequaled, in whom the President demonstrated full confidence — marshalled the arguments for the blockade and refused to be moved, the blockade became a formidable alternative.

Second, Robert Kennedy — the President's closest confidant — was unwilling to see his brother become a "Tojo." His arguments against the air strike on moral grounds struck a chord in the President. Moreover, once his brother had stated these arguments so forcefully, the President could not have chosen his initially preferred course without, in effect, agreeing to become what RFK had condemned.

The President learned of the missiles on Tuesday morning. On Wednesday morning, in order to mask our discovery from the Russians, the President flew to Connecticut to keep a campaign commitment, leaving RFK as the unofficial chairman of the group. By the time the President returned on Wednesday evening, a critical third piece had been added to the picture. McNamara had presented his argument for the blockade. Robert Kennedy and Sorensen had joined McNamara. A powerful coalition of the advisors in whom the President had the greatest confidence, and with whom his style was most compatible, had emerged.

Fourth, the coalition that had formed behind the President's initial preference gave him reason to pause. *Who* supported the air strike — the Chiefs, McCone, Rusk, Nitze, and Acheson — as much as *how* they supported it, counted. Fifth, a piece of inaccurate information, which no one probed, permitted the blockade advocates to fuel (potential) uncertainties in the President's mind. When the President returned to Washington Wednesday evening, RFK and Sorensen met him at the airport. Sorensen gave the President a four-page memorandum outlining the areas of agreement and disagreement. The strongest argument was that the air strike simply could not be surgical.[40] After a day of prodding and questioning, the air force

---

[40] Sorensen, *Kennedy,* p. 686.

had asserted that it could not guarantee the success of a surgical air strike limited to the missiles alone.

Thursday evening, the President convened the ExCom at the White House. He declared his tentative choice of the blockade and directed that preparations be made to put it into effect by Monday morning.[41] Though he raised a question about the possibility of a surgical air strike subsequently, he seems to have accepted the experts' opinion that this was no live option.[42] (Acceptance of this estimate suggests that he may have learned the lesson of the Bay of Pigs — "Never rely on experts" — less well than he supposed.)[43] But this information was incorrect. That no one probed this estimate during the first week of the crisis poses an interesting question for further investigation.

A coalition, including the President, thus emerged from the President's initial decision that something had to be done; McNamara, Robert Kennedy, and Sorensen's resistance to the air strike; incompatibility between the President and the air strike advocates; and an inaccurate piece of information. . . .[44]

17   *Variations in Agency Power*

FRANCIS E. ROURKE

While all administrative agencies have at least some of the political and professional assets upon which bureaucratic power depends, these agencies vary a great deal in their capacity to exercise

[41] *Ibid.*, p. 691.

[42] *Ibid.*, pp. 691–692.

[43] Schlesinger, *op. cit.*, p. 296.

[44] Space will not permit an account of the path from this coalition to the formal government decision on Saturday and action on Monday.

From Francis E. Rourke, *Bureaucracy, Politics, and Public Policy,* pp. 63–86, by permission of the author and Little, Brown and Company. Copyright © 1969 by Little, Brown and Company (Inc.).

influence over policy decisions. Some agencies are extraordinarily gifted in their ability to achieve their goals, while others often seem to be step-children of the executive branch. At the lowest ebb of its power, an agency may ultimately come to be "an object of contempt to its enemies and of despair to its friends." [1]

Several factors help to shape these variations in agency power. For one thing, agencies differ a great deal in the strength of their constituencies. Some organizations simply enjoy the support of more influential groups than others or have fewer powerful enemies. The nature of an agency's expertise is also of strategic importance, for not all bureaucratic skills command equal respect in the community. Along with these basic resources of constituency strength and expertise, two other factors are highly instrumental in determining the political effectiveness of an administrative agency. One is an agency's organizational vitality. Because of the nature of their mission or the dedication of their personnel, some agencies generate a good deal more energy than others. The second of these instrumental factors is the quality of leadership with which an agency is blessed. However well-endowed it may be in other respects, an agency that is not effectively led will fall far short of attaining the full measure of its potential influence.

While the various factors which help to shape differentials in agency power can thus be sorted out, there is no easy way in which the effectiveness of one source of power can be weighed against another. No common unit of measurement exists for making such comparisons. This is a familiar problem which arises in connection with all efforts to measure power, influence, or authority. [2] It is not, for example, very feasible to use the outcomes of disputes between agencies having apparently different sources of power as a test of the relative value of one kind of power as opposed to another. In the United States at least, the abundance of resources makes it possible to have power contests in which all participants gain at least some of their original objectives. In any case, a single agency may draw power from several different sources, and there is no way of telling how much of an agency's success should be attributed to constituency strength, bureaucratic expertise, organizational vitality, or skillful leadership.

[1] Norton E. Long, *The Polity* (Chicago: Rand McNally & Co., 1962), p. 50.
[2] See Robert A. Dahl, *Modern Political Analysis* (Englewood Cliffs, N.J.: Prentice-Hall, 1963), pp. 39–54.

ADMINISTRATIVE CONSTITUENCIES

The most obviously important characteristic of any agency's political following is its effective size. Differentials in agency power are often alleged to rest more than anything else on the number of people an agency serves as well as upon the strategic dispersion of this clientele around the country. In his comparison of the relative influence of the Corps of Engineers and the Bureau of Reclamation upon water resource policy, Arthur Maass traces the superior influence of the Corps precisely to the fact that it provides significant services to a larger and more strategically located constituency.[3] While the irrigation orientation of the Bureau has largely confined its activities to the Western part of the United States, where rainfall is often sparse, the Corps performs not only irrigation but also navigation, flood-control, harbor dredging, and other water resource functions which give it a substantial constituency in every section of the country.

The number of congressional districts or states in which an agency's activities are significant often provides a convenient measure of the dimensions of an agency's constituency, where this yardstick can be appropriately used. The power of the Department of Defense in American politics in recent years has often been calculated in precisely this way. Observers have linked the influence of the department with the number of congressional districts in which defense contracts are a significant factor in the local economy. A measure of the department's potential influence in the Senate rather than the House can be derived by identifying the number of states in which domestic industries are heavily dependent upon defense contracts.

Certainly, the size and dispersion of an agency's constituency have a very significant bearing upon the scope of its influence, and agencies are understandably interested in increasing the geographical spread of their clientele. The Department of the Interior, for example, has traditionally been regarded in American politics as devoted primarily to the interests of the West. The department's program heavily emphasizes water resource and public land man-

---

[3] Arthur A. Maass, *Muddy Waters* (Cambridge, Mass.: Harvard University Press, 1951).

agement activities that are chiefly of concern in the western states, and in deference to this geographical identification the Secretary of the Interior has customarily been selected from the West. More recently, however, with the establishment of the Bureau of Outdoor Recreation under its jurisdiction, the department has for the first time gained an administrative foothold in the metropolitan areas in the Northeast where both the population and the demand for outdoor recreation have enormously expanded. This new constituency gives the department an opportunity to serve substantial population groups in a part of the country in which it has not previously played a significant role.

The breadth of an agency's following is not, however, the sole determinant of its ability to provide an agency with political support. However large it may be, a clientele that is weak in certain other salient respects will not be in a position to give effective political assistance. A small clientele that is highly self-conscious and dedicated to the pursuit of certain tangible objectives which it shares with the agency can in the last analysis be much more helpful than a large clientele that has neither of these characteristics. For example, consumers as a group represent as large a following as any agency could reasonably hope to command and yet agencies representing consumers have always been notoriously weak in their political position, primarily because consumers lack self-consciousness as a group, are poorly organized, and generally do not have a strong identification with agencies set up to serve their interests.

Lack of cohesion on the part of its constituency may also be highly disadvantageous to an administrative agency. Throughout much of its early history, the National Labor Relations Board suffered greatly from the split in the ranks of the trade union movement it was trying to protect between the AFL and the CIO. The agency often found itself caught in a cross fire between these rival labor organizations even while it was trying to fend off attacks from employers hostile to its very existence.

It might be assumed ordinarily that as the size of an agency's clientele decreases, its ability to provide the agency with effective support will diminish. This does not, however, need to be the case, since a clientele that is dwindling may become, precisely because it is losing its own position of power in society, even more dependent upon a government agency and the services it provides, and hence more intensely devoted to it. The intensity of commitment of its clientele may thus be no less important to an executive agency than the size and cohesion of its following.

Of course, from the point of view of an administrative agency, there is no constituency worse than one whose members are not included within the American voting population. In its successive incarnations as ECA, MSA, FOA, ICA, and AID, the foreign aid agency has been gravely disadvantaged by the fact that it serves foreign groups which do not participate in American elections. In an effort to counter the weakness, the agency's promotional efforts have stressed the fact that many American economic interests benefit from goods produced in this country for eventual shipment overseas as part of foreign aid.

At the opposite extreme is a constituency such as the agricultural population which has always enjoyed a position of high prestige in American society. The view which Jefferson first articulated has never been seriously challenged in American or for that matter in any other society: "The proportion which the aggregate of the other classes of citizens bears in any State to that of its husbandmen, is the proportion of its unsound to its healthy parts." The most remarkable aspect of this attitude is that it has so strongly persisted even though each decade has seen a steady decline in the size of the farm population.[4]

Certainly the strong position of the Department of Agriculture in American bureaucray has not been appreciably weakened by this decline. The ability of the department to maintain its strength even in the face of a sharp contraction in the size of its clientele can partially be attributed to certain traditional characteristics of the American political system, particularly the overrepresentation of rural areas in legislative decisionmaking. It also mirrors the prestigious position of the farmer in American life, and the fact that so many urban residents share the farmers' image of themselves as a chosen people.

The structure of a constituency is also important in determining

[4] The literature bearing on this point is extensive. See, for example, A. Whitney Griswold, *Farming and Democracy* (New York: Harcourt, Brace, 1948), Richard Hofstadter, *The Age of Reform* (New York: Alfred A. Knopf, 1955), and Henry Nash Smith, *Virgin Land* (Cambridge, Mass.: Harvard University Press, 1950).

its value to an agency. As noted earlier, an administrative agency that derives most of its support from a single outside group often finds itself excessively dependent upon the group for political support. As a result the group may acquire the power to prevent an agency from pursuing goals that the organization regards as professionally desirable. There is no certainty that the objectives of a bureaucracy will always mesh with the goals of an interest group upon which it depends for political support. Hence, an agency generally prefers to draw its support from a variety of groups, no one of which possesses substantial control over it, while interest groups favor organizational arrangements which enable them to monopolize rather than share membership in an agency's constituency.

As it has been used in this discussion, the term constituency includes all groups that regard themselves or that are regarded by an agency as benefiting from its work. It is, of course, also possible for many groups on the outside to look upon the agency with hostility, or even to desire its extinction.[5] An agency's power thus rests on a favorable balance of attitudes toward it in the public. In this respect, regulatory agencies are usually worse off than agencies performing service functions. If it vigorously enforces the law it is charged to administer, a regulatory agency is bound to incur the displeasure of segments of the public upon which it imposes constraints. At the same time, the groups on whose behalf regulation is being carried on may be peevishly critical of the agency for not doing more to advance their interests, or, as often happens, these friendly groups may leave the agency to fend for itself once it has been established.

A service agency, on the other hand, ordinarily generates benefits

[5] Some definitions of constituency include hostile as well as friendly groups within their scope. Cf. Matthew Holden, Jr., "'Imperialism' in Bureaucracy," *The American Political Science Review* 60 (December 1966):944. In Holden's view, the constituency of any agency head includes "those who support his ends, those who oppose his ends, and those who wish to intervene for what he regards as 'irrelevant' purposes." Holden also looks upon groups of employees within the agency as "internal constituencies" from the point of view of an agency executive. Murray Edelman, on the other hand, defines administrative constituencies as "the groups which have the power to remove the incumbents or kill the organization if it does not respond to their wishes." See "Governmental Organization and Public Policy," *Public Administration Review* 12 (Autumn 1952):277. Unfortunately, from their point of view, not many groups served by an administrative agency actually have the power "to kill the organization if it does not respond to their wishes."

rather than restrictions upon the public, and the groups it serves usually constitute a solid core of support for the agency's survival and development. Of course, there are great differentials in constituency strength even among such service agencies. Taxpayer opposition to increasing the costs of any program is always possible, and this resistance is not evenly apportioned among all government services. Educational agencies, for example, carry on activities designed to achieve one of the most highly cherished values in American society, and they perform this role for all strata of society. Contrariwise, welfare agencies administer a function that sharply conflicts with the traditional American norm of individual self-reliance, and they perform it for lower-income groups that are unorganized, demoralized and often, as nonwhites, vulnerable to racial prejudice. The class as well as the geographical distribution of a clientele may thus be a strategic factor contributing to its influence.

But again, even with respect to a particular administrative function, there may be wide variations in constituency strength among different governmental jurisdictions. A school system in a large urban center may be buffeted constantly about by the conflicting demands of different neighborhoods for better services — a tension which is particularly acute today between white and nonwhite segments of the community. In a neighboring suburb, inhabited mainly by well-to-do citizens, the educational system may be at the pinnacle of the administrative pyramid — well financed, the teachers highly paid, and the constituency loyal and devoted to the welfare of the schools.

In summary, it can be said that the ideal administrative constituency from the point of view of an executive agency is large and well distributed throughout all strata of society or in every geographical section of the community. It should include devoted supporters who derive tangible benefit from the services an agency provides. However, an administrative agency should not be excessively dependent upon the support of any segment of its constituency, nor should it carry on activities that threaten the interests of substantial outside groups. Finally, the economic or social activities in which a constituency engages should be in accord with the most highly ranked values in the society. To the extent that it has these characteristics, an agency's constituency is in a position to give it effective support toward the achievement of its goals.

VARIETIES OF BUREAUCRATIC EXPERTISE

While all administrative agencies have some degree of expertise in the functions they perform, not all bureaucratic skills exact equal deference from the community. There are some areas in which the notion of expertise is lightly regarded. Or the amount of expertise available in the private sector of society may equal or outweigh that which a government organization commands. In cases of this sort, a public agency is not in a strong position to use its special skills as a source of influence over public policy.

Where there is a lack of respect for the intrinsic function which an agency performs, the search for clientele support can be particularly intense since a strong constituency is imperative for a public agency whose technical proficiency is not held in high esteem. In such a situation an agency may easily become what Burton Clark has described as a "precarious organization" — constantly obliged to curry public favor in order to survive.[6] In the California adult education program which Clark studied, the administrators involved found it very difficult to adhere to professional standards because of the constant need they faced to satisfy their clientele. Decisions on curriculum and personnel came to be based on student demands rather than professional criteria. As Clark explains it: "acceptance is sought on the basis of service rather than on intrinsic educational worth and professional competence."[7]

As a source of power, expertise reaches its fullest development in those organizations which have skills related to the survival of the society. Scientists and military officers, for example, are in a highly advantageous position today to command respect for their particular talents. Professionals in each of these groups exercise powers that may have "life-or-death" consequences for the citizen. In the case of the military professional, the deference which the public accords may be the product of fear as well as respect, since military organizations alone among public agencies have the capacity to take over physical control of the apparatus of the state.

The ascendancy of military professionals within the bureaucracy seems, however, to be a more pronounced characteristic of back-

[6] Burton R. Clark, "Organizational Adaptation and Precarious Values: A Case Study," *American Sociological Review* 21 (June 1956):327–336.
[7] *Ibid.*, p. 335.

ward than of advanced societies. In the so-called emerging nations, the military bureaucracy is in a commanding position in the state because it represents the only well-trained elite and is the most efficiently organized institution in the country.[8] In this context, the military bureaucracy is not subject to effective restraint by either a system of political parties or the countervailing power of civilian agencies. The temptation to seize control of the state is strong, and military coups have, therefore, been a prominent feature of the politics of underdeveloped nations.

In a highly industrialized society like the United States, however, with an extremely well-organized and highly literate population, the influence of the military is offset by that of a variety of other groups and organizations. The military is only one of many skilled professions, and its dominance even in the area of national security policy cannot be assured. The standing of any bureaucratic role is thus shaped in part by the stage of political development a society has reached.

It also varies a good deal from one period of time to another in any particular society. Prior to World War II, American foreign policy was very much the exclusive preserve of the professional diplomat. Following the outbreak of hostilities, however, the military began to exert increasing influence on foreign-policy decisions, and since the war a variety of other skill groups have also come to exercise influence over such decisions. As a result, the Department of State has been hard put in recent years to maintain its hegemony in the field of foreign policy. The skills of a diplomat may be much less relevant to the negotiation of a nuclear test ban treaty than those of a nuclear physicist.

Changes in the state of knowledge play an important part in bringing about these alterations in the status of a particular skill group. The emergence of the new managerial science since World War II — operations research, systems analysis, and a number of other associated techniques — has brought a new group of management specialists to the fore in public as well as private organizations. In the field of military policy these specialists have increasingly come to dominate decisions. Against such software weaponry as "cost-effectiveness" ratios, traditional military tactics as taught at

[8] See Lucian W. Pye, *Aspects of Political Development* (Boston: Little, Brown and Co., 1966), pp. 172–187.

West Point and Annapolis have proved virtually helpless. The hey-day of military ascendancy which the Joint Chiefs of Staff achieved during World War II [9] has been succeeded in more recent times by a Pentagon in which civilian strategists have as much influence as military professionals. Many of these civilians are graduates of Rand rather than West Point, and they have provided civilian policy-makers with an alternative source of expertise in wrestling with decisions on national security strategy.

Two characteristics are especially valuable in enhancing the in-fluence of any body of experts within bureaucracy. The first is the possession of a highly technical body of knowledge which the lay-man cannot readily master, and the second is a capacity to produce tangible achievements which the average man can easily recognize. This combination of obscurity in means and clarity of results seems an irresistible formula for success as far as any professional group is concerned.

In the period since World War II, the natural scientists have been the group most strongly exhibiting these two characteristics in bu-reaucracy. While these scientists may not be quite the "new priest-hood" some writers have claimed, still there is no doubt about the prestige and public respect in which the so-called hard sciences are today held.[10] This standing rests in part upon the awe with which scientific wizardry is regarded by the general public, and in part upon the fact that the natural sciences have been — in the areas of their central concern — so extraordinarily successful in obtaining results, whether in the development of nuclear weapons, the explo-ration of space, or the conquest of disease.

Among social scientists, only economists have achieved compara-ble standing in recent years in the prestige and influence of their ex-pertise in the framing of public policy.[11] This achievement is most highly visible in the increasing stature of the Council of Economic

[9] See Samuel P. Huntington, *The Soldier and the State* (Cambridge, Mass.: Harvard University Press, 1957), pp. 317–324.

[10] For an argument that scientists are in some sense a new "power elite" see Don K. Price, *The Scientific Estate* (Cambridge, Mass.: Harvard University Press, 1965), and Ralph E. Lapp, *The New Priesthood* (New York: Harper & Row, 1965). Cf. also, however, the searching critique of this elitist thesis by Daniel S. Greenberg, "The Myth of the Scientific Elite," *The Public Interest* 1 (Fall 1965):51–62.

[11] Cf. the discussion of this point in Harold L. Wilensky, *Organizational In-telligence* (New York: Basic Books, Inc., 1967), pp. 106–107.

Advisors — which is charged with chief responsibility for making recommendations to the President on the larger economic issues of the day, such as the maintenance of a high level of employment. But it is also apparent in the increasing use of economic skills in other areas of administration, such as the cost-benefit analysis which is coming to play a dominant role in making decisions on the allocation of budgetary resources among administrative agencies. As is the case with natural scientists, economists' growing power is a result of the specialized nature of their discipline — and the fact that they have demonstrated a capacity to help elected officials make the hard choices which the development of public policy entails.

ORGANIZATIONAL ESPRIT

In recent years, no agency of the national government . . . ascended more rapidly into the limelight or more quickly won the esteem of all sections of the community than the Peace Corps. Established in 1961 to help meet the need of the so-called emerging nations for trained manpower, the agency quickly established itself as one of the major successes of the Kennedy administration. Talented young men and women whose aspirations would not normally be directed toward the public service flocked to the Peace Corps from all directions in spite of the fact that the remuneration they received was meager and the conditions under which they were expected to work abroad were uncomfortable and often hazardous.

What this experience suggests is the enormous value an agency can obtain from the performance of a function which excites the imagination of the community. In an analysis of the structure and operation of bureaucratic systems, Amitai Etzioni identifies three kinds of power which organizations exercise over their members coercive, remunerative, and normative.[12] Coercive power is the threat or the actual use of physical control, remunerative control is the use of material rewards as incentives, and normative power rests on the manipulation of "esteem, prestige, and ritualistic symbols."

Looked at from the perspective of this analytical scheme, the Peace Corps presents a striking illustration of a normative organization in the public service. Its power rests on the enthusiasm it has

---

[12] See Amitai Etzioni, *A Comparative Analysis of Complex Organizations* (New York: Free Press of Glencoe, 1961).

been able to generate for its functions from both those who work for it and the community at large. It is not, of course, the only example available of a public agency with this kind of appeal. The marine corps and, in its early history at least, the air force generated a similar kind of zeal and dedication. Military organizations, with a distinctive tradition and a membership drawn from volunteers rather than conscripts, have traditionally provided the most vivid displays of normative commitment in public bureaucracy. The Peace Corps is an unusual demonstration of the capacity of a public agency to ignite enthusiasm without resort to regimental flags, legends of courage, feats of valor, or the other appeals of military life.

Another way to describe the power of an organization like the Peace Corps is to say that it is charismatic, insofar as it evokes a faith and enthusiasm that transcend rational calculation. However, this use of the term "charismatic" differs sharply from that of Max Weber — from whose work the concept of charisma in modern social science is largely derived. In Weber's view, bureaucracy and charisma were antithetical terms. Social movements which began under the leadership of a charismatic leader became bureaucracies as their functions were rationalized and routinized in formal organizations — the sect in the end became a church. "In its economic substructure, as in everything else," Weber wrote, "charismatic domination is the very opposite of bureaucratic domination." [13]

It is possible to discern within bureaucratic organizations themselves a tendency to move from an initial period of enthusiasm and energy to a subsequent stage when the organization becomes routinized and gradually loses a good deal of its original élan. If this transition cannot, in Weber's terminology, be said to mark an evolution from charisma to bureaucracy, it certainly bears a close resemblance to such a transformation. In his description of the "life cycle" of independent regulatory commissions of the national government, Marver Bernstein shows that once such agencies have gotten past an initial stage of youthful zeal, they undergo a process of devitalization which culminates in old age in a period of debility and decline. "Complacency and inertia appear as inevitable devolpments in the life cycle of a commission. Although tradition, precedent, and

---

[13] See H. H. Gerth and C. Wright Mills (Eds.), *From Max Weber: Essays in Sociology* (New York: Oxford University Press, 1946), p. 247.

custom can harden into blind routine in all types of social organization, the commission seems to be peculiarly susceptible to the disease of 'administrative arteriosclerosis.'" [14]

This tendency of established organizations to become wedded to routines and resistant to change has frequently been used to justify the creation of new institutions to administer innovative programs. The establishment by President Franklin D. Roosevelt of a variety of "alphabetical" agencies such as the WPA and the CC in the early 1930s has been widely interpreted as a step on his part to insure that New Deal programs would be carried on with vigor and enthusiasm, rather than being smothered in the red tape and lassitude with which existing agencies would approach their administration.

As far as Roosevelt was concerned, this problem presented itself in a particularly acute form in the case of the Department of Agriculture. Before Roosevelt's time, the Department was strongly committed to a philosophy of confining the national role in agriculture to educational activities channeled through the state extension agencies. The new programs Roosevelt contemplated involved a direct relationship between the national government and the farmer in such fields as rural electrification and soil conservation. Faced with this dilemma, Roosevelt's characteristically diplomatic solution was to establish his programs initially in independent agencies such as the Rural Electrification Administration and the Soil Conservation Service. Then, as these agencies gained sufficient administrative experience and outside political support to insure their viability, he allowed them to be incorporated into the department. By this time the agencies were too strong for the Department to sabotage their mission. Indeed, there was on the contrary reasonable expectation that the agencies might infuse the Department with their own more aggressive attitude toward agricultural administration.[15]

Organizational esprit depends to a large extent upon the development of an appropriate ideology or sense of mission on the part of an administrative agency both as a method of binding outside supporters to the agency and as a technique for intensifying the loyalty

[14] Marver H. Bernstein, *Regulating Business by Independent Commission* (Princeton, N.J.: Princeton University Press, 1955), p. 101.

[15] An analysis of Roosevelt's strategy with respect to administrative organization may be found in Arthur M. Schlesinger, Jr., *The Coming of the New Deal* (Boston: Houghton Mifflin, 1959), pp. 533–552.

of the organization's employees to its purposes. Some of the conservation agencies have developed almost a mystical sense of mission about their function in the administrative apparatus — the preservation of some priceless asset such as the forests, the soil, natural beauty, or historic monuments. This ideology is a powerful force not only in maintaining the esprit of conservation agencies, but also in heightening their impact upon the development of public policy.

Of course not all agencies perform functions which allow them to develop either a persuasive ideology or a sense of esprit. Any agency may seek through public relations activity to "glamorize" its role, but wholly artificial esprit is difficult to sustain. A great many agencies have a forceful sense of mission early in their history, but tend to lose this crusading spirit as they mature. A few agencies have managed to sustain it throughout much of their history, and cases of administrative renaissance are not entirely unknown. But where enthusiastic performance is sought for in the public service, the common practice has been to create new agencies in order to achieve it. This is one of many reasons why bureaucracies tend to multiply.

Administrative Statecraft

The role of leadership in shaping the success of any organization is as elusive as it is important. On frequent occasions the ability of an administrative agency to achieve its goals and to secure the resources necessary for its survival depends directly on the identity of its leader. Early in the Truman administration, Congress made it very clear that the Federal Security Agency would never obtain the status of an executive department as long as Oscar Ewing was at the head of the agency. When Eisenhower became President, and Ewing was succeeded by Oveta Culp Hobby, the proposal to transform the FSA into the Department of Health, Education, and Welfare quickly won congressional approval.

The story of Jesse Jones as Secretary of Commerce provides equally impressive evidence of the importance of leadership to an organization. During Jones's tenure as Commerce Secretary, his ability to command support in Congress and devoted allegiance from the business community was legendary. When Roosevelt removed Jones and appointed Henry A. Wallace as Secretary of Commerce in 1945, Congress immediately proceeded to remove from the department one of its most important constituent bureaus — the

Reconstruction Finance Corporation. And the decisive factor in bringing about this reduction in the scope of the department's jurisdiction was the replacement of Jones by Wallace.[16]

Of course, in appraising the role of leadership in an administrative agency, it should be recognized that leadership in public administration, like leadership in any organizational context, is to a large extent situational — dependent, that is, on factors in the environment other than the leader himself. Jones was successful as Secretary of Commerce in large part because his department served a business constituency that was strong in Congress, and still very powerful in the outside community, but that looked upon Jones as its only real protagonist in the executive branch. The influence Jones exercised was thus a product not only of his own capacities but of the circumstances which prevailed when he was in office. For the conservatives in Congress and the country, Jones was a solid and sensible figure in an otherwise radical administration. For President Roosevelt, Jones was a natural bridge to a constituency in which his administration was generally very weak. Jones's personal attributes thus fit perfectly the role he was called upon to play. He would have been far less successful as Secretary of Labor than he was as Secretary of Commerce, since none of his skills could have overcome easily the hostility in Congress and the business community toward the Department of Labor.

In more recent times Sargent Shriver was widely heralded as the model of successful leadership during his tenure as head of the Peace Corps, and many newspaper accounts appeared celebrating the dexterity with which he handled relations with Congress and the public in advancing the cause of the agency over which he presided. However, in 1965 Shriver took over responsibility for the Office of Economic Opportunity — an agency established to carry on "the war against poverty" in the United States. This assignment produced very little in the way of adulatory comment. But the presumption is strong that Shriver was no less able a leader in the Office of Economic Opportunity than he was in the Peace Corps. The critical change that occurred was in the nature of his assignment — from an agency carrying on generally popular activities abroad that did not threaten any important interests in the United

---

[16] For a brief but enlightening analysis of Jones's career as Secretary of Commerce, see Richard F. Fenno, *The President's Cabinet* (Cambridge, Mass.: Harvard University Press, 1959), pp. 234–247.

States to an agency caught in the turbulence of racial conflict and welfare politics in major American cities.

In short, while an institution is often described as the lengthened shadow of a man, it may be equally correct to say that an executive is the lengthened shadow of an institution, since his own prestige may largely reflect the appeal of the organization he commands. Consequently, an executive who values his reputation as a leader must choose well the institution in which he exercises his talents — to make certain that there is a match between his abilities and the institution's needs. Or better yet, an institution can be one of those rare organizations that so well meets the mood of its time that it is assured of success. But in the end an administrative executive, like Machiavelli's Prince, cannot escape the impact of chance upon the success of his career — being in the right place, at the right time, with the right tactic. As Machiavelli described the fate of leadership: "men are successful while they are in close harmony with Fortune, and when they are out of harmony, they are unsuccessful." [17]

But when this much has been said about the accidental factors which help to determine the success of leadership, it is nonetheless true that executives in quite similar positions in public bureaucracy often have varying degrees of success at their jobs. It seems reasonable to conclude, therefore, that the capacities of a leader can make a difference to an administrative agency and that there are certain skills associated with the effective performance of the executive role in an administrative organization which can be identified as contributing to a leader's success.

Leadership skills in the context of public bureaucracy are of principal value in two areas of an executive's responsibility: (1) externally, in insuring a favorable response to the agency from the outside groups and organizations which control resources upon which it depends; (2) internally, in maintaining the morale of employees of the agency and their commitment to its goals. In large organizations, these external and internal responsibilities of leadership are so complex and demanding that they customarily require considerable specialization, and the organization is in effect run by an executive cabinet in which some individuals are given responsibility for handling external relations, while the duties of others

[17] See *The Prince* in *Machiavelli, The Chief Works and Others,* translated by Allan Gilbert (Durham, N.C.: Duke University Press, 1965), I, 92.

relate primarily to the internal functioning of the institution. However, even under this cabinet system, the head of an agency retains responsibility for the success or failure of the organization, as well as the privilege of choosing his executive associates and of deciding which of his responsibilities he will delegate to them.

As far as the external responsibilities of leadership are concerned, all studies of this subject stress the importance of an executive's ability to create confidence in his own personal and technical capacities among those who control resources the agency needs. The executive must be in some sense a "trusted leader" upon whom others can rely. Fenno's work on the appropriations process suggests that the willingness of Congress to grant an agency the funds it needs to carry on its work is very much determined by the confidence legislators have in the head of the organization.[18]

What an agency head needs to know, therefore, is what techniques will help instill confidence in his abilities within his constituency. On this subject we have some guidelines especially in the area of an executive's relations with legislators — a key elite with which the heads of public agencies normally deal. Studies in this field agree that at appropriations hearings and in other contacts with lawmakers, the head of an agency should display such qualities as honesty and clarity in the presentation of his agency's needs, a passion for economy in the use of public funds, and simplicity and affability of manner in personal contacts.[19]

In executive-legislative relations, it is essential for an agency executive to recognize that Congressmen are in a highly vulnerable political position, subject as they are to removal from office by defeat at the polls. The least the head of any agency can do is avoid, whenever possible, decisions and actions by his agency that may be embarrassing to a Congressman in his own district. On the more positive side, he can take steps to lend the Congressman certain forms of political support. The agency can routinely provide help and information in handling problems which constituents bring to a Congressman, or it may help a Congressman advertise himself by arranging for a well-publicized trip to a field installation, or by allowing him to announce from his office the negotiation of a gov-

[18] Richard F. Fenno, *The Power of the Purse* (Boston: Little, Brown and Co., 1966), pp. 288–291.

[19] See in this regard *ibid.*, pp. 285–291, and Aaron Wildavsky, *The Politics of the Budgetary Process* (Boston: Little, Brown and Co., 1964), pp. 74–84.

ernment contract, or the establishment of an administrative facility that will redound to his credit in his district. If reciprocity is the unwritten if not altogether inviolable law of political life, an executive can reasonably expect that these administrative investments will bring a high rate of political return.

As important as any skill an executive may possess is an ability to communicate successfully with his constituency. Very often the language in which administrative policies are explained and defended is as important to their success as the policies themselves. In the field of higher education, for example, state university officials have frequently demonstrated great skill in the use of metaphors which will bring the distinctive needs of higher learning home to their agricultural constituencies. In a celebrated defense of academic freedom, the regents of the University of Wisconsin stressed their belief that "the great State University of Wisconsin should ever encourage that continual and fearless *sifting and winnowing* by which alone the truth can be found" (italics supplied). A similar sensitivity to the importance of using appropriate language in addressing a constituency was displayed in Texas where in protesting efforts to force the university to spend money from its reserve fund, an administrator vehemently declared that this policy would deprive the school of its "seed-corn." [20]

In all his relations with his various publics it is important that an executive not only have the qualities associated with leadership but that he display these qualities as dramatically as possible. Victor Thompson has stressed the importance of dramaturgy to the effective performance of the leader's role.[21] The successful executive must be skilled in impression management — the ability to convey to others a sense of his own capacities. State university presidents have in recent years concerned themselves not only with being more efficient but also with convincing others that they are running an efficient institution:

it is of vital importance that the state legislature and the tax-paying public . . . be convinced of the soundness of university operations. Under the pressures of competition from other state institutions, a large state university is often forced to put on a dramatic show of scientific

[20] Malcolm Moos and Francis E. Rourke, *The Campus and the State* (Baltimore: The Johns Hopkins Press, 1959), pp. 24–25.

[21] See Victor A. Thompson, *Modern Organization* (New York: Alfred A. Knopf, 1961), pp. 138–151.

objectivity in order to justify its requests for continued support, even though the dramatic props — elaborate formulas, statistical ratios, and so on — may have very little to do with the way in which decisions are actually made within the academic establishment. As one administrative vice-president remarked about the preparation of the university budget, "We simply use the displays that give us the best image . . ." [22]

As they have developed in recent years in higher education, techniques of scientific management may thus serve not so much to manage the university as to manage the impression that outsiders have about the university.

External relations occupy a good deal of the time and attention of the head of any administrative agency. Just as the duties of the President of the United States have increasingly come to center on foreign affairs so executives in public agencies find themselves drawn increasingly into community relations activity, negotiations with other organizations and a variety of other roles that involve the interaction between their organization and its environment. In the words of Herbert Simon:

Observation indicates that, as the higher levels are approached in administrative organizations, the administrator's "internal" task (his relations with the organization subordinate to him) decreases in importance relative to his "external" task (his relations with persons outside the organization). An ever larger part of his work may be subsumed under the heads of "public relations" and "promotion." [23]

But if external relations have become dominant in the performance of the executive role, internal responsibilities have by no means disappeared. Apart from attending to the purely housekeeping chores of management, an executive has such major internal responsibilities as arousing the enthusiasm and the energy of the organization's employees for its objectives, settling disputes and conflicts of interest within the organization, and generally serving as a catalytic agent for the continuous appraisal of existing programs, and the inauguration, whenever necessary, of innovations in policy.

Very often these external and internal responsibilities tend to pull an executive in opposite directions. Decisions he makes to maintain harmony with the outside world may alienate the organi-

[22] See Francis E. Rourke and Glenn E. Brooks, "The 'Managerial Revolution' in Higher Education," *Administrative Science Quarterly* 9 (September 1964):180–181.

[23] Herbert A. Simon, *Administrative Behavior* (New York: The Macmillan Co., 2nd ed., 1957), p. 217.

zation's employees. Conversely, the employees of an agency may push an executive in directions which make it more difficult to maintain good relations with outside groups. While he was Secretary of State, Dean Acheson was a staunch defender of Department of State employees against attacks on their loyalty in Congress — a position which did little to endear him in influential circles of the legislature. On the other hand, his successor, John Foster Dulles, improved his relations with Congress by taking certain steps to tighten security procedures in the department. Since some of these steps were regarded as detrimental to their interests by Department of State employees, Dulles improved the Department's external image at the price of seriously weakening his own standing with its staff.[24]

Hard choices of this kind confront an executive at every turn — the need to balance uncertain gains against certain losses, or perhaps to choose the lesser of two evils in a context in which the question of which is the lesser evil is precisely the issue in doubt. In the case of national agencies, an executive is confronted by a board of directors in the form of a congressional committee which has many members who — for partisan reasons — wish him ill rather than well. The President whom he nominally serves may well abandon him if he gets into trouble. The agency's employees are career bureaucrats who may choose to ignore or defy him, and who cannot easily be disciplined or dismissed. It is in this refractory environment that administrative statecraft must be carried on in the public service, and what is perhaps most remarkable is not that many fail, but that some succeed.

THE PURSUIT OF POWER

If the sources of administrative power are varied, so too are the motives which animate administrative agencies in their quest for primacy. Most clearly apparent is the desire of agencies to strengthen their position to enhance their ability to achieve such manifest goals as better medical care, a more effective system of crime control, or the prevention of water pollution. The statutory objectives of public agencies today are wide-ranging, and in order to fulfill its mission, every agency requires an adequate supply of resources to

[24] See in this regard Norman A. Graebner (Ed.), *An Uncertain Tradition: American Secretaries of State in the Twentieth Century* (New York: McGraw-Hill, 1961), pp. 267–308.

employ personnel and meet the other expenses of organizational life. These resources are easier for the strong to obtain than the weak, so power is sought not for its own sake but because it is an essential prerequisite for carrying on an effective program.

But along with these manifest goals by which agencies are inspired in their quest for power, certain other latent objectives are also commonly present. At the upper reaches of the hierarchy, agency executives may have a strong desire for power as a means of gratifying a personal need for status and the other perquisites of office. On the part of rank-and-file personnel, the pursuit of power may be primarily designed to insure the continuation of certain more tangible rewards which are important to them as civil servants, including adequate salaries, pensions, working conditions, and fringe benefits. The preservation and improvement of these remunerative incentives have become the special responsibility of public employee organizations.[25]

These varied motives for which power is sought are not, of course, necessarily incompatible. An agency may be most capable of serving the public interest when it is led by an ambitious chief executive, who may, while using the agency as a springboard for advancing his own career, bring it to new levels of achievement in its capacity for public service. A private vice can, as Adam Smith long ago noted, often be transformed into a public virtue. The community may also be as well served if rank-and-file employees are allowed to gratify their continuing desire for improvements in remuneration and working conditions. There are certainly reasonable grounds for believing that satisfied employees will be more efficient than those who cherish grievances. Public and private interests may thus dovetail neatly together, in the best of all possible administrative worlds.

There are, however, other less attractive possibilities. The personal goals of agency employees may gain a distinct priority over the actual purposes for which the agency was created. This distortion occurs in its worst form in cases of administrative corruption,

[25] The divergence between the goals of individuals and the goals of the organizations of which they are members is a recurring theme in organization theory. See especially the work of Chris Argyris, *Personality and Organization: The Conflict Between System and the Individual* (New York: Harper, 1957), and *Interpersonal Competence and Organizational Effectiveness* (Homewood, Ill.: Dorsey Press, 1962).

where some members of a law-enforcement agency, for example, look upon its power not as a means of protecting the safety of the public, but as an instrument for extorting tribute from the individuals engaged in the illegal activity they are supposed to be suppressing. In situations of this kind, the needs of the public recede altogether, and administrative power is sought merely to advance the private goals of agency employees.

Of course, the private interests which members of an administrative agency serve need not necessarily be their own. As noted earlier, there are many public agencies which, either in their initial establishment or eventual development, exist mainly as satellite organizations for outside groups. A licensing board, for example, may be set up for the manifest public purpose of insuring that certain professional standards are adhered to in the practice of a particular skill. But in actual fact the latent function of such an agency may be that of limiting entry into the profession to protect the economic position of present members of the group, thus inflicting costs upon the public it is supposed to serve.

Less obvious but no less difficult are the cases in which public organizations are in a position to justify their pursuit of power on the basis of disinterested criteria such as service to the public, when in point of fact, power is sought only to advance the interests of the organization's members. In this category would be pessimistic assessments by the armed forces of a potential enemy's capabilities and intentions which are contrived in order to pressure the public into supporting an expansion in the strength of the military.

Whatever its motives may be in seeking greater authority, an agency must constantly reckon with the fact that an expansion in jurisdiction does not always result in an expansion in power. While bureaucracies are often pictured as being implacably imperialist in their desire to expand their jurisdiction, in actual fact there are occasions when an agency may increase its power by narrowing, or refusing to expand, the scope of its legal authority. According to Sayre and Kaufman, for example, the agencies in New York City's government

. . . compete to avoid program assignments that are especially difficult and controversial. The Commissioner of Hospitals and the Commissioner of Correction have both tried to prevent lodging responsibility for treatment of narcotics addicts in their departments, and the Department of

Health has been restive under burdens of building inspection the Commissioner and the Board of Health would generally prefer to have placed entirely on the Department of Buildings.[26]

Thus, in the quest for power an agency's strategy has to be one of optimizing rather than maximizing its jurisdiction. Activities that have weak political support, are inordinately expensive, or that divert an agency from its essential purposes represent liabilities rather than assets from the point of view of an agency's power balance.

Perhaps the most embarrassing kind of jurisdiction an agency can acquire is control over an activity that is anathema to its own constituency. This was the unhappy fate of the Department of Labor in 1963, when it was put in charge of administering the Landrum-Griffin Act, a statute designed to protect union members from abuses of power by their own officers. Prior to its enactment this legislation had been bitterly fought by the labor organizations that represent the Department's chief source of outside support, and since 1963 the Department of Labor has discharged its responsibilities in this area with a notable lack of enthusiasm.[27] In cases of this kind, administration of the law may become in fact nullification of the law, or, as some would put it, sabotage of its intent.

It should be borne in mind that executive agencies, like all contestants in the struggle for power, operate with imperfect knowledge regarding the kinds of strategy that will advance their interests. An agency may, for example, strongly resist measures which it feels will reduce its authority, only to find, when the changes actually take place, that no such effects have occurred. In advancing or protecting its power interests, as on other matters, an executive agency thus operates within the limits of what Herbert Simon calls "bounded rationality" [28] . . . the course of action best calculated to achieve its objectives is not always clear to it.

[26] Wallace S. Sayre and Herbert Kaufman, *Governing New York City* (New York: Russell Sage Foundation, 1960), p. 262.

[27] A similar case involving the failure of the Federal Power Commission to enforce the Natural Gas Act is cited by Holden, *op. cit.*, p. 945.

[28] See Herbert Simon, *Models of Man* (New York: John Wiley & Sons, Inc., 1957), pp. 196–206.

V

BUREAUCRATIC POLITICS
AND ADMINISTRATIVE REFORM

Efforts to reform public administration in the United States have largely centered on management problems connected with the organization and operation of government agencies, such activities as the hiring of personnel, the handling of funds, and the division of labor among various segments of the organization. The focus has been on the efficient use of the men, money, and materials entrusted to government agencies to achieve the goals of these organizations at a minimum cost to the taxpayers. Underlying most such reform efforts has been a view of the administrative system as entirely separate from the needs and pressures of the political process.

I

This image of administration liberated from political influence has dominated the field of personnel reform for nearly a century. Since Congress passed the Pendleton Act in 1883, reformers have sought to isolate the hiring and firing of administrative personnel from the machinations of political parties. These efforts have been crowned with success, at least at the national level. Political parties are no longer able to make wholesale use of jobs in the federal government as rewards for deserving party members, however incompetent these appointees might be for these positions.

However, in "The Growth of the Federal Personnel System," Herbert Kaufman shows that the success of reformers in purging the civil service of the influence that political parties had once exerted soon threatened a serious erosion in public control over bureaucratic decision-making in the national government. (Not to mention, as he also demonstrates, that personnel reform has not always had happy results from the viewpoint of managerial efficiency.) As a result, recent years have seen some tendency to return to earlier practice. Presidents have been authorized to make an increased number of top-level appointments on the basis of political loyalty. It has slowly been recognized that responsiveness to public control, as well as competence in official duties, is an indispensable characteristic of the bureaucrat in a democratic society.

On the urban scene, the consequences of reform in personnel administration have been even more dramatic. As Theodore J. Lowi shows in "Machine Politics — Old and New," boss-rule under Tammany was eliminated from New York politics at the cost of leaving each of the city's major bureaucracies virtually free of outside control. As a result, programs these bureaucracies disapprove of can only be carried on with great difficulty, and problems they are not interested in may suffer total neglect. New York is perhaps unique in the tenacious autonomy of its municipal employee groups, yet the problems which it presents may well prefigure difficulties that will become increasingly important in other cities as well as in national politics.

II

In the case of fiscal administration, the reform movement has consistently flirted with the notion that the budgetary process can be structured entirely around such neutral criteria as efficiency and productivity. In his "Political Implications of Budgetary Reform," Aaron Wildavsky challenges this belief. He argues that no system of budgeting can be devised that will not have political or policy effects.[1] Ulti-

---

[1] Wildavsky is thus highly critical of the latest reform in national budgetary practices, the planning-programming-budgeting system (PPBS). See Aaron Wildavsky, "Rescuing Policy Analysis from PPBS," *Public Administration Review* 29 (March/April 1969): 189–

mately, decisions on how the government is to spend money are political decisions. No budgetary theory can ignore the choices involved in the budget, choices deeply affected by the shifting weight of political influence in Congress and in the public at large, as well as by changes in popular conceptions of what is important to spend money for. Budgeting, at least as it bears on the central issue of allocating expenditures among various competing programs, is inextricably linked with politics in the sense of power and politics in the sense of policy.

Organizational reform reveals a similar pattern, as described by Harold Seidman in "The Politics of Government Organization." Reformers have long sought to win acceptance for what they regard as completely nonpolitical principles of administrative organization, such as the centralization of administrative authority at the top of executive agencies and the grouping of like functions of government into cohesive departments. But efforts to apply these so-called rational principles of organization in redesigning administrative structures inevitably meet with resistance from those who regard them as having far-reaching political effects. Many agencies feel that changes in their administrative location will threaten to effect a significant loss in their status and ability to influence policy. Moreover, the groups they serve, including both outside organizations and legislative committees, commonly look upon such changes as reducing their own access to, and influence over, policy deliberations.

To be sure, these perceptions of the consequences of administrative reform for politics and policy are not always accurate. In administrative reorganization, for example, many effects that opponents anticipate from such changes never occur. An agency's power is not greatly affected by a shift in its administrative location or structure, and its clientele groups enjoy no less access and influence than they had previously enjoyed. Moreover, much alteration in operating procedures can be accomplished without arousing substan-

---

202. For a defense of PPBS, see in the same issue (pp. 137–151), Allen Schick, "Systems Politics and Systems Budgeting."

tial political concerns — in personnel training and records management, for instance. But means affect ends in public administration as elsewhere, and it is not unreasonable to expect that reforms making significant changes in organizational instruments may have a profound impact on the goals achieved through executive operations.

18 The Growth of the Federal Personnel System

HERBERT KAUFMAN

NEUTRALIZING THE CIVIL SERVICE (1883–1954)

The Attack on Spoils. A great many things were blamed on the spoils system during the fight to overthrow it. Every evidence of dishonesty. Every display of incompetence. Every suggestion of inefficiency. Everything low and mean and degrading that ever occurred in the government service was blamed on the spoils system. Indeed, one merit system enthusiast, looking back to the days of spoils, even charged that the spoils system encouraged prostitution:

Some young women in despair, losing hope at the loss of their jobs, went wrong on the town, for Washington like other cities big and little had its red light district. . . .

It is said that young women suddenly deprived of their positions under the spoils system were sometimes driven by extremity to those notorious resorts.

Oh! the pity of it. Strangers in a strange city unexpectedly turned out of office, their salary then too small to permit of savings, without funds or friends, the amiable madam's [sic] of the oldest trade in the world hospitally [sic] extended a welcome to these unfortunate recruits, and the folks back home unknowingly continued to enjoy the wages of sin of an erring daughter whom of course they still thought a Government employee.

It was not really necessary to resort to near-hysterical accusations to discredit spoils. The disadvantages of this means of staffing government agencies were profound and obvious enough not to require

From Herbert Kaufman, "The Growth of the Federal Personnel System," in Wallace S. Sayre, Editor, *The Federal Government Service*, Second Edition © 1965 by The American Assembly, Columbia University, New York, New York. Reprinted by permission of Prentice-Hall, Inc., Englewood Cliffs, N.J.

artistic heightening. In the long run, the government service tended to deteriorate under these conditions. Spoils may have democratized politics; it threatened to degenerate administration as it continued completely unchecked. The government, it is true, continued to do its job under spoils — but at what cost? For how long could it have continued to do so after the rise of specialization? How well was it working?

The spoils system put a premium on the creation of extra jobs — both to provide additional political currency and also to lighten the workload so that loyal political partisans would have time for their assigned political tasks.

It resulted in the employment of many individuals who were not qualified to perform the duties for which they were hired.

It tempted government officials to use their official positions for personal gain, for they had generally only four years in which to reap the harvest for which they had labored long and hard in the political vineyards.

It meant that a good deal of energy went into the orientation and basic training of a new work force every four years.

It reduced the President to the level of petty job broker, and diverted his strength and attention from important matters of state to the dispensation of hundreds of posts under the greatest pressure. The President gained bargaining leverage, but at the price of his health and vigor, his peace of mind, and the dignity and decorum of his high office. The executive mansion was besieged. The chief executive could not escape to protect either the nation's welfare or his own sanity.

All these concomitants of spoils were clearly visible even to the most dispassionate observer. They moved men of conscience and goodwill to strive for reform.

The Beginnings of Reform. The reformers adopted a simple but drastic formula to correct the defects of the civil service system. Since they ascribed the defects almost entirely to politically motivated appointments and removals, they proposed to take these powers out of the hands of the politicians. They planned to vest the control of these personnel actions in a relatively independent nonpolitical body that would administer examinations to screen applicants for vacancies, and that would act to prevent dismissal for purely political reasons. The politicians were accused of corrupting the public service; the reformer's remedy was to isolate the public service from their machinations. . . .

Neutrality through Isolation. The provisions of the Civil Service Act of 1883 reflect the reformer's conviction that power to make appointments had to be transferred in large part, if not entirely, from political officers to a nonpolitical agency as they believed it had been in England. . . .

What the law did, in effect, was to substitute the Commission for congressional and party officials in providing appointment advice to the President and his department heads. The politicians had determined who would be in the public service on the basis of the political contributions made by the applicants; the Commission would now make the same determination, but on the basis of fitness for office evaluated by examinations. . . .

The New Dilemmas

The Line Administrators Complain. In recent years, as the merit system began to push toward its upper limits, words of criticism have been heard from the very people the system was designed to assist and protect — the line administrators. Top management personnel of the line agencies, their organizations now protected against the raids of the spoilsmen, have begun to pray for deliverance from their guardians. They do not deny that it would be impossible to conduct effective administrative operations if their staffs were inexpert because of the influence of politics, but they add that good administration is difficult also if personnel management is taken partly out of their hands.

No adequate explanation of this seeming paradox is possible unless two closely related facts are taken into account. One is . . . that the federal government moved into areas calling for increasingly intensive specialization on the part of its work force. The other is that the component elements of the civil service, developing a continuity (as a result of the merit system) and a sense of the importance and difficulty of their work (as a result of specialization), began to display an awareness of themselves as identifiable bodies in society and a deep interest in expanding and perfecting the programs they administered; in a word, they gradually came to exhibit the characteristics of a series of sizable bureaucracies. Party loyalty of the patronage days gave way to program and professional loyalty.

As a result, the members of the line agencies, from top to bottom, grew more intolerant of incompetence than even the reformers; they developed a greater interest than the reformers in the ability of their own membership. In the first place, dedicated as they are to the welfare of their agencies and their programs, they are unwilling to see these jeopardized by unproficiency; they have an ideological stake to preserve. In the second place, the esprit de corps of the organizations and their prestige in the community engendered insistence by members of line organizations upon capable personnel; identification with, and pride in, his group constitutes another stake for each civil servant. In the third place, as government workers became more and more skilled and professional, they tended to grow resentful of newcomers who received the same rewards without the same qualifications; this was another investment for them to keep safe. All in all, then, the forces at work among government employees thrust in the direction of higher attainment. To be sure, there are tendencies in the *other* direction, too, generated by the new conditions of government work. Members of tight-knit organizations become emotionally attached to each other and to the old ways of doing things, and when it becomes necessary to make any changes in either or both, strong currents of resistance appear; hardening of administrative arteries is another facet of bureaucratization. But the fact remains that federal government employment, considered overall, has become more like a profession, and federal officials are as concerned about professional standards for their membership as anyone else.

Now, when the officers of the line agencies try to take personnel actions considered routine in the business world, they are on occasion prevented from doing what they want by the interpretations placed on laws, rules, and regulations by the staff of the Civil Service Commission. Often therefore, before even making a move, agencies check with the Commission staff to see if the proposal will meet with disapproval. And even if they secure approval, it is often slow in coming; delays are chronic. Let them try to fill a vacancy, to transfer a man, to promote someone, to increase an employee's pay by changing the position-class to which his job is allocated, to take any of a host of such ordinary steps, and they encounter the Commission.[1]

[1] Dismissal for other than political or religious reasons, as well as other forms of discipline are not, as is often popularly believed, impossible under the competitive system. They can be and are invoked by administrative officers, al-

To a line officer, this hardly makes sense. He is not less anxious than the Commission to protect the merit system. Moreover, he is apt to feel he knows the employment situation in his technical field a good deal better than anyone on the Commission. Yet he feels hemmed in from every side. The labyrinthine procedures developed to keep politics out of administration are alleged to have grown into prisons for administrators, and many administrators charge that they, like the spoilsmen, are treated by the Commission as the enemy. Their every move is suspect; the very machinery constructed to promote energetic, creative, imaginative administration, they bewail, now obstructs it. This complaint is common in Washington; it is an old story in administrative circles.

Bureaucracy and the Powers of Government. At the same time that the professionalization of the service was producing dissatisfaction with the Civil Service Commission among line administrators, a kind of uneasiness sprang up among other students and practitioners of American government.

The great, sprawling complex of organizations that constitutes the executive branch is, as we have seen, a patchwork. It was put together by bits and pieces, each added as the need for it was felt, piled on the rest without any real effort at system or order; as one outstanding administrative committee once put it, it grew like a farm — a wing added to the house now, a new barn put up later, a shed built some other time, a silo at one stage, a corn crib at another, until it was spread over the landscape in a haphazard and thoroughly confusing way. America's pragmatic genius assembled this crazy quilt because problems were attacked as they arose; it might have been done more tidily had we been functioning on a smaller scale, but we were conquering a vast and rich continent, and the rough edges of the structures we built in the process could be smoothed off whenever there was time. Besides, through the spoils system, the parties exerted substantial influence on the shape of American public administration; the parties were, and remain, highly decentralized, and it was almost inevitable, therefore, that they should help produce a fragmented pattern.

Each fragment, despite its formal subordinancy to the President,[2]

---

though relatively infrequently because the process is often laborious and time-consuming before it is over.

[2] Including it should be noted, the Civil Service Commission.

became a local center of power. Congress, not out of preference but out of necessity delegated to them authority to "sub-legislate" — that is, to issue, within the framework provided by statute, rules and regulations binding upon the people to whom they applied — and to make administrative adjudications — that is, to decide cases involving individual citizens in a quasi-judicial fashion. At first, the courts attacked this blurring of what had traditionally been considered the boundaries of the separate legislative, executive, and judicial branches, but eventually, reluctantly admitted the inevitability of the new phenomenon in view of the needs of an industrial civilization, and administrative law took its place beside the common law, the law of equity, and statutory law. For a long time, each agency secured its own appropriations directly from Congress; there was no central review in either the executive or legislative branches. Each agency became influential with respect to the formulation of legislation in its own sphere of expertness, and much of the legislation enacted by Congress originates with the agencies themselves. Every segment of the executive branch has thus become a decisionmaking center, and if every decision, considered individually, is not of great significance, all of them taken in the aggregate are of tremendous importance.

Congress, too, is fragmented; the real work of Congress is done in its numerous committees, and it is in the committees that much of the real legislative power resides. With a decentralized party system, a diffused legislature, a splintered executive, and a plethora of interest groups exerting pressure at all these points, there was for a long time no place at all in the government where a coordinated policy could be worked out and a unified set of plans devised for accomplishing the ends selected. The operation of the government in each policy area devolved upon clusters of administrative agencies, congressional committees, and interest groups.[3]

One consequence of this arrangement — or nonarrangement — with its lack of central control and direction, was the rise of familiar administrative defects in a most acute form. Agencies not only duplicated each other's work; one would sometimes unwittingly undo what others had carefully done. They not only pursued contradictory ends; they sometimes became involved in administrative wars

[3] This applies to the Civil Service Commission, too, whose support in Congress and among reform organizations enhances its independence of the President.

of incredible bitterness and long duration over the shaping of policy and its execution.

A second consequence was the appearance of "self-directing bureaucracies," the agencies that began to function almost autonomously, behaving less like parts of a large team than as individual, independent establishments. With the end of the spoils system, the civil service has been growing steadily into a corps of specialists who outlast political officers. The politicians come and go; the civil servants remain. The transients are amateurs, laymen; the permanent body is expert. In the relations between the two groups, it was often the political officers who felt themselves at a disadvantage, psychologically, factually, technically. Political control declined somewhat in force; some agencies went into virtual freewheeling and others partially so.

If it were not for the rise of this autonomy, the defects of unplanned administrative growth might be easier to remedy; if it were easier to control all the executive agencies, it might be simpler to do away with the clashes and contradictions and other inefficiencies that characterize the executive branch. It is not surprising, therefore, that insulation of the civil service from political influence came under questioning. Is it possible, ask some political scientists, that insulation from political influence contributes to insulation from political control (a problem that never occurred under the spoils system)? Is it possible, inquire some administrative experts, that the way our system of personnel administration operates deprives the President, as chief administrator of the nation, of an important tool of management? Neither political scientists nor administrative experts advocate return to the spoils system, nor do they ascribe to one cause a complex phenomenon that is obviously the product of a large number of things. All that their questions imply is that the triumph of the merit system may not be without its own administrative difficulties.

Problems of Party and Policy Leadership. But administrative problems were not the only ones intensified by the rise of the isolated personnel system. . . . Jobs in the government service have long been used as political currency by Presidents, enabling them to establish their authority as leader of their parties and to provide leadership in the formulation and execution of policy; our fragmented legislative body is far less able to perform these functions. Up to now, every President has found some device to provide himself with the necessary currency. But the merit system has been pushed almost to its limit now, and the likelihood of the rise of a parallel bureaucracy comparable to that built under President Roosevelt seems low. The supply of currency of this kind is thus almost at an end — as long as our chief executives continue to respect the practices that have now become personnel traditions.

There is perhaps insufficient evidence to reach any hard and fast conclusions about the impact of this state of affairs on presidential-congressional relations, but there is enough to warrant some concern about the attenuation of leadership in the federal government today and the tendency of the government to become paralyzed as a result of conflict among its component political (as well as administrative) units or as a consequence of the simultaneous pursuit of mutually contradictory ends by its political (as well as administrative) constituent elements. It appears to be more than a coincidence that these symptoms should manifest themselves just at the time the patronage has been reduced to a very low point. That is not to say patronage is the only device that can keep our governmental system from flying apart, but the decline of patronage brought in its train many consequences besides those advertised by the reformers, and it is important to keep these in view in order to maintain perspective on the questions with which we are here concerned.

The Rise of Anti-isolationism. It appears to the political scientists and administrative experts that a single remedy might help meliorate the complaints of the line administrators, the lack of coordination in government and parties, the declining ability of political officers to control the increasingly specialized bureaucracy, and the ebb of governmental leadership. That remedy, they say, is reintegration of all the tools of management in the hands of administrators at every level. Even political control, they contend, would be easier to restore if fragmentation were reduced. They (one is almost tempted to speak of them as the counterreformists) have therefore turned their energies to an overhaul of the administrative machinery of the federal government with an eye to effecting the remedy they propose.

Strengthening the President — perhaps we should say the Presidency, as an institution rather than a man — constitutes the core of their recommendations. They have concentrated more heavily on the presidency alone than on the lower levels of administration as a matter of tactics and strategy, although they are interested in all levels; more than half their total battle would be won if they could succeed at the presidential level. They have concentrated on the executive branch because, under our system of government, it is the natural center for political and administrative integration. Constitutionally, the President is the head of the administration, and, in all likelihood, if the Constitution had not endowed him with that power, the course of events would have done so; the need for a strong executive has become not a matter of free choice but something imposed by the pressure of modern history. Moreover, the President and Vice-President are the only officers of the federal government elected by the people of the entire country; no other elected public official anywhere in the United States has a constituency even remotely approaching the size of theirs. It was inevitable that the new movement should gravitate toward the chief executive.

This movement has by no means been confined to personnel administration; on the contrary, the management of the civil service is only a part of it. The first target was the installation of an executive budget — a budget system giving the President some control over the program and financial planning of all the agencies under his command, and, by this means, enabling him to provide coordination and balance for the executive branch as a whole. A second target of the proponents of a stronger presidency was the acquisition by the President of authority to reorganize the executive branch of government by transferring and consolidating units of departments. A third target was building up the executive office of the President as an instrument of managerial leadership.

All of these targets have been fulfilled in substantial degree; the last thirty-five years have seen the adoption of the Budget and Accounting Acts, the Reorganization Acts, and the growth of the executive office. The anti-isolationists scored heavily in these areas.

Personnel Administration as a Phase of Anti-isolationism. Establishing the President in a position to provide the principal initiative in personnel policies and to direct and supervise the federal work force was another of the targets, set up for the same purpose as all the others — to strengthen him sufficiently to discharge his political and administrative responsibilities. Here, the progress of anti-isolationism has been less pronounced. The most forthright proposal for action to this end was the recommendation by the Committee on Administrative Management in 1937 that the Civil Service Commission be abolished entirely, the responsibility for personnel management assigned to a personnel director serving in the President's immediate official family, and the guardianship of the merit system charged to a Civil Service Board with advisory and investigatory powers but no administrative authority. This measure was designed to return to the chief executive the personnel powers that were his in form, but that in substance were actually wielded by a Civil Service Commission functioning, like other specialized agencies, with remarkable independence. A single officer, close to the President and the problems of the line agencies, would be more apt to interpret its mission in terms of program accomplishments, it was contended, than in terms of technical compliance with detailed regulations regardless of the effect on administration. In any event, the change in the composition and location of the personnel agency would have had a symbolic value for strengthening the President that was not to be overlooked in calculating the desirability of the suggested reorganization.

Nothing came of this 1937 proposal, however, and the first major change in the Civil Service Commission's structure did not take place until 1949. Accepting the recommendations of the Hoover Commission, President Truman offered a Reorganization Plan (under the provisions of the Reorganization Act) which Congress allowed to go into effect; it separated the administrative functions of the Civil Service Commission (examination, classification, enforcement, internal operation, etc.) from its rule-making and appellate duties. The administrative functions were assigned to the Chairman of the Commission alone, the others to the Chairman and two additional Commissioners sitting as the Commission. The Chairman is assisted by an Executive Director. Under President Eisenhower, moreover, the Chairman was moved into the White House and invited to attend cabinet meetings, thus bringing him into closer contact with the heads of the line agencies than had been the case when there was a Liaison Officer for Personnel Management on the White House staff whose job it was to keep the Commission apprised of developments; the present Chairman is in constant personal touch with events, events he now has a hand in shaping. So the government moved toward the goal of the anti-isolationists.

There were other steps in the same direction. The Classification Act of 1949 authorized allocation of positions to position-classes by agencies without prior reference to the Commission (though subject to post-audit and revision by the Commission, and even to revocation of the allocation authority). The Commission granted agencies a larger role in the examining process, and in other personnel management practices, subject to its supervision. It also strengthened its field organization — it operates through fourteen regional offices — to speed service to the nine-tenths of the federal bureaucracy located outside Washington. At every level, integration of the personnel process with the other tools and responsibilities of management was being accomplished gradually. . . .

Some have recoiled from the doctrines of this school of thought. They deny isolation of personnel administration at present, pointing out that the President can remove Commissioners at will. They dispute the charge that the Civil Service Commission has caused problems of control. They question some of the complaints. But most of all, they express the conviction that the course of action proposed in the name of integration would lead ultimately to the return of the spoils system and the loss of the accomplishments of three-quarters of a century.

And here the situation stands today. In the days of the fight against the spoilsmen, it was not difficult for men concerned with good government to choose their sides. But now that a different issue is involved, they may be found in both camps. Here, plainly, is a problem for long and careful thought.

The End of the Cycle. The history of the federal government service began with emphasis on ability to serve — tempered, it is true, by concern for the old soldiers, the old civil servants, the claims of the states to proportional representation in the government service, and for political loyalties, but with heavier emphasis on ability than any other criterion. Jackson altered the emphasis; he put the stress on political service. But he did not forget the other criteria altogether, and neither did the other Presidents in the days of spoils. Nevertheless, while their practices resulted in the democratization of American politics and administration, they introduced evils that became intolerable. The reformers succeeded in driving out spoils by isolating the civil service from politics, and ability was once more enthroned in the highest position, although some of the other criteria continued to win recognition. Yet as the reformers moved closer to full attainment of their goals, even opponents of the spoils system began to develop anxieties about control of the vast administrative machine that had developed, and professional administrators complained that they were prevented from operating effectively because of the web of Civil Service Commission regulations and surveillance constricting them. A move to restore personnel administration from an isolated position to a place as an integral part of the President's administrative powers has sprung up to solve these problems. But some of the reformers warn of a return to the spoils system. Are we about to start the same cycle again?

Of one thing we may be sure at the outset: In a changing world, there will be no permanent solution, no panacea. Every formula will become outdated before long. The question that must be answered is, what kind of system will satisfy our present requirements and the needs we can see in the near future?

19   *Machine Politics—Old and New*

THEODORE J. LOWI

New York city government, like government in almost all large American cities except Chicago, is a product of Reform. It is difficult to understand these cities without understanding the two strains of ideology that guided local Reform movements throughout the past three-quarters of a century. *Populism* and *efficiency,* once the foundation of most local insurgency, are now almost universally triumphant. These two tenets are now the orthodoxy in local practice.

Populism was originally a statement of the evils of every form of bigness in the city, including big business, big churches, big labor, as well as big political organizations. Decentralization was an ulti-

From Theodore J. Lowi, "Machine Politics — Old and New," reprinted by permission of the author and the publisher, The University of Chicago Press, from *The Public Interest,* No. 9 (Fall 1967), pp. 83–92. Copyright © 1967 National Affairs, Inc. This extract covers pages 85–89.

mate goal. In modern form, it has tended to come down to the aim of eliminating political parties, partisanship, and if possible "politics" itself.

Efficiency provided the positive program to replace that which is excised by populist surgery. The doctrine calls essentially for the centralization and rationalization of government activities and services to accompany the decentralization of power. Some Reformers assumed that services do not constitute power. Others assumed the problem away altogether by positing a neutral civil servant who would not abuse centralized government but who could use it professionally to reap the economies effected by rationalization and by specialization. That was the secret of the business system; and, after all, the city is rather like a business. ("There is no Republican or Democratic way to clean a street.")

While there are many inconsistent assumptions and goals between the doctrines of populism and efficiency, they lived well together. Their coexistence was supported by the fact that different wings of the large, progressive movement they generated were responsible for each. Populism was largely the province of the working class, "progressive" wing. Doctrines of efficiency were very much the responsibility of the upper class wing. Populism resided with the politician-activists. Efficiency was developed by the intellectuals, including several distinguished university presidents, such as Seth Low, Andrew Dickson White, Harold Dodd, and, preeminently, Woodrow Wilson, who, while still a professor of political science, wrote a classic essay proclaiming the virtues of applying Prussian principles of administration in the United States.

These two great ideas were, by a strange and wonderful chemistry, combined into a movement whose influence forms a major chapter of American history. Charters and laws have been enacted that consistently insulate city government from politics, meaning party politics. It has become increasingly necessary, with each passing decade, to grant each bureaucratic agency autonomy to do the job as each commissioner saw fit, as increasingly appointments were made of professionals in each agency's fields.

On into the 1960s, the merit system extends itself "upward, outward, and downward," to use the Reformers' own rhetoric. Recruitment to the top posts is more and more frequent from the ranks of those who have made careers in their agencies, party backgrounds increasingly being a mark of automatic disqualification. Reform has succeeded in raising public demand for political morality and in making "politics" a dirty word. A "good press" for mayors results from their determination to avoid intervening in the affairs of one department after another. The typical modern mayor is all the more eager to cooperate because this provides an opportunity to delegate responsibility. Absolution-before-the-fact for government agencies has become part of the mayoral swearing-in ceremony.

Reform has triumphed and the cities are better run than ever before. But that is, unfortunately, not the end of the story, nor would it have been the end of the story even had there been no Negro revolution. The triumph of Reform really ends in paradox: *Cities like New York became well-run but ungoverned.*

THE NEW MACHINES

Politics under Reform are not abolished. Only their form is altered. *The legacy of Reform is the bureaucratic city-state.* Destruction of the party foundation of the mayoralty cleaned up many cities but also destroyed the basis for sustained, central, popularly-based action. This capacity, with all its faults, was replaced by the power of professionalized agencies. But this has meant creation of new bases of power. Bureaucratic agencies are not neutral; they are only independent.

Modernization and Reform in New York and other cities has meant replacement of Old Machines with New Machines. The bureaucracies — that is, the professionally organized, autonomous career agencies — are the New Machines.

Sociologically, the Old Machine was a combination of rational goals and fraternal loyalty. The cement of the organization was trust and discipline created out of long years of service, probation, and testing, slow promotion through the ranks, and centralized control over the means of reward. Its power in the community was based upon services rendered to the community.

Sociologically, the New Machine is almost exactly the same sort of an organization. But there are also significant differences. The New Machines are more numerous, in any given city. They are functional rather than geographic in their scope. They rely on formal authority rather than upon majority acquiescence. And they probably work with a minimum of graft and corruption. But these differences do not alter their definition; they only help to explain why the New Machine is such a successful form of organization.

The New Machines are machines because they are relatively ir-responsible structures of power. That is, each agency shapes impor-tant public policies, yet the leadership of each is relatively self-perpetuating and not readily subject to the controls of any higher authority.

The New Machines are machines in that the power of each, while resting ultimately upon services rendered to the community, de-pends upon its cohesiveness as a small minority in the midst of the vast dispersion of the multitude.

The modern city has become well-run but ungoverned because it has, according to Wallace Sayre and Herbert Kaufman, become comprised of "islands of functional power" before which the modern mayor stands denuded of authority. No mayor of a modern city has predictable means of determining whether the bosses of the New Machines — the bureau chiefs and the career commissioners — will be loyal to anything but their agency, its work, and related profes-sional norms. Our modern mayor has been turned into the likes of a French Fourth Republic Premier facing an array of intransigent parties in the National Assembly. These modern machines, more monolithic by far than their ancient brethren, are entrenched by law, and are supported by tradition, the slavish loyalty of the news-papers, the educated masses, the dedicated civic groups, and, most of all, by the organized clientele groups enjoying access under exist-ing arrangements.

ORGANIZED DECENTRALIZATION

The Reform response to the possibility of an inconsistency be-tween running a city and governing it has been to assume the exist-ence of the Neutral Specialist, the bureaucratic equivalent to law's Rational Man. The assumption is that, if men know their own spe-cialties well enough, they are capable of reasoning out solutions to problems they share with men of equal but different technical com-petencies. That is a very shaky assumption indeed. Charles Frank-el's analysis of such an assumption in Europe provides an appropriate setting for a closer look at it in modern New York; ". . . different [technical] elites disagree with each other; the ques-tions with which specialists deal spill over into areas where they are *not* specialists, and they must either hazard amateur opinions or ignore such larger issues, which is no better . . ."

During the 1950s, government experts began to recognize that, despite vast increases in efficiency flowing from the defeat of the Old Machine, New York city government was somehow lacking. These concerns culminated in the 1961 Charter, in which the office of Mayor was strengthened in many impressive ways. But it was quickly discovered that no amount of formal centralization could definitively overcome the real decentralization around the Mayor. It was an organized disorganization, which made a mockery of the new Charter. The following examples, although drawn from New York, are of virtually universal application:

1. Welfare problems always involve several of any city's largest agencies, including Health, Welfare, Hospitals, etc. Yet during more than forty years, successive mayors of New York failed to reorient the Department of Health away from a "regulative" toward a "service" concept of organization. And many new aspects of welfare must be set up in new agencies if they are to be set up at all. The new poverty programs were set up very slowly in all the big cities — except Chicago.

2. Water pollution control has been "shared" by such city agencies as the Departments of Health, Parks, Public Works, Sanitation, Water Supply, and so on. No large city, least of all New York, has an effective program to combat even the local contributions to pollution. The same is true of air pollution control, although for some years New York has had a separate department for this purpose.

3. Land-use patterns are influenced one way or another by a large variety of highly professional agencies. It has proven virtually impossible in any city for one of these agencies to impose its criteria on the others. In New York, the opening of Staten Island by the Narrows Bridge, in what may be the last large urban frontier, found the city with no plan for the revolution that is taking place in property values and land uses in that borough.

4. Transportation is also the province of agencies too numerous to list. Strong mayors throughout the country have been unable to prevent each from going its separate way. To take just one example: New York pursued a vast off-street parking program, at a cost of nearly $4,000 per parking space, at the very moment when local rail lines were going bankrupt.

5. Enforcement of civil rights is imposed upon almost all city agencies by virtue of federal, state, and local legislation. But efforts to set up public, then City Council, review of police processes in New York have been successfully opposed by professional police officials. Efforts to try pairing and busing on a very marginal, ex-

perimental basis have failed. The Police Commissioner resigned at the very suggestion that values other than professional police values be imposed upon the Department, even when the imposition came via the respected tradition of "legislative oversight." The Superintendent of Education, an "outsider," was forced out; he was replaced by a career administrator. One education journalist at that time said: "Often . . . a policy proclaimed by the Board [of Education], without the advice and consent of the professionals, is quickly turned into mere paper policy . . . The veto power through passive resistance by professional administrators is virtually unbeatable. . . ."

The decentralization of city government toward its career bureaucracies has resulted in great efficiency for the activities around which each bureaucracy was organized. The city is indeed well-run. But what of those activities around which bureaucracies are not organized, or those which fall between or among agencies' jurisdictions? For these, as suggested by the cases above, the cities are suffering either stalemate or elephantiasis — an affliction whereby a particular activity, say, urban renewal or parkways, gets pushed to its ultimate "success" totally without regard to its importance compared to the missions of other agencies. In these as well as in other senses, the cities are ungoverned. . . .

20   Political Implications of Budgetary Reform

AARON WILDAVSKY

A large part of the literature of budgeting in the United States is concerned with reform. The goals of the proposed reforms are couched in similar language — economy, efficiency, improve-

From Aaron Wildavsky, "Political Implications of Budgetary Reform," reprinted by permission of the author and The American Society for Public Administration from *Public Administration Review* 21 (Autumn 1961):183–190. For a fuller treatment of this subject, see also by Wildavsky, *The Politics of the Budgetary Process* (Boston: Little, Brown and Co., 1964).

ment, or just better budgeting. The President, the Congress and its committees, administrative agencies, even the interested citizenry are all to gain by some change in the way the budget is formulated, presented, or evaluated. There is little or no realization among the reformers, however, that any effective change in budgetary relationships must necessarily alter the outcomes of the budgetary process. Otherwise, why bother? Far from being a neutral matter of "better budgeting," proposed reforms inevitably contain important implications for the political system, that is for the "who gets what" of governmental decisions. What are some of the major political implications of budgetary reform and where should we look to increase our knowledge about how the budget is made? We begin with the noblest vision of reform: the development of a normative theory of budgeting that would provide the basis for allocating funds among competing activities.

A Normative Theory of Budgeting?

In 1940, in what is still the best discussion of the subject, V. O. Key lamented "The Lack of a Budgetary Theory." He called for a theory which would help answer the basic question of budgeting on the expenditure side: "On what basis shall it be decided to allocate X dollars to Activity A instead of Activity B?" [1] Although several attempts have been made to meet this challenge,[2] not one has come close to succeeding. No progress has been made for the excellent reason that the task, as posed, is impossible to fulfill.[3] The search for an unrealizable goal indicates serious weaknesses in prevailing conceptions of the budget.

If a normative theory of budgeting is to be more than an academic exercise, it must actually guide the making of governmental decisions. The items of expenditures which are passed by Congress, enacted into law, and spent must in large measure conform to the theory if it is to have any practical effect. This is tantamount to

---

[1] V. O. Key, Jr., "The Lack of a Budgetary Theory," *The American Political Science Review* 34 (December 1940):1137–1144.

[2] Verne B. Lewis, "Toward a Theory of Budgeting," *Public Administration Review* 12 (Winter 1952):42–54; "Symposium on Budgetary Theory," *Public Administration Review* 10 (Spring 1954):20–31; Arthur Smithies, *The Budgetary Process in the United States* (New York, 1955).

[3] Key, in fact, shies away from the implications of his question and indicates keen awareness of the political problems involved. But the question has been posed by subsequent authors largely in the terms in which he framed it.

prescribing that virtually all the activities of government be carried on according to the theory. For whatever the government does must be paid for from public funds; it is difficult to think of any policy which can be carried out without money.

The budget is the lifeblood of the government, the financial reflection of what the government does or intends to do. A theory which contains criteria for determining what ought to be in the budget is nothing less than a theory stating what the government ought to do. If we substitute the words "what the government ought to do" for the words "ought to be in the budget," it becomes clear that a normative theory of budgeting would be a comprehensive and specific political theory detailing what the government's activities ought to be at a particular time. A normative theory of budgeting, therefore, is utopian in the fullest sense of that word; its accomplishment and acceptance would mean the end of conflict over the government's role in society.

By suppressing dissent, totalitarian regimes enforce their normative theory of budgeting on others. Presumably, we reject this solution to the problem of conflict in society and insist on democratic procedures. How then arrive at a theory of budgeting which is something more than one man's preferences?

The crucial aspect of budgeting is whose preferences are to prevail in disputes about which activities are to be carried on and to what degree, in the light of limited resources. The problem is not only "how shall budgetary benefits be maximized?" as if it made no difference who received them, but also "who shall receive budgetary benefits and how much?" One may purport to solve the problem of budgeting by proposing a normative theory (or a welfare function or a hierarchy of values) which specifies a method for maximizing returns for budgetary expenditures. In the absence of ability to impose a set of preferred policies on others, however, this solution breaks down. It amounts to no more than saying that if you can persuade others to agree with you, then you will have achieved agreement. Or it begs the question of what kind of policies will be fed into the scheme by assuming that these are agreed upon. Yet we hardly need argue that a state of universal agreement has not yet arisen.

Another way of avoiding the problem of budgeting is to treat society as a single organism with a consistent set of desires and a life of its own, much as a single consumer might be assumed to have a stable demand and indifference schedule. Instead of revenue being raised and the budget being spent by and for many individuals who may have their own preferences and feelings, as is surely the case, these processes are treated, in effect, as if a single individual were the only one concerned. This approach avoids the central problems of social conflict, of somehow aggregating different preferences so that a decision may emerge. How can we compare the worth of expenditures for irrigation to certain farmers with the worth of widening a highway to motorists and the desirability of aiding old people to pay medical bills as against the degree of safety provided by an expanded defense program?

The process we have developed for dealing with interpersonal comparisons in government is not economic but political. Conflicts are resolved (under agreed upon rules) by translating different preferences through the political system into units called votes or into types of authority like a veto power. There need not be (and there is not) full agreement on goals or the preferential weights to be accorded to different goals. Congressmen directly threaten, compromise, and trade favors in regard to policies in which values are implicitly weighted, and then agree to register the results according to the rules for tallying votes.

The burden of calculation is enormously reduced for three primary reasons: first, only the small number of alternatives which are politically feasible at any one time are considered; second, these policies in a democracy typically differ only in small increments from previous policies on which there is a store of relevant information; and third, each participant may ordinarily assume that he need consider only his preferences and those of his powerful opponents since the American political system works to assure that every significant interest has representation at some key point. Since only a relatively few interest groups contend on any given issue and no single item is considered in conjunction with all others (because budgets are made in bits and pieces), a huge and confusing array of interests is not activated all at once.

In the American context, a typical result is that bargaining takes place among many dispersed centers of influence and that favors are swapped as in the case of logrolling public works appropriations. Since there is no one group of men who can necessarily impose their preferences upon others within the American political system, special coalitions are formed to support or oppose specific policies. Support is sought in this system of fragmented power at numerous centers of influence — congressional committees, the congressional leadership, the President, the Budget Bureau, interdepartmental committees, departments, bureaus, private groups, and so on. Nowhere does a single authority have power to determine what is going to be in the budget.

THE POLITICS IN BUDGET REFORM

The seeming irrationalities [4] of a political system which does not provide for even formal consideration of the budget as a whole (except by the President who cannot control the final result) has led to many attacks and proposals for reform. The tradition of reform in America is a noble one, not easily to be denied. But in this case it is doomed to failure because it is aimed at the wrong target. If the present budgetary process is rightly or wrongly deemed unsatisfactory, then one must alter in some respect the political system of which the budget is but an expression. It makes no sense to speak as if one could make drastic changes in budgeting without also altering the distribution of influence. But this task is inevitably so formidable (though the reformers are not directly conscious of it) that most adversaries prefer to speak of changing the budgetary process, as if by some subtle alchemy the irrefractible political element could be transformed into a more malleable substance.

The reader who objects to being taken thus far only to be told the obvious truth that the budget is inextricably linked to the political system would have a just complaint if the implications of this remark were truly recognized in the literature on budgeting. But this is not so. One implication is that by far the most significant way of influencing the budget is to introduce basic political changes (or to wait for secular changes like the growing industrialization of the South). Provide the President with more powers enabling him to control the votes of his party in Congress; enable a small group of

[4] See Charles E. Lindblom, "The Science of 'Muddling' Through," *Public Administration Review,* Vol. 19 (Spring, 1959), pp. 79–88, for a description and criticism of the comprehensive method. See also his "Decision-Making in Taxation and Expenditure" in National Bureau of Economic Research, *Public Finances: Needs, Sources, and Utilization* (Princeton, 1961), pp. 295–327, and his "Policy Analysis," *American Economic Review* 48 (June 1958):298–312.

Congressmen to command a majority of votes on all occasions so that they can push their program through. Then you will have exerted a profound influence on the content of the budget.

A second implication is that no significant change can be made in the budgetary process without affecting the political process. There would be no point in tinkering with the budgetary machinery if, at the end, the pattern of budgetary decisions was precisely the same as before. On the contrary, reform has little justification unless it results in different kinds of decisions and, when and if this has been accomplished, the play of political forces has necessarily been altered. Enabling some political forces to gain at the expense of others requires the explicit introduction and defense of value premises which are ordinarily missing from proposals for budgetary reform.

Since the budget represents conflicts over whose preferences shall prevail, the third implication is that one cannot speak of "better budgeting" without considering who benefits and who loses or demonstrating that no one loses. Just as the supposedly objective criterion of "efficiency" has been shown to have normative implications,[5] so a "better budget" may well be a cloak for hidden policy preferences. To propose that the President be given an item veto, for example, means an attempt to increase the influence of the particular interests which gain superior access to the chief executive rather than, say, to the Congress. Only if one eliminates the element of conflict over expenditures, can it be assumed that a reform which enables an official to do a better job from his point of view is simply "good" without considering the policy implications for others.

Arthur Smithies may stand as a typical proponent of a typical reform. Identifying rationality with a comprehensive overview of the budget by a single person or group, Smithies despairs of the fragmented approach taken by Congress and proposes a remedy. He suggests that a Joint (congressional) Budget Policy Committee be formed and empowered to consider all proposals for revenue and expenditure in a single package and that their decisions be made binding by a concurrent resolution. And he presents his reform as a moderate proposal to improve the rationality of the budget process.[6] If the proposed Joint Committee were unable to secure the passage

[5] Dwight Waldo, *The Administrative State* (New York, 1948); Herbert A. Simon, "The Criterion of Efficiency," in *Administrative Behavior*, 2nd ed. (New York, 1957), pp. 172–197.

[6] Smithies, *op. cit.*, pp. 192–193 ff.

of its recommendations, as would surely be the case, it would have gone to enormous trouble without accomplishing anything but a public revelation of futility. The impotence of the Joint Committee on the Legislative Budget,[7] the breakdown of the single congressional attempt to develop a comprehensive legislative budget,[8] and the failure of congressional attempts to control the Council of Economic Advisors [9] and the Budget Bureau,[10] all stem from the same cause. There is no cohesive group in Congress capable of using these devices to affect decision making by imposing its preferences on a majority of Congressmen. Smithies' budgetary reform presupposes a completely different political system from the one which exists in the United States. To be sure, there is a name for a committee which imposes its will on the legislature and tolerates no rival committees — it is called a *cabinet* on the British model. In the guise of a procedural change in the preparation of the budget by Congress, Smithies is actually proposing a revolutionary move which would mean the virtual introduction of the British parliamentary system if it were successful.

Smithies suggests that his proposals would be helpful to the President. But the membership of the Joint Committee would be made up largely of conservatives from safe districts who are not dependent on the President, who come from a different constituency than he does, but with whom he must deal in order to get any money for his programs. Should the Joint Committee ever be able to command a two-thirds vote of the Congress, it could virtually ignore the President

[7]Avery Leiserson, "Coordination of the Federal Budgetary and Appropriations Procedures under the Legislative Reorganization Act of 1946," *National Tax Journal* 1 (June 1948):118–126.

[8] Robert Ash Wallace, "Congressional Control of the Budget," *Midwest Journal of Political Science* 3 (May 1959):160–162; Dalmas H. Nelson, "The Omnibus Appropriations Act of 1950," *Journal of Politics* 15 (May 1953):274–288; Representative John Phillips, "The Hadacol of the Budget Makers," *National Tax Journal* 4 (September 1951):255–268.

[9] Roy Blough, "The Role of the Economist in Federal Policy-Making," *University of Illinois Bulletin*, Vol. 51 (November 1953); Lester Seligman, "Presidential Leadership: The Inner Circle and Institutionalization," *Journal of Politics* 18 (August 1956):410–426; Edwin G. Nourse, *Economics in the Public Service: Administrative Aspects of the Employment Act* (New York, 1953); Ronald C. Hood, "Reorganizing the Council of Economic Advisors," *Political Science Quarterly* 69 (September 1954):413–437.

[10] Fritz Morstein Marx, "The Bureau of the Budget: Its Evolution and Present Role II," *The American Political Science Review* 39 (October 1945):363–398; Richard E. Neustadt, "The Presidency and Legislation: The Growth of Central Clearance," *ibid.*, 48 (September 1954):631–671; Seligman, *op. cit.*

in matters of domestic policy and run the executive branch so that it is accountable only to the committee. . . .

WHAT DO WE KNOW ABOUT BUDGETING?

The overriding concern of the literature on budgeting with normative theory and reform has tended to obscure the fact that we know very little about it. Aside from the now classical articles on congressional oversight of administration by Arthur Macmahon,[11] an excellent study of internal budgetary procedures in the army by Frederick C. Mosher,[12] and an interesting case history by Kathryn S. Arnow,[13] there is virtually nothing of substance about how or why budgetary decisions are actually made. Of course, the general literature on decision making in national government provides some valuable propositions, but it is not keyed in to the budgetary process. Yet the opportunities for developing and testing important propositions about budgetary decisions are extraordinarily good and I would like to suggest a few of the many possible approaches here.

How do various agencies decide how much to ask for? Most agencies cannot simply ask for everything they would like to have. If they continually ask for much more than they can get, their opinions are automatically discounted and they risk a loss of confidence by the Budget Bureau and Appropriations subcommittees which damages the prospects of their highest priority items. The agencies cannot even ask for all that they are authorized to spend because their authorizations commonly run way ahead of any realistic expectation of achievement. At the same time, they do not wish to sell themselves short. The result is that the men who make this choice (an official title is no certain guide to whom they are) seek signals from the environment — supporting interests, their own personnel, current events, last year's actions, attitudes of Congressmen, and so on — to arrive at a composite estimate of "what will go." A combination of interviews, case studies, and direct observation should enable the researcher to determine what these signals are, to construct propositions accounting for the agencies budgetary position, and to generally recreate the environment out of which these choices come.

[11] Arthur W. Macmahon, "Congressional Oversight of Administration," *Political Science Quarterly* 58 (June, September 1943):161–190, 380–414.

[12] Frederick C. Mosher, *Program Budgeting:* Theory and Practice, with Particular Reference to the U.S. Department of the Army (Public Administrative Serivce, 1954).

[13] *The Department of Commerce Field Offices,* Inter-University Case Series No. 21 (Alabama, 1954).

Once having decided what they would like to get, how do agencies go about trying to achieve their objectives? Today, we do not even have a preliminary list of the most common strategies used by participants in trying to influence budgetary outcomes. Again, the techniques listed above should bring the necessary data to light.

Perhaps a few examples will demonstrate the importance of understanding budgetary strategies. There are times when an agency wishes to cut its own budget because it has lost faith in a program, for internal disciplinary reasons, or because it would like to use the money elsewhere. If the agency is particularly well endowed with effective clientele groups, however, it may not only fail in this purpose but may actually see the appropriation increased as this threat mobilizes the affected interests. One budget officer informed me that he tried to convince the Budget Bureau to undertake two projects which the agency did not want but which several influential Congressmen felt strongly about. Otherwise, the official argued, the Congressmen would secure their desires by offering additional projects to their colleagues. The Budget Bureau turned him down and the result was nine unwanted projects instead of two.

The appearance of a budget may take on considerable importance, a circumstance which is often neglected by proponents of program budgeting. Suppose that an agency has strong clientele backing for individual projects. It is likely to gain by presenting them separately so that any cut may be readily identified and support easily mobilized. Lumping a large number of items together may facilitate cuts on an across-the-board basis. Items lacking support, on the other hand, may do better by being placed in large categories so that it is more difficult to single them out for deeper slashes. . . .

Another approach would be to locate and segregate classes of administrative officials who are found by observation to have or not to have the confidence of the appropriations committees and to seek to explain the differences. For if there is any one thing which participants in budgeting are likely to stress, it is the importance of maintaining relations of confidence and they are highly conscious of what this requires. Since it appears from preliminary investigation that the difference is not accounted for by the popularity of the agency or its programs, it is possible that applications of some gross psychological and skill categories would reveal interesting results.

Many participants in budgeting (in the agencies, Congress, the Budget Bureau) speak of somehow having arrived at a total figure which represents an agency's or an activity's "fair share" of the budget. The fact that a fair share concept exists may go a long way toward explaining the degree of informal coordination that exists among the participants in budgeting. Investigation of how these figures are arrived at and communicated would help us understand how notions of limits (ceilings and floors) enter into budgetary decisions. A minimum effort in this direction would require the compilation of appropriations histories of various agencies and programs rather than just individual case histories which concentrate on some specific event or moment in time. Investigation of the Tennessee Valley Authority's experience in securing electric power appropriations, over a twenty-five-year period, for example, reveals patterns and presents explanatory possibilities which would not otherwise be available.[14]

By its very nature the budgetary process presents excellent opportunities for the use of quantitative data although these must be used with great caution and with special attention to their theoretical relevance. Richard Fenno has collected figures on thirty-seven bureaus dealing with domestic policies from 1947 to 1958 from their initial estimates to decisions by the Budget Bureau, appropriations committees in both houses, conference committees, and floor action. Using these figures he expects to go beyond the usual facile generalizations that the House cuts and the Senate raises bureau estimates, to the much more interesting question of determining the conditions under which the patterns that do exist actually obtain.[15] Although such data do not by any means tell the whole story, they can be used to check generalizations about patterns of floor action or conference committee action which would not otherwise be possible.

After giving the matter considerable thought, I have decided that it would not be fruitful to devise a measure which would ostensibly give an objective rank-ordering of bureaus and departments according to their degree of success in securing appropriations. The first measure which might be used would be to compare an agency's initial requests with its actual appropriations. The difficulty here is

[14] See Aaron B. Wildavsky, "TVA and Power Politics," *The American Political Science Review* 55 (September 1961):576–590.

[15] From a research proposal kindly lent me by Richard Fenno. See also his excellent paper, "The House Appropriations Committee as a Political System: The Problem of Integration," [*The American Political Science Review* 56 (June 1962):310–324].

that agency estimates are not merely a measure of their desire but also include a guess as to what they can reasonably expect to get. The agency which succeeds in getting most of what it desires, therefore, may be the one which is best at figuring out what it is likely to get. A better measure, perhaps, would be an agency's record in securing appropriations calculated as percentages above or below previous years' appropriations. But this standard also leads to serious problems. There are fortuitous events — sputnik, a drought, advances in scientific knowledge — which are beyond the control of an agency but which may have a vital bearing on its success in getting appropriations. Indeed, some "affluent agencies" like the National Institutes of Health may find that there is little they can do to stop vast amounts of money from coming in; they may not even be able to cut their own budgets when they want to do so. Furthermore, agencies generally carry on a wide variety of programs and the total figures may hide the fact that some are doing very well and others quite poorly. Thus it would be necessary to validate the measure by an intensive study of each agency's appropriations history and this would appear to make the original computation unnecessary.

The purpose of this suggested research . . . is to formulate empirically valid propositions which will be useful in constructing theories (general explanations) accounting for the operation and outcomes of the budgetary process. A theory of influence would describe the power relationships among the participants, explain why some are more successful than others in achieving their budgetary goals, state the conditions under which various strategies are or are not efficacious, and in this way account for the pattern of budgetary decisions.

With such a theory, it would become possible to specify the advantages which some participants gain under the existing system, to predict the consequences of contemplated changes on the distribution of influence, and to anticipate sources of opposition. Possibly, those desiring change might then suggest a strategy to overcome the expected resistance. But they would not, in their scholarly role, accuse their opponents of irrationality in not wishing to have their throats cut. . . .

21   The Politics of Government Organization

HAROLD SEIDMAN

Organizational arrangements are not neutral. We do not organize in a vacuum. Organization is one way of expressing national commitment, influencing program direction, and ordering priorities. Organizational arrangements tend to give some interests, some perspectives, more effective access to those with decisionmaking authority, whether they be in the Congress or in the executive branch. As Richard Neustadt has pointed out: "In political government, the means can matter quite as much as the ends; they often matter more." [1]

Institutional location and environment, administrative arrangements and type of organization, can raise significant political questions concerning the distribution and balance of power between the executive branch and the Congress; the federal government and state and local governments; states and cities; the federal government and organized interest groups, particularly the principal beneficiaries of federal programs; and finally, among the components of the executive establishment itself, including the President's relationship to the departments and the bureaucracy.

If our democratic system is to be responsive to the needs of *all* our people, organization structure and administrative arrangements need to so balance the competing interests within given program areas that none is immune to public control and capable of excluding less powerful segments of our society from effective participation in the system and an equitable share of its benefits. Failure to maintain this balance has contributed to the present malaise.

President Eisenhower in his farewell address to the nation warned against "the acquisition of unwarranted influence, whether sought

Adapted from *Politics, Position, and Power: The Dynamics of Federal Organization* by Harold Seidman. Copyright © 1970 by Oxford University Press, Inc. Reprinted by permission. Footnotes are renumbered.

[1] Richard E. Neustadt, *Presidential Power — The Politics of Leadership* (New York: John Wiley & Sons, Inc., 1960), p. 47.

or unsought, by the military-industrial complex." Other complexes, notably the science-education and agricultural establishments, wield power equal to or exceeding that of the perhaps overly dramatized military-industrial combine. Scientific research is said to be the only pork barrel for which the pigs determine who gets the pork.

The political implications of organization structure were recognized as early as 1789 when the states endeavored to control the extension of federal power by limiting the creation of executive departments. In 1849 the bill to establish the Department of the Interior was opposed because "it meant the further extension of Federal authority to the detriment of the states." [2] Opposition to the establishment of the Department of Housing and Urban Development in the 1960s stemmed from much the same concern.

Application of "economy and efficiency" as the criteria for government organization can produce serious distortions, if political and environmental factors are ignored. It led the first Hoover Commission to proceed from the indisputable finding that the Farmers Home Administration's functions duplicated and overlapped those of the Farm Credit Administration and Agricultural Extension Service to the seemingly logical conclusion that the Administration ought to be liquidated and its functions divided between its two competitors. The conclusion was obviously faulty to anyone in the least familiar with the histories of the Farm Credit Administration and the Extension Service as creatures of the American Farm Bureau Federation and the most conservative elements in the agricultural community. The Farm Bureau was proud of its role in scuttling the Rural Resettlement Administration and Farm Security Administration, the immediate predecessors of the FHA.[3] If there were ever a case of letting the goats loose in the cabbage patch, this was it. The FHA was created to furnish special assistance to farmers who constitute marginal risks and possess little political clout. Commissioners Acheson, Pollock, and Rowe observed in their dissent that "the purpose of the Farmers Home Administration is to make

[2] Lloyd M. Short, *The Development of National Administrative Organization in the United States* (Baltimore: The Johns Hopkins Press, 1923), p. 89.

[3] For excellent analyses of the role played by the American Farm Bureau Federation in organizational politics see Sidney Baldwin, *Poverty and Politics*, University of North Carolina Press, 1968; Philip Selznick, *TVA and the Grass Roots*, University of California Press, 1949.

'good' tenant farmers out of 'poor' tenant farmers, and not to restrict credit to 'good' tenant farmers who can probably obtain credit from other sources." [4]

Some now question whether the Farmers Home Administration or any other agency within a department so conceived and so organized as the Department of Agriculture can respond adequately to the needs of the rural poor in the South, most of whom are black. It was no concidence that the 1968 Poor People's Campaign in Washington singled out the Department of Agriculture for special attention. The Citizens Board of Inquiry into Hunger and Malnutrition in the United States asserted that the Department of Agriculture and the congressional Agriculture Committees are "dominated by a concern for maximizing agricultural income, especially within the big production categories. Other objectives always yield to this one . . . almost never does our agricultural policy take a direct concern with the interests of consumers." [5] The Board proposed reorganization and removal of food programs from Agriculture's jurisdiction as the answer.

Powerful groups in the commercial banking, research, and educational communities regard overlapping and duplication not as vices, but positive virtues. The American Bankers Association through the years has successfully blocked efforts to consolidate bank supervisory and examining functions in a single federal agency. The division of responsibility among the Comptroller of the Currency, the Federal Deposit Insurance Corporation, and the Federal Reserve Board is viewed by the ABA as "wholly in keeping with the broad principle that the success and strength of democracy in America is largely due to the sound safeguards afforded by the wisely conceived checks and balances which pervade our composite governmental system." [6] The system is defended because banks retain the option of changing their federal supervisors and thus gaining "some possible relief from unduly stringent examinations." [7]

[4] The Commission on Organization of the Executive Branch of the Government, "Federal Business Enterprises," A Report to the Congress, March 1949, p. 102.

[5] Reprinted in hearings before the Subcommittee on Executive Reorganization of the Senate Committee on Government Operations on "Modernizing the Federal Government," January–May 1968, p. 355.

[6] American Bankers Association, "Reply to Questionnaire of U.S. Senate Committee on Banking and Currency," April 1941, p. 65.

[7] Ibid., p. 67.

Whatever advantages may have been gained by these "checks and balances" now appear to be more than offset by the loss of power within the councils of government. Without a single spokesman, the common interests of the commercial banks may be obscured in a chorus of discordant voices. This was a matter of little importance when most commercial banks enjoyed de facto monopolies and did not face competition from newly chartered commercial banks and an aggressive, politically wise savings and loan industry. The commercial banks are now in a position where they might be better served by organizational arrangements designed to stimulate and influence, not prevent, federal action. Unwillingness to abandon long cherished positions is not the exclusive disease of government bureaucracies.

Overlapping and duplication among federal agencies making research grants do not alarm scientists and educators. On the contrary, diversity in support is held essential to maximize the opportunities for obtaining federal funds and to minimize the dangers of federal control. The Committee on Science and Public Policy of the National Academy of Sciences strongly endorsed a "plural system" which has many roots for its authority "and many alternative administrative means of solving a given problem." [8]

Assignment of administrative jurisdiction can be a key factor in determining program direction and ultimate success or failure. Each agency has its own culture and internal set of loyalties and values which are likely to guide its actions and influence its policies. A number of satellites grow up and around and outside the institution and develop a mutual dependence. Private bureaucracies in Washington now almost completely parallel the public bureaucracies in those program areas where the federal government contracts for services, regulates private enterprise, or provides some form of financial assistance.

Shared loyalties and outlook knit together the institutional fabric. They are the foundation of those intangibles which make for institutional morale and pride. Without them, functions could not be decentralized and delegated with the confidence that policies will be administered consistently and uniformly. But because people believe what they are doing is important and the way they have been

[8] National Academy of Science, "Federal Support of Basic Research in Institutions of Higher Learning," Washington, D.C., 1964.

taught to do it is right, they are slow to accept change. Institutional responses are highly predictable, particularly to new ideas which conflict with institutional values and may pose a potential threat to organizational power and survival. Knowledgeable Budget Bureau officials estimate that agency positions on any major policy issue can be forecast with nearly 100 per cent accuracy, regardless of the administration in power.

There is an ever-present danger that innovative programs which challenge accepted norms, demand new skills and approaches, and create conflicts with agency constituencies will be assimilated into the "system" and their purposes muffled or distorted. One way to kill a program is to house it in a hostile or unsympathetic environment.

The Congress tacked a rider to the 1953 RFC Liquidation Act authorizing the President to designate an agency to make loans to public bodies for the construction or acquisition of public facilities.[9] Budget Bureau staff recommended that the Housing and Home Finance Agency be designated because its mission was most closely related to urban and community development, but the then Budget Director preferred Treasury "because it wouldn't make the loans." Treasury obviously would be less susceptible to pressure from state capitols and city halls and could be expected to apply strict banking criteria in reviewing loan applications. The final solution was not to make any designation. The Congress solved the problem by enacting legislation vesting program responsibility in the Housing and Finance Agency.

In their zeal to construct neat and uncluttered organization charts, professional reorganizers and reorganization commissions tend to downgrade, when they do not wholly ignore, environmental influences. Certainly, the poverty program would have been different, whether better or worse depends on one's point of view, if, as many advocated, responsibility at the outset had been given either to the Department of Health, Education, and Welfare or, the choice of the big-city mayors, the Department of Housing and Urban Development. Creation of a new agency is likely to present fewer problems than reform of an old one and enables the President and the Congress to finesse competing jurisdictional claims. Compromise arrangements are possible, and program seedlings under some circumstances can take root and grow within established depart-

---

[9] Reconstruction Finance Corporation Liquidation Act, 1953 (40 U.S.C. 459).

ments if protected during the developmental period by a self-contained relatively autonomous status.

Adherence to the principle of organization according to major purposes provides no automatic answers. Herbert Hoover would have resolved the problem by having the Congress define "major purpose" and then leaving it to the President to reorganize executive agencies in accordance with their purposes as set forth in law.[10] Granted that Mr. Hoover made this proposal in 1924, when federal programs were simple by today's standards, it is incredibly naive.

Federal programs are likely to have multiple purposes. Disagreements as to priorities among diverse and sometimes conflicting objectives are a major source of current controversies. Is the major purpose of the food stamp program to dispose of surplus agricultural commodities or to feed the poor? Is mass transportation a transportation or an urban development program? Are loans for college housing a housing or education function? Should the federal water pollution control program have as its principal objective health protection, or should it be concerned more broadly with the development of water resources?

Major purposes cannot be ascertained by scientific or economic analysis. Determination of major purpose represents a value judgment, and a transitory one at that. What is a secondary purpose for one, is a major purpose for another. To quote Miles's law: "Where one stands depends on where one sits." [11] Major purposes are not constants but variables shifting with the ebb and tide of our national needs and aspirations.

Debates about organizational type also may mask basic differences over strategy and objectives. Orthodox theory postulates that all federal agencies, with the possible exception of the independent regulatory commissions, be grouped under a limited number of single-headed executive departments and consequently ignores the other possible forms of organization. Except for the regulatory commissions and government corporations, the Hoover Commissions and President's Committee on Administrative Management took little

[10] Library of Congress [*A Compilation of Basic Information on the Reorganization of the Executive Branch of the Government of the United States 1912–1947* (Washington, D.C.: Government Printing Office, 1947)], p. 1216.

[11] Attributed to Rufus Miles, formerly Assistant Secretary for Administration, Department of Health, Education, and Welfare.

interest in the typology of organization — a disinterest shared by most students of public administration.

The significance of institutional type has been underrated. . . . The differences among . . . institutional types are more a matter of convention and tradition than legal prescriptions. Yet some have acquired a "mystique" which can profoundly influence public attitudes and executive and congressional behavior for good or ill. Institutional type can be crucial in determining who controls — the President, the Congress, or the so-called "special interests."

Institutional type, for example, was a major issue when Congress authorized the Marshall Plan. Republicans wanted the plan administered by a government corporation because by definition it would be more "businesslike." [12] A corporation would also make it more difficult for the State Department to meddle in the European recovery program. The compromise was to establish an independent agency outside the State Department and to authorize creation of a corporation, if and when needed. . . .

Up to now we have been discussing mainly the strategic implications of executive branch organization. But power relationships are not always involved in organization decisions. The President, the Congress, and even outside groups may use organizational means to obtain some immediate tactical advantage. . . .

Presidents have continued to employ committees and commissions to capture and contain the opposition. Committees and commissions can also offer an immediate, visible response in times of national catastrophe, such as the assassinations of President Kennedy and Senator Kennedy or the Watts riot. Study commissions are employed as a kind of tranquillizer to quiet public and congressional agitation about such matters as pesticides, crime, and public scandals. Attention, it is hoped, will be diverted to other issues by the time the commissions report. . . .

Prestigious commissions can also build public support for controversial courses of action. What is wanted is endorsement, not advice, although "run-away" commissions are not unknown. On sensitive issues such as congressional pay, where Congressmen are politically vulnerable, a commission report helps to take them off the hook.

[12] House Select Committee on Foreign Aid, "Preliminary Report Eleven — Comparative Analysis of Suggested Plans of Foreign Aid," November 22, 1947.

Both Presidents Kennedy and Johnson used commissions to support legislation to increase executive, congressional, and judicial salaries.[13]

Interagency committees sometimes create an impression of neatness and order within the executive establishment, even when a President cannot or will not resolve the basic differences and jurisdictional conflicts. If differences surface publicly and become embarrassing to the administration, the President's reflex reaction is to appoint another committee or to reorganize existing committees. The pressure is almost overwhelming "to do something" which might do some good and certainly will do no harm. No President can confess that he is stumped by a problem.

Pressure for immediate, tangible answers to highly complex problems may result in reorganizations. President Eisenhower's first response to the national trauma caused by the Soviet Union's successful launching of Sputnik in 1957 was to appoint a special assistant to the President for Science and Technology and to transfer the Science Advisory Committee from the Office of Defense Mobilization to the White House office.

Reorganization may provide a convenient way to dump an unwanted official, particularly one with strong congressional or constituency ties. The maneuver is not always successful, as was seen with Secretary Rusk's abortive plan to abolish the Department's Bureau of Security and Consular Affairs. Mr. Abba Schwartz's version of this incident is highly colored, but there is no question that Secretary Rusk's timing was influenced by his desire to shift Mr. Schwartz from the Bureau directorship to another post. The Bureau of Security and Consular Affairs was the brainchild of Senator Joseph McCarthy, and the Bureau of the Budget had targeted it for reorganization long before Mr. Schwartz arrived on the scene.

Use of reorganization to by-pass a troublesome committee or subcommittee chairman in the Congress can also be hazardous when it does not succeed. Transfer of civil defense activities from the Office of Civil and Defense Mobilization to the Secretary of Defense in 1961 was expected as an incidental benefit to remove the shelter program from the jurisdiction of an unfriendly appropriations sub-

[13] For a perceptive analysis see Elizabeth D. Drew, "How to Govern (or Avoid It) by Commission," *Atlantic Monthly*, May 1968.

committee chairman.[14] Albert Thomas, however, had the power to retain jurisdiction to the great discomfiture of the civil defense officials.

Organization choices may be motivated almost entirely by a desire to exclude billions in expenditures from budget tabulations. The 1969 budget was the first to include trust funds and mixed-ownership government corporations in the administrative budget. President Eisenhower's 1955 proposal to create a Federal Highway Corporation for financing the construction of the National System of Interstate Highways was deliberately designed to keep the authorized payments of $25 billion out of the budget totals. The proposal was later abandoned when it was found that establishment of a highway trust fund could serve the same purpose. Conversion of the Federal National Mortgage Association from a wholly-owned to a mixed-ownership government corporation in 1954 also had as its principal appeal the appearance of a multi-billion-dollar budget reduction. When the ground rules were changed with the 1969 budget, legislation was enacted to turn the Federal National Mortgage Association into a "government sponsored private corporation" so as to keep its expenditures out of the budget.

A new name and a new look may be necessary to save a program with little political appeal, particularly one which congressional supporters find difficult to sell to their constituents. At times reorganization supplies the rationale needed by a congressman to explain his vote. The frequent reorganization and re-naming of the foreign aid agency reflect efforts to bolster congressional support and to demonstrate presidential interest, rather than to introduce new policies and improve management. There have been no less than eight successive foreign aid agencies — from the Economic Cooperation Administration in 1948 to the Agency for International Development in 1961 — until 1961 an average of a new agency oftener than every two years.[15]

For many organization is a symbol. Federal councils on aging, mental retardation, physical fitness, consumers, and the arts, for example, are more important as evidence of national concern than as molders of federal policies.

[14] Executive Order No. 10952, July 20, 1961.
[15] Michael K. O'Leary, *The Politics of American Foreign Aid* (New York: Atherton Press, 1967), p. 117.

Some seek the creation of new federal agencies or reorganizations to enhance their status in the outside community. The demand for an independent National Archives disassociated from the government's "housekeeper," the General Services Administration, in part stems from the achivists' desire to improve their standing as a scholarly profession. Several years ago the firemen's association sought Bureau of the Budget support for a Federal Fire Academy. While the academy would not fulfill any identifiable federal need, it would place firemen on a par with policemen, who had a federal "sponsor" in the Federal Bureau of Investigation, and thus strengthen their bargaining position in dealing with mayors and city councils.

The Congress is highly skilled in the tactical uses of organization and reorganization. If you come from a district with a jet airport, establishment of an Office of Noise Abatement in the Department of Transportation has tremendous voter appeal. Even though there is doubt that a separate office could do much to reduce noise levels, at least it offers a place where congressmen can send constituent complaints. While the administration was able to defeat an amendment to the Department of Transportation bill to create such an office on the valid grounds that aircraft noise was a research and development and traffic control problem, Secretary Alan Boyd later found it expedient to create an Office of Noise Abatement by administrative action. Congressmen are more susceptible to pressures from sectional, economic, and professional interests than the President, and these often become translated into organizational responses.

Economy and efficiency are demonstrably not the prime purposes of public administration. Mr. Justice Brandeis emphasized that "the doctrine of separation of powers was adopted by the Constitution in 1787, not to promote efficiency but to preclude the exercise of arbitrary power." [16] The basic issues of federal organization and administration relate to power: who shall control it and to what ends?

The questions that now urgently confront us are as old as the Republic itself. How can we maintain a government structure and ad-

---

[16] Cited in Lewis Meriam and Lawrence F. Schmeckebier, *Reorganization of the National Government* (Washington, D.C.: The Brookings Institution, 1939), p. 132.

ministrative system which reconcile liberty with justice and institutional and personal freedom with the general welfare?

What we are observing today are the strains and tensions inevitably produced by revolutionary changes in the federal government's role and its relationships to other levels of government, institutions of higher learning and other nonprofit institutions, and the private sector. Dividing lines have become increasingly blurred. It is no longer easy to determine where federal responsibilities end and those of state and local governments and private institutions begin. These changes began with the "New Deal" in the 1930s, but the most dramatic developments have occurred since 1961.

Organizational ills are not easily diagnosed. Organization problems are often merely symptoms of growing pains or more deep-seated organic disease. Institutions do not perform well when called upon to accomplish significant transformations in the economic and social structure of our society within a one- or two-year time frame. Yet this is exactly what we have done in the poverty and model cities programs. In piling one new program on top of another, we have tended to ignore the need to find or develop the necessary managerial capability at all levels of government and have overloaded the system.

Yardsticks for measuring organizational health are admittedly inadequate and may be misleading. Strong public and congressional criticism may reflect effective performance, not the reverse. Servile obedience to congressional and constituency pressures, or inaction, may win more influential "friends" and supporters than vigorous pursuit of the public interest.

Growth has been a factor. Expeditures for major social programs, such as health and education, have tripled since 1961 and now exceed $18 billion a year. In 1961 the federal government had no programs for disadvantaged school children. One million children were enrolled in the Head Start and Head Start follow-through programs in 1968. Federal Aid to state and local governments has more than quadrupled from about $7 billion in 1961 to an estimated $28 billion in 1970. In the same period annual expenditures for research and development have increased from approximately $9 billion to over $16 billion.

As a percentage of gross national product, federal outlays for civilian programs — apart from interest on the debt, veterans programs, and the costs of the Post Office — rose from 1 per cent or less in the 1920s to about 5 per cent in immediate postwar years to almost 10 per cent in fiscal 1969.[17]

These increases would not be significant, if they represented in the main stepped up spending for traditional programs (welfare payments, price supports, veterans benefits, public works, highway construction) which could be smoothly channeled through the comfortable time-worn, single-purpose, single-agency groove. But the new programs to combat poverty, air and water pollution, and urban blight rewrote the ground rules. Under these programs, the federal government directly participates in specific projects in states and communities and acts as a co-equal partner with state and local governments, either individually or as members of joint federal-state organizations such as the Appalachia Regional Commission. These programs call for participation by many federal agencies and cut across established jurisdictional lines at all levels of government.

The Hoover Commission solution of "placing related functions cheek-by-jowl" so that "the overlaps can be eliminated, and of even greater importance coordinated policies can be developed" is not workable when you must combine the major purpose programs — health, education, manpower, housing — in alleviating the social and economic ills of a specific region, city, or neighborhood. We could regionalize the executive branch, as some have proposed, but Congressmen, governors, and mayors would be unwilling to accept such a concentration of power in any one federal agency. Such modest proposals as those to establish HUD "urban expediters" in key cities are viewed with suspicion. If one official could control the flow of federal funds into a region, he would be in a position to dictate state and local policies.

Senator Robert Kennedy posed the fundamental question when he asked: "Do the agencies of Government have the will and determination and ability to form and carry out programs which cut across departmental lines, which are tailored to no administrative convenience but the overriding need to get things done?" [18]

Straight lines of authority and accountability cannot be established in a nonhierarchical system. The federal government is compelled to rely increasingly for accomplishment of its goals on

[17] Charles L. Schultz, *The Politics and Economics of Public Spending* (Washington, D.C.: The Brookings Institution, 1968), p. 15.

[18] Senate Committee on Government Operations, hearings on "Federal Role in Urban Affairs," 1967, p. 40.

cooperation by non-federal institutions which are not legally responsible to the President and subject to his direction. Federal powers are limited to those agreed upon and enumerated in negotiated contracts. Success of the foreign aid, atomic energy, space, and defense research and development programs depends almost as much on performance by contractors as by the government's own employees. About 80 per cent of federal expenditures for research and development are made through non-federal institutions, under either grants or contracts.[19] The government since 1948 has caused to be organized and wholly financed a host of university and industry sponsored research centers and so-called not-for-profit corporations for the sole purpose of providing services to the government. Legally these are private organizations, but many, such as the Institute for Defense Analyses, Aerospace Corporation, Urban Institute, Lincoln Laboratory, and Oak Ridge National Laboratory, have more in common with traditional government agencies than with private institutions.

Fundamentalist dogmas were developed for a different universe — for the federal government as it existed in the 1920s and early 1930s. It was a time when Herbert Hoover could be told by one of his predecessors as Secretary of Commerce that the "job would not require more than two hours of work a day. Indeed that was all the time that former secretaries devoted to it. Putting the fish to bed at night and turning on the lights around the coast were possibly the major concepts of the office." [20] In the 1920s the Department of Commerce was engaged in what were then typical government services: collection and dissemination of statistics, preparation of charts and maps, operation of light houses, issuance of patents, and licensing, inspection, and regulation. Except for public works projects, timber, grazing and minerals rights, agricultural loans, and land permits, the federal government had little power to confer or withhold economic benefits. Federal intervention in the economy was indirect through economic regulation, the tariff, fiscal, monetary, and credit policies.

Government and business regarded each other as adversaries, not as potential partners. Theodore Roosevelt argued that establish-

[19] U.S. Bureau of the Budget, "Report to the President on Contracting for Research and Development," April 30, 1962.

[20] Herbert C. Hoover [*The Memoirs of Herbert Hoover, The Cabinet and the Presidency, 1920–1933* (New York: The Macmillan Co., 1952)], p. 42.

ment of a Department of Commerce would represent "an advance toward dealing with and exercising supervision over the whole subject of the great corporations doing an interstate business." [21] Roosevelt considered that the Secretary's first duty would be to regulate commerce and industry, rather than to act as a spokesman for their interests.

The regulatory approach reached its high-water mark with the New Deal. To the Interstate Commerce Commission, Federal Trade Commission, and Federal Power Commission, there were added the Securities and Exchange Commission, Federal Communications Commission, Civil Aeronautics Board, U.S. Maritime Commission, and the National Labor Relations Board. As far as the regulated industries were concerned, except for maritime and aviation subsidies, the less the federal government did the better. Tactics were defensive and designed to weaken, capture, and control the regulators. . . .

In the years since World War II, the federal table has become crowded with dependents, each clamoring to be fed and demanding the biggest slice of pie. Where before the federal government was tolerated as a nuisance or at best a marginal customer, major industries, universities, and other institutions have now come to depend on federal funds for survival.

In contrast to the situation in World War II, and even that during the Korean War, a large share of defense production is performed by highly specialized defense contractors, many of whose products bear little resemblance to civilian items, and who have had little experience outside defense production. For many companies their only important customer is the United States government. Fifteen companies derive more than half of their business from United States government contracts. For Lockheed Aircraft, McDonnell Douglas, AVCO, Newport News Shipbuilding, and Thiokol, government purchases account for more than 70 per cent of sales. [22]

In 1955–56 the total capital and recurrent expenditure by all higher educational institutions in the United States was $4.1 billion, of which 12 per cent, including research and development support, was supplied by the federal government. In 1967 the figure

[21] Library of Congress, *op. cit.*, pp. 1205–1206.
[22] *Congressional Quarterly*, Special Report on "The Military-Industrial Complex," May 24, 1968.

was $16.8 billion, of which 23 per cent, including research support and loans, was from federal sources. The President of the Carnegie Corporation predicts that by 1975 the federal share will rise to 50 per cent. [23]

The federal government currently finances almost three-quarters of university research. Scientists insist that a constantly rising level of federal support is essential to maintain our national position. Budget cutbacks cause near hysteria with rumors that sixteen private medical colleges and ten dental schools might have to close.[24]

States and cities see no solution to their critical financial problems other than more federal money. Federal aid has risen as a proportion of state and local revenues from 12.0 per cent in 1958 to 17.4 per cent in 1969.

The federal government may not be loved, but its capacity to raise revenues is greatly envied. Industry interests, however, may go beyond money. Otto Klima, Jr., and Gibson Wolfe, for example, advocate one federal agency with overview and program responsibility for all of this nation's interests in the oceans primarily as a means of helping United States industry by providing it with better decisional criteria.[25]

Unlike the regulated industries, it is not enough for these federal dependents to maintain a strong defensive posture. Under our system of checks and balances, it is relatively easy to block action. It is far more difficult to persuade the executive branch and the Congress to do something, particularly when there are strong competing demands for limited resources. Offense demands a new team and a different strategy. Some industries, such as the railroads, have been penalized because they were too slow in getting their defensive team off the field.

Each of the dependents endeavors to manipulate the organization structure and assignment of program responsibilities so as to maximize its ability to obtain federal funds and to minimize federal interference in the allocation and use of funds. Scientists had these objectives in mind when they developed their original design for the National Science Foundation. Farm organizations were inspired

[23] *Congressional Record*, May 1, 1968, p. E3631.
[24] Victor Cohn, "U.S. Science Is Feeling Budget Pinch," *The Washington Post*, August, 4, 1968.
[25] Otto Klima, Jr., and Gibson M. Wolfe, "The Oceans: Organizing for Action," *Harvard Business Review*, May–June, 1968.

by identical motives when they convinced President Eisenhower to support legislation which provided independent financing for the farm credit system and immunized it to effective federal control. Not all dependents have been as successful as the farm credit organizations in gaining the four freedoms: freedom from financial control by the Congress, freedom from independent audit by the Comptroller General, freedom from budget review by the President, and freedom to use Federal funds. But for many these freedoms remain the goals.

The struggle for power and position has contributed to fragmentation of the executive branch structure and the proliferation of categorical programs. By narrowing the constituency, agencies are made more susceptible to domination by their clientele groups and congressional committees.[26] Efforts to narrow the constituencies have been accompanied by demands for independent status or autonomy within the departmental structure.

Programs are packaged in such a way as to elicit congressional and clientele support. General programs have far less political appeal than specific programs. Support can be mobilized more readily for federal programs to combat heart disease, blindness, cancer, and mental illness, than for such fields as microbiology or for general health programs. For this reason in 1955 the National Microbiological Institute was renamed the National Institute of Allergy and Infectious Diseases. As was explained at the time, the Institute had been handicapped in making its case to the Appropriations Committees because "no one ever died of microbiology."[27]

It would be a mistake to assume, however, that dependents always have the wisdom to know what is in their own best interests. The maritime unions have become so obsessed with the idea that an independent maritime agency would solve all of their problems that they have ignored the plain fact that any transportation agency outside the Department of Transportation would be in a very weak competitive position. . . .

The issue of dependence vs. subservience is at the heart of our present dilemma. How can we reconcile a growing federal involvement in all aspects of our national life with the maintenance of

[26] For a brilliant analysis of the significance of constituencies see Grant McConnell, *Private Power and American Democracy* (New York: Alfred A. Knopf, 1967).
[27] *The New York Times,* December 14, 1969.

deeply cherished pluralistic values? The typical answer is that offered by Alan Pifer, President of the Carnegie Corporation.[28] He proposed the creation of a federal center for higher education which would "depend heavily in all its activities on men and women co-opted from the colleges and universities *so that it is as much of higher education itself as it is of government*" (italics supplied).

Few would dispute that federal domination of science and education would be undesirable. Yet grave risks are run when public power is exercised by agricultural, scientific, and educational elites who are more concerned with advancing their own interests and the interests of the institutions they represent than the public interest. Serious distortions and inequities may occur in the allocation of funds among those eligible for assistance. Vested interests are created which are resistant to change and the reordering of priorities to meet new national needs. . . .

[28] Alan Pifer, Speech to the Association of American Colleges, January 16, 1968, reprinted in *Congressional Record*, May 1, 1968, p. E.3631.

VI

PUBLIC CONTROL OVER BUREAUCRATIC POWER

Making the decisions and actions of bureaucratic organizations responsive to the needs and preferences of the community has long been a central concern in America as in other democratic societies. In large part this has been viewed as a matter of restraining the unwarranted use of power by executive agencies. Fears have been strong that government officials will employ their authority to infringe on the liberties of individual citizens and private organizations. Much attention has thus been given to developing controls to insure that these officials stay within the limits of their legal authority.

I

In the view of some observers, checks on the excessive use of bureaucratic power can only come from bureaucrats themselves — a system, so to speak, of administrative self-restraint. Carl J. Friedrich argues for reliance on such inner checks in his "Public Policy and the Nature of Administrative Responsibility." As he sees it, the expertise and professional skill of the bureaucrat are so formidable that no untrained lay politician or group can ever hope to oversee effectively the decisions that bureaucrats are called upon to make. "Under the best arrangements," he contends, "a considerable margin of irresponsible conduct of administrative activities is inevitable."

311

Friedrich also defends the far more questionable proposition that public opinion is most effective as a control over administrative behavior when it is taken into account at the initiative of bureaucrats themselves, as they anticipate probable public reactions to projected policies in their own deliberations. What his analysis at this point neglects is the possibility that administrative agencies may perceive only that image of public opinion it suits them to see — an image that may be altogether out of touch with reality. Moreover, the bureaucrat can, through the dissemination of information and the skillful use of publicity, use the communications media to shape the very public opinion by which he is supposed, in theory at least, to be controlled.

The notion that inner checks suffice as a method of controlling bureaucratic behavior is subjected to sharp criticism by Herman Finer in "Administrative Responsibility in Democratic Government." It is Finer's view that "reliance on an official's conscience may be reliance on an official's accomplice," since "the political and administrative history of all ages . . . has demonstrated without the shadow of a doubt that sooner or later there is an abuse of power when external punitive controls are lacking." Finer thus insists on the subordination of bureaucrats in policy-making. Policy is only legitimate when it meets with acquiescence from the public or its elected representatives.

To some extent the differences spelled out in this debate between Friedrich and Finer are differences of emphasis. Friedrich stresses the importance of internal checks over the decisions and actions of bureaucrats — certainly an appropriate emphasis for those areas of administrative behavior in which it is not feasible to expect external controls to be constantly in force. Seen in this light, external and internal controls do not substitute for, but complement, one another. Yet one enduring legacy of this now-classic controversy is Finer's firm insistence on the indispensability of external controls. Inner checks work as well as they do precisely because they are supported by the threat of external sanctions, and if this threat were ever removed, internal restraints might soon wither away.

II

Both Friedrich and Finer recognize that bureaucrats may misuse their power not by exceeding their authority but by failing to do what the law commands — provide the services or exercise the regulatory authority within an agency's responsibility. But their argument accents the excessive use of bureaucratic power and how it can be prevented. This was certainly a characteristic view of the problem of bureaucratic power during the 1930s and 1940s as Western societies moved from a predominantly laissez faire economy to a society in which government agencies began to intervene in a pervasive way in social and economic life.

As the modern activist state emerged, it became increasingly clear that bureaucratic organizations may suffer not from excessive zeal in using their powers but from inadequate enthusiasm in pursuing the goals for which they were created. Groups looking to an executive agency for services and assistance often feel that the agency is primarily interested in safeguarding the career interests and working conditions of its own employees and, in the case of regulatory programs, is unduly deferential to the business firms it should be supervising.[1]

The failure of bureaucratic organizations to pursue their goals vigorously has led to a reappraisal of some fundamental assumptions about what makes public organizations perform well. It has, for example, commonly been assumed that bureaucratic effectiveness can best be secured by eliminating overlap or duplication of governmental functions and assigning the responsibility for carrying on a particular program to a single agency.

In an original and stimulating essay, "Redundancy, Rationality, and the Problem of Duplication and Overlap," Martin Landau proposes a radically new way of thinking about the design of the executive branch. He suggests that the public is best served by an organizational arrangement

---

[1] For recent evidence of concern over this problem, see the investigation by Ralph Nader and his associates into the operations of the federal regulatory agencies.

in which several agencies perform the same task — a "redundant" system, as he puts it, in which overlap and duplication are regarded not as vices but as virtues. Such redundancy will provide much greater assurance that a governmental function will be carried out than a system in which a single agency is given sole responsibility for it.

Landau's analysis would draw warm support from those who are disappointed with some recent efforts to obtain a more effective bureaucracy by the traditional method of consolidating activities in the executive establishment. The unification of the armed forces in the United States following World War II is now seen by some observers as having made the military services much less responsive to public control than was the case when they were divided into separate departments.[2] More recently, the gathering together of various social service programs into a single Department of Health, Education, and Welfare has had similarly disappointing results. A monopoly in public bureaucracy seems as disadvantageous for the public as monopoly power in private industry. As a result, support has increased for allowing executive agencies to compete in performing the same or similar functions as a means of making them more responsive to the community. The idea of organizational redundancy has for the first time won intellectual respectability in the sphere of public bureaucracy.

Keeping bureaucratic organizations responsive to the public remains, however, an elusive goal. In "Symbols and Political Quiescence," Murray Edelman shows how regula-

---

[2] For a description of this earlier rivalry and its consequences for public control of the military bureaucracy, see Samuel P. Huntington, "Interservice Competition and the Political Roles of the Armed Services," *American Political Science Review* 55 (March 1961):40–52. Before unification occurred, the branches of the armed services struggled as fiercely among themselves as they did with foreign adversaries, in a continuing effort to achieve a preeminent position in the defense establishment. According to Huntington this competition had the striking and altogether unintended result of greatly bolstering civilian control of the military. Civilian officials were able to divide and conquer — to gain military support for certain policies they favored by playing off one segment of the military against another. Military rivalry for civilian support was thus the foundation of civilian control over defense policy.

tory agencies established to safeguard the consumer from economic exploitation can, in fact, facilitate such predatory activity. A major result of establishing regulatory agencies may be to lull the public into the comforting, but erroneous, belief that something is being done on its behalf, and thus to provide a screen behind which things can go on as they have. Edelman applies the term "quiescence" to this false sense of security on the part of the public. This quiescence is induced by a failure to distinguish between the goals an agency appears to be seeking and the interests actually being served by the policies it is carrying out.

22 *Public Policy and the Nature of Administrative Responsibility*

CARL J. FRIEDRICH

The starting point of any study of responsibility must be that even under the best arrangements a considerable margin of irresponsible conduct of administrative activities is inevitable. For if a responsible person is one who is answerable for his acts to some other person or body, who has to give an account of his doings (Oxford English Dictionary), it should be clear without further argument that there must be some agreement between such a responsible agent and his principal concerning the action in hand or at least the end to be achieved. When one considers the complexity of modern governmental activities, it is at once evident that such agreement can only be partial and incomplete, no matter who is involved. Once the electorate and legislative assemblies are seen, not through the smoke screen of traditional prejudice, but as they are, it is evident that such principals cannot effectively bring about the responsible conduct of public affairs, unless elaborate techniques make explicit what purposes and activities are involved in all the many different phases of public policy. It is at this point that the decisive importance of policy determination becomes apparent. Too often it is taken for granted that as long as we can keep the government from doing wrong we have made it responsible. What is more important is to insure effective action by any sort. To stimulate initiative, even at the risk of mistakes, must nowadays never be lost sight of as a task in making the government's services responsible. An official should be as responsible for inaction as for wrong action; certainly the average voter will criticize the government as severely for one as for the other. . . .

POLICYMAKING AND POLICY EXECUTION

It has long been customary to distinguish between policy-making and policy execution. Frank J. Goodnow, in his well-known work, *Politics and Administration,* undertook to build an almost absolute distinction upon this functional difference.

There are, then, in all governmental systems two primary or ultimate functions of government, viz. the expression of the will of the state and the execution of that will. There are also in all states separate organs, each of which is mainly busied with the discharge of one of these functions. These functions are, respectively, Politics and Administration.[1]

But while the distinction has a great deal of value as a relative matter of emphasis it cannot any longer be accepted in this absolute form. Admittedly, this misleading distinction has become a fetish, a stereotype in the minds of theorists and practitioners alike. The result has been a great deal of confusion and argument. The reason for making this distinction an absolute antithesis is probably to be found in building it upon the metaphysical, if not abstruse, idea of a will of the state. This neo-Hegelian (and Fascist) notion is purely speculative. Even if the concept "state" is retained — and I personally see no good ground for it — the idea that this state has a will immediately entangles one in all the difficulties of assuming a group personality or something akin to it.[2] In other words, a problem which is already complicated enough by itself — that is, how a public policy is adopted and carried out — is bogged down by a vast ideological superstructure which contributes little or nothing to its solution. Take a case like the AAA [Agricultural Adjustment Administration] . . . adopted . . . [to help] the farmer weather the storm

[1] Frank J. Goodnow, *Politics and Administration* (New York, 1900), p. 22.
[2] See Carl J. Friedrich, *Constitutional Government and Politics* (New York, 1936), pp. 29 ff. and elsewhere.

of the depression. This admittedly was AAA's broad purpose. To accomplish this purpose, crop reduction, price-fixing, and a number of lesser devices were adopted. Crop reduction in turn led to processing taxes. Processing taxes required reports by the processors, inspection of their plants. Crop reduction itself necessitated reports by the farmers, so-called work sheets, and agreements between them and the government as to what was to be done, and so forth and so on. What here is politics, and what administration? Will anyone understand better the complex processes involved in the articulation of this important public policy if we talk about the expression and the execution of the state will? The concrete patterns of public policy formation and execution reveal that politics and administration are not two mutually exclusive boxes, or absolute distinctions, but that they are two closely linked aspects of the same process. Public policy, to put it flatly, is a continuous process, the formation of which is inseparable from its execution. Public policy is being formed as it is being executed, and it is likewise being executed as it is being formed. Politics and administration play a continuous role in both formation and execution, though there is probably more politics in the formation of policy, more administration in the execution of it. Insofar as particular individuals or groups are gaining or losing power or control in a given area, there is politics; insofar as officials act or propose action in the name of public interest, there is administration.

The same problem may be considered from another angle. Policies in the common meaning of the term are decisions about what to do or not to do in given situations. It is characteristic of our age that most legislation is looked upon as policy-deciding. Hence policy-making in the broad sense is not supposed to be part of administration. While these propositions are true in a general way, they tend to obscure two important facts, namely, (1) that many policies are not ordained with a stroke of the legislative or dictatorial pen but evolve slowly over long periods of time, and (2) that administrative officials participate continuously and significantly in this process of evolving policy. To commence with the latter fact, it is evident that in the process of doing something the administrator may discover another and better way of accomplishing the same result, or he discovers that the thing cannot be done at all, or that something else has to be done first, before the desired step can be taken. In our recent agricultural policy, examples of all these "administrative" policy determinations can be cited, as likewise in our social security policy. The discussions now taking place in both fields amply illustrate these points. What is more, such administrative participation alone renders policymaking a continuous process, so much in a state of flux that it is difficult, if not impossible, to state with precision what the policy in any given field is at any particular time. But, if this is true, it follows as a corollary that public policy will often be contradictory and conflicting in its effects upon society. Our mythmakers, of course, remain adamant in proclaiming that this should not be so, and let it go at that. It is hard to disagree with them, but we still have to face the question of responsibility, seeing that policies are in fact contradictory and conflicting. Who is responsible for what, and to whom? To what extent does such responsibility affect the actual conduct of affairs? A complex pattern appears when we attempt to answer such questions.

Some time ago I pointed out that administrative responsibility had not kept pace with our administrative tasks. In relying upon the political responsibility of policymaking persons and bodies, we had lost sight of the deeper issues involved. At that time I wrote:

> . . . autocratic and arbitrary abuse of power has characterized the officialdom of a government service bound only by the dictates of conscience. Nor has the political responsibility based upon the election of legislatures and chief executives succeeded in permeating a highly technical, differentiated government service any more than the religious responsibility of well-intentioned kings. Even a good and pious king would be discredited by arbitrary "bureaucrats"; even a high-minded legislature or an aspiring chief executive pursuing the public interest would be thwarted by a restive officialdom.

An offended commentator from the British Isles exclaimed loudly that if I imagined that to be true of England I was "simply wrong." But I think it would be easy to show that the officials of a seventeenth-century prince were more responsible, i.e., answerable, to him, their sovereign, than the officials of any modern democracy are as yet to the people, their supposed sovereign. In the comparison there was no judgment as to the positive amount of responsibility found in either. Admittedly, many commentators have dwelt at length upon the frequently irresponsible conduct of public affairs in Great Britain and elsewhere. . . .

A DUAL STANDARD OF ADMINISTRATIVE RESPONSIBILITY

But are there any possible arrangements under which the exercise of such discretionary power can be made more responsible? The difficulties are evidently very great. Before we go any further in suggesting institutional safeguards, it becomes necessary to elucidate a bit more the actual psychic conditions which might predispose any agent toward responsible conduct. Palpably, a modern administrator is in many cases dealing with problems so novel and complex that they call for the highest creative ability. This need for creative solutions effectively focuses attention upon the need for action. The pious formulas about the will of the people are all very well, but when it comes to these issues of social maladjustment the popular will has little content, except the desire to see such maladjustments removed. A solution which fails in this regard, or which causes new and perhaps greater maladjustments, is bad; we have a right to call such a policy irresponsible if it can be shown that it was adopted without proper regard to the existing sum of human knowledge concerning the technical issues involved; we also have a right to call it irresponsible if it can be shown that it was adopted without proper regard for existing preferences in the community, and more particularly its prevailing majority. Consequently, the responsible administrator is one who is responsive to these two dominant factors: technical knowledge and popular sentiment. Any policy which violates either standard, or which fails to crystallize in spite of their urgent imperatives, renders the official responsible for it liable to the charge of irresponsible conduct.

In writing of the first of these factors, technical knowledge, I said some years ago:

Administrative officials seeking to apply scientific "standards" have to account for their action in terms of a somewhat rationalized and previously established set of hypotheses. Any deviation from these hypotheses will be subjected to thorough scrutiny by their colleagues in what is known as the "fellowship of science." . . . If a specific designation were desirable, it might be well to call this type of responsibility "functional" and "objective," as contrasted with the general and "subjective" types, such as religious, moral and political responsibility. For in the former case, action is tested in terms of relatively objective problems which, if their presence is not evident, can be demonstrated to exist, since they refer to specific functions. Subjective elements appear wherever the possibility of relatively voluntary choice enters in, and here political responsibility is the only method which will insure action in accordance with popular preference.[3]

Similarly, John M. Gaus writes:

The responsibility of the civil servant to the standards of his profession, in so far as those standards make for the public interest, may be given official recognition. . . . Certainly, in the system of government which is now emerging, one important kind of responsibility will be that which the individual civil servant recognizes as due to the standards and ideals of his profession. This is "his inner check." [4]

Yet this view has been objected to as inconceivable by one who claimed that he could not see how the term "responsibility" could be applied except where the governed have the power to dismiss or at least seriously damage the officeholder.[5] Thus, with one stroke of the pen, all the permanent officials of the British government, as well as our own and other supposedly popular governments, are once and for all rendered irresponsible. According to this commentator, political responsibility alone is "objective," because it involves a control by a body external to the one who is responsible. He also claims that its standards may be stated with finality and exactitude and its rewards and punishments made peremptory. For all of which British foreign policy leading up to Munich no doubt provides a particularly illuminating illustration.

It seems like an argument over words. The words, as a matter of fact, do not matter particularly. If you happen to feel that the word "objective" spells praise, and the word "subjective" blame, it may be better to speak of "technical" as contrasted with "political" responsibility, or perhaps "functional" and "political" will appeal. Whether we call it "objective" or "functional" or "technical," the fact remains that throughout the length and breadth of our technical civilization there is arising a type of responsibility on the part of the permanent administrator, the man who is called upon to seek and find the creative solutions for our crying technical needs, which cannot be effectively enforced except by fellow-technicians who are capable of judging his policy in terms of the scientific knowledge bearing upon

[3] Carl J. Friedrich, "Responsible Government Service under the American Constitution," *Problems of the American Public Service* (New York, 1935), p. 38.

[4] John M. Gaus, "The Responsibility of Public Administration," *The Frontiers of Public Administration* (Chicago, 1936), pp. 39–40.

[5] Herman Finer, "Better Government Personnel," *Political Science Quarterly* 51, No. 4 (December 1936):569ff., esp. pp. 580 ff.

it. "Nature's laws are always enforced," and a public policy which neglects them is bound to come to grief, no matter how eloquently it may be advocated. . . .

POLITICAL RESPONSIBILITY

The foregoing reflections must not deceive us, however, into believing that a public policy may be pursued just because the technicians are agreed on its desirability. Responsible public policy has to follow a double standard, as we stated before. We are entirely agreed that technical responsibility is not sufficient to keep a civil service wholesome and zealous, and that political responsibility is needed to produce truly responsible policy in a popular government. Discarding the wishful thinking of those who would tell us that Great Britain has solved this difficult problem, it is first necessary to repeat that such truly responsible policy is a noble goal rather than an actual achievement at the present time, and may forever remain so. All institutional safeguards designed to make public policy thus truly responsible represent approximations, and not very near approximations at that. One reason is the intrusion of party politics, already discussed; another is the tremendous difficulty which the public encounters in trying to grasp the broader implications of policy issues, such as foreign affairs, agriculture, and labor today. Concerning unemployment, all the general public really is sure about is that it should disappear. . . .

THE ROLE OF CITIZEN-PARTICIPATION

There are, of course, those who would altogether deny the impact of the people or its representatives, whether Congress or Parliament, upon the emerging policies. Such observers assert that even the most far-reaching of public policies are often formed by executive agencies under the pressure of circumstances and are merely legalized by subsequent legislation. It was thus recently put by an able student of our labor policy:

It is a problem for the bureaucracy to foresee a situation and evolve a solution which will break gradually upon the political consciousness and be sufficiently entrenched so that its formal adoption in the legislative chamber is not an embarcation upon an uncharted sea.

Lest our British friends rush in to tell us that this is another American heresy, let me hasten to add that a similar view is even more common among British students of these matters, and quite naturally, since the role of the permanent administrative group in the drafting of legislation is so much more openly acknowledged under the cabinet system of government. Indeed, apropos the previously quoted address of Sir Josiah Stamp, the commentator in *The Times* felt it necessary to remark upon the neglect of Parliament which Sir Josiah's views seemed to spell. Nor is this trend so very novel. Long before the war Sir Eyre Crowe, a leading permanent official of the Foreign Office, once wrote a confidential memorandum on parliamentary and public influence upon the course of British foreign policy. He stated that there was very little or none; he could recall only one instance, the Venezuela imbroglio, when the Foreign Office had been obliged to change its policy in response to public opinion. But it is our opinion that Sir Eyre Crowe, as well as all others who maintain the virtual aloofness of the permanent administrator from politics, are deceiving themselves. It is our view that such officials are more or less responsible to the people and its representatives, the press and Parliament, right along. Sir Eyre Crowe forgot that policymaking officials deliberated almost daily upon what would be the reaction of the public to this, the reaction of Parliament to that move. By correctly anticipating these reactions, the Foreign Office avoided getting embroiled and having to reverse its course. Who can say, then, that it was free from influence by Parliament and the public?

The same thing would, I believe, be found to be true here. The mere knowledge that the representative assemblies can stop a policy from going forward, that a row in the public press may destroy all chances of initiating an activity which the administrator holds to be desirable, will make him keenly interested in and desirous of anticipating the reactions of public and Parliament or Congress alike. Too little attention has been directed to the fact that political influence works most effectively through such anticipation, rather than through the reversal of policies after they have been adopted. But while the press and Parliament still provide very potent sources of influence, and hence their reactions are keenly watched by policy-formulating officials, newer and equally potent instruments have been developed in recent years. Through its informational services, administrative officials have begun to tap independent sources of insight into the views and reactions of the general public which are increasingly important in guiding them towards the making of public policy in a responsible fashion.

It is quite common to look upon the informational services which are being developed in this country at the present time as largely devoted to the handing-out of routine news items to the daily press. A more comprehensive discussion of these activities is not intended here. Their many-sided function is being increasingly recognized. In fields with novel policies to administer, such as Social Security or AAA, educational and promotional functions are being recognized. But along with all this outward flow of information on emerging policies, there is an ever-increasing quantity of intake. This intake of all sorts of communicable views, opinions, facts, and criticisms is becoming a potent factor in the shaping of public policy, particularly in areas where the government is entering new or experimental ground. But even in established realms of governmental activity new lines of approach are being pushed as a result of the activity of informational services. It is the function of the administrator to make every conceivable effort toward the enforcement of the law which he is called upon to administer. The authoritarian tradition of the past was inclined to take the attitude that it was up to the citizen to find out what the law was; if he did not, it was just too bad. Ignorance was no excuse. This conception of the government as mere police is quite outmoded, though undoubtedly many government offices are still administered according to such outworn notions. The modern conception of government as the largest "public service" with vast and diversified activities to administer cannot be made to work in such terms. The continuously changing pattern of our society requires that the administrator be responsive to whatever trends may be affecting his activities. Laws do not embody static and universal truths; they represent expedient policies which are subject to continous change and must be so considered. Instead of administering according to precedent, the responsible administrator today works according to anticipation. Within the limits of existing laws, it is the function of the administrator to do everything possible which will make the legislation work. The idea of enforcing commands yields to the idea of effectuating policy. For most of the policies of a modern government, at any rate under democratic conditions, require collaboration rather than force for their accomplishment.

It is very natural that policies which are novel in their creative impact upon society should elicit a great many diverse public reactions. These will flow into the administrative offices in the form of inquiries, criticisms, and suggestions. Under democratic conditions, the average citizen feels entirely free to communicate with the government, because he considers it his own. According to the traditional conception of representative government, such communications would be sent to the citizen's representative in Congress or Parliament, who in turn would make them the basis of suitable action, official or unofficial inquiries, remarks in the debates of the House, and so on. A great deal of public reaction still takes this form, and, while elected Representatives at times are inclined to feel that their mail is getting to be too much of a good thing, they would surely be agreed that the more important communications of this kind constitute an intrinsically valuable source of information and guidance. In Great Britain, the question hour still serves this purpose fairly well. In the United States much would depend upon the Representative's being a member of the strategically important committees. However, the great pressure of legislative work has made it increasingly difficult for parliamentarians to attend to such matters. Moreover, a citizen, no matter how competent or well-informed, would be handicapped if his views were patently different from those of the representatives, whether for political or technical reasons. It is evident that in these and similar situations the citizen has become more and more accustomed to turn directly to the administrator. . . .

Put quite broadly, it may be said that the public relations work of the administrative agencies has the task of anticipating clashes between the administrative efforts at effectuating a policy and the set habits of thought and behavior of the public which constitutes its "environment." There is, we might say, a laudable tendency here to adopt the department store slogan: "The customer is always right." For if such friction develops, the presumption exists that there is a flaw in the policy or in the methods by which the policy is being administered. Many questions asked of the information services of important federal agencies have no answer. The questions raise issues of policy which either have not been anticipated, or at least have not been settled by the administrative officer involved, or reported back to Congress for settlement. . . .

CONCLUSION

The ways, then, by which a measure of genuine responsibility can be secured under modern conditions appear to be manifold, and they must all be utilized for achieving the best effect. No mere reliance upon some one traditional device, like the dependence of the cabinet upon majority support in Parliament, or popular election of the chief executive (neither of which exists in Switzerland), can be accepted as satisfactory evidence. At best, responsibility in a democracy will remain fragmentary because of the indistinct voice of the principal whose agents the officials are supposed to be — the vast heterogeneous masses composing the people. Even the greatest faith in the common man (and I am prepared to carry this very far) cannot any longer justify a simple acceptance of the mythology of "the will of the people." Still, if all the different devices are kept operative and new ones developed as opportunity offers, democratic government by pooling many different interests and points of view continues to provide the nearest approximation to a policy-making process which will give the "right" results. Right policies are policies which seem right to the community at large and at the same time do not violate "objective" scientific standards. Only thus can public policy contribute to what the people consider their happiness.

23   *Administrative Responsibility in Democratic Government*

HERMAN FINER

Administrative responsibility is not less important to democrative government than administrative efficiency; it is even a contributor to efficiency in the long run. Indeed, it is tempting to argue

From Herman Finer, "Administrative Responsibility in Democratic Government," reprinted by permission of The American Society for Public Administration from *Public Administration Review* 1 (Summer 1941):335–350. This article was written as a reply to the argument presented by Carl J. Friedrich in the preceding selection.

that the first requisite is responsibility, and if that is properly insti-
tuted efficiency will follow. Elaboration of this point should be unnecessary in the era and under the stress of the events which now
make up our days.

To the subject of administrative responsibility, Professor Carl J.
Friedrich has made several interesting and sagacious contributions,
and he deserves our gratitude for having reintroduced its discussion
among primary problems. Yet these contributions have by no means
said the last word on the subject. Indeed, he has put forward a number of propositions which must arouse earnest dissent. . . .

My chief difference with Professor Friedrich was and is my insistence upon distinguishing responsibility as an arrangement of
correction and punishment even up to dismissal both of politicians
and officials, while he believed and believes in reliance upon responsibility as a sense of responsibility, largely unsanctioned, except
by diference or loyalty to professional standards. I still maintain my
belief while in a more recent article * Professor Friedrich still maintains his, so far as I am able to follow his argument. I propose therefore to treat the subject in two divisions, first, a more extended
version of my own beliefs and, second, a critical examination of his
article.

I

Most of the things I have to say are extremely elementary, but
since it has been possible for a writer of eminence to discount their
significance I may be forgiven for reaffirming them. The modern
state is concerned with a vast sphere of services of a mixed nature.
They are repressive, controlling, remedial, and go as far as the actual conduct of industrial, commercial, and agricultural operations.
The state, which used to be negative — that is to say which was
concerned to abolish its own earlier interventions and reduce such
controls as ancient and medieval polity had caused it to undertake
— has for some decades now abandoned laissez faire and can be
called ministrant. Its work ranges over practically every sector of
modern individual and social interest, from sheer police work, in
the sense of apprehending and punishing assaults on person, peace,
and property, to the actual ownership and management of utilities.

* [See the preceding essay, "Public Policy and the Nature of Administrative
Responsibility. — Ed.]

I need not dwell on this point further, nor upon the range and detailed intensity of the state's operation, nor the large percentage of men and women among the gainfully occupied population it employs in the strategic positions in society. The weight and immensity and domination of this behemoth, for our good as well as for our control, are well known to all of us. But academic persons are less subject to the power of the colossus than the worker, the economic entrepreneur, the sick and the needy of all kinds. The academic person is therefore likely to regard the weight of the administrator's hand as not needing to be stayed or directed by the public custodian.

Are the servants of the public to decide their own course, or is their course of action to be decided by a body outside themselves? My answer is that the servants of the public are not to decide their own course; they are to be responsible to the elected representatives of the public, and these are to determine the course of action of the public servants to the most minute degree that is technically feasible. Both of these propositions are important: the main proposition of responsibility, as well as the limitation and auxiliary institutions implied in the phrase, "that is technically feasible." This kind of responsibility is what democracy means; and though there may be other devices which provide "good" government, I cannot yield on the cardinal issue of democratic government. In the ensuing discussion I have in mind that there is the dual problem of securing the responsibility of officials, (a) through the courts and disciplinary controls within the hierarchy of the administrative departments, and also (b) through the authority exercised over officials by responsible ministers based on sanctions exercised by the representative assembly. In one way or another this dual control obtains in all the democratic countries, though naturally its purposes and procedures vary from country to country.

What are we to mean by responsibility? There are two definitions. First, responsibility may mean that X is accountable for Y to Z. Second, responsibility may mean an inward personal sense of moral obligation. In the first definition the essence is the externality of the agency or persons to whom an account is to be rendered, and it can mean very little without that agency having authority over X, determining the lines of X's obligation and the terms of its continuance or revocation. The second definition puts the emphasis on the conscience of the agent, and it follows from the definition that if he commits an error it is an error only when recognized by his own conscience, and that the punishment of the agent will be merely the twinges thereof. The one implies public execution; the other harakiri. While reliance on an official's conscience may be reliance on an official's accomplice, in democratic administration all parties, official, public, and Parliament, will breathe more freely if a censor is in the offing. . . .

Democratic governments, in attempting to secure the responsibility of politicians and officeholders to the people, have founded themselves broadly upon the recognition of three doctrines. First, the mastership of the public, in the sense that politicians and employees are working not for the good of the public in the sense of what the public *needs*, but of the *wants* of the public as expressed by the public. Second, recognition that this mastership needs institutions, and particularly the centrality of an elected organ, for its expression and the exertion of its authority. More important than these two is the third notion, namely, that the function of the public and of its elected institutions is not merely the exhibition of its mastership by informing governments and officials of what it wants, but the authority and power to exercise an effect upon the course which the latter are to pursue, the power to exact obedience to orders. The Soviet government claimed (in the years when the claim seemed profitable to it internationally) that it was a democratic government; but its claim was supported by two arguments only, that the government worked for the good of the people, their economic well-being, and that the people were allowed to inform the government of their will through a multitude of institutions. The Soviet government never sought to employ with any cogency the third and really vital argument that it could be made to conform to the people's will by the people and against its own will. This last alone is responsibility in democratic government.

Democratic government proceeded upon the lines mentioned because the political and administrative history of all ages, the benevolent as well as the tyrannical, the theological as well as the secular, has demonstrated without the shadow of a doubt that sooner or later there is an abuse of power when external punitive controls are lacking. This abuse of power has shown itself roughly in three ways. Governments and officials have been guilty of nonfeasance,[1]

[1] I use the terms nonfeasance and malfeasance in a common sense, not a legal sense — they are convenient.

that is to say, they have not done what law or custom required them to do owing to laziness, ignorance, or want of care for their charges, or corrupt influence. Again there may be malfeasance, where a duty is carried out, but is carried out with waste and damage because of ignorance, negligence, and technical incompetence. Third, there is what may be called *over*feasance, where a duty is undertaken beyond what law and custom oblige or empower; overfeasance may result from dictatorial temper, the vanity and ambition of the jack in office, or genuine, sincere, public-spirited zeal. As a matter of fact, the doctrine of the separation of powers as developed by Montesquieu was as much concerned with the aberrations of public-spirited zeal on the part of the executive as with the other classes of the abuse of power. Indeed, his phrase deserves to be put into the center of every modern discussion of administrative responsibility, *virtue itself hath need of limits.* We in public administration must beware of the too good man as well as the too bad; each in his own way may give the public what it doesn't want. If we wish the public to want things that are better in our estimation, there is a stronger case for teaching the public than for the imposition of our zealotry. A system which gives the "good" man freedom of action, in the expectation of benefiting from all the "good" he has in him, must sooner or later (since no man is without faults) cause his faults to be loaded on to the public also.

As a consequence of bitter experience and sad reflection, democratic governments have gradually devised the responsible executive and an elected assembly which enacts the responsibility. Within the system, there has been a particular concentration on the subservience of the officials to the legislature, ultimately through ministers and cabinet in a cabinet system, and through the chief executive where the separation of powers is the essential form of the organization of authority. Where officials have been or are spoilsmen, the need for holding them to subservience is particularly acute, since the spoilsman has not even a professional preparation to act as a support and guide and guarantee of capacity. With career men, the capacity may be present. What is needed, however, is not technical capacity per se, but technical capacity in the service of the public welfare as defined by the public and its authorized representatives.

Legislatures and public have realized that officials are monopolist no less than the grand men of business who have arrogated to themselves the exclusive control of the manufacture or sale of a commodity and therewith the domination, without appeal by the victim, of an entire sector of national life. The philosophy and experience of the Sherman Anti-Trust Act have significant applications to administrative procedures in public administration. The official participates in the monopoly of a service to society so outstanding that it has been taken over from a potential private monopolist by the government. This monopoly is exercisable through a sovereign agency armed with all the force of society and subject to no appeal outside the institutions which the government itself creates. This is to be subject to a potentially grievous servitude.

How grievous can be surmised in one or both of two ways. One can reflect on the merits of competitive industry which satisfies the consumers best as to price and quality and variety while it remains competitive, so that the consumer can cast a more than daily vote most effectively for the producer he prefers by buying his goods or services, and expel the others from office by *not* buying from them. One can notice, too, how producers, on the plea of "service before self" and the like, attempt to escape consumer's control; and memories are stirred of Adam Smith's dig at traders who affect to trade "for the public good." Or, second, one can have experience at first hand, not merely of the coercive side of public monopolies, say the contract powers of a municipal electricity undertaking, but of its administration of charitable undertakings, say in the feeding of school children or hospital management. The conceit of Caesar making concessions *ex gratia* to "subjects" can be noticed too palpably.

To overcome the potential evils flowing from public monopoly, democratic governments have set up various controls. It is these controls, and especially their modern deficiencies, which seem to have worried Professor Friedrich into a position where he practically throws the baby out with the bath. He feels that there is need of some elasticity in the power of the official, some discretion, some space for the "inner check," and he sees also that existent controls (either intentionally or by the accident of their own institutional deficiencies) do actually leave some latitude to the official. He argues therefore that heavy and, indeed, primary reliance in the making of public policy and its execution should be placed on *moral* responsibility, and he pooh-poohs the efficacy of and need for political responsibility. He gives the impression of stepping over the dead body of political responsibility to grasp the promissory incandescence of the moral variety.

Let us review the chief controls exercised over politicians and officials in democratic government, and their deficiencies and the remedy of these deficiencies. In traversing their inadequacies I am dealing with those loopholes for administrative discretion or the policymaking power of officials which have given Professor Friedrich so much concern. First, the legislative definition of the duties and powers of officials may not be precise because the legislators were not very clear about what they wanted. It is doubtful, for example, whether the planning clauses in the TVA statute represented any clarity of purpose in the legislative mind. Legislative draftsmanship may be slipshod. Or the statute may be simply misunderstood, thus offering latitude to officials. If all the items of administrative determination arising out of the elbowroom allowed by these causes were gathered together they would no doubt be considerable. Since this latitude exists, it calls for one or both of the available remedies: the continuing control of the representative and judicial agencies over the official and an omnipresent sense of duty *to the public* on the part of the official. But the remedy is not, as Professor Friedrich suggests, the institution of specific legislative policies which may please the heart of the technical expert or the technocrat. I again insist upon subservience, for I still am of the belief with Rousseau that the people can be unwise but cannot be wrong. The devices for securing the continuing responsiveness of the official are, of course, the law courts, the procedure of criticism, question, debate, and fact-finding, and parliamentary control of the purse within the assembly, and, in the United States, the election of executive or administrative officials and their recall.

It has been suggested by Professor Laski that to overcome judicial bias in the interpretation of social legislation a preamble might be set at the head of every statute so that the intention of it should be rendered less mistakable.[2] Such a device might serve the purpose of making the official amenable to the legislature, except that I have grave doubts whether the legislature can express its intention any better in a preamble than it does in the particulars of the whole statute.

Next, the enormous congestion of modern legislative assemblies

[2] Committee on Ministers' Powers, *Report, 1932, Addendum.*

and the heritage of antiquated procedure mean that a sufficiently frequent review of legislation and its administrative outcrops cannot be secured to remedy, or to punish, or to act by power of anticipation on the official mind. But these are not insuperable problems and there is no need for us, seeing contemporary deficiencies, to jettison political responsibility prematurely.

Third, there may be a want of understanding by members of Parliament and congressmen of technical issues involved in the law and the administration, and this shortcoming has meant a leaning upon the supply of these things available in public employees. But the growth of advisory bodies, formal and informal, in the major governments of our own time has tremendously limited the need to rely wholly upon official initiative. Attention to the further development of advisory bodies is the line of progress here, not surely the handing over of our fate to officials who, by the way, are themselves only too grateful for instruction by such bodies.[3]

It is true, further, that the exercise of the power of control by the legislature, such for example as Congress's detailed attention to and itemization of financial appropriations, may destroy movement, flexibility, and the like, on the part of the administration. This point is stressed by Professor Friedrich; queerly enough, he does not deduce from this criticism that a more rational parliamentary procedure is required, but that there is need of more administrative discretion. He even goes to the inexplicable extreme of proposing that some action is better than none, whatever the action is!

In short, these various drawbacks of political control can be remedied. They can be highly improved, and it is therefore unnecessary to proceed along the line definitely approved by Professor Friedrich of more administrative policymaking. As a democrat, I should incline to the belief that the remedying of these drawbacks is precisely our task for the future. The legitimate conclusion from the analysis of the relationship between Parliament and administration is not that the administration should be given its head, but on the contrary that legislative bodies should be improved. Conceding the power of officials we may discover the remedy in the improvement of the quality of political parties and elections, if our minds are ready to explore.

Even then I am willing to admit an external agency could not

[3] Cf. R. V. Vernon and N. Mansergh, *Advisory Bodies* (London, 1941).

attend to every administrative particular without introducing an element of coercion and fear into administration which might damage originality, joy in work, the capacity for creative suggestion, and day-by-day flexibility. No external agency could do this; and none that we know would want to. But because some latitude must be given — both owing to the technical impossibility of complete political coverage, and the wise recognition that the permitted latitude can be used for technically good policy which though not immediately acclaimed or wanted may become so in a short while upon demonstration to the public — there is no need to overstress the auxiliaries to political control. Such auxiliaries as approved by Professor Friedrich are: referenda by government departments, public relations offices, consultation of academic colleagues in order to temper "partisan extravagance," "education and promotional functions," the administrative scrutiny of a Congressman's mail. These are harmless enough.

But when Professor Friedrich advocates the official's responsibility to "the fellowship of science," the discard of official anonymity, the entry of the official into the political arena as an advocate of policy and teacher of fact versus "partisan extravagance," the result to be feared is the enhancement of official conceit and what has come to be known as "the new despotism." It seems to me that in Professor Friedrich's article a theoretical aberration regarding the value of devices for eliciting public opinion, auxiliary to the medium of the legislative assembly, has led to pushing these auxiliaries into the principal place. Where the external, propelling, remedial, and punitive power of legislative bodies and administrative superiors acting after the administrative event, and upon the imagination of the official before it (and therefore relying upon fear), is weak, other techniques can be and have been added. . . .

All these devices have their value, but let it be remembered that they do not and cannot commit and compel the official to change his course. Officials may, in spite of them, still think that what they are doing is for the good of the public, although the public is too ignorant to recognize what is for its good. However, the more the official knows of public reactions the better. My qualm is that the official is very likely to give himself the benefit of the doubt where the information he elicits admits of doubt, whereas when the legislative assembly asserts an opinion it also asserts a command. . . .

Besides these arrangements the official may be kept responsive to the will of the legislative assembly by all the devices of legal responsibility. This point need not be adumbrated in any detail as it has been the subject of so many recent analyses and proposals for reform in the standard works of administrative law. . . . In addition, there is the regular intradepartmental discipline resting upon the professional prospects and career, the salary, the retirement pay, and the chances of promotion, transfer, distinction, and honors, or vice versa, of the civil servant, going right up the hierarchy to those who are in direct contact with the secretaries of departments and the chief executive in the United States and the permanent secretaries and the ministers in Great Britain.

Even when the best has been accomplished with all this mechanism and the rewards, punishments, and incentives by which it functions, there may be still a gap between the controls and those official actions which would give the greatest public satisfaction. We should do all we can to reduce this gap to its minimum. Where our powers reach an impasse we will be obliged to rely upon two ways out: the education of the official and the influence of his professional organizations.

As for education — which should be part of the official's training before entry and then should be continued in various ways after entry [4] — besides the purpose of technical excellence, it should be shaped to make the official aware of the basic importance of his responsibility to the parliamentary assembly, and the errors into which he will be liable to fall unless he makes this his criterion. He should realize the dangers in the belief that he has a mission to act for the good of the public outside the declared or clearly deducible intention of the representative assembly. No one in his right mind would deny the importance of suggestions persuasively presented by the expert; but there is a world of difference between acknowledging the value of such suggestions and following the path of increasing administrative independence simply because there is *faute de mieux* already some independence.

Again, my own studies in the field of the professional organizations of local and central government officials in Great Britain have taught me what a great power for the good can be exercised by them.[5] Besides keeping members up to the mark and up-to-date in

[4] Cf. Finer, *The British Civil Service* (London, 1937), pp. 243 *et seq.*
[5] Cf. *Municipal Trading* (London, 1941), especially the last two chapters, for a development of this point.

the exercise of their profession, they do embody a sense of responsibility in the second sense in which we use that term, as devotion to the highest standards of a craft or to a special body of people in the community — such as the consumers of electricity or passengers on petrol or trolley buses, or the frequenters of public baths, or the payers of income tax. They engender and develop this sense of responsibility, and it is a valuable product. But even with this we must require principally and austerely the subservience of the public official. Without this requirement, we shall gradually slip into a new version of taxation without representation. There will result the development of a profession or corporate spirit, and bodies which at first are beneficial in their freshness become what Rousseau and Hobbes have called "worms in the entrails of the body politic." We shall become subject to what has, in a short time, almost always been to the detriment of the public welfare — producer's control of the products, the services, the commodities which the producer thinks are good for the consumer and therefore ought to be produced at the consumer's expense, though the consumer does not want the services or commodities in question and strongly prefers something else. . . .

II

The foregoing critical analysis of Professor Friedrich's view on administrative responsibility . . . shows, I think, its untenability both in its main drift and in most of its particular secondary though related aspects. The analysis reveals the following propositions as cogent and justifiable, in contradiction to Professor Friedrich's contentions.

Never was the political responsibility of officials so momentous a necessity as in our own era. Moral responsibility is likely to operate in direct proportion to the strictness and efficiency of political responsibility, and to fall away into all sorts of perversions when the latter is weakly enforced. While professional standards, duty to the public, and pursuit of technological efficiency are factors in sound administrative operation, they are but ingredients, and not continuously motivating factors, of sound policy, and they require public and political control and direction.

The public and the political assemblies are adequately sagacious to direct policy — they know not only where the shoe pinches, but have a shrewd idea as to the last and leather of their footwear: and where they lack technical knowledge their officials are appointed to offer it to them for their guidance, and not to secure official domination; and within these limits the practice of giving administrative lattitude to officials is sound.

Contemporary devices to secure closer cooperation of officials with public and legislatures are properly auxiliaries to and not substitutes for political control of public officials through exertion of the sovereign authority of the public. Thus, political responsibility is the major concern of those who work for healthy relationships between the officials and the public, and moral responsibility, although a valuable conception and institutional form, is minor and subsidiary.

24   Redundancy, Rationality, and the Problem of Duplication and Overlap

MARTIN LANDAU

Not so long ago I experienced an emergency landing. We had been aloft only a short time when the pilot announced some mechanical failure. As we headed toward the nearest airport, the man behind me, no less frightened than I, said to his companion, "Here's where my luck runs out." A few minutes later we touched down to a safe landing amidst foam trucks and asbestos-clad fire fighters.

On the ground I ran into the pilot and asked him about the trouble. His response was vague, but he did indicate that something

From Martin Landau, "Redundancy, Rationality, and the Problem of Duplication and Overlap," reprinted by permission of the author and The American Society for Public Administration from *Public Administration Review* 29 (July/August 1969):346–358. Some footnotes are renumbered.

had been wrong with the rudder. How, then, was he able to direct and land the plane? He replied that the situation had not really been as ominous as it had seemed: the emergency routines we had followed were necessary precautions and he had been able to compensate for the impairment of the rudder by utilizing additional features of the aircraft. There were, he said, safety factors built into all planes.

Happily, such matters had not been left to chance, luck, as we say. For a commercial airliner is a very redundant system, a fact which accounts for its reliability of performance; a fact which also accounts for its adaptability.

A PARADOX

The English language presents us with a striking curiosity. Its lexicons establish an instance of *redundancy* as a "liability" and yet it is precisely the liberal use of redundancy that provides linguistic expression with an extraordinary measure of "reliability."

The Definition

In the context of ordinary language, redundancy is said to exist whenever there is an excess or superfluity of anything. The excess may be of parts, of rules, of words, . . . of anything. *Excess,* as defined lexically, is something which is more than the normal, the required, the usual, the specified. It is useless, superfluous, needless — terms which are variously employed to define *redundancy.*

This linguistic habit directs a negative judgment. It points to features of a situation which are of no value, which are wasteful, which are bad. The force of this habit is immediately to be seen by noting that the synonyms for the adjective *excessive* are: immoderate, intemperate, inordinate, extravagant, exorbitant, and extreme. If we need a time scale here, we can note that excessive has been used to define redundancy for some 400 years.

Accordingly, to say of a person's speech that it is redundant is not to extend a compliment. To observe an excess of parts is to observe an unnecessary duplication which, almost automatically, is seen as waste. To confront an excess of rules is, naturally, to make unhappy contact with red tape. And so on. In each case, more than is necessary is apparent, a condition which is sometimes regarded as affluent but more often as profligate. It is rarely regarded as economic and even less often as efficient. Indeed, there are many who seem to make *zero redundancy* the measure of both economy and efficiency. And if this condition is not fully realizable in practice, it nevertheless stands as the optimal state to be attained.

So powerful is this convention, that when Harry Nyquist introduced "redundancy" as a technical term in information theory, it referred to the useless portions of a message — those which could be eliminated without any loss of information. Nyquist sought a nonredundant system, one which would permit the transmission of information with the absolutely minimal number of signs that could possibly be employed.[1] Today, however, this goal is no longer entertained. It has been set aside: not because it is impossible of achievement, but because its realization would, in fact, increase the probability of failure — of false, misleading, and distorted messages.

The Use of Redundancy

Consider this essay. I write it because I have a statement to make, one which I think is deserving of interest. And, as befalls anyone who wishes to send a message of this kind, several doubts assail me. To begin with, it is possible that my statement is not worth sending, but upon reflection I think it is. Then, I may not be able to make myself understood. My thoughts and/or my phraseology may be quite unclear and I know that to be understood requires a clarity of expression. I am also aware that I know most about what I want to say, but I am not sure that I can present my position in such a way as to enable the reader to receive it exactly as I want him to. Nor am I any more certain of my reader who, for many reasons beyond my control, may misinterpret what I write and receive an erroneous impression.

These are some of the uncertainties which face me as I seek to communicate. The possibility of misunderstanding, of an inability to make contact, of breakdown, is inescapable. I anticipate this and I work to lessen the risk all along the line. It would be helpful, of course, if I could deploy a decision system specifically designed to do so; statistics perhaps. It does, after all, permit the making of decisions under conditions of uncertainty with the least possible

[1] J. R. Pierce, *Symbols, Signals and Noise* (New York: Harper, 1961), pp. 35–39. Also, see chapters 7 and 8.

error.[2] But I have not ordered this paper, nor can I, in such a manner as to make use of its powers. Happily, however, I am not without other resources.

Notice that the paragraphs I have written are quite repetitious. I repeat directly and indirectly, and I did this in all similar circumstances before I "knew" that simple repetition is the easiest way to introduce redundancy and that redundancy is a powerful device for the suppression of error. I employ more words than the "absolute minimum" and I arrange them according to a larger number of grammatical rules than are ideally necessary, all of this not to waste space but to insure reliability of communication.[3] If the overall uncertainty factor could be eliminated, I would (theoretically) write with zero redundancy. But then, strangely enough, there would be no way to detect error should one arise.[4] This, of course, is an idle speculation, because no language is without redundancy.[5] Even our most precise scientific languages contain redundancies, and this statement is true for purely formal languages as well.[6]

It is, thus, virtually impossible to eliminate all duplication. And given the state of my knowledge at this point, it is rather fortuitous that the language I must employ is loaded with both a semantic and syntactical redundancy that comes naturally to me. In time I may be able to communicate on this problem with more certainty, with a more logical and precise syntax, with less multiplicity of meanings; then, the type of redundancy needed would change, the amount would diminish, and the risk of inconsistency would lessen. Now, however, a resort to the vernacular and I need not apologize

---

[2] Irwin D. J. Bross, *Design for Decision* (New York: Macmillan, 1953).

[3] So, too, we repeat observations. The more observations, the less the uncertainty.

[4] See J. R. Pierce, *op. cit.*, chaps. 7 and 8. Also see Colin Cherry, *On Human Communication* (New York: Science Editions, 1961), pp. 180–185.

[5] The English language is estimated to be between 50 to 65 percent redundant. The language employed in control tower–pilot communication is about 95 percent redundant.

[6] It suffices to note that it is precisely the property of redundancy in a formal logic that permits deductive inference. Given a set of algebraic equations, e.g., we can deduce the solution by acting in accordance with the appropriate syntactical rules. This solution is *implicit* in the set of equations and can thereby be deduced. It contains "no more information" than the original equations and constitutes a redundancy (repetition) that is present but not obvious. See Cherry, *op. cit.*, pp. 221–231. Also, see Herbert A . Simon, "The Architecture of Complexity," *Proceedings of the American Philosophical Society* 106 (1962):478–479.

for this. On the contrary, "the rules we call grammar and syntax . . . supplement and duplicate each other, providing a great margin of safety." [7] While I must exercise care so as not to be incoherent, I can nevertheless break some of these rules without destroying or critically damaging the communication process itself. Nor need it be stressed that the redundancy of both our grammar and lexicon are sources of great creativity and innovation.

PUBLIC ADMINISTRATION AND REDUNDANCY

It is, however, the lexical evaluation of redundancy which prevails in public administration. Indeed, this view is to be seen as programmatic in such revitalization movements as Taylorism and scientific management. These demanded the wholesale removal of duplication and overlap as they pressed for "streamlined organizations" that would operate with the absolutely minimal number of units that could possibly be employed in the performance of a task. Zero redundancy constituted the measure of optimal efficiency and this ideal, fortified by a scarcity of resources and an abundance of precedent, has informed both the theory and practice of public administration since the earliest days of the reform movement. Now, of course, we possess new vocabularies, direct our attention to management control systems, and seize upon such new technologies as PPBS [Planning-Programming-Budgeting System]. But our perspective remains fully as Utopian as it was a half-century ago. [8]

For the plain fact is that no amount of effort has yet been able to produce, even for limited time-spans, the precise mutually exclusive differentiation of activity that administrative integrationists long for . . . In the last thirty years we have observed massive efforts to reduce duplication: we have moved from the radical reconstructions which followed upon the Roosevelt and Hoover commissions to the institution of continuous executive reorganization — only to find that duplication and overlap are as conspicuous today as they have ever been. . . .

. . . The removal of redundancy is rarely, if ever, challenged in the technology of public administration. It is an article of faith, a commanding precept: and if its injunctions cannot be followed today, one can always dream of tomorrow. Those controversies that do

[7] Cherry, *ibid.*, p. 19
[8] Dwight Waldo, *The Administrative State* (New York: Ronald Press, 1948), pp. 37–38.

arise generally concern the manner in which repair is to be effected
and are not expressed any more differently than when Francis W.
Coker cast a skeptical eye on the dogmas of administration. The
doubts he raised turned on whether more might be accomplished
through an incremental strategy than by a process of radical integration. But with respect to the need to "eliminate duplication and
overlapping," [9] he felt obliged to state, "No serious exception can be
taken to this principle." [10]

In what follows, I shall exercise a theoretical option and take
such exception. I cannot argue the case in full here, but I shall try
to show that there are good grounds for suggesting that efforts to improve public administration by eliminating duplication and overlap
would, if successful, produce just the opposite effect. That so many
attempts have failed should perhaps alert us to what sociologists
would call the "latent function" of this type of redundancy. This
possibility alone is sufficient warrant for transforming a precept into
a problem.

REDUNDANCY AND ERROR SUPPRESSION: RELIABILITY

There is, however, an additional reason for doing so.

The reader will observe that the phenomenon of "duplication" is
no longer left to chance in the study of language. Nor is it overlooked in the design of automobiles, computers, and aircraft; the
latter are reliable to the extent that they are redundant — and we
have all had occasion to note that a good deal of the controversy
over "safe cars" has had to do with the introduction of this feature as
a standard element of design, as with the dual braking system, for
example. That is, there is now a developing theory of redundancy,
and while it was originally conceived of in the domains of information science (including computer technology) and natural automata
(neural networks), it appears to have very wide application. In
many areas, therefore, "over-engineering," "reserve power," and
"safety-factors" of all sorts need no longer be dealt with intuitively.

But what of large-scale formal organization: can it be engaged in
terms of this theory? The answer, of course, cannot be had a priori,
but the attempt to do so is well under way, precipitated quite natu-

---

[9] Once again this is a goal of the newly proposed "Hoover Commission"; see
Public Administration News, August 1967, p. 2.

[10] "Dogmas of Administrative Reform," *The American Political Science
Review*, Vol. 16 (August 1922).

rally by our propensity to draw from such cognate languages as systems analysis, cybernetics, and information theory — in particular, the latter. Fashion aside, however, "this comparison need not be a sterile metaphorical analogy," as Rapoport and Horvath note, for all organizations have "neural physiologies" in the sense that they are unthinkable "without internal communication, integration and control." [11] Marschak, in the same vein, proposes that an organization is to be defined by the rules which determine the sets of messages that can be received by its different members. Any given system, thus, "states who should do what in response to what." [12]

Upon reflection, it makes a good deal of sense to regard a large-scale organization as a vast and complicated information system. It is, after all, necessarily and continuously engaged in the transmission and reception of messages. But it is an awfully noisy system. Its codes, classification rules, are not unambiguous; its internal arrangements are not perfect; the course of its messages are neither consistent nor constant — nor are the messages themselves. Error occurs at the point of origin, where a message is selected from a whole ensemble of signs (stimuli), and at the point of reception. The language which is employed is notoriously vague and the "variable human," [13] acting both as sender and receiver, often transforms the relation between a sign and its referent into a mystery. In an organizational system one can never be sure that either members or clientele can be reached without error or distortion. The transmission of information is, indeed, a very risky business.[14] Against this backdrop, the demand for control by central officers can clearly be seen as a demand for increased reliability (predictability) of response — and this means a reduction of uncertainty.

In public administration the standard policy for improving the performance characteristics of an administrative agency has rested upon the classical axiom that the reliability and efficiency of an op-

[11] Anatol Rapoport and William J. Horvath, "Thoughts on Organization Theory and a Review of Two Conferences," *General Systems Yearbook* (1959):91.

[12] Jacob Marschak, "Economic Planning and the Cost of Thinking," *Social Research* 33 (Summer 1966):157–158. Also, see John T. Dorsey, Jr., "The Information-Energy Model," in F. Heady and S. Stokes (Eds.), *Papers in Comparative Public Administration* (Ann Arbor, Mich.: Institute of Public Administration, 1962).

[13] The phrase is James D. Thompson's. *Organizations in Actions* (New York: McGraw-Hill, 1967), see chapter 8.

[14] This, incidentally, is a redundant sentence.

erating system, man or machine, is dependent on the reliability and efficiency of each of its parts, including linkages. Improvement, therefore, calls for a system to be broken down (decomposed or analyzed) into its most basic units, these to be worked on to the point of infallibility. So much success has attended this procedure, especially as regards machine-based systems, that it not only constitutes a sound problem-solving paradigm, but is often generalized into a good common-sense rule. About the only limitations which are imposed on its application are those which derive from market conditions, the law of diminishing returns, and the state of the art.

Yet it is doubtful that the risk of failure can be removed in this manner even in the most advanced technologies. No matter how much a part is perfected, there is always the chance that it will fail. In some cases, many in fact, this is a tolerable risk — the unit involved may not be a basic component and the consequences of failure may be minimal. But where a system is important, and where it is made dependent upon operating parts that are organized into a tight means-end chain, the problem becomes acute. In such systems, especially when large, there is a tendency for even minor errors to be so amplified along the length of the chain as to make the end-result quite unreliable. In formal organizations this tendency can be expressed in terms of "the absorption of uncertainty." [15] The failure, then, of a single part can mean the failure of the entire system: as when the breakdown of a switching circuit blacks out an entire region or the failure of a duty officer to heed radar readings permits a force of unidentified aircraft to attack Pearl Harbor with devastating success. The latter case, it will be recognized, constitutes a stark illustration of the uncertainty principle. Here it was not the *evidence* which was transmitted, only the *inferences*.[16] In complex and tightly ordered systems the cost of error can run very high.

This is the context in which the theory of redundancy bulks so large. For it sets aside the doctrine that ties the reliability of a system to the perfectability of parts and thereby approaches the pragmatics of systems in action much more realistically. That is, it accepts the inherent limitations of any organization by treating any

[15] James G. March, Herbert A. Simon, and Harold Guetzkow, *Organizations* (New York: John Wiley, 1958), pp. 164–166. I am indebted to Aaron Wildavsky for this suggestion.

[16] *Ibid.*, p. 165.

and all parts, regardless of their degree of perfection,[17] as risky actors. The practical implications of this shift in orientation is immediately to be seen when the following question is asked: Is it possible to take a set of individually unreliable units and form them into a system "with any arbitrarily high reliability"?[18] Can we, in other words, build an organization that is more reliable than any of its parts?

The answer, *mirabile dictu*, is yes. In what is now a truly classical paper, Von Neumann demonstrated that it could be done by adding sufficient redundancy.[19] Developments in this domain move swiftly and where before we could only resort to an intuitive and rather pragmatic redundancy, there now exist powerful theorems which can be applied with far greater certainty and much less waste.[20] This, it can be said, is a cardinal feature of "systems analysis" — all too often overlooked.

The theory itself is a rather complicated set of formulations and it serves no purpose to dwell upon it in any great detail. Yet there is one theorem that must be indicated because of the profound effect it can have on organizational design: that the probability of failure in a system decreases exponentially as redundancy factors are increased. Increasing reliability in this manner, of course, raises the price to be paid and if fail-safe conditions are to be reached, the cost may be prohibitive. But an immediate corollary of the theorem eases this problem for it requires only arithmetic increases in redundancy to yield geometric increases in reliability. Costs may then be quite manageable.

The application of this formula, however, depends upon the

[17] It is assumed, of course, that any component meets a specified standard of performance.

[18] Jagjit Singh, *Information Theory, Language and Cybernetics* (New York: Dover Publications, 1966), p. 173.

[19] John Von Neumann, "Probabilistic Logics and the Synthesis of Reliable Organizations from Unreliable Components," in C. E. Shannon and J. McCarthy (Eds.), *Automata Studies* (Princeton, N. J.: Princeton University Press, 1956). Also, see C. E. Shannon and W. Weaver, *The Mathematical Theory of Communication* (Urbana: University of Illinois Press, 1949). And see Pierce, *op. cit.*, chap. 8; Singh, *op. cit.*, chaps. 4 and 5; and Cherry, *op. cit.*, chap. 5.

[20] W. H. Pierce, "Redundancy in Computers," *Scientific American*, Vol. 210 (February 1964). Also, see W. S. McCulloch, "The Reliability of Biological Systems," in M. G. Yovitz and S. Cameron (Eds.), *Self-Organizing Systems* (New York: Pergamon Press, 1960); and Singh, *op. cit.*, chaps. 10–12. And see Robert Gordon, "Optimum Component Redundancy for Maximum System Reliability," *Operations Research*, Vol. 5 (1957).

ability to construct a system so that it satisfies those conditions which permit the laws of probability to apply, in this case, the multiplication theorem or the product rule for independent events: alternatively, the failure of parts must be random and statistically independent (unrelated). In practical terms, therefore, a system must be so arranged that when parts fail, they do so unpredictably and in such manner *that they cannot and do not impair other parts*, as in the dual braking system of a car. If each braking assembly is not completely separated from the other, the redundancy is not waste, it becomes a very dangerous addition: when it fails it is likely (perhaps certain) to damage the other assembly. So much for a theorem which has to do with duplication. We turn now to "overlapping."

"Overlapping"

Generally employed to denote biological organisms (neural physiologies, in particular), "self-organizing systems" command fully as much attention in the study of redundancy as computing machines and communication networks. There is nothing surprising about this since the theory of redundancy is a theory of system reliability. And self-organizing systems exhibit a degree of reliability that is so far superior to anything we can build as to prompt theorists to suggest "that the richly redundant networks of biological organisms must have capabilities beyond anything our theories can yet explain." [21] In Von Neumann's phrasing, they "contain the necessary arrangements to diagnose errors as they occur, to readjust the organism so as to minimize the effects of errors, and finally to correct or to block permanently the faulty component." Error refers here to malfunction, and Von Neumann states that there is now little doubt that they are "able to operate even when malfunctions set in . . . [while] their subsequent tendency is to remove them." [22] Pierce adds that they are able to improve reliability when errors are common even as they improve their capabilities when errors are infrequent. [23]

---

[21] Pierce, *op. cit.*, p. 112.

[22] John Von Neumann, "The General and Logical Theory of Automata," in James R. Newman, *The World of Mathematics* (New York: Simon and Schuster, 1956), IV, 2085–2086.

[23] Pierce, *op. cit.*

Equipotentiality

How, precisely, this works remains an object of inquiry. But it seems clear that such systems possess a fantastic number of parallel hookups of many different types. McCulloch, in commenting on the reliability of biological organisms, speaks of redundancies of codes, of channels, of calculation, and of potential command, noting that each serves differently. "The reliability you can buy with redundancy of calculation cannot be bought with redundancy of code or channel." [24] To these we can add the property of "equipotentiality" which provides the system with an extraordinary adaptive power.

Equipotentiality, interestingly enough, is often referred to as "overlapping." [25] It denotes the tendency of neural networks to resist that kind of precise differentiation of function which is mutually exclusive. Even in the case of highly specialized subsystems the tendency is restricted but not lost. There appears to be some "overlap" at all times which enables residual parts or subsidiary centers to "take over," though somewhat less efficiently, the functions of those which have been damaged. It is this overlap [26] that permits the organism to exhibit a high degree of adaptability, i.e., to change its behavior in accordance with changes in stimuli.

DUPLICATION AND OVERLAP: POLITICS

And this is why it may be quite *irrational* to greet the appearance of duplication and overlap by automatically moving to excise and redefine. To unify the defense departments, or the several independent information-gathering services of the government, or the large number of agencies engaged in technical assistance, or the various antipoverty programs, or the miscellany of agencies concerned with transportation, or the great variety of federal, state, and local administrations that function in the same areas may rob the system of its necessary supports. It can be hypothesized that it is precisely such redundancies that allow for the delicate process of

[24] McCulloch, *op. cit.*, p. 265.

[25] Singh, *op. cit.*, pp. 246–247, 323.

[26] It is interesting to note that learning machines, machines which "interpret their environment," are built upon this principle. They are much more flexible than computers and "can rise to occasions not foreseen by programmed instructions." *Ibid.*, p. 225.

mutual adjustment, of self-regulation, by means of which the whole system can sustain severe local injuries and still function creditably.

Hypothesis? — perhaps it is more than that. If, of course, "men were angels," the systems they constitute would be foolproof. But they are not; and this is the fact that stands at the foundation of the organization created in Philadelphia. For the charter of the national system is a patent illustration of redundancy. Look at it: separation of powers, federalism, checks and balances, concurrent powers, double legislatures, overlapping terms of office, the Bill of Rights, the veto, the override, judicial review, and a host of similar arrangements. Here is a system that cannot be described except in terms of duplication and overlap — of a redundancy of channel, code, calculation, and command.

These are the redundancies which prompt public administration theorists to regard this system as quite inefficient — if not irrational. Where they wish one unambiguous code, there are many and these are hardly unequivocal; where they seek a unity of command, there is a redundancy of command; and so on. As a decision system, the organization of government certainly appears to be inferior to that which underlays program budgeting — which is why we see an expressed longing for a "wholesale revision of the federal structure." After all, as some programmers see it, the objectives of the architects of the Constitution were as much political as economic, and their economics "had a philosophic rather than managerial or operational character. The decision-making structure came . . . under the influence of objectives other than rationality of choice." [27] And, as Smithies has noted, "It is fundamental to our culture that rational choice is better than irrational choice." [28]

It is not possible, however, to determine whether a choice is rational except in terms of systemic context and goal. A course of action may be perfectly rational in one sphere and perfectly silly in another. It is only when context and goal are rendered nonproblematical that objective evaluations of competing decision systems can be had. If these factors cannot be bracketed, then assessments of decision systems are of necessity assignments of priority to specific sets of values. To say, therefore, that rational choice is fundamental

[27] Roland N. McKean and Melvin Anshen, "Limitations, Risks and Problems," in Novick, *op. cit.*, p. 287.
[28] Arthur Smithies, "Conceptual Framework for the Program Budget," *ibid.*, p. 24.

to our culture is either to say nothing or, as in the context of administration, to urge that economic rationality is intrinsically superior to political rationality. In this case it should be clear, economic rationality is equated to scientific rationality and we are being told, without restriction, that the rules of scientific decisionmaking are not simply different, they are best. We need not wonder why scientific management programs have always had the appearance of an ideology.

But there is more than one kind of "rationality," including the rationality of redundancy. Theoretically, there can be as many rationalities as there are systems — which is why phenomenologists have urged that rationality not be treated solely as a methodological principle but as "empirically problematical material" as well. In this respect Garfinkle has demonstrated that there are profound differences between "common sense" and "scientific" rationalities — of such an order that the two cannot be ranked. Indeed, it might give us all pause to observe what happens when the maxims of ideal scientific procedure are introduced willy-nilly into the everyday situation; what they do is to disrupt its continuities and multiply its anomic features.[29] In short, they disorganize an organized state.

Moreover, there is an element of paradox in the effort to extend these maxims to government at large. Most of us are influenced, if not absorbed, by the notion of "system," and this statement obviously includes economizers. Among the most fundamental elements of systems analysis, however, is the concept of systemic relevance. And the criteria which establish relevance are the criteria which mark boundaries. This means that any methodology is to be valued only to the extent that it achieves systemically relevant goals and such goals, to be at all sensible, must be desired state conditions which are in reach and which are field determined. Otherwise, they are idle fantasies or simply Utopian. If, of course, boundaries enlarge so as to permit what was heretofore irrelevant, this can only be learned by experience. Under such an expansion, methodologies which were once inappropriate may become extremely valuable. As Hamilton was wont to say, "means ought to be proportional to the end."[30]

[29] Harold Garfinkle, "The Rational Properties of Scientific and Common-Sense Activities," *Behavioral Science,* Vol. 5 (1960), and *Studies in Ethnomethodology* (Englewood Cliffs, N.J.: Prentice-Hall, 1967), chap. 2.
[30] *The Federalist,* No. 31.

Auxiliary Precautions

The constitution-makers, it appears, were eminently "rational." They chose wisely and they did so under hazardous conditions. They knew that they were "organizing" a system in the face of great uncertainty. We need not list the profound and abiding cleavages which existed nor the intense fears which were displayed: *The Federalist* alone makes this clear. But it also instructs that in fabricating the constitution, the architects were ever mindful of the grave possibility of failure and sought a system which could perform in the face of error — which could manage to provide a stable set of decision rules for an exceedingly unstable circumstance. And they found their answer in Newton's Third Law.[31] Experience, Madison wrote, has taught mankind the necessity for *auxiliary precautions:* these were to be had "by so contriving the internal structure of government so that its several constituent parts, may by their mutual relations, be the means of keeping each other in their proper places."[32] The principle of action and reaction, of checks and balances, turns out to have been, in organization terms, the principle of interwoven and competing redundancies.

"That which is redundant is, to the extent that it is redundant, stable. It is therefore reliable."[33] One hundred and seventy-nine years have passed since the original design, and save for one massive failure, the system has withstood the severest of shocks — and may well continue to do so even in the face of today's unprecedented problems. We like to say that it is the oldest constitutional government in the world, yet it remains a novelty. It seems to have worked like a "self-organizing" system exhibiting both the performance reliability and adaptability that such systems display. Marked by a redundancy of law, of power and command, of structure and linkage — *the whole has appeared as more reliable than any of its parts.* Where one part has failed another has taken over, and even when duplicates were not there to be employed, the presence of equipotentiality, of overlapping functions, permitted the load to be assumed elsewhere, however imperfectly. Scholars have for years spoken of the "cyclical character" of intragovernmental arrange-

[31] Martin Landau, "On the Use of Metaphor in Political Analysis," *Social Research*, Vol. 28 (Autumn 1961).
[32] *The Federalist*, No. 51, emphasis added; see also Nos. 47 and 48.
[33] McCulloch, *op. cit.*, p. 265.

ments, of a "pendulum of checks and balances," frequently pointing to this phenomenon as an adaptive response. The "uncertain content" (jurisdiction) of the various parts of government just will not allow it to sit still and the hyphenated phrases we are forced to use in describing government are indicative of the extent of its equipotentiality. Even when such reference is pejorative, as often happens in the instance of "judicial-legislation," such a concept points to an overlap which enables adaptation. *Baker* v. *Carr* is a recent illustration of this kind of self-regulation.[34] The boss, the historical master of an "invisible government," was a redundancy that developed to offset the failures of local government,[35] and this would not have been possible but for the redundancy of party. Senator Mike Mansfield, speaking on the floor of the Senate, warns his colleagues that if they do not act, other branches of government will:

It is clear that when one road to this end fails, others will unfold as indeed they have unfolded. If the process is ignored in legislative channels, it will not necessarily be blocked in other channels — in the executive branch and in the courts.[36]

And the President has been severely criticized because he has radically curtailed the number of channels, formal and informal, that are employed for purposes of control. Richard Neustadt, after describing the extraordinary redundancy which marked FDR's administration, concludes the presidency cannot function effectively without competing information sources.[37]

Nor need any of this be gainsaid by the compelling movement toward centralization. Although this is an empirical problem which I have only begun to investigate, there is some basis for suggesting that this trend constitutes a replacement of historically accepted types of redundancies by those which may be more appropriate to the existent task environment. Because such changes involve command or control, they do not occur without sharp and often protracted conflict — as can be seen in the bitter controversy between the Senate Foreign Relations Committee and the President. This,

[34] See Martin Landau, "Baker v. Carr and the Ghost of Federalism," in G. Schubert (Ed.), *Reapportionment* (New York: Scribners, 1964).

[35] Robert K. Merton, "Manifest and Latent Function, in *Social Theory and Social Structure* (Glencoe, N.Y.: The Free Press, 1957).

[36] Quoted by Marquis Childs, *New York Post*, May 10, 1962.

[37] Richard E. Neustadt, *Presidential Power* (New York: John Wiley, 1960), chap. 7.

to be sure, is exacerbated by differences over Vietnam policy, but it necessarily involves competing redundancies. However this is settled, the organization of government in this country, at least until now, demands attention: it seems to have brought an extraordinary amount of reliability and adaptability through its extensive parallel networks (duplication) and equipotential parts (overlap).

Indeed, it is a curiosity to observe the extent to which redundancy theorists resort to political metaphor. Their designs eschew single-line arrangements and they employ a system of multiplexing (multiple lines in parallel) which operates in accordance with the principle of "majority rule." Such devices are known as "vote-takers" which abide by the rules of "democratic suffrage." As Von Neumann put it, they are "majority organs." And Pierce remarks that, "It is as though there were a nation in which no citizen could be trusted, and accordingly, several citizens were required to act together in making decisions, executing orders or delivering messages." [38] But there are times when equally weighted votes are not as effective as one might desire. Under such circumstances, redundancy theorists provide for an "aristocratic suffrage" by assigning unequal weights to decisionmakers. What is most interesting here is that this assignment is made in proportion to a decisionmaker's reliability as tested under performance conditions and is adjusted continuously in accordance with the record.[39] More immediately, however, the use of such metaphor bespeaks an implicit grasp of the power of redundancy in politics.

PUBLIC ADMINISTRATION

Not so for public administration, however.

Its prevailing notions of organizational rationality are built upon contrary assumptions. Where the "rationality" of politics derives from the fact that a system can be more reliable (more responsive, more predictable) than any of its parts, public administration has postulated that a system can be no more than the sum of its parts: reliable components, thus, add up to a reliable system and *per contra*.

The logic of this position, to iterate, calls for each role to be perfected, each bureau to be exactly delimited, each linkage to articulate unfailingly, and each line of communication to be noiseless —

[38] Pierce, *op. cit.*, p. 105–106. Also, see Singh, *op. cit.*, p. 176.
[39] Which appears as a sound principle for constituting "elites."

all to produce one interlocking system, one means-end chain which possesses the absolutely minimum number of links, and which culminates at a central control point. For the public administration rationalist, the optimal organization consists of units that are wholly compatible, precisely connected, fully determined, and, therefore, perfectly reliable. The model which represents this dream is that of a linear organization in which everything is arrayed in tandem.[40] It is as if the entire house is to be wired in series.

If the analogy holds, and it does to a considerable extent — especially as regards communication processes, organizational systems of this sort are a form of administrative *brinkmanship*. They are extraordinary gambles. When one bulb blows, everything goes. Ordering parts in series makes them so dependent upon each other that any single failure can break the system. It is the old story of "For want of a nail . . . the battle was lost." Other illustrations: each of us can supply any number of instances of rather serious disruptions because of a faulty part, a malfunctioning actor, a noisy channel. Serial arrangements have the property of intensifying error.

In fact, they may be conducive to error — and to all sorts of problems. For they presuppose the human actor is a linear element and can, therefore, produce outputs in proportion to inputs, and on schedule. There is no doubt, of course, that the human actor can perform "indifferently" over a very wide task environment and under very diverse conditions: otherwise, large-scale formal organization as we know it would not be able to maintain itself.[41] But we have come to learn, and at sad cost, that even if serial demands fall within an actor's "zone of acceptance," there are limits to his linearity. The strains imposed can be too much, the burden of error can be too great — in short, he can be overloaded. A ready resort to a "rational calculus," which places actors in serial interdependence on the assumption of linearity, courts trouble. As against optimum performance, it may beget even less than a satisficing one. Indeed, it is more likely to breed a "resistance" which ultimately results in a sharply reduced zone of acceptance. And this reduction may be so severe as to constitute a direct challenge to organizational authority. In this circumstance, organizational expenditures to secure

---

[40] Thompson refers to this organizational pattern as the "long-linked technology" involving "serial interdependence," *op. cit.*, pp. 18–19.

[41] *Ibid.*, pp. 105–106. Also, see Herbert Simon, *Administrative Behavior* (New York: Macmillan, 1947).

compliance may be far more than the cost of parallel hookups which do not require perfectability to increase reliability and which, thereby, reduce strain.

There are additional risks as well — not the least of which is an intensification of the "displacement of goals." [42] Because each part assumes so weighty a responsibility in the system, exacting controls are required. Rules, therefore, assume even more importance than they ordinarily do. And the more precise they are, the better the control. There is, then, an even greater possibility that strict and slavish adherence to regulations will obtain. The burden of error is sufficient to prompt a refusal to exercise discretion when an untoward situation arises. This holds *a fortiori* in a government organization which is bound by rules that have the force of law: for a mistake in interpretation may place action outside the limits of the rule and render it *ultra vires*. Under such strictures there will neither be the "taking advantage of a technicality" or of a "loophole" — and it is a practice such as this one which often constitutes an adaptive response to an urgent problem.

But, beyond this, the "rationality of redundancy" assumes considerable praxiological force when it is noted that the typical organizational pattern which the administrative rationalist proposes is invariably the ideal organizational structure for synoptic or programmed decisionmaking.[43]

To be sure, this type of decision process stands as the perfect form of problem solving. It is, on analysis, modeled on the deductive chain of a fully axiomatized theory. Where it holds, all that is needed to "decide" is to compute the solution — the correct course of action. It can only obtain, however, under conditions of certainty, in a circumstance that Herbert Simon has called a "closed set of variables." [44] For public administration, this means that the environ-

[42] Robert Merton, "Bureaucratic Structure and Personality," in Merton *et al.*, (Eds.), *Reader in Bureaucracy* (Glencoe, N.Y.: The Free Press, 1952).

[43] I take both terms as synonyms for the same concept. See David Braybrooke and Charles E. Lindblom, *A Strategy for Decision* (New York: The Free Press, 1963), and Herbert Simon, *The New Science of Management Decision* (New York: Harper, 1960). "Computation decision" is still another name employed by James Thompson and Arthur Tuden; see "Strategies, Structures, and Processes of Organizational Decision" in *Comparative Studies in Administration* (Pittsburgh: University of Pittsburgh Press, 1959).

[44] If the situation is one in which we do not have certainty but we are able to measure (accurately) the probability distributions of the outcomes of each alternative course of action, the situation can be treated as "closed."

ment has been fully and correctly described, that preferred state conditions are unequivocal, and that the instruments necessary to produce preferred states are at hand. Said alternatively, certainty exists as to fact and value, instrumentation and outcome, means and ends. All that needs to be known is known and no ambiguities prevail. If there is any doubt on either side of the equation, then a forced programmed process is no more than an instance of "Gresham's Law." It will drive out the very activity which is needed to produce knowledge: in organizational terms, operational agencies that have not mastered their task environment will be sealed off from it.[45]

Now there are many areas of administration which admit of the logic of programming, with respect to which we can apply the rather powerful "closed decision systems" we already possess. Not to do so is a witless act, for it is an absurdity to refuse to deploy knowledge which is at hand. But there is a question as to how much of the domain of public administration can be covered in this manner.[46] Conditions of certainty, or near certainty, appear to be rare facts in the life of a public agency, and when they exist, their scope is likely to be severely restricted. If so, it is not very rational to design organizations to pursue decision strategies that can comprehend only a small portion of their activities. On the contrary, it is a very sensible rule to construct organizations so that they can cope with uncertainty as to fact and disagreement over values.

If facts are in question, then we simply do not have knowledge of the appropriate means to use in seeking an outcome. We may have hunches and rules of thumb and we may write elaborate plans which anticipate all conceivable outcomes, but these are only hypotheses. It is, therefore, an obvious and "rational calculus" to employ a pragmatic and experimental procedure: that is, a policy of redundancy which permits several, and competing, strategies to be

[45] This is especially so with respect to serial designs, since they can only operate under closure. See Thompson, *op. cit.*, p. 19, Prop. 2.1: Under norms of rationality, organizations seek to seal off their core technologies from environmental influences.

[46] The history of science and technology indicates that as we gain more knowledge we open new areas of uncertainty. Which is why, I suspect, that Simon says that "many, perhaps most of the problems that have to be handled at middle and high levels of management" will probably never be amenable to mathematical treatment. Herbert Simon, *The New Science of Management Decision, op. cit.*, p. 21.

followed both simultaneously and separately. Separately, because the moment a plan is put into effect it constitutes an experiment, and unless we introduce "controls" we cannot determine which course of action is best. And as difficult as it may be to apply this policy in an ongoing agency, so is it necessary. It can be seen, then, that any attempt to "program" solutions prematurely is the height of folly. Managements may do this in the interest of economy and control, but the economy will be false and the control a ritual — for we are acting, and organizing, as if we "know" when we do not. It is a striking phenomenon of organizational life (and elsewhere, of course) that we often present the appearance of "rationality" when we do not know what we are doing or why. Operating personnel will not find this last statement amiss.

Alternatives

If the value side is open, we can either fight, slam it shut, or negotiate. It would take us too far afield to discuss conflict here, and we can dispatch the arbitrary closure of value differences by suggesting that it breeds conflict — up to and including "administrative sabotage" — a possibility that programmers must always be alert to. But if there exist differences as to preferences, and the parties involved value the existence of the organization, it makes good sense to compromise, to negotiate differences, to be "political." . . . This process, we know, is a widespread practice in public administration. The Inter-University Case Program, if it has demonstrated anything, points up "the intricate process of negotiation, mutual accommodation, and reconciliation of competing values . . ." which mark all of the agencies thus far studied.[47] As a decision system, negotiation avoids the precise, mutually exclusive definitions of value that are necessary to any synoptic procedure. This cardinal rule of bargaining has been generated by years of extensive experience, especially in labor-management relations, and is based upon the fact that such clarification of values serves only to extend and intensify disagreement.[48] It, therefore, requires the redundancy of ambiguity, surplus

[47] Herbert Kaufman, "The Next Step in Case Studies," *Public Administration Review* 18 (Winter 1958):55.

[48] Charles Lindblom offers an appropriate maxim in this regard: Do not try to clarify values if the parties can agree on policies. "Some Limitations on

meaning, for it is precisely such surplus that permits values to overlap the parties in dispute providing thereby some common ground for agreement.

There are, then, a number of decision systems,[49] each of which calls for a different organizational perspective. None, however, can do without redundancy. Whatever claims are made for programmed decisionmaking, it is to be recognized that if its organizational structure consisted only of the "absolutely minimal number of parts," error could not be detected. As against pragmatics and negotiation, there is little doubt that reliable performance requires lesser amounts of redundancy. But the task remains to learn to distinguish between inefficient redundancies and those that are constructive and reinforcing — and this includes the kind of knowledge which will permit the introduction of redundancies so that they can work to increase both reliability and adaptability. This task, needless to say, attends pragmatics and negotiation as well, for they are redundant by their nature.

A FINAL NOTE

The appearance, therefore, of duplication and overlap in administrative agencies are not necessarily signs of waste and inefficiency. On the contrary, it is becoming increasingly evident that large-scale organizations function as self-organizing systems and tend to develop their own parallel circuits: not the least of which is the transformation of such "residual" parts as "informal groups," into constructive redundancies. Where we are sometimes prone to regard such groups as sources of pathology, they may be compensating for the deficiencies of the formal organization in the same way that the "boss" once did.

At one and the same time, thus, redundancy serves many vital functions in the conduct of public administration. It provides safety factors, permits flexible responses to anomalous situations and provides a creative potential for those who are able to see it. If there is

---

Rationality" in Carl J. Friedrich (Ed.), *Rational Decision* (New York: Atherton Press, 1964).

[49] The system of classification that I have employed is based upon Thompson and Tuden, *op. cit.* My own explication of their formulations is to be found in "Decision Theory and Comparative Public Administration," *Comparative Political Studies,* Vol. 1 (July 1968).

no duplication, if there is no overlap, if there is no ambiguity, an organization will neither be able to suppress error nor generate alternate routes of action.[50] In short, it will be most unreliable and least flexible, sluggish, as we now say.

"Streamlining an agency," "consolidating similar functions," "eliminating duplication," and "commonality" are powerful slogans which possess an obvious appeal. But it is just possible that their achievement would deprive an agency of the properties it needs most — those which allow rules to be broken and units to operate defectively without doing critical injury to the agency as a whole. Accordingly, it would be far more constructive, even under conditions of scarcity, to lay aside easy slogans and turn attention to a principle which lessens risks without foreclosing opportunity.

25   Symbols and Political Quiescence

MURRAY EDELMAN

Few forms of explanation of political phenomena are more common than the assertion that the success of some group was facilitated by the "apathy" of other groups with opposing interests. If apathy is not an observable phenomenon in a political context because it connotes an individual's mental state, quiescence is observ-

---

[50] As an immediate illustration, an agency often encounters situations which require prompt and necessary action. Where rules duplicate and overlap, safety factors exist. If one set of rules fails or does not cover the situation, an alternate route can be found or rules can be stretched — broadly interpreted. The problem, again, is to eliminate an inefficient profusion and to provide efficient redundancy.

From Murray Edelman, "Symbols and Political Quiescence," reprinted by permission of the author and The American Political Science Association from *The American Political Science Review* 54 (September 1960):695–704. Some footnotes are renumbered.

able. It is the purpose of this paper to specify some conditions associated with political quiescence in the formation of business regulation policies. Although the same general conditions are apparently applicable to the formation of public policies in any area, the argument and the examples used here focus upon the field of government regulation of business in order to make the paper manageable and to permit more intensive treatment.

Political quiescence toward a policy area can be assumed to be a function either of lack of interest — whether it is simple indifference or stems rather from a sense of futility about the practical prospects of securing obviously desirable changes — or of the satisfaction of whatever interest the quiescent group may have in the policy in question. Our concern here is with the forms of satisfaction. In analyzing the various means by which it can come to pass, the following discussion distinguishes between interests in resources (whether goods or freedoms to act) and interests in symbols connoting the suppression of threats to the group in question. Few political scientists would doubt, on the basis of common-sense evidence, that public policies have value to interested groups both as symbols and as instruments for the allocation of more tangible values. The political process has been much less thoroughly studied as a purveyor of symbols, however; and there is a good deal of evidence, to be presented below, that symbols are a more central component of the process than is commonly recognized in political scientists' explicit or implicit models.[1]

Three related hypotheses will be considered:

(1) The interests of organized groups in tangible resources or in substantive power are less easily satiable than are interests in symbolic reassurance.

(2) Necessary conditions associated with the occurrence of the latter type of interest are:

- (a) the existence of economic conditions in some measure threatening the security of a large group;
- (b) the absence of organization for the purpose of furthering the common interest of that group;
- (c) widespread political responses suggesting the prevalence of

[1] Harold Lasswell is a major exception, and some of his contributions will be noted.

inaccurate, oversimplified, and distorted perceptions of the issue.

(3) The pattern of political activity represented by lack of organization, distorted perception, interests in symbolic reassurance, and quiescence is a key element in the ability of organized groups to use political agencies in order to make good their claims on tangible resources and power, thus continuing the threat to the unorganized.

Available evidence bearing on these hypotheses will be marshalled as follows. First, some widely accepted propositions regarding group claims, quiescence, and techniques for satisfying group interests in governmental regulation of business will be summarized. Next, some pertinent experimental and empirical findings of other disciplines will be considered. Finally the paper will explore the possibility of integrating the various findings and applying them to the propositions listed above.

I

If the regulatory process is examined in terms of a divergence between political and legal promises on the one hand and resource allocations and group reactions on the other hand, the largely symbolic character of the entire process becomes apparent. What do the studies of government regulation of business tell us of the role and functions of that amorphous group who have an interest in these policies in the sense that they are affected by them, but who are not rationally organized to pursue their interest? The following generalizations would probably be accepted by most students, perhaps with occasional changes of emphasis:

(1) Tangible resources and benefits are frequently not distributed to unorganized political group interests as promised in regulatory statutes and the propaganda attending their enactment.

This is not true of legal fictions, but rather of the values held out to (or demanded by) groups which regard themselves as disadvantaged and which presumably anticipate benefits from a regulatory policy. There is virtually unanimous agreement among students of the anti-trust laws, the Clayton and Federal Trade Commission acts, the Interstate Commerce acts, the public utility statutes and the right-to-work laws, for example, that through much of the history of their administration these statutes have been ineffective in the sense that many of the values they promised have not in fact been realized. The story has not been uniform, of course; but the general point hardly needs detailed documentation at this late date. Herring,[2] Leiserson,[3] Truman,[4] and Bernstein [5] all conclude that few regulatory policies have been pursued unless they proved acceptable to the regulated groups or served the interests of these groups. Within the past decade Redford,[6] Bernstein [7] and others have offered a "life cycle" theory of regulatory history, showing a more or less regular pattern of loss of vigor by regulatory agencies. For purposes of the present argument it need not be assumed that this always happens but only that it frequently happens in important cases.[8]

(2) When it does happen, the deprived groups often display little tendency to protest or to assert their awareness of the deprivation.

The fervent display of public wrath, or enthusiasm, in the course of the initial legislative attack on forces seen as threatening "the little man" is a common American spectacle. It is about as predictable as the subsequent lapse of the same fervor. Again, it does not always occur, but it happens often enough to call for thorough explanation. The leading students of regulatory processes have all remarked upon it; but most of these scholars, who ordinarily display a close regard for rigor and full exploration, dismiss this highly significant political behavior rather casually. Thus, Redford declares

[2] E. Pendleton Herring, *Public Administration and the Public Interest* (New York, 1936), p. 213.

[3] Avery Leiserson, *Administrative Regulations: A Study in Representation of Interests* (Chicago: University of Chicago Press, 1942), p. 14.

[4] David Truman, *The Governmental Process* (New York, 1951), chap. 5.

[5] Marver Bernstein, *Regulating Business by Independent Commissions* (Princeton, N.J.: Princeton University Press, 1955), chap. 3.

[6] Emmette S. Redford, *Administration of National Economic Control* (New York, 1952), pp. 385–386.

[7] *Op. cit.*, note 5 above.

[8] In addition to the statements in these analytical treatments of the administrative process, evidence for the proposition that regulatory statutes often fail to have their promised consequences in terms of resource allocation are found in general studies of government regulation of business and in empirical research on particular statutes. As an example of the former see Clair Wilcox, *Public Policies toward Business* (Chicago, 1955). As examples of the latter see Frederic Meyers, *"Right to Work" in Practice* (New York: Fund for the Republic, 1959); Walton Hamilton and Irene Till, *Antitrust in Action*, TNEC Monograph 16 (Washington, D.C.: Government Printing Office, 1940).

that, "In the course of time the administrator finds that the initial public drive and congressional sentiment behind his directive has wilted and that political support for change from the existing pattern is lacking." [9]

Although the presumed beneficiaries of regulatory legislation often show little or no concern with its failure to protect them, they are nevertheless assumed to constitute a potential base of political support for the retention of these statutes in the law books. The professional politician is probably quite correct when he acts on the assumption that his advocacy of this regulatory legislation, in principle, is a widely popular move, even though actual resource allocations inconsistent with the promise of the statutes are met with quiescence. These responses (support of the statute; apathy toward failure to allocate resources as the statute promises) define the meanings of the law so far as the presumed beneficiaries are concerned.[10] It is the frequent inconsistency between the two types of response that is puzzling.

(3) The most intensive dissemination of symbols commonly attends the enactment of legislation which is most meaningless in its effects upon resource allocation. In the legislative history of particular regulatory statutes the provisions least significant for resource allocation are most widely publicized and the most significant provisions are least widely publicized.

The statutes listed under Proposition 1 as having promised something substantially different from what was delivered are also the ones which have been most intensively publicized as symbolizing protection of widely shared interests. Trust-busting, "Labor's Magna

[9] Redford, op. cit., p. 383. Similar explanations appear in Herring, op. cit., p. 227, and Bernstein, op. cit., pp. 82–83. Some writers have briefly suggested more rigorous explanations, consistent with the hypotheses discussed in this paper, though they do not consider the possible role of interests in symbolic reassurance. Thus Truman calls attention to organizational factors, emphasizing the ineffectiveness of interest groups "whose interactions on the basis of the interest are not sufficiently frequent or stabilized to produce an intervening organization and whose multiple memberships, on the same account, are a constant threat to the strength of the claim." Truman, op. cit., p. 441. Multiple group memberships are, of course, characteristic of individuals in all organizations, stable and unstable; and "infrequent interactions" is a phenomenon that itself calls for explanation if a common interest is recognized. Bernstein, loc. cit., refers to the "undramatic nature" of administration and to the assumption that the administrative agency will protect the public.

[10] Cf. the discussion of meaning in George Herbert Mead, Mind, Self and Society (Chicago: University of Chicago Press, 1934), pp. 78–79.

Carta" (the Clayton Act), protection against price discrimination and deceptive trade practices, protection against execessive public utility charges, tight control of union bureaucracies (or, by other groups, the "slave labor law"), federal income taxation according to "ability to pay," are the terms and symbols widely disseminated to the public as descriptive of much of the leading federal and state regulation of the last seven decades; and they are precisely the descriptions shown by careful students to be most misleading. Nor is it any less misleading if one quotes the exact language of the most widely publicized specific provisions of these laws: Section 1 of the Sherman Act, Sections 6 and 20 of the Clayton Act, or the closed shop, secondary boycott, or emergency strike provisions of Taft-Hartley, for example. In none of these instances would a reading of either the text of the statutory provision or the attendant claims and publicity enable an observer to predict even the direction of future regulatory policy, let alone its precise objectives.

Other features of these statutes also stand as the symbols of threats stalemated, if not checkmated, by the forces of right and justice. Typically, a preamble (which does not pretend to be more than symbolic, even in legal theory) includes strong assurances that the public or the public interest will be protected. And the most widely publicized regulatory provisions always include other non-operational standards connoting fairness, balance, or equity.

If one asks, on the other hand, for examples of changes in resource allocations that have been influenced substantially and directly by public policy, it quickly appears that the outstanding examples have been publicized relatively little. One thinks of such legislation as the silver purchase provisions; the court definitions of the word "lawful" in the Clayton Act's labor sections; the procedural provisions of Taft-Hartley and the Railway Labor Act; the severe postwar cuts in Grazing Service appropriations; and changes in the parity formula requiring that such items as interest, taxes, freight rates and wages be included as components of the index of prices paid by farmers.

Illuminating descriptions of the operational meaning of statutory mandates are found in Truman's study and in Earl Latham's *The Group Basis of Politics*.[11] Both emphasize the importance of con-

---

[11] Truman, *op. cit.*, pp. 439–446; Earl Latham, *The Group Basis of Politics* (Ithaca, N.Y.: Cornell University Press, 1952), chap. 1.

tending groups and organizations in day-to-day decisionmaking as the dynamic element in policy formation; and both distinguish this element from statutory language as such.[12]

We are only beginning to get some serious studies of the familiarity of voters with current public issues and of the intensity of their feelings about issues; but successful political professionals have evidently long acted on the assumption that there is in fact relatively little familiarity, that expressions of deep concern are rare, that quiescence is common, and that, in general, the Congressman can count upon stereotyped reactions rather than persistent, organized pursuit of material interests on the part of most constituents.[13]

(4) Policies severely denying resources to large numbers of people can be pursued indefinitely without serious controversy.

The silver purchase policy, the farm policy, and a great many other subsidies are obvious examples. The anti-trust laws, utility regulations, and other statutes ostensibly intended to protect the small operator or the consumer are less obvious examples; though there is ample evidence, some of it cited below, that these usually support the proposition as well.

The federal income tax law offers a rather neat example of the divergence between a widely publicized symbol and actual resource allocation patterns. The historic constitutional struggle leading up to the Sixteenth Amendment, the warm defenses of the principle of ability to pay, and the frequent attacks upon the principle through such widely discussed proposals as that for a 25 percent limit on rates have made the federal tax law a major symbol of justice. While the fervent rhetoric from both sides turns upon the symbol of a progressive tax and bolsters the assumption that the system is highly progressive, the bite of the law into people's resources depends upon quite other provisions and activities that are little publicized and that often seriously qualify its progressive character. Special tax treatments arise from such devices as family partnerships, gifts *inter vivos*, income-splitting, multiple trusts, percentage depletion, and deferred compensation.

[12] The writer has explored this effect in labor legislation in "Interest Representation and Labor Law Administration," *Labor Law Journal* 9 (1958):218–226.

[13] Evidence for these propositions is contained in the writer's study of congressional representation, still not completed or published. See also Lewis A. Dexter, "Candidates Must Make the Issues and Give Them Meaning," *Public Opinion Quarterly* 10 (1955–56):408–414.

Tax evasion alone goes far toward making the symbol of "ability to pay" hollow semantically though potent symbolically. While 95 percent of income from wages and salaries is taxed as provided by law, taxes are actually collected on only 67 percent of taxable income from interest, dividends, and fiduciary investments and on only about 36 percent of taxable farm income.[14] By and large, the recipients of larger incomes can most easily benefit from exemptions, avoidances and evasions. This may be desirable public policy, but it certainly marks a disparity between symbol and effect upon resources.

II

These phenomena are significant for the study of the political process for two reasons. First, there is a substantial degree of consistency in the group interest patterns associated with policies on highly diverse subject matters. Second, they suggest that nonrational reaction to symbols among people sharing a common governmental interest is a key element in the process. The disciplines of sociology, social psychology, and semantics have produced some pertinent data on the second point; and to some of this material we turn next.

Harold Lasswell wrote three decades ago that "[P]olitics is the process by which the irrational bases of society are brought out into the open." He marshalled some support in case studies for several propositions that have since been confirmed with richer and more direct experimental evidence. "The rational and dialectical phases of politics," he said, "are subsidiary to the process of redefining an emotional consensus." He argued that "widespread and disturbing changes in the life-situation of many members of society" produce adjustment problems which are resolved largely through symbolization; and he suggested that "[P]olitical demands probably bear but a limited relevance to social needs." [15]

The frame of reference suggested by these statements is sometimes accepted by political scientists today when they study voting behavior and when they analyze the legislative process. Its bearing

[14] Randolph E. Paul, "Erosion of the Tax Base and Rate Structure," in Joint Committee on Economic Report, *Federal Tax Policy for Economic Growth and Stability*, 84th Congress, 1st Session, 1955, pp. 123–138.

[15] *Psychopathology and Politics* (Chicago: University of Chicago Press, 1930), pp. 184, 185.

on policy formation in the administrative process is not so widely recognized. It is true that cognition and rationality are central to administrative procedures to a degree not true of legislation or voting. But this is not at all the same thing as saying that administrative policies or administrative politics are necessarily insulated from the "process of redefining an emotional consensus."

Let us consider now some experimental findings and conclusions specifying conditions under which groups or personality types are prone to respond strongly to symbolic appeals and to distort or ignore reality in a fashion that can be politically significant.

(1) People read their own meanings into situations that are unclear or provocative of emotion. As phrased by Fensterheim, "The less well defined the stimulus situation, or the more emotionally laden, the greater will be the contribution of the perceiver." [16] This proposition is no longer doubted by psychologists. It is the justification for so-called projective techniques and is supported by a great deal of experimental evidence.

Now it is precisely in emotionally laden and poorly defined situations that the most widely and loudly publicized public regulatory policies are launched and administered. If, as we have every reason to suppose, there is little cognitive familiarity with issues, the "interest" of most of the public is likely to be a function of other sociopsychological factors. What these other factors are is suggested by certain additional findings.

(2) It is characteristic of large numbers of people in our society that they see and think in terms of stereotypes, personalization, and oversimplifications; that they cannot recognize or tolerate ambiguous and complex situations; and that they accordingly respond chiefly to symbols that oversimplify and distort. This form of behavior (together with other characteristics less relevant to the political process) is especially likely to occur where there is insecurity

[16] Herbert Fensterheim, "The Influence of Value Systems on the Perception of People," *Journal of Abnormal and Social Psychology* 48 (1953):93. Fensterheim cites the following studies in support of the proposition: D. Krech and R. S. Crutchfield, *Theory and Problems of Social Psychology* (New York, 1948); A. S. Luchins, "An Evaluation of Some Current Criticisms of Gestalt Psychological Work on Perception," *Psychological Review* 58 (1951):69–95; J. S. Bruner, "One Kind of Perception: A Reply to Professor Luchins," *Psychological Review* 58 (1951):306–312; and the chapters by Bruner, Frenkel-Brunswik, and Klein in R. R. Blake and G. V. Ramsey, *Perception: An Approach to Personality* (New York, 1951). See also Charles Osgood, Percy Tannenbaum, and George Suci, *The Measurement of Meaning* (Urbana: University of Illinois Press, 1957).

occasioned by failure to adjust to real or perceived problems.[17] Frenkel-Brunswik has noted that "such objective factors as economic conditions" may contribute to the appearance of the syndrome, and hence to its importance as a widespread group phenomenon attending the formulation of public policy.[18] Such behavior is sufficiently persistent and widespread to be politically significant only when there is social reinforcement of faith in the symbol. When insecurity is individual, without communication and reinforcement from others, there is little correlation with ethnocentricity or its characteristics.[19]

A different kind of study suggests the extent to which reality can become irrelevant for persons very strongly committed to an emotion-satisfying symbol. Festinger and his associates, as participant-observers, studied a group of fifteen persons who were persuaded that the world would come to an end on a particular day in 1956 and that they as believers would be carried away in a flying saucer. With few exceptions the participants refused to give up their belief even after the appointed day had passed. The Festinger study concludes that commitment to a belief is likely to be strengthened and reaffirmed in the face of clear disproof of its validity where there is a strong prior commitment (many of the individuals involved had actually given away their worldly goods) and where there is continuing social support of the commitment by others (two members who lost faith lived in environments in which they had no further contact with fellow members of the group; those who retained their faith had continued to see each other). What we know of previous messianic movements of this sort supports this hypothesis.[20]

(3) Emotional commitment to a symbol is associated with con-

---

[17] Among the leading general and experimental studies dealing with the phenomenon are: M. Rokeach, "Generalized Mental Rigidity as a Factor in Ethnocentrism," *Journal of Abnormal and Social Psychology* 43 (1948):259–277; R. R. Canning and J. M. Baker, "Effect of the Group on Authoritarian and Non-authoritarian Persons," *American Journal of Sociology* 64 (1959):579–581; A. H. Maslow, "The Authoritarian Character Structure," *Journal of Social Psychology* 18 (1943):403; T. W. Adorno and others, *The Authoritarian Personality* (New York, 1950); Gerhart Saenger, *The Psychology of Prejudice* (New York, 1953), pp. 123–138; Erich Fromm, *Escape from Freedom* (New York, 1941); R. K. Merton, *Mass Persuasion* (New York, 1950).

[18] Else Frenkel-Brunswik, "Interaction of Psychological and Sociological Factors in Political Behavior," [*The American Political Science Review*] 46 (1952):44–65.

[19] Adorno, *op. cit.*

[20] Leon Festinger, Henry Riecken, and Stanley Shachter, *When Prophecy Fails* (Minneapolis: University of Minnesota Press, 1956).

tentment and quiescence regarding problems that would otherwise arouse concern.

It is a striking fact that this effect has been noticed and stressed by careful observers in a number of disparate fields, using quite different data and methods. Adorno reports it as an important finding of the *Authoritarian Personality* study:

Since political and economic events make themselves felt apparently down to the most private and intimate realms of the individual, there is reliance upon stereotype and similar avoidances of reality to alleviate psychologically the feeling of anxiety and uncertainty and provide the individual with the illusion of some kind of intellectual security.[21]

In addition to the support it gets from psychological experiment, the phenomenon has been remarked by scholars in the fields of semantics, organizational theory, and political science. Albert Salomon points out that "Manipulation of social images makes it possible for members of society to believe that they live not in a jungle, but in a well organized and good society." [22] Harold Lasswell put it as follows:

It should not be hastily assumed that because a particular set of controversies passes out of the public mind that the implied problems were solved in any fundamental sense. Quite often a solution is a magical solution which changes nothing in the conditions affecting the tension level of the commuity, and which merely permits the community to distract its attention to another set of equally irrelevant symbols. The number of statutes which pass the legislature or the number of decrees which are handed down by the executive, but which change nothing in the permanent practices of society, is a rough index of the role of magic in politics. . . . Political symbolization has its catharsis function. . . .[23]

Chester Barnard, an uncommonly astute analyst of his own long experience as an executive, concluded that:

Neither authority nor cooperative disposition . . . will stand much overt division on formal issues in the present stage of human development. Most laws, executive orders, decisions, etc., are in effect formal notice that all is well — there is agreement, authority is not questioned.[24] . . .

[21] Adorno, *op. cit.*, p. 665.

[22] Albert Salomon, "Symbols and Images in the Constitution of Society," in L. Bryson, L. Finkelstein, H. Hoagland, and R. M. MacIver (Eds.), *Symbols and Society* (New York, 1955), p. 110.

[23] Lasswell, *op. cit.*, p. 195.

[24] Chester I. Barnard, *The Functions of the Executive* (Cambridge, Mass.: Harvard University Press, 1938), p. 226.

III

These studies offer a basis for understanding more clearly what it is that different types of groups expect from government and under what circumstances they are likely to be satisfied or restive about what is forthcoming. Two broad patterns of group interest activity vis-à-vis public regulatory policy are evidently identifiable on the basis of these various modes of observing the social scene. The two patterns may be summarized in the following shorthand fashion:

(1) Pattern A: a relatively high degree of organization — rational, cognitive procedures — precise information — an effective interest in specifically identified, tangible resources — a favorably perceived strategic position with respect to reference groups — relatively small numbers.

(2) Pattern B: shared interest in improvement of status through protest activity — an unfavorably perceived strategic position with respect to reference groups — distorted, stereotyped, inexact information and perception — response to symbols connoting suppression of threats — relative ineffectiveness in securing tangible resources through political activity — little organization for purposeful action — quiescence — relatively large numbers.

It is very likely misleading to assume that some of these observations can be regarded as causes or consequences of others. That they often occur together is both a more accurate observation and more significant. It is also evident that each of the patterns is realized in different degrees at different times.

While political scientists and students of organizational theory have gone far toward a sophisticated description and analysis of Pattern A, there is far less agreement and precision in describing and analyzing Pattern B and in explaining how it intermeshes with Pattern A.

The most common explanation of the relative inability of large numbers of people to realize their economic aspirations in public policy is in terms of invisibility. The explanation is usually implicit rather than explicit, but it evidently assumes that public regulatory policy facilitating the exploitation of resources by knowledgeable organized groups (usually the "regulated") at the expense of taxpayers, consumers, or other unorganized groups is possible only because the latter do not know it is happening. What is invisible to them does not arouse interest or political sanctions.

On a superficial level of explanation this assumption is no doubt valid. But it is an example of the danger to the social scientist of failure to inquire transactionally: of assuming, in this instance, (1) that an answer to a questioner, or a questionnaire, about what an individual "knows" of a regulatory policy at any point in time is in any sense equivalent to specification of a group political interest; and (2) that the sum of many individual knowings (or not-knowings) as reported to a questioner is a *cause* of effective (or ineffective) organization, rather than a consequence of it, or simply a concomitant phase of the same environment. If one is interested in policy formation, what count are the assumptions of legislators and administrators about the determinants of future political disaffection and political sanctions. Observable political behavior, as well as psychological findings, reveals something of these assumptions.

There is, in fact, persuasive evidence of the reality of a political interest, defined in this way, in continuing assurances of protection against economic forces understood as powerful and threatening. The most relevant evidence lies in the continuing utility of old political issues in campaigns. Monopoly and economic concentration, anti-trust policy, public utility regulation, banking controls, and curbs on management and labor are themes that party professionals regard as good for votes in one campaign after another, and doubtless with good reason. They know that these are areas in which concern is easily stirred. In evaluating allegations that the public has lost "interest" in these policies the politician has only to ask himself how much apathy would remain if an effort were made formally to repeal the anti-trust, public utility, banking, or labor laws. The answers and the point become clear at once.

The laws may be repealed in effect by administrative policy, budgetary starvation, or other little publicized means; but the laws as symbols must stand because they satisfy interests that are very strong indeed: interests that politicians fear will be expressed actively if a large number of voters are led to believe that their shield against a threat has been removed.

More than that, it is only as symbols of this sort that these statutes have utility to most of the voters. If they function as reassurances that threats in the economic environment are under control, their indirect effect is to permit greater exploitation of tangible resources by the organized groups concerned than would be possible if the

legal symbols were absent. Those who are deprived become defenders of the very system of law which permits the exploiters of
resources to act effectively.

To say this is not to assume that everyone objectively affected by
a policy is simply quiescent rather than apathetic or even completely unaware of the issue. It is to say that those who are potentially able and willing to apply political sanctions constitute the
politically significant group. It is to suggest as well that incumbent
or aspiring Congressmen are less concerned with individual constituents' familiarity or unfamiliarity with an issue as of any given moment than with the possibility that the interest of a substantial
number of them *could* be aroused and organized if he should cast
a potentially unpopular vote on a bill or if a change in their economic situations should occur. The shrewder and more effective
politicians probably appreciate intuitively the validity of the psychological finding noted earlier: that where public understanding is
vague and information rare, interests in reassurance will be all the
more potent and all the more susceptible to manipulation by political symbols.

The groups that succeed in using official agencies as instrumentalities to gain the resources they want are invariably organized so
as to procure and analyze pertinent information and then act rationally. Most voters affected by the regulatory policy are certain on
the other hand to secure distorted information, inadequate for intelligent planning of tactics or strategy.

We have already noted that it is one of the demonstrable functions of symbolization that it induces a feeling of well-being: the
resolution of tension. Not only is this a major function of widely
publicized regulatory statutes, but it is also a major function of their
administration. Some of the most widely publicized administrative
activities can most confidently be expected to convey a misleading
sense of well-being to the onlooker because they suggest vigorous
activity while in fact signifying inactivity or protection of the "regulated."

One form this phenomenon takes is noisy attacks on trivia. The
Federal Trade Commission, for example, has long been noted for its
hit-and-miss attacks on many relatively small firms involved in deceptive advertising or unfair trade practices while it continues to
overlook much of the really significant activity it is ostensibly es-

372   MURRAY EDELMAN

tablished to regulate: monopoly, interlocking directorates, and so on.[25]

Another form it takes is prolonged, repeated, well-publicized attention to a significant problem which is never solved. An excellent example is the approach of the FCC to surveillance of program content in general and to discussions of public issues on the air in particular. In the postwar period we have had the Blue Book, the Mayflower Policy, the abolition of the Mayflower Policy, and the announcement of a substitute policy; but the radio or television licensee is in practice perfectly free, as he has been all along, to editorialize, with or without opportunity for opposing views to be heard, or to eschew serious discussion of public affairs entirely.

The most obvious kinds of dissemination of symbolic satisfactions are to be found in administrative dicta accompanying decisions and orders, in press releases, and in annual reports. It is as common here as in labor arbitration to "give the rhetoric to one side and the decision to the other." Nowhere does the FCC wax so emphatic in emphasizing public service responsibility, for example, as in decisions permitting greater concentration of control in an area, condoning license transfers at inflated prices, refusing to impose sanctions for flagrantly sacrificing program quality to profits, and so on.[26]

The integral connection is apparent between symbolic satisfaction of the disorganized, on the one hand, and the success of the organized, on the other, in using governmental instrumentalities as aids in securing the tangible resources they claim.

Public policy may usefully be understood as the resultant of the interplay among groups.[27] But the political and socio-psychological processes discussed here mean that groups which would otherwise present claims upon resources may be rendered quiescent instead by their success in securing nontangible values. Far from represent-

25 Cf. Wilcox, op. cit., pp. 281, 252–255.

26 Many examples may be found in the writer's study entitled The Licensing of Radio Services in the United States, 1927 to 1947 (Urbana: University of Illinois Press, 1950).

27 For discussions of the utility of this view to social scientists, see Arthur F. Bentley, The Process of Government (1908; New York: The Principia Press, reprint 1949); Truman, op. cit. But cf. Stanley Rothman, "Systematic Political Theory," [The American Political Science Review] 54 (March 1960):15–33.

ing an obstacle to organized producers and sellers, they become defenders of the very system of law which permits the organized to pursue their interests effectively, at the expense of the disorganized or unorganized.

Thurman Arnold has pointed out how the anti-trust laws perform precisely this function:

The actual result of the antitrust laws was to promote the growth of great industrial organizations by deflecting the attack on them into purely moral and ceremonial channels . . . every scheme for direct control broke to pieces on the great protective rock of the antitrust laws. . . .

The antitrust laws remained as a most important symbol. Whenever anyone demanded practical regulation, they formed an effective moral obstacle, since all the liberals would answer with a demand that the antitrust laws be enforced. Men like Senator Borah founded political careers on the continuance of such crusades, which were entirely futile but enormously picturesque, and which paid big dividends in terms of personal prestige.[28]

Arnold's subsequent career as Chief of the Anti-trust Division of the Department of Justice did as much to prove his point as his writings. For a five-year period he instilled unprecedented vigor into the Division, and his efforts were widely publicized. He thereby unquestionably made the laws a more important symbol of the protection of the public; but despite his impressive intentions and talents, monopoly, concentration of capital, and restraint of trade were not seriously threatened or affected.

This is not to suggest that signs or symbols in themselves have any magical force as narcotics. They are, rather, the only means by which groups not in a position to analyze a complex situation rationally may adjust themselves to it, through stereotypization, oversimplification, and reassurance.

There have, of course, been many instances of effective administration and enforcement of regulatory statutes. In each such instance it will be found that organized groups have had an informed interest in effective administration. Sometimes the existence of these groups is explicable as a holdover from the campaign for legislative enactment of the basic statute; and often the initial administrative appointees are informed, dedicated adherents of these interests. They

[28] *The Folklore of Capitalism* (New Haven: Yale University Press, 1937), pp. 212, 215, 216.

are thus in a position to secure pertinent data and to act strategically, helping furnish "organization" to the groups they represent. Sometimes the resources involved are such that there is organization on both sides; or the more effective organization may be on the "reform" side. The securities exchange legislation is an illuminating example, for after Richard Whitney's conviction for embezzlement key officials of the New York Stock Exchange recognized their own interest in supporting controls over less scrupulous elements. This interest configuration doubtless explains the relative popularity of the SEC both with regulated groups and with organized liberal groups.

IV

The evidence considered here suggests that we can make an encouraging start toward defining the conditions in which myth and symbolic reassurance become key elements in the governmental process. The conditions [29] are present in substantial degree in many policy areas other than business regulation. They may well be maximal in the foreign policy area, and a similar approach to the study of foreign policy formation would doubtless be revealing.

Because the requisite conditions are always present in some degree, every instance of policy formulation involves a "mix" of symbolic effect and rational reflection of interests in resources, though one or the other phenomenon may be dominant in any particular case. One type of mix is exemplified by such governmental programs outside the business regulation field as public education and social security. There can be no doubt that these programs do confer important tangible benefits upon a very wide public, very much as they promise to do. They do so for the reasons suggested earlier. Business organizations, labor organizations, teachers' organizations, and other organized groups benefit from these programs and have historically served to fucus public attention upon the resources to be gained or lost. Their task has been all the easier because the techniques for achieving the benefits are fairly readily recognizable.

But the financing of these same programs involves public policies of a different order. Here the symbol of "free" education and other

---

[29] They are listed above under "Pattern B."

benefits, the complexity of the revenue and administrative structure, and the absence of organization have facilitated the emergence of highly regressive payroll, property, and head taxes as the major sources of revenue. Thus, business organizations, which by and large support the public schools that provide their trained personnel and the social security programs that minimize the costs of industrial pensions, pay relatively little for these services; while the direct beneficiaries of the "free" programs pay a relatively high proportion of the costs. Careful analysis of the "mix" in particular programs should prove illuminating.

If the conditions facilitating symbolic reassurance are correctly specified, there is reason to question some common assumptions about strategic variables in policy formulation and reason also to devise some more imaginative models in designing research in this area. The theory discussed here suggests, for example, a tie between the emergence of conditions promoting interests in symbolic reassurance and widened freedom of policy maneuver for those attempting to assert leadership over the affected group. It implies that the number of adherents of a political interest may have more to do with whether the political benefit offered is tangible or symbolic than with the quantity or quality of tangible resources allocated. It suggests that the factors that explain voting behavior can be quite different from the factors that explain resource allocations through government. The fact that large numbers of people are objectively affected by a governmental program may actually serve in some contexts to weaken their capacity to exert a political claim upon tangible values.

A number of recent writers, to take another example, have suggested that it is the "independence" of the independent regulatory commissions which chiefly accounts for their tendency to become tools of the groups they regulate. The hypotheses suggested here apply to regulatory programs administered in cabinet departments as well; and their operation is discernible in some of these programs when the specified conditions are present. The Grazing Service and the Anti-trust Division are examples.

In terms of research design, the implications of the analysis probably lie chiefly in the direction of emphasizing an integral tie of political behavior to underlying and extensive social interaction. Analysts of political dynamics must have a theory of relevance; but the directly relevant may run farther afield than has sometimes been assumed. Political activities of all kinds require the most exhaustive scrutiny to ascertain whether their chief function is symbolic or substantive. The "what" of Lasswell's famous definition of politics is a complex universe in itself.

VII

CITIZEN PARTICIPATION
IN BUREAUCRACY

A striking development in the recent history of public administration in the United States has been the growing interest in citizen participation in bureaucracy as a technique for making executive organizations more responsive to the groups they serve. The goal of citizen participation has been a major ideological commitment tying together many activities undertaken in connection with the war on poverty. By some of those involved in programs carried on by the Office of Economic Opportunity, the development of an effective system of citizen participation in bureaucratic decisionmaking has been regarded as even more important than the actual delivery of services to the poor.

I

In "Administrative Decentralization and Political Power," Herbert Kaufman examines the current movement for greater citizen participation in administration from a historical perspective. As Kaufman notes, the demand for public involvement in bureaucracy has been a long-standing tradition in American politics. In the nineteenth century, when the tasks of administration were comparatively simple, such demands were satisfied by the annual election of a variety of local administrative officials and the appointment of lay boards and commissions to run administrative agencies. Executive agencies, however, have become increasingly professionalized, with expert staffs dominating the making as well as the execution of policy, and lay boards have either been abolished or reduced to the role of ratifying policies decided by their staffs.

Current efforts at promoting citizen participation in administration can thus be regarded as an attempt to restore an old tradition. Citizen participation is being urged, however, in an environment far different from the rural setting that once prevailed, where administrators and ordinary citizens were alike in talent and background. American society has become urbanized, and the personnel in the agencies in which representation is sought are separated from their clientele not only by wide disparities in educational training and economic status, but often by the barrier of race as well. Black citizens represent a large part of the population served by the poverty agencies in which the demand for citizen participation is centered.

Gideon Sjoberg, Richard A. Brymer, and Buford Farris, the authors of "Bureaucracy and the Lower Class," point up some disadvantages with which the poor are burdened in dealing with the bureaucracies they encounter in ghetto areas. The lower-class person "lacks knowledge of the rules of the game." As compared with middle- or upper-class citizens, the client in a poverty area "stands in awe of bureaucratic regulations and frequently is unaware that he has a legal and moral claim to certain rights and privileges." Finally, the impersonality of bureaucracy presents communication problems for the poor, whereas "middle-class persons are better able to relate to others within an impersonal context."

The authors also identify some alternative organizational forms that might be useful in closing the gap between bureaucracy and the poor. The demand for such organizational innovation has grown in modern politics because of pressures not only from the clientele of executive agencies but also from the lower ranks of employees who want a greater voice in decision-making than is customary in public organizations.

II

Michael Lipsky has drawn attention to what he calls "street-level" bureaucrats — administrative officials who deal with a clientele "consisting predominantly of minority groups and other stigmatized individuals."[1] Lipsky believes that in such ghetto areas bureaucrats commonly work with inadequate resources, feel a sense of danger in the environment in which they are operating, and are frequently uncertain about exactly what is expected of them. In such a setting the bureaucrat can be regarded as no less a victim of his environment than the client.

In any case the pressure they receive from clients has triggered growing resistance from agency employees, who regard client demands as threats to their own professional standing and economic security. The result in many cities has been increasingly militant opposition by employee unions to any innovation designed to enhance community control over areas of decisionmaking previously left to bureaucratic determination.

This opposition is outlined by Frances Fox Piven in "Militant Civil Servants in New York City." Bureaucratic organizations in New York and other urban centers are threatening to withhold services on which the community depends either to defeat proposals for community control or to extract other concessions from elected officials. This form of direct bureaucratic coercion is not much seen in national politics, but the effectiveness with which the weapon is being employed on the urban scene will certainly encourage its use in other areas of government as well.

The threat to cripple a city by denying it a vital service is a form of bureaucratic power quite different from the expertise and constituency mobilization described in the first sections of this book. If the efforts of clientele groups to secure a greater role in bureaucratic decisionmaking can be described as "revolutionary," then the attempts of agency employees to protect their own position appear as a counter-revolutionary response to the challenge of the new politics.

[1] Michael Lipsky, "Toward a Theory of Street-Level Bureaucracy," a paper presented at the 1969 Annual Meeting of the American Political Science Association.

26　Administrative Decentralization
and Political Power

Herbert Kaufman

Curious as it may seem today, bureaucrats in the '30s were
regarded by many as heroes in the struggles for a better social order. As late as 1945, Paul Appleby, a prominent New Deal official,
felt impelled to dedicate a book to "Bill Bureaucrat," [1] and much of
the literature of professional and academic public administration
had a confident, approving, consensual tone.

By mid-'50s it was possible to discern emerging conflicts of doctrine and practice among those who previously applauded and defended bureaucrats. A major shift of outlook and values in governmental design seemed to be taking place.

It was not the first such shift to occur in our history. On the contrary, the administrative history of our governmental machinery can
be construed as a succession of shifts of this kind, each brought
about by a change in emphasis among three values: representativeness, politically neutral competence, and executive leadership.[2]

From Herbert Kaufman, "Administrative Decentralization and Political Power,"
reprinted by permission of the author and The American Society for Public
Administration from *Public Administration Review* 29 (January/February
1969):3–15. Some footnotes are renumbered.

[1] Paul H. Appleby, *Big Democracy* (New York: Alfred A. Knopf, 1945).
Actually, the dedication was "To John Citizen and Bill Bureaucrat."

[2] Herbert Kaufman, "Emerging Conflicts in the Doctrines of Public Administration," *The American Political Science Review* 50, No. 4 (December
1956):1073.

None of these values was ever totally neglected in any of our past modifications of governmental design, but each enjoyed greater emphasis than the others in different periods.

Thus, for example, our earliest political institutions at all levels can be interpreted as reactions against executive dominance in the colonial era. Later on, extreme reliance was placed on representative mechanisms, which made the post-Revolutionary years an interval of great power for legislatures and elective officials and of comparative weakness for executives in most jurisdictions. By the middle of the nineteenth century, however, legislative supremacy, the long ballot, and the spoils system resulted in widespread disillusionment with our political institutions, which in turn gave impetus to efforts to take administration out of politics by lodging it in independent boards and commissions and by introducing the merit system to break the hold of parties on the bureaucracies. But the fragmentation of government reduced both efficiency and representativeness, and the search for unification led to the popularly elected chief executives; the twentieth century was marked by a rapid growth in their powers.

This is not to say the values are pursued abstractly, as ends in themselves, or that there is universal agreement on which should be emphasized at any given time. On the contrary, different segments of the population feel differentially disadvantaged by the governmental machinery in operation at any given moment, and agitate for structural changes to improve their position — i.e., to increase their influence — in the system. Discontent on the part of various groups is thus the dynamic force that motivates the quest for new forms. Some groups feel resentful because they consider themselves inadequately represented; some feel frustrated because, though they are influential in forming policy, the policy decisions seem to be dissipated by the political biases or the technical incompetence of the public bureaucracies; some feel thwarted by lack of leadership to weld the numerous parts of government into a coherent, unified team that can get things done. At different points in time, enough people (not necessarily a numerical majority) will be persuaded by one or another of these discontents to support remedial action — increased representativeness, better and politically neutral bureaucracies, or stronger chief executives as the case may be. But emphasis on one remedy over a prolonged period merely accumulates the other discontents until new remedies gain enough support to be put into effect, and no totally stable solution has yet been devised. So the constant shift in emphasis goes on.

No matter how vigorous the pursuit of any one value at any given time, the other two are never obliterated. And no matter how determined the quest for any one value, it is never realized as fully as its most extreme advocates would like. Even after a century of efforts to strengthen neutral competence and executive leadership, partisan influence still retains great vitality and executive institutions at all levels of government are still remarkably fragmented. And after a century of denigration of "politics," politicians, and "special interests," representativeness is still a powerful force in American government. But in that century of building professional bureaucracies and executive capacities for leadership, the need for new modes of representation designed to keep pace with new economic, social, and political developments did not arouse equal concern. Partly for this reason, and partly because the burgeoning of large-scale organizations in every area of life contributes to the sensation of individual helplessness, recent years have witnessed an upsurge of a sense of alienation on the part of many people, to a feeling that they as individuals cannot effectively register their own preferences on the decisions emanating from the organs of government. These people have begun to demand redress of the balance among the three values, with special attention to the deficiencies in representativeness.

CURRENT DISSATISFACTION

America is not wanting in arrangements for representation. More than half a million public offices are still elective.[3] Legislatures and individual legislators retain immense powers, and do not hesitate to wield them liberally. Parties are still strong and attentive to the claims of many constituencies. Interest groups are numerous and press their demands through myriad channels. The mass media serve as watchdogs of governmental operations. Administrative agencies incorporate manifold procedures for representation into their decisionmaking processes, including quasi-judicial and quasi-

[3] U.S. Bureau of the Census, *1967 Census of Governments,* Vol. 6, *Popularly Elected Officials of State and Local Governments,* pp. 1 ff.

legislative hearings, representative or bipartisan administrative boards, and advisory bodies.[4] Opportunities for participation in political decisions are plentiful. Why, then, is there dissatisfaction with these arrangements?

Fundamentally, because substantial (though minority) segments of the population apparently believe the political, economic, and social systems have not delivered to them fair — even minimally fair — shares of the system's benefits and rewards, and because they think they cannot win their appropriate shares in those benefits and rewards through the political institutions of the country as these are now constituted. These people are not mollified by assurances that the characteristics of the system thwarting them also thwart selfish and extremist interests; it appears to them that only the powerful get attention, and that the already powerful are helped by the system to deny influence to all who now lack it. Thus, the system itself, and not just evil men who abuse it, is discredited.

At least three characteristics of the system contribute heavily to this impression on the part of the deprived: first, existing representative organs are capable of giving only quite general mandates to administrative agencies, yet it is in the day-to-day decisions and actions of officials and employees in the lower levels that individual citizens perceive the policies. There are often gross discrepancies between the promise of the programs (as construed by the populace to be served) and performance — sometimes because the expectations of the populace are unrealistically optimistic, sometimes because programs are impeded by difficulties that could not be foreseen, and sometimes because bureaucracies are too bound by habit or timidity to alter their customary behavior in any but the most modest ways.[5]

Second, the pluralistic nature of the political system provides abundant opportunities for vetoes by opponents of change. Each proposed innovation must run a gamut of obstacles, and ends as a product of bargains and compromises. So change usually comes

[4] Avery Leiserson, *Administrative Regulation: A Study in Representation of Group Interests* (Chicago: University of Chicago Press, 1942).

[5] See, for instance, the criticism of professional bureaucracy and the demand for "public participation" in resource management decisions by Yale Law School Professor Charles A. Reich in his *Bureaucracy and the Forests* (Santa Barbara, Calif.: Center for the Study of Democratic Institutions, 1962).

slowly, by small advances, in bits and pieces. Those who regard particular problems as requiring urgent, immediate action are prone to condemn a system that behaves so "sluggishly."

Third, the scale of organization in our society has grown so large that only through large-scale organization does it seem possible to have a significant impact. This impression alone is enough to make individual people feel helplessly overwhelmed by huge, impersonal machines indifferent to their uniqueness and their humanity. In addition, however, some interests — notably those of Negroes and of youth — have recently begun to develop the organizational skills to mobilize their political resources only to find that it takes time to build channels of access to political structures. Rather than wait for admission to these structures — where, incidentally, they are likely to encounter larger, more experienced, well-entrenched organizations opposed to them — these groups, while continuing to strive for recognition in the older institutions, have adopted a strategy of deriding those institutions and seeking to build new ones in which they can have greater, perhaps dominant, influence.

Thus, the plenitude of traditional modes of representation no longer suffices; the existing methods do not adequately accommodate many of the demands upon them. Just as the adaptation of governmental design during the past century has gravitated toward furnishing expertise and leadership, so it is now under pressure from several quarters to accord a greater role to representativeness.

Increasing Representativeness through Administrative Change

The quest for representativeness in this generation centers primarily on administrative agencies. Since administrative agencies have grown dramatically in size, function, and authority in the middle third of this century, this is hardly surprising. Chief executives, legislatures, and courts make more decisions of *sweeping* effect, but the agencies make a far greater number of decisions affecting individual citizens in *intimate* ways. In them lies the source of much present unrest; in them, therefore, the remedies are sought.

One type of proposal for making administrative agencies more representative is traditional in character; situating spokesmen for the interests affected in strategic positions within the organizations.

Often, this means nothing more than filling vacancies on existing boards and commissions with appointees enjoying the confidence of, or perhaps even chosen by, those interests.[6] In the case of the controversial police review boards, it involves injecting into administrative structures new bodies, dominated by ethnic minority groups or their friends, to survey and constrain bureaucratic behavior. Architecturally, such plans do not require drastic modifications of existing organizations, and their objectives could probably be met by changes in personnel at high organizational levels.

More unorthodox, but swiftly gaining acceptance, is the concept of a centralized governmental complaint bureau, clothed with legal powers of investigation, to look into citizen complaints against administrative agencies and to correct inequities and abuses — the office of "ombudsman." [7] Once, it was chiefly through his representative in the appropriate legislative body, or through the local unit of his political party, that a citizen of modest status and means petitioned for a remedy of a grievance. But professionalization of administration and the insulation of bureaucrats from party politics have reduced the ability of the parties to be of real help, and the constituencies of legislators have grown so large that they rarely intervene in more than a *pro forma* fashion on behalf of most individual constituents. Today, some observers contend that only a specialized, fulltime official, wise in the ways of bureaucracy, having a vested interest in correcting its errors, and supported by adequate staff and authority, can perform this function effectively; apparently, it takes a bureaucrat to control a bureaucrat. Advocates of this proposed new agency defend it on the grounds that it would constitute a channel of representation for people who now have no satisfactory alternative.

[6] For example, *The New York Times* reported on November 29, 1967, that "A [New York City] citizen group demanded yesterday that a Negro and a Puerto Rican be named to the city's nine-man Community Mental Health Board." And a high-ranking city antipoverty administrator (suspended for failing to file tax returns) went on a hunger strike to dramatize his demand that Puerto Ricans be named to the Board of Education, the State Board of Regents, the citywide Model Cities Advisory Committee, the Civil Service Commission, and the City Housing Authority (*The New York Times,* June 29, 1968).

[7] Walter Gellhorn, *When Americans Complain* (Cambridge, Mass.: Harvard University Press, 1966), and *Ombudsmen and Others* (Cambridge, Mass.: Harvard University Press, 1966); Stanley Anderson (Ed.), *Ombudsmen for American Government* (Englewood Cliffs, N.J.: Prentice-Hall, 1968).

The most sweeping expression of the unrest over lack of representativeness is the growing demand for extreme administrative decentralization, frequently coupled with insistence on local clientele domination of the decentralized organizations. Dramatic manifestations of this movement occurred in the antipoverty program and in education.

In the antipoverty program the original legislation included a provision that community action be "developed, conducted, and administered with maximum feasible participation of residents of the areas and members of the groups served." Initially by interpretation of the Office of Economic Opportunity, and later by statute, the provision was construed to mean that community action boards should try to allot some of their chairs to the poor, so that the poor would have a voice in the highest policy councils of the community programs. Whatever the original intent of the drafters of the phrase (about which there is some disagreement), it has come to mean the program is to be run in substantial degree *by* the poor, not merely *for* the poor.[8]

In public education the new trend is exemplified by recent events in New York City. During 1967, demands for decentralization of the municipal school system gathered force swiftly: Leaders in the state legislature urged it. Three separate public reports recommended it in the strongest possible terms. The mayor endorsed the principle unequivocally. When concrete proposals were introduced into the legislature the following year, however, vehement opposition from the teachers' union, the school administrators' association, and the City Board of Education resulted in modification of many of the provisions the objectors found unacceptable. The measure ultimately enacted emerged weaker than the plans favored by the advocates of decentralization, but it was a major step in their direction; the thrust toward decentralization and neighborhood control of schools was slowed but not stopped, and resistance, however determined and forceful, seemed destined to give way over a broad front.

The outcry has not been limited to the war on poverty and to education. It was taken up in public housing when the Secretary of Housing and Urban Development unveiled a program to modernize low-rent projects that included an augmented role for tenants in

[8] See the article by S. M. Miller [*Public Administration Review* 29 (January/February 1969):15–24].

their operation.[9] At a meeting of the American Institute of Planners, a dissenting group, calling itself Planners for Equal Opportunity, demanded a larger place for the poor in city planning, and exhorted its members to engage in "advocate planning," which is to say expert counsel for neighborhood associations unhappy with official plans for renewal in their areas. . . .

A meeting of Americans for Democratic Action was warned by Daniel P. Moynihan, an outspoken liberal, that "Liberals must divest themselves of the notion that the nation, especially the cities of the nation, can be run from agencies in Washington.[10] Senator Robert F. Kennedy, campaigning for the Democratic presidential nomination in Los Angeles, promised audiences a revolution in the distribution of political power that would, among other things, reduce the authority of the federal bureaucracy in Washington. "I want," he said, "the control over your destinies to be decided by the people in Watts, not by those of us who are in Washington." [11] Richard M. Nixon similarly urged the federal government to relinquish some of its powers to state and local governments, voluntary associations, and individuals, saying, "One reason people are shouting so loudly today is that it's far from where they are to where the power is," and that power should be brought closer to them rather than exercised from remote centers. . . .

[9] *The New York Times,* November 18, 1967. John W. Gardner, former Secretary of Health, Education, and Welfare, and currently chairman of the Urban Coalition, went even further and urged a larger role for Negroes in helping solve the urban crisis generally (*The New York Times,* May 6, 1968).

[10] *The New York Times,* September 24, 1967. But he criticized school decentralization a short time later (*The New York Times,* June 5, 1968).

[11] *The Washington Post,* March 26, 1968. See also the arguments of a former foreign service officer for "dismantling the present overgrown bureaucratic apparatus" in Washington, Gordon Tullock, *The Politics of Bureaucracy* (Washington, D.C.: Public Affairs Press, 1965), chap. 25. That liberals have thus adopted a position taken by conservatives in New Deal days is an irony to which attention has been drawn by James Q. Wilson, "The Bureaucracy Problem," *The Public Interest* 2, No. 6 (Winter 1967):3–4. Note the similarities between the new liberal language and the position of former Governor George C. Wallace of Alabama: "I would," he said, "bring all those briefcase-toting bureaucrats in the Department of Health, Education, and Welfare to Washington and throw their briefcases in the Potomac River. . . ." *The New York Times,* February 9, 1968. His attack on bureaucrats is, of course, based on their zeal in defense of civil rights; the liberals' indictment is constructed on a diametrically opposite appraisal. The impulse toward decentralization thus comes from both the political right and the political left for entirely different reasons — but with combined force.

In short, "decentralization" of administration is in the air every-where.[12] While it is sometimes defended on grounds of efficiency, it is more frequently justified in terms of effective popular partici-pation in government. Reformers of earlier generations succeeded in raising the level of expertise and professionalism in the bureauc-racies, and to a lesser extent, in improving capacity of chief execu-tives to control the administrative arms of government. Now, people are once again turning their attention to representativeness, and are trying to elevate it to a more prominent place in the governmental scheme of things.

THE CONTINUING SEARCH FOR LEADERSHIP

Public bureaucracies are under fire not only from critics outside the machinery of government, but also from inside. Chief execu-tives who once championed measures to insulate the bureaucracies from partisan politics as steps toward enlarging their own control over administrative agencies discovered that these measures did not make the agencies more responsive to executive direction; rather, they increased agency independence. This independence, in turn, makes it difficult for the executives to secure enthusiastic adoption of new approaches to social problems; money pumped into new programs administered by established agencies tends to be used more for intensification of traditional ways of operating than for inventive departures from familiar patterns. Furthermore, it results in massive problems of coordination of effort, and even in dissipation of energies in interbureau rivalries. Consequently, just as segments of the public are upset by the alleged unresponsiveness of administration to their demands, so chief executives have been increasingly concerned about the unresponsivenss of agencies to their leadership.

We may therefore look forward to new waves of administrative reorganization proposals. One principal thrust of the movement will, as in the past, be toward rationalizing, enlarging, and strength-ening the executive-office staffs of the heads of governmental units at all levels, and toward building up the staffs of the administrators who report directly to the heads. More and more, chief executives

---

[12] Like all slogans, it means different things to different people, however. It is a much more complex and ambiguous concept than it seems; see note [17], below.

will reach out for new devices to coordinate policy decisions, to work up fresh programs to deal with emergent problems, and to maintain the momentum of innovations adopted.[13] Executive offices will be redesigned; the U.S. Bureau of the Budget, for example, has only recently undergone a major reorganization.[14] New vigor will be applied to the exploration of "superdepartments," with the Department of Defense as a prototype; Mayor Lindsay, for instance, has expended much political capital on introducing this concept into the government of New York City. Programming-planning-budgeting systems, in many variants, will continue to spread.[15] There will be a new burst of literature calling attention to the relative powerlessness of our highest public executives.[16]

Another stream of recommendations will urge strengthening executive leadership through what its advocates will call "decentralization," but which, in fact, is better characterized as organization by

[13] The executive office of the President was created in 1939, when the federal budget was under $9 billion. It has grown since, but not nearly as much as the budget, now fifteen times larger and many hundreds of times more complex. Some reordering seems almost inevitable.

[14] U.S. Bureau of the Budget, "Work of the Steering Group on Evaluation of the Bureau of the Budget: A Staff Study," July 1967. The reorganization took effect shortly afterwards.

[15] The origins of PPBS are many and varied; see Allen Schick, "The Road to PPB," *Public Administration Review* 26, No. 4 (December 1966):243–258. But it was the system's utility to the Secretary of Defense from 1961 on in gaining control of his own department that gave widespread currency to the idea and induced the President to make it governmentwide in 1965; see U.S. Senate, 90th Congress, 1st Session (1967), Committee on Government Operations, Subcommittee on National Security and International Operations, *Program-Planning-Budgeting: Official Documents*, pp. 1–6, and *Program-Planning-Budgeting: Hearings, Part 1* (August 23, 1967). This new impetus will doubtless lead to adaptive imitation in other governments.

[16] Arthur M. Schlesinger, Jr., *A Thousand Days* (Boston: Houghton Mifflin, 1965), pp. 679–680, reports, "he [President Kennedy] had to get the government moving. He came to the White House at a time when the ability of the President to do this had suffered steady constriction. The clichés about the 'most powerful office on earth' had concealed the extent to which the mid-century Presidents had much less freedom of action than, say, Jackson or Lincoln or even Franklin Roosevelt. No doubt the mid-century Presidents could blow up the world, but at the same time they were increasingly hemmed in by the growing power of the bureaucracy and of Congress. The President understood this." Similarly, President Johnson's assistant for domestic programs, Joseph A. Califano, Jr., . . . complained publicly of the limitations of presidential power, observing that the powers of the office have not kept pace with its growing responsibilities; *The Washington Post*, May 6, 1968.

area as opposed to the present almost exclusive organization by functional departments and bureaus.[17] The justification for it will be couched in terms of efficiency — the need to speed decisions in the field without referral to headquarters and without loss of coordination among field personnel in different bureaus. The consequences will extend further, however, because areal officers in the field would give top executives lines of communication and control alternative to existing functional channels, thus actually strengthening central authority. At the federal level, this will mean renewed attempts to set up much stronger regional representatives of the heads of cabinet departments than any we have had in the past. It will also mean intensified efforts to establish regional presidential representatives in the field.[18] Similarly, we may anticipate Governors and their department heads will follow the same strategies with respect to regions within the states. At the local level, Mayor Lindsay has already sought — with very limited success — to win approval for "little city halls" throughout New York. Distinctively American versions of the European prefect may yet make an appearance.

In short, dissatisfaction with public bureaucracies will furnish ammunition for the defenders of executive leadership as well as for the proponents of increased representation of the consumers of public services. The bureaucracies will be pressed from both above and below.

CONFLICT AND COALITION

Sources of Conflict

It has long been recognized that much public policy is shaped largely by clusters of bureaus, their organized clienteles, and legislative committees and legislators specializing in each public

---

[17] James W. Fesler, *Area and Administration* (University, Ala.: University of Alabama Press, 1949), especially pp. 8–18, and "Approaches to the Understanding of Decentralization," *Journal of Politics* 27, No. 3 (August 1965):557–561. See also the essay by John D. Millett, "Field Organization and Staff Supervision," in *New Horizons in Public Administration: A Symposium* (University, Ala.: University of Alabama Press, 1945), pp. 98–118.

[18] Fesler, *op. cit.*, pp. 88–89. Fesler's writing on this subject anticipated long in advance the problems that were to engender a more general awareness when programs of the New Frontier and the Great Society overwhelmed the administrative machinery.

function [19] — health, education, welfare, etc. The arguments for strengthening chief executives and their department heads vis-à-vis the clusters are based chiefly on the need to offset the resulting fragmentation of government by introducing sufficient central direction to unify the policies and administration of these separate centers of power. The arguments for new modes of participation by the public in these centers rest on the conviction that hitherto excluded and unorganized interests have little to say about decisions that affect them profoundly. But it is most unlikely that the arguments of either kind will be warmly received by those already in key positions in each decision center.

They will resist not simply out of abstract jealousy of their own power or stubborn unwillingness to share their influence with each other, though these motives will doubtless not be absent. They will oppose because, in addition, the proposed reforms threaten those values which present arrangements protect. Bureau chiefs and the organized bureaucracies perceive intervention by political executives as the intrusion of partisan politics into fields from which doctrine has for many years held that politics should be excluded; they see jeopardy for the competence nurtured so carefully and painfully against political distortion or extinction. Similarly, opening the system to lay members of local communities looks like a negation of the expertise built up by the specialist. Legislators regard strong regional officials responsive to chief executives and their cabinets as executive attempts to invade legislative districts and usurp the representative function of legislative bodies. In like fashion, local control of administrative programs could conceivably weaken the representative basis of legislative institutions, a development that men of goodwill may fear for quite public-spirited reasons.

So the champions of executive leadership and evangelists of expanded representativeness have many obstacles to overcome before they have their respective ways. For example, Congress has been cautious about presidential recommendations of added funds and personnel for the heads of cabinet departments, and has always looked with suspicion on so relatively innocuous an innova-

[19] See J. Leiper Freeman, *The Political Process: Executive Bureau-Legislative Committee Relations* (New York: Random House, rev. ed., 1965), and the works therein cited in chapter one.

tion as field offices for the Bureau of the Budget.[20] The Office of Economic Opportunity in the executive office of the President always operated chiefly through established bureaus and engaged in independent administration only in limited ways; gradually, through delegation, it has been relinquishing its control over programs to the bureaus and the future of even those few programs it manages directly is uncertain. Moreover, its community-action program aroused resentment among both Congressmen and local executives, to whom the action agencies appeared as springboards for political rivals; consequently, legislation in 1967 authorized greater control of the agencies by local governments. In New York City, the mayor's "little city halls," which he presented as a device for bringing the people and their government closer together, were soundly defeated by a City Council (dominated by the opposite party) denouncing the plan as a strategy for establishing political clubhouses throughout the city at public expense.[21] And, when the plan for school decentralization appeared, the largest teachers' union and the Board of Education — which not long before had been at each other's throats in labor disputes — each took a similar firm stand against it. In Board-sponsored experiments with commuity control of schools in Harlem and in Brooklyn, the community leaders and the head of the same teachers' union engaged in acrimonious battles with each other. The reforms are not having an easy time of it. . . .

[20] Bureau of the Budget field offices were set up in mid-1943 but were eliminated in the early years of the Eisenhower administration. Recent efforts to revive them, even on a limited basis, ran into stiff opposition; see U.S. Senate, 90th Congress, 1st Session, Subcommittee of the Committee on Appropriations, *Hearings on H.R. 7501: Treasury, Post Office and Executive Office Appropriations for Fiscal Year 1968* (Washington, D.C.: Government Printing Office, 1967), pp. 973–990. Note especially the comments of Senator Monroney at p. 981: "The reason the committee cut your request for additional personnel last year was because it did not wish to have field offices established. . . . My impression was that we were afraid they would grow into a 50-state bureaucracy with state and regional offices."

[21] The mayor proposed thirty-five local mayor's offices soon after his inauguration; encountering opposition in the Board of Estimate, he tried to set up five by executive order, but the City Council refused to support him, and the comptroller refused to approve payment of their bills. The mayor tried again in May 1967, but was again rebuffed by the Council and the Board of Estimate. Eventually, four local offices were opened, but they were much weaker than was originally anticipated. For the time being, at least, the plan seems emasculated.

The Confluence of Representativeness and Leadership

. . . Groups clamoring for local control of administrative programs, confronted with the suspicion and resentment of bureaucracies and their legislative and interest-group allies, will probably discover that they get their most sympathetic hearings from chief executives, especially from big-city mayors. For such groups can provide the executive with the counterweights to the bureaucracies: they constitute an alternative channel of information about administrative performance, reducing executive dependence on the bureaucracies on the one hand and on the mass media (with their bias toward the sensational) on the other. The groups are a constituency that can be mobilized to help exert leverage on bureaucracies resistant to executive leadership. They furnish a direct conduit to localities from the executive mansions. They can serve as the nuclei of discrete, executive-oriented campaign organizations. Chief executives probably could not create the groups if they set out deliberately to do so, but it would be surprising if they did not eventually perceive the advantages of collaborating with them now that a variety of complaints has brought the groups spontaneously into being.

It will be an uneasy, mutually wary relationship. To neighborhood and community associations, the paradox of turning to remote chief executives in a quest for local control will be disturbing. To chief executives, the risk of opening a Pandora's box and releasing uncontrollable disintegrative forces will give pause. Yet each can gain so much from an alliance with the other that it is hard to avoid the feeling the attractions will overcome the anxieties. I do not mean to imply the alliance will be formal or structured. I mean only to suggest each side will turn to the other as appropriate occasions arise, and that the occasions will arise with increasing frequency in the years ahead. In this way, the new voices of representatives and the more familiar voices of executive leadership will be joined in a common challenge to those who speak for neutral competence and for older institutions of representation.

THE SUBSEQUENT PHASE OF THE CYCLE

So it seems reasonable to anticipate that "decentralization" of two types will indeed occur: concessions will be made to the demands for greater local influence on public programs, and there will be some headway toward establishing territorial officers with at least limited authority over field personnel of the functional bureaus.

It will not take long for the price of these changes to make itself felt. Decentralization will soon be followed by disparities in practice among the numerous small units, brought on by differences in human and financial resources, that will engender demands for central intervention to restore equality and balance and concerted action; the factors underlying the movement toward metropolitan units of government and toward conditional federal grants-in-aid will, in other words, reassert themselves. Decentralization will stand in the way of other goals, such as school integration (as did "states' rights" doctrines in other times). It will give rise to competition among the units that will be disastrous for many of them, which will find it more difficult to attract talent and money than others that start from a more advantageous position. In some units, strong factions may well succeed in reviving a new spoils system, thus lowering the quality of some vital services. Decentralization of public administration will not necessarily be accompanied by decentralization of the other institutions with which public units deal, such as unions of public employees, so that the local units may find themselves at a serious disadvantage in negotiations and unable to resist the pressures of special interests. Economies of scale, which are admittedly overstated very frequently, nevertheless do exist, and the multiplication of overhead costs in local units will divert some resources from substantive programs to administrative housekeeping. Initially, all these costs will be regarded by those concerned with representativeness as well worth paying, but the accumulation of such grievances over time will inspire a clamor for unification and consolidation.[22]

Similarly, area officials reporting directly to chief executives will soon develop autonomous bases of political power in the regions to which they are assigned. Rapid rotation from area to area will help

---

[22] Some anxieties about the costs of decentralization have already been voiced in Irving Kristol, "Decentralization for What?" *The Public Interest*, No. 11 (Spring 1968), p. 17, and echoed by Daniel P. Moynihan as he assailed school decentralization as likely to lead to segregated bureaucracies, *The New York Times*, June 5, 1968. Note also the dissents by Governors Rhodes and Rockefeller from a hearty endorsement of neighborhood subunits with limited powers of taxation and local self-government, Advisory Commission on Intergovernmental Relations, *op. cit.*, p. 21.

to reduce their independence, but the rate of rotation will decline because each new assignment will necessitate a period of familiarization with the new territory during which actions and decisions are held in abeyance, and because local interests, having established comparatively stable relationships with their regional officers, will protest and resist frequent transfers. As the regional officers get more and more involved in regional complexes, they will become more and more ambassadors from the regions to the chief executives instead of the executives' men in the regions.[23] Regional differences and competition will become sources of irritation and controversy. Moreover, regional posts may become convenient and effective springboards to elective office. At first these dangers will seem remote and therefore less important than the immediate gains, but time is likely to reverse the balance. . . .

27   *Bureaucracy and the Lower Class*

GIDEON SJOBERG, RICHARD A. BRYMER, AND
BUFORD FARRIS

. . . Sociologists have devoted little attention, on either the community or national level, to the impact of bureaucracy upon the stratification system. Yet our experience, based on research among lower-class Mexican-Americans in San Antonio, points to the critical role of bureaucratic organizations in sustaining social stratification. Sociologists frequently compare lower- and middle-class culture patterns, but they fail to recognize that bureaucratic

[23] Herbert Kaufman, *The Forest Ranger* (Baltimore: The Johns Hopkins Press, 1960), pp. 75–80.

From Gideon Sjoberg, Richard A. Brymer, and Buford Farris, "Bureaucracy and the Lower Class," reprinted by permission of the authors and the publisher from *Sociology and Social Research* 50 (April 1966):325–337. Footnotes are renumbered.

systems are the key medium through which the middle class maintains its advantaged position vis-à-vis the lower class.

Our analysis of the effect of the client-centered bureaucracy upon the lower class is cast in rather theoretical terms. However, illustrative materials from our research project and the writings of other scholars indicate the kinds of data that support our generalizations. After delineating the main elements of the bureaucratic model, we discuss the lower class from the perspective of the bureaucratic system and then bureaucracy from the viewpoint of the lower class. These materials set the stage for a consideration of various emergent organizational and political patterns in American society.

THE NATURE OF BUREAUCRACY

In the post–World War II era various sociologists [1] have questioned the utility of Weber's analysis of bureaucracy. Nevertheless, sociologists continue to assume that bureaucracy (as conceived by Weber) is positively associated with the continued development of an advanced industrial-urban order and that this bureaucracy is more or less inevitable.

Modern bureaucracies lay heavy stress upon rationality and efficiency. In order to attain these ends, men are called upon to work within a hierarchical system, with well-defined lines of authority, and within a differentiated social setting, with an elaborate division of labor that stresses the specialization of function. This hierarchy and division of labor are, in turn, sustained through a complex set of formalized rules which are to be administered in a highly impersonal and standardized manner. There is considerable centralization of authority, and as one moves from top to bottom there is greater specialization of function and adherence to the rules.

What is not as clearly recognized is that efficiency and rationality are predicated upon an explicit statement of the organization's goals. Only when an end is clearly stated can one determine the most efficient means for its attainment. Thus, because the corporate structure has had an explicit goal (i.e., profit), it has been quite successful in measuring the efficiency of its programs (i.e., means).

The corporate system has been the model that other bureaucracies have emulated. As a result, there has been considerable concern

[1] Peter Blau, *The Dynamics of Bureaucracy* (rev. ed., Chicago: University of Chicago Press, 1963), and Alvin Gouldner, *Patterns of Industrial Bureaucracy* (New York: The Free Press, 1965).

with efficiency within, say, the federal government. McNamara's reorganization of the U.S. Defense Department in the 1960s is a case in point. It is significant that McNamara . . . [drew] heavily upon the work of Hitch and McKean [2] in developing his program, for Hitch and McKean argue that organizational goals must be spelled out in rather concrete terms in order to measure the effectiveness of various programs. An understanding of the interrelationships among measurement, objectification of goals, and efficiency and rationality is essential if we are to assess the impact of bureaucratic structures upon the lower class.

ORIENTATIONS OF BUREAUCRACIES TOWARDS THE LOWER CLASS

Bureaucratic organizations frequently reinforce the class structure of the community and the nation through their staffing procedures. When a bureaucracy serves both upper- and lower-class groups, as does the school, the poorly qualified teachers tend to drift into lower-class neighborhoods, or, as frequently occurs, beginning teachers are placed in "hardship" districts, and then the most capable move up and out into upper-status school districts where higher salaries and superior working conditions usually prevail. Thus, the advancement of lower-class children is impeded not only because of their cultural background but because of the poor quality of their teachers.

In welfare bureaucracies, social workers have struggled to escape from their traditional identification with the poor, either by redefining their functions in order to serve middle-class clients or by moving away from clients into administrative posts. Once again, evidence suggests that the lower class comes to be served by the least qualified personnel.

In addition to staffing arrangements, the bureaucracy's method of selecting clients reinforces the class system. At this point we must remember that bureaucracies are under constant pressure to define their goals so that the efficiency of their programs can be measured. But unlike corporate systems, client-centered bureaucracies experience grave difficulties in specifying their goals and evaluating their efficiency. The client-centered bureaucracies meet the demands

---

[2] Charles J. Hitch and Roland N. McKean, *The Economics of Defense in the Nuclear Age* (Cambridge, Mass.: Harvard University Press, 1960).

placed upon them through the use of simplified operational definitions. Universities, for instance, do not judge their effectiveness in
terms of producing "educated men" but according to the ratings of
their students on national tests, the number of students who gain
special awards, etc. These operational criteria reflect the orientation
or view of persons in positions of authority within the bureaucracy
and the broader society. In turn, these criteria become the basis for
the selection of clients. Through this procedure, a bureaucratic
organization can ensure its success, and it can more readily demonstrate to the power structure that the community or society is "getting something for its money." The bureaucracy's success is likely
to lead to an increase in funds and expanded activities. It follows
that client-centered bureaucracies often find it advantageous to
avoid lower-class clients who are likely to handicap the organization
in the attainment of its goals.[3]

Several illustrations should clarify our argument. The federal Job
Corps program has been viewed as one means for alleviating the
unemployment problem among youth, especially those in the lower
class. This program has sought to train disadvantaged youths in
various occupational skills. The success of the Job Corps is apparently to be evaluated according to the number of trainees who enter the industrial labor force. Consequently, the organization has
sought to select those youths who have internalized some of the
middle-class norms of upward mobility and who are likely to succeed in the occupational system. The Job Corps bypasses many persons who in theory stand in greatest need of assistance; for example,
potential "troublemakers" — young men with criminal records — are
not accepted as trainees. Because of this selection process the Job
Corps leadership will likely be able to claim success and to convince Congressmen that the program should be continued and perhaps broadened.

A more subtle form of client selection can be found in child guidance clinics. Here clients are often accepted in terms of their "receptivity" to therapy.[4] However, this criterion favors those persons who
have been socialized into the middle-class value orientation held by,

[3] See, e.g., Martin Rein, "The Strange Case of Public Dependency," *Trans-
action* 2 (March–April 1965):16–23.
[4] Based on the personal observations of Buford Farris who, as a social
worker, has had extensive contact with these agencies.

for example, the clinic staff and the social groups who pay the bill. The poor, especially the families from ethnic groups within the lower class, who according to the ideal norms of these agencies should receive the greatest amount of attention, are quietly shunted aside. Moreover, one study has indicated a positive association between the social status of the client and the social status of the professional worker handling the case in the agency.[5]

The procedures by which school systems cope with their clients are perhaps central to understanding the community and national class system, for the educational variable is becoming increasingly significant in sustaining or advancing one's status. At this point we are concerned with the differential treatment of clients by the organization once they have been accepted.

School systems frequently employ IQ tests and similar instruments in their evaluation of pupils. These tests, however, have been constructed in such a manner that they articulate with the values, beliefs, and knowledge of the middle class and the demands of the power elements of the society. That these tests are used to make early judgments on the ability of pupils serves to support the existing class system. Lower-class pupils often come to be defined as "dull," and, through a kind of self-fulfilling prophecy, this definition of the situation structures the students' future career. In fact, school counselors frequently interpret test scores according to their middle-class expectations; they, therefore, tend to discourage lower-class pupils from attending college even when their scores are relatively high.[6]

It is significant that the New York City school system has been forced to abandon the use of IQ tests.[7] It appears that the traditionally disadvantaged groups such as Negroes and Puerto Ricans have attained sufficient political power to challenge those methods that

[5] Raymond G. Hunt, Orville Gurrslin, and Jack L. Roach, "Social Status and Psychiatric Service in a Child Guidance Clinic," *American Sociological Review* 23 (February 1958):81–83.

[6] Aaron Cirourel and John I. Kitsuse, *The Educational Decision-Makers* (Indianapolis: Bobbs-Merrill Co., 1963). For a general discussion of the bureaucratization of the school system see Dean Harper, "The Growth of Bureaucracy in School Systems," *American Journal of Economics and Sociology* 23 (July 1965):261–271.

[7] Fred M. Hechinger, "I.Q. Test Ban," *The New York Times*, March 8, 1964, Section E, p. 7; Fred H. Hechinger, "Testing at Issue," *The New York Times*, November 1, 1964, Section E, p. 9.

the school bureaucracy has used for determining success, methods that have been oriented to middle-class rather than lower-class norms.

Bureaucratized school systems place the lower-class clients at a disadvantage in still other ways. Various types of standardization or categorization, which are a product of middle-class expectations and which are viewed as essential for maintaining efficiency, limit the school's ability to adjust to the "needs" of lower-class pupils. We know of a special class, for example, that was established for the purpose of teaching lower-class and problem children, but in which the rules demanded that the teacher follow the same teaching plan employed in other classes in the school.

Actually, bureaucratic structures socialize the incumbents of roles in such a manner that they are frequently incapable of understanding the world-view of the lower-class client. Discussions of the bureaucratic personality, such as those by Merton and Presthus,[8] have given but scant attention to the difficulty of the bureaucrat's taking the role of the lower-class other. For as a result of his role commitment, the bureaucrat tends to impose his own expectations and interpretations of reality upon the client. He often comes to view the norms of the system as invariant. And bureaucrats in the lower echelons, those who have the greatest amount of contact with lower-class clients, are also the most bound by the rules. Faced with recalcitrant clients or clients having divergent value orientations, the typical office holder will say in effect, "If only clients would act properly, everything would be all right, and we could get on with our work."

The bureaucrat, oriented as he is to the middle- or upper-class life styles, usually lacks knowledge about the lower-class client's subculture. Moreover, he finds it difficult to step outside his formalized role. If he seeks to take the role of the client — in the sense of understanding the latter's belief and value system — he will ultimately have to challenge or at least question some of the rules that govern the operation of the system of which he is a part. For if he understands why clients act the way they do, he is likely to recognize that they have valid reasons for objecting to his conception of reality or, more specifically, to some of the bureaucratic regulations.

---

[8] Robert K. Merton, *Social Theory and Social Structure* (rev. ed., New York: The Free Press, 1957), pp. 195–206, and Robert Presthus, *The Organizational Society* (New York: Vintage Books, 1965).

Consequently, bureaucratic organizations tend to penalize those of their members who "overidentify" with clients.

Social workers who overidentify with their clients or teachers who overidentify with their students are considered to be indulging in nonprofessional action. Such action, so the reasoning runs, makes it impossible for the professional to adhere to the ideal norms of universalism and objectivity and thus to assist his clients effectively. Professional norms such as these reinforce those bureaucratic norms that impose barriers upon the lower-class person's advancement in the social order.

The controls exerted by the bureaucrats over members of the lower class are intensified because the office holders are constantly called upon to normalize and stabilize the system with an eye to maintaining the proper public image. One means of stabilizing and rationalizing the system's performance is to work within the context of established rules or categories. But to cope really effectively with such deviants as juvenile delinquents, the schools would have to alter radically their time-honored categories. Our experience suggests, however, that school systems stifle the grievances of deviant or lower-class groups, for these grievances, at least implicitly, challenge the bureaucratic norms that are supported by the groups that determine public policy.

The general insensitivity of bureaucracies to lower-class persons and their problems is highlighted in the "custodial function" adopted by many mental hospitals and even slum schools.[9] Because the bureaucracy's normative system runs counter to (or at best ignores) the norms and values of the lower class, a minimum of attention is given to socializing clients into the bureaucratic — or broader societal — norms. Bureaucratic systems adjust to this situation through the caretaker function.

ORIENTATIONS OF THE LOWER CLASS
TOWARDS BUREAUCRACIES

Just as significant as the bureaucracy's orientation towards the lower class is the latter's orientation toward the bureaucracy. Our investigations, particularly depth interviews of Mexican-American

[9] See, e.g., Ivan C. Belknap, *Human Problems of a State Mental Hospital* (New York: McGraw-Hill Book Co., 1956); Fred M. Hechinger, "Poor Marks for Slum Schools," *The New York Times,* December 12, 1965, Section E, p. 9; Kenneth Clark, *Dark Ghetto* (New York: Harper and Row, 1965), chap. 6.

families in San Antonio, support the conclusion of other social scientists — that members of the lower class encounter serious difficulties when they attempt to understand or to cope with the normative
order of bureaucratic systems.

First and foremost, the lower-class person simply lacks knowledge
of the rules of the game. Middle-class persons generally learn how
to manipulate bureaucratic rules to their advantage and even to
acquire special "favors" by working through the "private" or "backstage" (as opposed to the "public") sector of the bureaucratic organization. Middle-class parents teach by example as they intervene
with various officials — e.g., the police or school teachers — to protect the family's social position in the community. In contrast, the
lower-class person stands in awe of bureaucratic regulations and frequently is unaware that he has a legal and moral claim to certain
rights and privileges. More often, however, it is the lack of knowledge of the system's technicalities and backstage regions that is
responsible for the lower-class person's inability to manipulate a
bureaucratic system to his advantage.

We mentioned earlier that in its lower echelons the bureaucracy
is highly specialized and governed by numerous regulations. Therefore, the lower-class person, whose knowledge of the system is least
adequate, must interact with the very officials who are most constrained by the formal rules. This situation is complicated by the
fact that the problems the lower-class person faces are difficult to
treat in isolation. The lack of steady employment, of education, and
of medical care, for example, interlock in complex ways. Yet, the
lower-class client encounters officials who examine only one facet of
his difficulties and who, in the ideal, treat all cases in a similar
fashion. After one agency (or official) has dealt with the special
problem assigned it, the client is then referred to another agency
which will consider another facet of the situation. It follows that
no official is able to view the lower-class client as a whole person,
and thus he is unable to point up to the client how he might use his
strengths to overcome his weaknesses.

Middle-class persons, on the other hand, are in a position to deal
with higher-status officeholders, who are less encumbered by the
rules and thus can examine their clients' problems in holistic terms.
Delinquents from middle-class homes, for instance, are more apt
than those from lower-class surroundings to be judged by officials
according to their overall performance — both past and present.

The cleavage between modern bureaucracies and the lower class is intensified by various cultural differences. Gans,[10] for example, has found that lower-class persons typically relate to one another in a personal manner. Middle-class persons are better able to relate to others within an impersonal context. Thus, members of the lower class face a greater gulf when they attempt to communicate with middle-class bureaucrats who ideally must administer rules according to impersonal, universalistic norms.

This divergence between the lower class and bureaucratic officialdom in patterns of social interaction simply makes it more difficult for a lower-class person to acquire knowledge of how the system operates. It is not surprising that under these circumstances members of the lower class often experience a sense of powerlessness or alienation. This alienation in turn reinforces and is reinforced by the sense of fatalism that is an integral part of "the culture of poverty." [11] That is, those who live in the world of the lower class account for events in the social sphere in terms of spiritual forces, chance, luck, and the like; they have little or no sense of control over their own destiny.

Because bureaucratic officials find it difficult to understand the perspective of lower-class clients and because lower-class persons must increasingly cope with highly specialized and technically oriented systems, the social distance between the bureaucratically skilled members of American society and some elements of the lower class may well be increasing rather than decreasing.[12] A kind of "circular causation," in Myrdal's terms,[13] is at work, as various social forces tend to exaggerate the schism between at least some sectors of the lower class and the upper socioeconomic groups who control the bureaucratic organizations.

ORGANIZATIONAL IMPLICATIONS

The dilemmas of client-centered bureaucracies which deal with lower-class persons are reflected in a variety of programs designed to

[10] Herbert Gans, *The Urban Villagers* (New York: The Free Press, 1965).

[11] See, e.g., various essays in Frank Riessman, Jerome Cohen, and Arthur Pearl (Eds.), *Mental Health of the Poor* (New York: The Free Press, 1964).

[12] U.S. Bureau of the Census, *Current Population Reprint Series P-60. No. 47, Income in 1964 of Families and Persons in the United States* (Washington, D.C.: Government Printing Office, 1965).

[13] Gunnar Myrdal, *Economic Theory and Under-Developed Regions* (London: Gerald Duckworth and Co., 1957), pp. 16–20.

eliminate poverty, juvenile delinquency, and other social problems. By examining these programs we can clarify some of the relationships between bureaucracy and the lower class discussed above and can bring to light other issues as well.

There have been two broad strategies for resolving the problems faced by the lower class on the national, state, and local levels. The dominant strategy emphasizes increased bureaucratization. The second approach, of theoretical rather than practical import at the present time, calls for a fundamental restructuring of client-centered bureaucracies.

1. The primary means of overcoming the problems that have been associated with the lower class has been more and more bureaucracy. This pattern has taken two forms.

a. The social problems of the lower class that have resisted solution (in terms of the values and beliefs of the dominant groups in society) are to be resolved through expansion of existing bureaucratic structures or the addition of new ones. This has been the main thrust of most legislation on both the national and the state levels since the 1930s. The programs initiated during the New Deal era have reached their fruition in President Johnson's "Great Society." In one sense the problems generated by bureaucracy are to be met by more bureaucracy.

The efforts to resolve social problems through bureaucratization have proliferated in the nongovernmental sector as well. For example, some programs — e.g., the YMCA Detached Workers Program in Chicago [14] — seek to combat delinquency among lower-class groups by fitting youth into an organizational apparatus.

The sociologist Glazer [15] views this organizational revolution as the basis of the new utopia. It is the model towards which men should strive. He, like many other sociologists, considers an industrial-urban order to be equivalent with a bureaucratic social order.

b. A small group of persons believe that the problems of the lower class require a counter-organizational solution. The Mobilization for Youth program in New York — as it has been interpreted by

[14] Charles N. Cooper, "The Chicago YMCA Detached Workers: Current Status of an Action Program," Paper presented at a joint session of the annual meeting of the Society for the Study of Social Problems and American Sociological Association, Los Angeles, California, August 1963.

[15] Nathan Glazer, "The Good Society," *Commentary* 36 (September 1963):226–234.

some social workers — is an instructive case in point.[16] Here a number of social workers, perhaps as a reaction to their traditional overidentification with middle-class norms, have been attempting to organize the poor in order to counter the problems generated by entrenched bureaucracies. In theory the new bureaucratic systems should side with the poor against the established bureaucracies which are controlled by the upper socioeconomic groups.

2. Along with this trend towards bureaucratization, there have been increased efforts to remake bureaucratic structures or to create nonbureaucratic systems in order to attain certain ends.[17]

a. Although the therapeutic community in the mental health field has not been specifically designed for lower-class clients, this development has been spurred by the sociological descriptions of custodial hospitals that have cared for lower-class patients. These highly bureaucratized systems have fallen far short of their stated goals; indeed, they have done much to stifle communication between therapists and patients.[18] The therapeutic community, which in extreme form calls for a complete breakdown of status barriers between therapist and patient, has thus emerged as a new organizational form in order to further the treatment of patients.

Somewhat similar communities have emerged in other areas as well. The Provo Experiment[19] with juvenile delinquents has displayed some of the characteristics of the therapeutic community. In at least the early stages of their contacts with delinquents, the workers in this project have placed considerable reliance upon informal groups (in sharp contrast to, say, the bureaucratized reformatory) as a mechanism for revising the delinquent's orientation.

b. In a similar vein, there have been efforts to set up organizations along collegial lines. Some writers, like Litwak, seem to regard this type of system as a "professional bureaucracy."[20] But if we take the Weberian model as our starting point, the very notion of a pro-

---

[16] See, e.g., Charles F. Grosser, "Community Development Programs Serving the Urban Poor," *Social Work* 10 (July 1965):15–21.

[17] There has been considerable interest in reorganizing corporate bureaucracy in recent years, but this material does not bear directly upon the problems at hand.

[18] See, e.g., Belknap, *op. cit.*

[19] LaMar T. Empey and Jerome Rabow, "The Provo Experiment in Delinquency Prevention," *American Sociological Review* 26 (October 1961):679–695.

[20] Eugene Litwak, "Models of Bureaucracy Which Permit Conflict," *American Journal of Sociology* 57 (September 1961):177–184.

fessional bureaucracy is a contradiction of terms. The collegial organization and the bureaucratic system are built on divergent principles. The former stresses, for example, equality among office-holders and the need for generalists rather than specialists. The generalist, unencumbered by highly formalized rules, can view clients in holistic terms and thus examine their weaknesses relative to their strengths. There emerges here a type of rationality that is not encompassed by Weber's notions of "formal rationality" (typical of bureaucratic systems) and "substantive rationality" (typical of traditional paternalistic systems).[21]

Some mental hospitals are apparently being built along collegial lines — as a compromise between a bureaucratic system and a therapeutic community.[22] Our experience in a neighborhood agency indicates that a collegial organization is necessary if social workers are to function as "mediators" between divergent class elements.[23] Workers within a bureaucratic welfare agency, as depicted by Wilensky and Lebeaux,[24] must take the class structure (as defined by the upper socioeconomic groups) as their frame of reference. Because bureaucratic functionaries find it difficult to understand the role orientations of lower-class others, they can not mediate effectively between elements of different social classes.

Overall, the trends in the development of nonbureaucratic organizations suggest a close association between the system's internal structure and its relationships with clients. These trends also support our contention that bureaucratic systems have not been successful in working with lower-class clients.

POLITICAL IMPLICATIONS

The tensions generated by the bureaucratic solution to current social problems are highlighted by the efforts to resolve the difficulties encountered by the Negro lower class. The debate generated by

21 *From Max Weber,* trans. and ed. by H. H. Gerth and C. Wright Mills (New York: Oxford University Press, 1946).

22 Research being carried out by James Otis Smith, J. Kenneth Benson and Gideon Sjoberg as part of the Timberlawn Foundation Research Project, Dallas, Texas, will bear diretcly upon this issue.

23 Gideon Sjoberg, "The Rise of the 'Mediator Society'," Presidential address delivered at the annual meeting of the Southwestern Sociological Association, Dallas, Texas, March 1964, examines the overall role of mediators in modern society.

24 Harold L. Wilensky and Charles N. Lebeaux, *Industrial Society and Social Welfare* (New York: The Free Press, 1965), pp. 238–240.

the "Moynihan Report" is of special theoretical interest.[25] (This Report, issued by the U.S Department of Labor, was written by Daniel P. Moynihan, although he is not formally listed as author.) Moynihan argues that the family structure of the lower-class Negro — which is mother-dominated and highly unstable by societal standards — must be revised if Negroes are to adapt to the industrial-urban order or the bureaucratic school systems, economic organizations, etc.

Elements of the Negro leadership have sharply attacked the Moynihan Report. They believe that instead of restructuring the lower-class Negro family we must remake modern bureaucratic systems so that these will be more responsive to the "needs" of the Negro lower class.

Moynihan's position is in keeping with that of many sociologists who accept present-day structural arrangements as more or less inevitable. Sociologists often argue that social problems arise because lower-class individuals or families are committed to sociocultural patterns that make it difficult for them to accommodate to the demands of industrial-urban organizations. Although some scholars have analyzed the dysfunctions of bureaucratic systems,[26] they rarely, if ever, assume that basic structural reorganization is necessary or possible. But the Weberian model may not be a rational or efficient organization for coping with many of the problems that have emerged (and will emerge) in an advanced industrial order where the problems of production have been resolved and the issues dealt with by client-centered organizations loom increasingly larger.

Sociologists must reexamine their basic premises if they are to grasp the nature of current social trends. For one thing, politics in a post-welfare, advanced industrial-urban order may become oriented around pro-bureaucratic and anti-bureaucratic ideologies. The rumblings of minorities (including some intellectuals in England, the United States, and Sweden) suggest that this type of political struggle may be in the offing. It is of interest, for example, that in the United States elements of the New Left — e.g., Students for a

[25] U.S. Department of Labor, *The Case for National Action* (Washington, D.C.: Government Printing Office, 1965). For reactions to this essay see: "The Negro Family: Visceral Reaction," *Newsweek* 60 (December 6, 1965):38–40, and John Herbers, "Moynihan Hopeful U.S. Will Adopt a Policy of Promoting Family Stability," *The New York Times,* December 12, 1965, p. 74.

[26] See, e.g., Harry Cohen, *The Demonics of Bureaucracy* (Ames: Iowa State University Press, 1965).

Democratic Society — share a common "devil" — the bureaucratic system — with elements of the right wing. We would hypothesize that some relationship exists between these ideological concerns and the problems of client-centered bureaucracies. Certainly, these developments are worthy of serious sociological investigation — and before, not after, the fact.

CONCLUSIONS

Evidence indicates that modern bureaucracies, especially client-centered ones, stand between lower-class and upper-status (particularly middle-class) persons. These groups do not encounter one another within a vacuum but rather within an organizational, bureaucratic context. Even when they meet in relatively informal situations, the bureaucratic orientation of the middle-class person structures his response to the lower-class individual. It is through their positions in the key bureaucracies that the higher-status groups maintain their social advantages and even at times foster bureaucratic procedures that impede the advancement of lower-class persons into positions of privilege. While our illustrative data are limited to the United States, many of our generalizations seem to hold for other industrial-urban orders as well. . . .

28   *Militant Civil Servants in New York City*

FRANCES FOX PIVEN

Not long ago, thousands of people massed in front of New York's City Hall and sang "Solidarity Forever." The image was of workers marching against Pinkertons. But the ranks were middle-

From Frances Fox Piven, "Militant Civil Servants in New York City," reprinted by permission of the author and the publishers from *Transaction*, 7 (November 1969):24–28, 55. Copyright © November, 1969, by TRANS-action, Inc., New Brunswick, New Jersey.

class civil servants, and their solidarity was directed against the Black and Puerto Rican poor. The issue on this occasion was school decentralization, but that is only one of a host of issues currently galvanizing White civil servants and dividing them from the enlarging minorities in the cities.

The rising militancy of public employees needs no documenting here. New York's 60,000 school teachers have been shutting down the school system regularly; this fall it was the Day Care Center workers; slowdowns by police and firemen are becoming commonplace. And if public employees are more militant in New York, where they are the most numerous and best organized, public unions across the country are catching up. Teachers prevented schools from opening this fall in Illinois, Ohio, Indiana, Massachusetts, Pennsylvania, New Hampshire, Michigan, New York, Pennsylvania, Connecticut, Rhode Island, Wisconsin, Minnesota, Utah and Tennessee. Last year Detroit's police were hit by the "blue flu"; while Cleveland's police threatened outright rebellion against Mayor Carl B. Stokes. In Atlanta the firemen went on strike; in Newark the police and firemen simultaneously called in sick.

These events are not, as they are sometimes described, simply contests between unions and the "general public." The keenest struggle is with residents of the central-city ghettos (who in any case now form a substantial segment of the "general public" in most big cities). Police, firemen, teachers and public-welfare workers increasingly complain about "harassment" in the ghettos. For their part, growing numbers of the Black poor view police, firemen, teachers, public-welfare workers and other city employees as their oppressors.

The emerging conflict is not difficult to explain. Whites and Blacks are pitted against each other in a struggle for the occupational and political benefits attached to public employment. Whites now have the bulk of these benefits, and Blacks want a greater share of them. Nor is it only jobs that are at stake. Organized public employees have become a powerful force shaping the policies of municipal agencies, but the policies that suit employees often run counter to ghetto interests. We may be entering another phase in the long and tragic history of antagonism between the Black poor and the White working class in America.

THE ETHNIC STAKE-OUT

Municipal jobs have always been an important resource in the cultivation of political power. As successive waves of immigrants settled in the cities, their votes were exchanged for jobs and other favors, permitting established party leaders to develop and maintain control despite the disruptive potential of new and unaffiliated populations. The exchange also facilitated the integration of immigrant groups into the economic and political structures of the city, yielding them both a measure of influence and some occupational rewards. Public employment was a major channel of mobility for the Italian, the Irish and the Jew, each of whom, by successively taking over whole sectors of the public services, gave various municipal agencies their distinctly ethnic coloration. Now Blacks are the newcomers. But they come at a time when public employment has been preempted by older groups and is held fast through civil-service provisions and collective-bargaining contracts. Most public jobs are no longer allocated in exchange for political allegiance, but through a "merit" system based on formal qualifications.

The development of the civil-service merit system in municipalities at the turn of the century (the federal government adopted it in 1883) is usually credited to the efforts of reformers who sought to improve the quality of municipal services, to eliminate graft and to dislodge machine leaders. At least some of the employees in all cities with more than 500,000 inhabitants are now under civil service; in about half of these cities, virtually all employees have such protections.

Although the civil service originated in the struggle between party leaders and reformers for control of public employment, it launched municipal employees as an independent force. As municipal services expanded, the enlarging numbers of public employees began to form associations. Often these originated as benevolent societies, such as New York's Patrolmen's Benevolent Association which formed in the 1890s. Protected by the merit system, these organizations of public employees gradually gained some influence in their own right, and they exerted that influence at both the municipal and the state level to shape legislation and to monitor personnel policies so as to protect and advance their occupational interests.

Shortly after World War I, when the trade union movement was growing rapidly, public employees made their first major thrust toward unionization in the famous Boston police strike. About 1,100 of the 1,400-man force struck, goaded by the refusal of city officials to grant pay raises despite rapid inflation and despite the favorable recommendations of a commission appointed to appraise police demands. The strike precipitated widespread disorder in the streets of Boston. Official reactions were swift and savage. Calvin Coolidge, then Governor, became a national hero as he moved to break the strike under the banner, "There is no right to strike against the public safety by anybody, anywhere, anytime." Virtually the entire police force was fired (and the few loyal men were granted pay raises). More important, the numerous police unions that had sprouted up in other cities, many of them affiliated with the American Federation of Labor, were scuttled. Public unionism did not recover its impetus until well after World War II.

In the meantime, civil-service associations relied mainly on lobbying to press their interests and, as their membership grew, they became an effective force in party politics. Although the mode of their involvement in party politics varied from place to place and from time to time, the sheer numbers of organized public employees made political leaders loath to ignore them. One measure of their impact is the number of major party leaders who rose from their ranks. In New York City, for example, Mayor William O'Dwyer was a former policeman; Abe Beame, the Democratic candidate for mayor in 1965, was a former schoolteacher, and Paul Screvane, his competitor for the Democratic mayoralty nomination in that same year, began as a sanitation worker.

PUBLIC UNIONISM

Now unionism is on the rise again, signalling a new phase in the political development of public employee groups. It is even spreading rapidly to the more professional services, such as education and welfare, whose employees have traditionally resisted the working-class connotation of unionism. The American Federation of Teachers has organized so many teachers as to force the National Educational Association, which considers itself a professional association, into a militant stance (including endorsing boycotts and strikes by its members). In New York, firemen last year successfully wrested the right to strike from their parent International Association of Firefighters, and the Patrolmen's Benevolent Association is exploring the possibility of an affiliation with the AFL-CIO. The American Federation of State, County, and Municipal Employees — half of whose members work for municipalities — is one of the fastest-growing affiliates of the AFL-CIO, having increased its membership by 70 percent in the last four years. Overall, unions of public employees are adding 1,000 new members every working day, according to a member of the National Labor Relations Board.

By becoming part of the labor movement, public employees are augmenting their influence in two ways. First, they can call for support from other unions, and that support can be a substantial force. New York's teachers were backed in the struggle against school decentralization by the Central Labor Council, which represents 1.2 million workers. (The Central Labor Council, headed by a top official from the electricians' union, and with an overwhelmingly white membership, also had its own interest in the school issue: the Board of Education disperses over $1 billion annually for maintenance and construction. Under a system of community control, contracts might be awarded to Black businesses or to contractors who hire Black workers. Some Black labor officials, seeing themselves allied against their own communities, broke ranks with the Central Labor Council over the decentralization issue.)

Unionism also means that public employees feel justified in using the disruptive leverage of the strike. Transit workers bring a metropolis to a standstill; teachers close down the schools; sanitation men bury a city under mounds of garbage. With each such crisis, the cry goes up for new legislative controls. But it is hard to see how laws will prevent strikes, unless the political climate becomes much more repressive. So far political leaders have been reluctant to invoke the full penalties permitted by existing law for fear of alienating organized labor. Thus New York State's Condon-Wadlin Law, enacted in 1947, was not used and was finally replaced by the "model" Taylor law which, as the experience of the last three years shows, works no better. Theodore Kheel, one of the nation's most noted labor arbitrators, in pronouncing the failure of the new law, pointed out that the state Public Employment Relations Board, established under the Taylor law to arbitrate disputes, took no action on either of the New York City teacher strikes. The New York Times concluded with alarm that "The virus of irresponsibility is racing through New York's unionized civil service," and "There is no end, short of draining the municipal treasury and turning taxpayers into refugees or relief recipients. . . ."

Public unions must be controlled, so the argument goes, because they are uniquely capable of paralyzing the cities and gouging the public as the price of restoring services. In a recent decision, New York's highest court held that a legislative classification differentiating between public and private industry was reasonable and constitutional, thus justifying prohibitions on the right of public employees to strike. The courts unanimously held that public employees could "by the exercise of naked power" obtain gains "wholly disproportionate to the services rendered by them."

As a practical matter, however, these distinctions between public and private employees do not hold up. Strikes in the public and private sectors rely on the same forms of leverage, though in varying degrees. Private-sector strikes result in economic losses, but so do strikes in the municipal services (for example, transit stoppages). Even teachers and welfare workers exert some economic pressure, although they rely more heavily on another form of leverage — the cries of a severely inconvenienced and discomfitted populace — to force government to settle their grievances. But private strikes of milk or fuel deliveries, of steel workers or transportation workers, also discomfit large sectors of the population and generate pressure for government to intervene and force a settlement.

Nor is it true that the coercive power of municipal unions enables them to obtain more favorable settlements than private unions. If, under the pressure of a strike in municipal services, the public is often unmindful of the impact of settlements on taxes, the public is equally unmindful of the eventual costs to consumers of settlements in the private sector. Industrial strikes are by no means necessarily less disruptive than public strikes or less coercive in pressing for a greater share of the public's dollar.

BLANKET SECURITY

Despite the continuing controversy over the right to strike, it is not the root of the trouble over municipal employment. Rather it is that the gains won by employees after long years of struggle now seem to be in jeopardy.

In fact, some groups of public employees had managed to secure substantial control over their working conditions long before they began to unionize, and in many cases long before comparable gains had been secured by workers in the private sector. These victories were won by intensive lobbying and by the assiduous cultivation of influence in the political parties at the municipal and state levels.

In the past, except where wages were concerned, other groups in the cities rarely became sufficiently aroused to block efforts by public employees to advance their interests. On issues such as tenure of working conditions or career advancement, and even retirement (which does not involve immediate costs) the civil services associations were able to make substantial strides by using conventional means of political influence.

First, with their jobs secured by the merit system, public workers in many agencies went on to win the principle of "promotion from within." This principle, together with promotion criteria that favored longevity, assured the career advancement of those already employed. But such a system of promotion, because it has the consequence of restricting outsiders to the bottom rank of public employment, is being opposed by new groups. When proponents of school decentralization insist that these requirements be waived to place Black people in supervisory or administrative positions, spokesmen for the New York school supervisors' association answer that it will "turn the clock back 100 years and reinstate the spoils system."

In some municipal agencies, moreover, newcomers are even barred from lower-level jobs. Building inspectors in New York City are required to have five years' experience in the building trades, but few Black people can get into the building trades. Police associations oppose any "lowering" of hiring standards, proposed as a way of facilitating entrance by minority groups, arguing that the complexity of modern law enforcement calls for even higher educational standards. (Police have even objected to lowering the physical height requirement, which now excludes many Puerto Ricans.) When New York City recently announced that impoverished people would be granted up to twelve extra points on civil-service tests for fifty low-paying jobs in anti-poverty agencies, the very meagerness of the concession cast in relief the system of exclusion it was to modify.

Public employees have also been successful in preempting some of the future resources of the city. Demands for improved retirement and pension plans, for example, are prominent: New York's transit workers recently settled for a contract that awarded pension pay on the basis of a time-and-a-half provision during their last year of employment, and the police are demanding the right to retire after fifteen years. Such benefits are often won more easily than wage demands, for it is less onerous for a mayor to make concessions payable under a later administration.

Obviously, elaborate entrance and promotion requirements now limit access by Blacks to municipal jobs. Indeed, one can almost measure the strength of public employee associations in different cities by their success in securing such requirements, and in keeping minority members out. In New York, where municipal workers are numerous and well organized, 90 percent of the teachers are White; in Detroit, Philadelphia, and Chicago, where municipal employees are not well organized, 25 to 40 percent of the teachers are Black.

MORTGAGED TREASURIES

The number of jobs at stake is vast, and Black demands are mounting. New York City employs 325,000 people, and personnel costs naturally account for the lion's share (about 60 percent) of a municipal budget topping $6 billion. And the share is growing: the number of public employees continues to rise (up 60 percent in New York City since the end of World War II), and wages and benefits are also rising. The question is not whether these costs are legitimate — but who will benefit by them. For as Blacks become more numerous in cities, they will come to power only to find the treasuries mortgaged to earlier groups.

Unionization has been important mainly (but not exclusively) in the area of wages, where public employees often lagged behind organized private workers. Relying as they did on political influence, they were blocked by taxpayer groups who usually opposed higher municipal salaries. However, with unionization and strike power, public employees are no longer dependent on the vicissitudes of interest-group politics to get higher wages, and so, as *The New York Times* notes with horror, they have begun to "leap frog" each other in salary demands.

Unionization is also enabling large numbers of municipal workers who hold less coveted jobs to move forward. By and large, hospital workers, clerks and janitors, for example, were left behind in the process of advancement through the civil services and through party politics. In New York City, many of these workers have now been

organized by District 37 of the State, County, and Municipal Employees Union. Furthermore, because these are low-paid, low-pres-
tige jobs, they are often held by Blacks who constitute about 25
percent of District 37's membership. (This helps to explain why
Victor Gotbaum, the outspoken head of District Council 37, bucked
the Central Labor Council in the school decentralization fight.) And
following the path of earlier public employee groups, District 37
is beginning to press for a series of civil service reforms to enable
its members to move up the municipal career ladder. The much
publicized struggles of the garbage workers in Memphis, and the
hospital workers in Charlotte are efforts by low-paid Blacks who, by
using militant union tactics, are making their first advances.

Competition for jobs and money is by no means the worst of the
struggle between the ghetto and public employees. In the course of
securing their occupational interests, some groups of public employees have come to exercise substantial control over their agencies,
and that control is now being challenged, too. The struggle over
school decentralization in a number of cities is a prime example.

Public employees have been able to win considerable influence
over the tasks they perform and other conditions of work. Many
civil-service positions are now enshrined in codified descriptions
which make both the job-holder and the work he performs relatively
invulnerable to outside interference, even by political leaders. Furthermore, substantial discretion is inherent in many civil-service
tasks, partly because legislative mandates are obscure, and partly
because many civil-service positions require the occupants to be
"professionals," enabling them to resist interference on the ground
that they are "experts."

Public employees often use both the codified protection of their
jobs and their powers of discretion to resist policy changes that alter
the nature of their work. When former Mayor Robert Wagner asked
the police department to patrol housing projects, the police refused
and were supported by the police commissioners. School personnel
effectively defeated desegregation policies by simply failing to inform ghetto parents of their right to enroll their children in White
schools, and by discouraging those parents who tried to do so. The
combined effect of procedural safeguards and professional discretion is suggested by the often-noted dilemma of a board of education
that is simultaneously too centralized and too decentralized: it is

hamstrung by regulations that seem to limit policy options, while its personnel retain the license to undermine central directives.

If some public employees have always had the ability to undermine policies, they now want the right to set policies, usually on the ground that as professionals they know what's best. Thus teachers recently demanded that the New York City Board of Education expand the "More Effective Schools" program, and that they be granted the right to remove "disruptive" children from their classrooms. Threatened by the efforts of ghetto parents to free their children from an unresponsive educational system, the union became the major force opposing school decentralization. Similarly, New York's striking welfare workers bargained for (but have not yet won) the right to join the commissioner in formulating agency policies, arguing that 8,000 case workers ought to have a say in policy decisions. The Patrolmen's Benevolent Association has begun issuing its own instructions to policemen on how the law should be enforced, to countermand Mayor John Lindsay's presumed indulgence of looters and demonstrators. And only through a full-scale public campaign was the mayor able to override the PBA's stubborn resistance to a "fourth platoon" permitting heavier scheduling of policemen during high crime hours. All of these ventures by the unions represent incursions on matters of municipal policy. That they are made under the banner of professional commitment to public service should not obscure the fact that they will entrench and enhance the position of the public employees involved.

In part, demands in the policy area are being provoked by the feeling among public employees that they must defend their agencies against Black assailants. The Black masses are very dependent on public services, but these services have been conspicuously unresponsive to them, and have even become instruments of White antagonism, as when police services take on the character of an army of occupation in the ghetto. The fierce fight waged by the New York Patrolmen's Benevolent Association against a civilian review board reveals the intensity of the conflict over the control of municipal agencies. In education and public welfare, the effect of cleavage between White staff and Black recipients are even more pervasive and tragic, for by blocking and distorting the delivery of these services White staffs virtually fix the life chances of the Black poor.

Jobs and services have always been the grist of urban politics. By entrenching and enlarging control over municipal agencies, White-controlled public-employee unions are also blocking a traditional avenue by which newcomers become assimilated into the urban political and economic system. Politicians who depend on the Black vote have not been oblivious to this obstruction. One response has been to generate new systems of services to be staffed by Blacks. By establishing these services under separate administrative auspices and by calling them "experimental," political leaders have tried to avoid aggravating White public employees. Thus the national Democratic administration which took office in 1960 created a series of new programs for the inner city in the fields of delinquency, mental health, poverty, education and the like. Federal guidelines required that Blacks have a large share of the new jobs and policy positions (e.g., "maximum feasible participation of the poor"). In general, these "demonstration" programs have been more responsive than traditional municipal agencies to Black interests. Of course, the White-dominated city bureaucracies fought for control of the new programs and sometimes won: at the least, they obtained a substantial share of the new funds as compensation. But regardless of who has control, the new programs are miniscule compared with existing municipal programs. If anything, the anti-poverty program has made more visible just how little Blacks do control, thus precipitating some of the current wrangles over control of traditional municipal programs.

IRONIES OF HISTORY

There are ironies in these developments. Reformers struggled to free municipal services from the vicissitudes of party politics; now some politicians are struggling to free municipal services from the vicissitudes of employee control. The advent . . . of the Lindsay administration in New York City is a good illustration, for it exposed and escalated the conflict between Blacks and Whites. Lindsay campaigned against the old Democratic regime to which the unions were tied. His election was made possible by the defection of almost half of the Black voters from Democratic ranks, and by middle- and upper-class support. It was to these groups that he appealed in his campaign and to which he is now trying to respond through his public posture and policies. To the Black voter, he has been a politician who walked in the ghetto streets, who allowed the welfare rolls to rise, who attempted to assert control over the police force and to decentralize the school system; to the middle and upper classes, he has been a reformer and innovator who revamped the city's bureaucratic structures and appointed prestigious outsiders to high administrative posts. Appeals to both constituencies led him to do battle with the public unions regularly, for these moves threaten the control exerted by employee groups over municipal services. These battles have activated race and ethnic loyalties so fierce as to seem to rupture the city; and the possibility that Lindsay has even alienated the largely liberal Jewish vote exposes the intensity of the struggles for control of municipal benefits. Similar alliances between the Black poor and affluent Whites are also appearing in other cities (Cleveland, Detroit, Gary) with similar reactions from public employees, and White ethnic groups generally. . . .

But the bitterest irony of all is that the struggle between Whites and Blacks is being played out within the narrow limits of the resources available in municipalities. There is nothing unreasonable in White employees' pressing to hold and expand the gains they have won, which in any case are not so munificent. What is unreasonable is that their gains are being made at the expense of Blacks, not at the expense of affluent and powerful sectors of the society. How to shift the struggle from the arena of municipal jobs and services to the arena in which national and corporate wealth are divvied up is hardly clear. But one thing is clear. The burden of shifting the struggle should not fall on Blacks, for they are only now getting their first chance at a share of what the city has to offer. Confined to the municipal sphere, Blacks will oppose the advances of the White unions and fight for what others got before them. And they may have cause to worry — not only that the stakes of municipal politics are limited, but that all of the stakes may be claimed before they have joined the game.